SAVING
THE
DIFFERENCES

CRISPIN WRIGHT

SAVING THE DIFFERENCES

Essays on Themes
from *Truth and Objectivity*

HARVARD UNIVERSITY PRESS · Cambridge, Massachusetts · London, England
2003

For Annalisa, Cyrus, Duncan, Jesper,

Lars Bo, Lars, Patrice, Patrick and Sven

Library of Congress Cataloging-in-Publication Data

Wright, Crispin, 1942–
    Saving the differences : essays on themes from Truth and
objectivity / Crispin Wright.
        p. cm.
    Includes bibliographical references (p.) and index.
    ISBN 0-674-01077-9 (alk. paper)
    1. Realism. I. Wright, Crispin, 1942– Truth and objectivity.
II. Title.

B835.W747 2003
121—dc21   2002191296

Contents

Contents

PREFACE

In his "Conversations with Wittgenstein" (Rush Rhees (1981), p. 171), M. C. Drury reports that Wittgenstein considered taking a line from *King Lear*, 'I'll teach you differences', as the motto for the *Philosophical Investigations*. The 'differences' he had in mind, of course, were not of the etiquette of rank and station which the Duke of Kent was keen to enforce, but differences in the role and function of superficially similar language games!—differences, in Wittgenstein's famous view, which those very similarities encourage us to overlook, thereby constituting a prime cause of philosophical misunderstandings and confusions. My book *Truth and Objectivity* was concerned with one (although a very general and of course contentious) instance of this Wittgensteinian thought: the idea that statement-making and susceptibility to ordinary propositional logic may be a relatively superficial aspect of discourses, masking deep differences in point of objectivity and the manner in which they relate to the real world. That idea calls for a philosophy of truth and truth-aptitude which allows the application of those notions to tolerate such deep differences, and an account of wherein the deep differences themselves consist. *Truth and Objectivity* made proposals in both those directions. The essays collected in the present volume prefigure, elaborate on or defend those proposals, or bring them to bear on specific regions of discourse. Since Wittgenstein decided not to use it, I have purloined the line from *Lear* as the motto for *my* book.

I have organised the essays into five groups. Part I contains, by way of introduction, a short précis of *Truth and Objectivity* together with my 1987 Gareth Evans Memorial Lecture in which I outlined earlier versions of its central ideas. Part II consists of essays and discussion notes written in response to the detailed reactions of reviewers of the book. Part III contains two essays on objectivity and truth in ethics. Four essays in Part IV enlarge on and defend the minimalist conception of truth proposed in *Truth and Objectivity,* as well as offering detailed discussion of coherentism and of the epistemic conception of truth defended by (and more recently renounced by) Hilary Putnam. The latter half of Essay 12, on Robert Brandom's 'assertibilism', is previously unpublished. Part V, finally, groups together three very recent essays on 'matters arising' in connection with response-dependence and Cognitive Command. All the previously published essays appear as originally save for occasional light editing for the sake of clarity. In addition to a bibliography of the references they contain, I have included a supplementary list of the most useful writings known to me which post-date *Truth and Objectivity* and criticise or apply to themes of my book, or pursue closely related ones. No conclusion should be drawn from what I may have omitted to include in this supplementary bibliography. No one can read everything; it is likely that I have overlooked a good number of relevant publications over the last decade. I would be pleased to hear of them from readers of the present volume.

Specific acknowledgements are separately noted, as originally, in each essay. Collectively, of course, the essays share the ancestry and so inherit the intellectual debts of *Truth and Objectivity* itself, and it is my pleasure to re-emphasise my gratitude to the various friends, colleagues and institutions acknowledged in the preface to that book. I take the opportunity to repair the omission of any mention there of the impetus to my thinking about realism which I brought away from my Princeton seminar in 1985–6. The prototype framework which emerged in the Evans Lecture one year later was the precipitate of the intense weekly attention to my ideas provided by, among others, Paul Benacerraf, the late David Lewis, Mark Johnston, Gideon Rosen and Michael Smith. A much more recent debt is owed to colleagues and students at the Mind and Language seminar at New York University, where, allotted a "thinker of the week" slot in three successive years in 1999–2001, I had the opportunity to present versions of the three essays in Part V, each of which profited immensely from the intensive critical scrutiny that forum characteristically provides.

My thanks to Cyrus Panjvani for indispensable help with the bibliographies, systematisation of references, and proofreading the typescript; and once again to Anne Cameron and Janet Kirk for its preparation. David Bemelmans once again did an immaculate job of copyediting and Marguerite Nesling provided her usual invaluable help to me in preparing the typescript's final form. My thanks to Donna Bouvier for her sure guidance through the final stages of proof correction. The book, which is dedicated to my nine very industrious and talented St. Andrews graduate students who have attained their Ph.D.'s during its preparation, has been put together during tenure of a Leverhulme Research Professorship, and I once again most gratefully acknowledge the support of the Leverhulme Trust.

Come, sir, arise, away! I'll teach you differences.
Away, away! If you will measure your lubber's length again, tarry:
but away! go to. Have you wisdom? So.

—*King Lear*, I, iv.

PART ONE

REALISM RECONFIGURED

It seemed best to begin my anthology with the précis of *Truth and Objectivity* I composed for the Philosophy and Phenomenological Research symposium on the book. But the other essay included in this part, though it antedates *Truth and Objectivity* by a number of years, also announces and motivates its programme, at least in broad outline, and may serve as introductory to it. It is the text of my Gareth Evans Memorial Lecture given in Oxford in the summer of 1987. It took shape as I began to think through the lessons of a seminar (Recent and Contemporary Philosophy) I'd given at Princeton the previous year. The first half of the seminar was given over to discussion of a debate between realists and anti-realists in the Dummettian mould and its connection to issues concerning rule-following and the objectivity of meaning. But in the second part I planned to press beyond those issues—which had already of course been much discussed—and to focus on a type of realist/anti-realist dispute typified by the older expressivist tradition in ethics and to try to get clearer about the best articulation of the theoretical framework required by that form of dispute. The plan was to focus on a number of instances of the relevant kind of anti-realist impulse—besides expressivism in ethics, I had in mind instrumentalism in the philosophy of science, projectivist conceptions of modality, and Wittgenstein's critique of private language taken in the traditional, pre-Kripkean way as epitomised at *Philosophical Investigations* §158—and to work towards an account of what it would be for the propositional surface of a region of discourse to mask an underlying non-propositional nature and of how that circumstance might be recognised. The seminar got nowhere near as far as I had hoped—a not uncommon experience for visitors to Princeton at that time—but by the end I had convinced myself that no solid theoretical framework for the expressivist direction could be provided, and that, so far from trying to make out a contrast between propositional surface and the dealing in genuine propositions, apt to be true or false, anti-realism would do better to focus on explaining how a discourse's possession of a genuinely propositional character could consist with both realist and anti-realist views of it and how what was really at stake between those views had, in general, nothing to do with whether a discourse provided for the assertion of genuine propositions, apt to be true or false. Essay 2 outlines some of the reasons, in the form of objections to Simon Blackburn's opposed *quasi-realist* approach, which led me to this way of looking at the matter. It goes on to outline a prototypical version of the constraint of cognitive command (therein called 'rational command') and a second realism-relevant crux turning on whether, if it is assumed that a target discourse deals in genuinely objective, independent states of affairs, it's possible to explain how it is that human minds are able to keep cognitive track of them. This crux was dropped by the time of *Truth and Objectivity*, when I had come to think that it was superseded by considerations of Width of Cosmological Role. The essay concludes by prefiguring a form of the Euthyphro Contrast and emphasising the distance between the forms of anti-realism which it might serve to corral and anything that might serve as a metaphysical basis for the more traditional expressivist (or quasi-realist) programme.

1

Précis of *Truth and Objectivity*

The terms 'realism' and 'anti-realism' loom large in modern philosophy—indeed 'anti-realism' is of very recent (probably Michael Dummett's) invention—but the metaphysical disputes which they have come to caption are as old as philosophy itself, and as stubborn. Why so little progress? Why does a broadly realist view about, say, ethics or mathematics or theoretical physics remain so obdurately contestable and contested? One possible explanation, favoured by a number of recently influential writers, is that the debates are bad: that they reflect a confused hankering after a chimerical kind of objectivity, a kind of 'sideways on' view of our thought and practices and their relation to what is external to them. Elements of this idea can be found in writers as otherwise diverse as McDowell and Rorty.[1] Another suggestion is that the debates are sustained only by the inability, or refusal, of their protagonists to see that objectionable presuppositions, or oversights, are shared by both sides—that a clear-headed perception of, for instance, the permeation of all our thought by *evaluations,* even hard-headed, natural scientific thought, as

1. The metaphor of the 'sideways on' view is coined in McDowell (1994), p. 35.

Putnam has urged, or the far-reaching implications of Wittgenstein's discussion of following a rule effectively deconstruct the contrast between the opposing positions.

Truth and Objectivity is written in reaction to these views. Its hypothesis is that, in seeking to explain the obduracy of the debates in question, we need not look farther than the usual suspects: unclarity about how best to formulate the issues involved and consequential oversimplifications and misdirection of argumentative effort. I propose a framework for this kind of dispute which both proscribes, as misconceived, certain traditional anti-realist 'paradigms'—ways of defining the anti-realist position—and allows that a plurality of distinct, though related, considerations may properly motivate—though perhaps to differing degrees—the kind of conception of a discourse to which realists are drawn: a conception which would view its characteristic claims as fitted for representation of aspects of a reality not of our making, and the characteristic intention of those who practise the discourse as being to succeed in such representation.

My starting point is the recommendation of *minimalist* conceptions of truth-aptitude and of truth. The minimalist view about truth, in brief, is that it is necessary and sufficient, in order for a predicate to qualify as a truth predicate, that it satisfy each of a basic set of platitudes about truth: the platitudes, for instance, that to assert a statement is to present it as true; that 'S' is true if and only if S (the Disquotational Scheme); that statements which are apt for truth have negations which are likewise; that truth is one thing, justification another; that to be true is to correspond to the facts; and so on.[2] Minimalism about truth-aptitude, likewise briefly summarised, comprises the twin contentions (i) that any assertoric discourse will allow the definition upon its statements of a predicate which qualifies as a truth predicate in the light of the minimalist proposal about truth; and (ii) that a discourse should be reckoned as assertoric just in case its ingredient sentences are subject to certain minimal constraints of syntax—

2. The inclusion of Correspondence as a platitude may seem surprising. I remark briefly on it below.

embeddability within negation, the conditional, contexts of propositional attitude, and so on—and of discipline: their use must be governed by agreed standards of warrant.

With each of these minimalisms in place, almost all of the areas which have traditionally provoked realist/anti-realist debate—ethics, aesthetics, intentional psychology, mathematics, theoretical science, and so on—will turn out to traffic in truth-evaluable contents, which moreover, when the disciplinary standards proper to the discourse are satisfied, we are going to be entitled to claim to be true. So two traditional anti-realist paradigms are immediately under pressure: *expressivism*—the denial that a target discourse, despite an apparently assertoric surface, really deals in truth-evaluable contents—is not going to be an option; and the *error theorist,* like John Mackie on ethics or Hartry Field on mathematics, though not out of the game straight away, will have his work cut out to make the charge of global error stick: typically, he will have to make out some systematic shortfall between the standards of warrant that actually inform the discourse in question and the notion of truth that actually applies therein, so that claims of truth, based on satisfaction of the former, can emerge as systematically misconceived.

Minimalism about truth, as I conceive it, is spiritually akin to but supersedes the well-known deflationary conception of truth which, I argue in the first chapter of *Truth and Objectivity,* is sound in its instinct that it does not, metaphysically, take very much for a discourse to qualify as truth-apt, nor for us to be entitled to claim that many of its statements are true, but unsound in the contention that 'true' does not express a genuine property. For the minimalist, truth is a property, inasmuch as there is always something in which the truth of a true statement, from whatever region of discourse, consists. However, as the last remark of the preceding paragraph may have suggested, this is not a commitment to the idea that truth is uniform across all areas of our thought. Any truth predicate, in whatever area, will satisfy the minimal platitudes—that's what *makes* it a truth predicate. But the truth predicates in different areas of thought may in addition exhibit differences—differences in, broadly speaking, the kind of circumstance that constitutes their applying, when they apply—and it is these differences which help to give content to realist and anti-realist intuitions and open them up to discussion. The suggestion, in other words, is that the justification of realist or anti-realist inclinations about a particular area is to be sought by attending to the characteristics, in various respects, of the local truth predicate. The main body of the argument of *Truth and Objectivity* is taken up with outlining and exploring a number of such cruces: a number of realism-relevant ways in which what is involved in a statement's being true may differ depending on the region of discourse to which it belongs.

An important idea for this purpose is that of a statement's being *superassertible*. A statement is superassertible if some actually accessible state of information—a state of information which this world, constituted as it is, would generate in a suitably receptive, investigating subject—justifies its assertion, and will continue to do so no matter how enlarged upon or improved. Whether this notion unconditionally satisfies the basic platitudes about truth is a complex question, turning in part upon one's antecedent views: in particular, superassertibility will not seem to satisfy the Disquotational Scheme in an area where the notion of truth is taken to be evidentially unconstrained. But I argue that superassertibility will satisfy the minimal platitudes in any area where—as perhaps in the case of comedy, or ethics—we conceive that any truth must be *knowable in principle*. I therefore propose that the view that truth is, globally, superassertibility should be the distinctive thesis of the semantic form of anti-realism which Dummett has argued is the most fruitful way to interpret the stance of the mathematical intuitionists, and which he has done so much to force philosophers to take seriously more generally. By the same token, one appropriate channel for the development of realist intuition about a region of discourse is via argument that truth there *cannot* satisfactorily be construed as superassertibility.

There are at least two ways such an argument might be relevantly accomplished. One is to show that the two notions are potentially divergent in extension—that truth potentially outruns superassertibility. Since the superassertibility of a superassertible statement has to be something for which (defeasible) evidence is in principle available, this can be accomplished by showing that the local truth predicate is essentially evidentially unconstrained. And just that, of course, is a characteristic contention of the kind of realist whom Dummett envisages as opposing the intuitionistic kind of anti-realist. But another possibility for the realist about a given area is to argue that, even granting that its truth predicate is—or may be—extensionally coincident with superassertibility, the latter is still a poor interpretation of the former because the truth of such statements actually provides the *explanatory ground* of their superassertibility, that is, stands to it rather in the manner in which the base of a disposition stands to its manifestation. This is the issue raised by what I term the *Euthyphro Contrast*.

Other relevant cruces may be elicited by dwelling on the Correspondence Platitude: that truth is correspondence to fact. The nomenclature may seem tendentious. But the fact is that, naturally interpreted, the claim that truth is correspondence to fact is not a contentious metaphysical thesis but a consequence of the minimal platitudes for truth. In addition, however, it is open to robust interpretations, and the clarification and justification of such interpretations for particular regions of discourse provides another avenue whereby realism may define and seek to support itself. I envisage two ways in which such clarification might be accomplished: by working on the notion of correspondence, so as to justify thinking of it as a substantial, representational relation; and by working on the second term, 'the facts', in such a way as to justify thinking of them as substantial, external states of affairs. The constraints of *Cognitive Command* and of *Width of Cosmological Role* are intended to illustrate the kinds of clarification that pursuit of these strategies might respectively involve. It is an a priori truth that a pair of devices—cameras, copy machines, tape recorders—whose function it is to produce representations of certain self-standing external states of affairs and which are each capable of doing so successfully within the same tolerances, cannot both have functioned as they ought if their respective outputs sufficiently diverge. Correspondingly, it must be a priori true of us, in any region of thought where our beliefs are the products of genuinely representational cognitive function, that differences of opinion—where not within the tolerances permitted by various relevant kinds of vagueness—have to involve some form of cognitive shortcoming. That, roughly formulated, is the Cognitive Command constraint. When it is satisfied, the notion of correspondence featuring in the Correspondence Platitude derives additional, realism-relevant substance. The constraint is presented both as independently plausible and as a crystallisation of the intuitively perceived crux which receives its more usual expression, especially in ethics, in the idea that something important about objectivity is reflected by convergence (or divergence) of opinions within and across cultures.

In similar fashion, the crux of Width of Cosmological Role is intended to place a control upon the intuitive idea that the subject matter of a certain discourse is, in a realism-relevant way, *self-standing*, that it deals in facts which are independent and substantial. Just such an idea, in the moral case, is at work in Gilbert Harman's claim, contested by such writers as David Wiggins and Nicholas Sturgeon, that moral states of affairs, to their disadvantage, do not feature in the best explanations of moral beliefs in the ways in which, for instance, physical states of affairs feature in the explanations of our physical beliefs. This seems to me to involve a misinterpretation of something valid. The right question to ask about moral states of affairs is not whether citation of them will contribute towards the best explanation of our moral beliefs, but *what else* citation of them can contribute towards explaining. It is when the states of affairs of a certain realm are active in other spheres than the doxastic, so to speak, that we are forced to think of them as self-standing, as more than merely the correlates of our true beliefs which the Correspondence Platitude demands. The Width of Cosmological Role of (the subject matter of) a discourse is the measure of the extent to which the states of affairs with which it distinctively deals live up to this demand.

Minimalism about truth, and truth-aptitude, and issues to do with superassertibility are the focus of the first two chapters of *Truth and Objectivity*. The shape of the recommended general framework for thinking about realism and anti-realism, and the Cognitive Command constraint in particular, emerge in chapter 3, to which is appended an extended discussion of the Euthyphro Contrast. Chapter 4 is concerned with certain difficulties to do with Cognitive Command: a threatened trivialisation of the notion, subverting the distinction between minimally truth-apt discourses and those which exert Cognitive Command, is warded off, and an argument that, to the contrary and owing to the theoretically conditioned character of all observation, *no* discourse actually passes the test is developed in detail. I still regard this latter argument as a major problem. Chapter 5 focuses on the Harman–Wiggins–Sturgeon debate and Width of Cosmological Role.

It is left to the final chapter to consider the neutralisation of the debate between realist and anti-realist which some have felt is implicitly accomplished by Wittgenstein's discussion of following a rule. One version of this idea, elicitable from John McDowell's writings on Wittgenstein, is considered and rejected. But there is a different, very simple train of thought which proves surprisingly durable. This says that, whatever exactly Wittgenstein's dialectic accomplishes, it surely imposes some kind of dilution of a realist conception of rules and meanings. Accordingly, since truth is a function of meaning, that dilution, whatever exactly it is supposed to be, has likewise to apply to all ascriptions of truth, whatever their subject matter. The rule-following considerations would accordingly seem to set an upper bound on the robustness of the realism which is available anywhere: one cannot be more robustly realist about any discourse than the rule-following considerations allow one to be about judgements concerning meanings, rules and what complies with them. And if, in particular, one takes the effect of Wittgenstein's discussion to be that such judgements are merely minimally truth-apt, and exhibit no other realism-relevant features, then mere minimal truth-aptitude must be the story everywhere. The final chapter of *Truth and Objectivity* is concerned with the development of this intuitive threat to its programme up to a point where it is clear at least that the difficulty does not succumb to the most immediate rejoinders. However, it is argued that, as a worst-case scenario, minimalism about rules and meanings will still permit the formulation of versions of the various cruces and will not, except in the one case of Evidence Transcendence, predetermine how particular discourses fare in relation to them. The real worry, I suggest, is not that the needed contrasts may be subverted or that all our thinking may turn out to occupy some uniform station, far removed from classical realist aspiration, but that the *interest* of the distinctions which we may yet be able to draw may be lost—that it may be possible to save the traditional debates only at the price of depriving them of the metaphysical import that their protagonists want to think they have. I regard this matter as wide open.

2 Realism, Anti-Realism, Irrealism, Quasi-Realism

I

It is, as is familiar, difficult to be precise about what is involved in realism. The realist in us wants to hold to a certain sort of very general view about our place in the world, a view that, as I have put it elsewhere, mixes modesty with presumption.[1] On the one hand, it is supposed, modestly, that how matters stand in the world, what opinions about it are true, is settled independently of whatever germane beliefs are held by actual people.[2] On the other, we presume to think that we are capable of arriving at the right concepts with which to capture at least a substantial part of the truth, and that our cognitive capacities can and do very often put us in position to know the truth, or at least to believe it with ample justification. The unique attraction of realism is the nice balance of feasibility and dignity that it offers to

1. In the introduction to Wright (1993a), which elaborates many of the themes of parts I and II of this essay.

2. A qualification even of this formulation would be necessary to make space for realism about self-intimating mental states.

our quest for knowledge. Greater modesty would mean doubts about the capacity of our cognitive procedures to determine what is true—or even about our capacity to conceptualise the truth—and so would be a slide in the direction of scepticism. Greater presumption would mean calling into question, one way or another, the autonomy of truth, and so would be a slide in the direction of idealism. To the extent that we are serious about the pursuit of truth, we are unlikely to be attracted by either tendency. We want the mountain to be climbable, but we also want it to be a real mountain, not some sort of reification of aspects of ourselves.

It is a remarkable phenomenon that an issue of this degree of abstractness, whose proper formulation is so unclear that it is prima facie hazy what shape a relevant debate about it might assume, can so command intellectual curiosity. The conviction that a real issue is being presented is the conviction that metaphysics, in the most traditional sense, is possible: that there are genuine questions about the objectivity of human intellectual endeavour, and about the constitution of reality, which it falls to the traditional philosophical methods of critical reflection and analysis to resolve, if resolution is possible. This conviction may be baseless and may yet be shown to be so by the application of just those methods. But we should work very hard before drawing that conclusion. The intellectual satisfaction associated with properly formulating and responding to these questions will be far greater than that of a repudiation of them, however well motivated.

In any case, it is evident that progress can be consequent only on some clarifications, perhaps in unexpected directions. One deservedly influential attempt at such a clarification has been Michael Dummett's.[3] I begin by indicating certain causes for dissatisfaction with Dummett's proposal, and will then try to consider what more generally apt analysis of realism may be appropriate if the metaphysi-

3. See especially essays 1, 10, 14 and 21 in Dummett (1978); chap. 20 of Dummett (1981); and Dummett (1976).

cal issues are to emerge both as reasonably definite in content and as (at least potentially) tractable. I am bound to confess to a certain pessimism about the ultimate possibility of this project. But my suggestions here must, in any case, be sketchy. And the thought is always consoling that, often in philosophy, it is more instructive to travel than to get anywhere.

II

No one has to be a realist, or not *tout court*. It is open to us to regard only some of our commitments as apt to engage with reality in the appropriate way. Realism about theoretical science, for example, need not commit one to realism about pure mathematics—and, indeed, one may wish to be only eclectically realist within science, taking an anti-realist view of quantum theory, for instance. Dummett's original view was that the distinctive and proper thesis of realism about a particular genre of statements is that each of them is determinately either true or false—that the principle of bivalence holds good for them. The point of the proposal is best appreciated if we concentrate on a class of statements—say, those concerning the past beyond living memory—for whose truth values we cannot guarantee to be able to get evidence one way or the other. Holding that bivalence is valid for such statements is holding that each is, nevertheless, guaranteed to be true or false. It would appear to follow that what confers truth or falsity on such a statement must be something separate from and independent of whatever makes for the availability of evidence for the statement's truth value—if anything does. Hence, in particular, such a statement's being true cannot be the same thing as its meeting even our most refined criteria for its truth. The truth is, thus, independent of human opinion, which is the key realist notion.[4]

4. Again, a qualification is called for, to make space for realism about statements that *concern* human opinion.

This line of thought has its problems,[5] but here I shall assume that it is in good order as far as it goes. That, however, does not seem to be far enough. One drawback of Dummett's proposal, remarked by a number of commentators, is that a Dummettian 'realist' about a given class of statements may also be a reductionist about them. Someone who held, for instance, that statements about the mental may be exhaustively analysed in behavioural terms could also consistently hold that the analysis would be bivalence-preserving; anyway, they would have to hold, presumably, that the analysis would respect the lack of any guarantee of available evidence, one way or the other, for such statements. But such a view would hardly involve what we think of as realism about the *mental*. Dummett, it should be emphasised, has never been under any illusions about this[6] and would be content to add, I think, that realism must be a view about what makes for the truth of statements when they are literally and non-reductively construed. But a more serious worry concerns vagueness. If the members of the germane class of statements are vague, then we precisely do not want to hold that each of them is guaranteed to be determinately either true or false. At the same time, vague statements are capable of truth and falsity, and a realist conception ought to be possible, it seems, of what makes for the state of affairs when they do possess determinate truth values.[7]

One response would be to suggest that, when bivalence is inappropriate for this sort of reason, Dummett's proposal should reduce, in effect, to the claim that truth may be *evidence-transcendent*: the truth of a statement, vague or otherwise, need have no connection with the

---

5. As it stands, it involves a *non sequitur,* generated by substituting into an opaque context: 'it is guaranteed that P' and 'it is not guaranteed that Q' do not entail the falsity of the biconditional: P ↔ Q. See Wright (1993a), chap. 16, section 1.

6. See, for example, essays 10 and 21 in Dummett (1978).

7. Dummett notes the problem posed by vagueness for his original account of realism in chap. 20 of Dummett (1981), p. 440. This chapter substantially qualifies the original account (though for somewhat different reasons). For a useful discussion of the new account, see the appendix to Rasmussen and Ravnkinde (1982).

availability of any ground, even in principle, for believing it to be true. I believe that the appropriateness of so construing truth is the deep question that Dummett's writings on the topic raise, and that such a construal is, indeed, a cardinal feature of certain realist positions, notably the Cartesian philosophy of mind, the Platonist philosophy of mathematics, and certain forms of scientific realism. But it leaves the realist with no opinion to hold when it comes to statements for which evidence, one way or the other, can be guaranteed to be available—effectively decidable mathematical statements, for instance, or a statement concerning the observable outcome of an experiment. More important still, it represents as the distinctive realist thesis something that someone might well want to oppose, though still wishing to endorse the spirit of realism. *Anti-realism,* in the sense associated with Dummett's work, is exactly the view that the notion of truth cannot intelligibly be evidentially unconstrained—or the view, at least, that once it is so unconstrained, it is no longer in terms of *truth* conditions that the meanings of the statements in question can be interpreted. But someone who believes that has, so far, no motive to forswear all use of the notion of truth (whatever exactly that would involve), unless it is supposed that truth is always and essentially epistemically unconstrained—a supposition that falls foul of evident fact that, for a great many types of statements, we can make no sense of the idea of their being true if we have to suppose that evidence for their truth is not, at least in principle, available. Indeed, in contrast to the direction of much of Dummett's work on this topic, it is not clear that a general anti-realist semantics must be other than truth-conditional, provided the truth of a statement is always taken to require the availability of evidence for its truth. The point remains that it ought to be possible to take a realist view of what makes for the truth or falsity of statements whose truth values are not conceived as evidence-transcendent. Dummett's anti-realist, who wishes to urge that truth value should never be so conceived, seems to have no motive to reject realism in this more basic sense.

But what is more basic sense? It would pass for a platitude, I think, that whether or not a statement, envisaged as uttered on a particular occasion, would express a truth is a function only of the content it would have on that occasion and the state of the world in relevant respects. The more basic kind of realism involves, I suggest, the assumption of a sort of *mechanical* view of this platitude. Truth values are, so to speak, ground out on the interface between language and reality. What thought a particular sentence would express in a particular context depends only on the semantics of the language and germane features of the context. Whether that thought is true depends only on which thought it is and germane features of the world. At neither point does human judgement or response come into the picture. To be sure, the semantics of the language depends on institution; it is we who built the machine. But, once built, it runs by itself. Thus, of any particular statement of sufficiently definite sense, it is determinate whether it expresses a truth in any particular context, irrespective of any judgement we may make about the matter. A basic realist thought is that wherever there is truth, it is, in this way, *investigation-independent*.

Since this conception builds no epistemic constraints into the factors that determine truth, it will no doubt come easily to someone who subscribes to it to suppose that truth can transcend all evidence. And since no provision seems to be made whereby reality can fail to determine truth values, so long as the statements concerned are of sufficiently definite sense, bivalence, too, will be a natural adjunct. But the conception is completely general, available both for the class of statements whose truth we conceive as requiring the availability of evidence for their truth and for its complement. And it does nothing to alter the essential character of this conception of truth to superimpose whatever verificationist constraints we please.

The conception remains very much at the level of metaphor. But at least it is clear that realism, as characterised by it, has two quite distinct areas of obligation. The belief that a class of statements are apt to possess investigation-independent truth values depends on regarding meaning as strongly objective: what constitutes correct use of an expression in particular circumstances has to be thought of as settled somehow independently of anyone's actual dispositions of response to those circumstances. What fits the meaning is one thing; what, if anything, we are inclined to say is another; and any correspondence between the two is merely contingent. Naturally, one feels there has to be something to this thought, that if the notion of meaning, and with it the notions of truth and error, are not to collapse, there must be space for *some* kind of contrast between proper use of an expression and that use to which people may actually incline. But it is quite another question whether only a realist conception of the objectivity of meaning can avoid such a collapse. Wittgenstein assimilated the relationship between meaning and practice to that between character and behaviour.[8] The parallel is suggestive: it is quite consistent with our attaching sense to the idea of someone's action being out of character to regard what it is true to say about character—as we do—as a function of the way the subject is actually inclined to behave. But I shall not consider further what notion of the objectivity of meaning may be appropriate to the realist's purpose.[9] My point is merely that someone who inclines to the 'more basic' realism owes an account of the matter.

A philosopher who had no qualms about the objectivity of meaning as such, however, might still be dissatisfied with this kind of realism about a particular class of statements. If there are to be things that it would be correct to say, irrespective of what anyone is actually inclined to say, then—in accordance with the platitude—a contribution is called for from 'the state of the world in relevant respects'. Historically, the various forms of anti-realism, in different areas of philosophy, have been fuelled mainly by doubts about the capacity of the world to make the necessary contribution. One class of such

8. Wittgenstein (1964) I, §13.

9. For more on the objectivity of meaning, see Wright (1986c) and (1987b).

To avoid misunderstanding, let me emphasise that I see no commitment to the objectivity of meaning issuing from acceptance of the platitude as such. It all depends on what we see as determining the contents that, with assistance from the world and in accordance with the platitude, determine truth values. See Wright (1986c), pp. 273–4, reprinted as chapter 3 of *Rails to Infinity* (Wright (2001b)).

proposals is associated with more or less austere, empiricism-inspired theories of concept formation. Hume, for instance, believed that there is no way whereby we can form a properly perspicuous notion of causation except at the cost of not including all the features that popular thought attributes to it. Hence, understood as popularly intended, statements involving the notion of causation are of insufficiently definite sense, in the Humean view, to take on determinate truth values. Since they nevertheless play a relatively determinate role in our ordinary thought and language, the proper account must be that their role is not to 'correspond to the facts'—we can attain no satisfactory conception of the relevant 'facts'—but is a non-descriptive one. The instrumentalism about scientific-theoretical statements espoused by many positivists had an essentially similar rationale: a preferred theory of meaning—here, the conviction that all significant descriptive language must ultimately be analysable into a vocabulary of sense experience—transpired not to have the resources to accommodate such statements within the sanctuary of fact-stating respectability.

This kind of proposal has its primary motivation in the theory of meaning. The reality of causation, or of certain sorts of theoretical entities, is called into question only because it is doubted that we can form any genuine concepts of what such things could be. A second kind of proposal, to similar effect, has a more basic ontological motivation. Although it is true that non-descriptive theories of moral and aesthetic valuation, for instance, can be and were stimulated by positivistic views about meaning, they have, nevertheless, retained an attraction for many who find no virtue in positivism. Such philosophers simply find it metaphysically incredible, as it were, that the world might actually contain objective values to which our moral, aesthetic, and other value judgements may be seen as some sort of cognitive response. It is found baffling what kind of thing an objective value could be—in what the objective value of a situation could reside—and what part of our nature might justifiably be considered sensitive to such a commodity. The alternative to so murky and pretentious a view of, for example, moral language is, again, to account for what appear to be its genuine assertions in terms of their possession of some other non-descriptive role.[10]

There are, no doubt, other kinds of motives for similar tendencies. The general conception to which they give rise is that the range and variety of our declarative discourse somehow outstrips the categories of states of affairs that are genuinely exemplified by reality. We apparently talk as if there were moral, or scientific-theoretical, or pure mathematical states of affairs, but in truth there are not. One response to that conviction, of course, would be to dismiss the 'language games' in question as mythology. What is common to the forms of anti-realism in which we are interested here is that they eschew that response: what might be taken to be mythological descriptions are credited, instead, with some sort of different but valid role. I shall reserve the term *irrealism* as a marker for these tendencies in general, preferring 'projectivism' for a proper subclass of irrealist proposals with which we shall be concerned later. What opposes irrealism with respect to a particular class of statements is the view that the world is furnished to play the part in the determination of their truth values which the platitude calls for, that there really are states of affairs of the appropriate species.[11]

III

Our concern, then, is with the philosophical topology of irrealism. What precisely are the commitments of irrealism concerning a particular class of statements? How best might it be supported? Is it

10. A fascinating example of the second sort of proposal is provided, of course, by Saul Kripke's interpretation of Wittgenstein on rule-following and meaning in Kripke (1982).

11. However, someone who so opposes irrealism (about a particular class of statements) need not endorse the objectivity of meaning unless, contrary to my own belief, the platitude requires it, so need not be a realist in the 'more basic' sense described in section II of this essay.

ultimately coherent? For a time, during the hegemony of so-called linguistic philosophy, the irrealist tendency seemed to be channelled exclusively into various forms of *expressive* theory. Expressive theories were proposed not merely of judgements of value, but of claims about truth and about causation, professions of knowledge, descriptions of actions as voluntary, and much else.[12] The point of the notion of 'expression' here is precisely its contrast with and exclusion of assertion, properly so regarded. When one expresses something in this sense, the intention was, one makes no claim about reality,[13] even

12. Thus, Austin on knowledge:

[S]aying 'I know' is taking a new plunge. But it is *not* saying 'I have performed a specially striking feat of cognition, superior, in the same scale as believing and being sure, even to being merely quite sure': for there *is* nothing in that scale superior to being quite sure. Just as promising is not something superior, in the same scale as hoping and intending, even to merely fully intending: for there *is* nothing in that scale superior to fully intending. When I say 'I know', I *give others my word*: I *give others my authority for saying* that 'S is P'. (Austin (1970), p. 99)

Compare Strawson on truth:

The sentence 'What the policeman said is true' has no use *except* to confirm the policeman's story; but [it] does not say anything further *about* the policeman's story . . . It is a device for confirming the story without telling it again. So, in general, in using such expressions, we are confirming, underwriting, agreeing with, what somebody has said; but . . . we are not making any assertion additional to theirs; and are *never* using 'is true' to talk *about* something which is *what they said*, or the sentences they used in saying it. (Strawson (1949), p. 93)

But the classic example is Ayer on morals:

If I say to someone, 'You acted wrongly in stealing that money', I am not stating anything more than if I had simply said, 'You stole that money'. In adding that this action is wrong, I am not making any further statement about it. I am simply evincing my moral disapproval of it. It is as if I had said, 'You stole that money', in a peculiar tone of horror, or written it with the addition of some special exclamation marks. (Ayer (1936), p. 107)

13. More accurately: no *additional* claim beyond the clause embedded within the expressive vocabulary if—as, for instance, in each of the examples cited in note 12— there is one.

though the syntax of the utterance is superficially that of a genuine assertion, apt to agree or fail to agree with some putative state of affairs.

The principal difficulties encountered by these theories were twofold. First, many of the positive suggestions concerning *what* was being expressed, or more generally what, in enunciating an 'expression', people were doing, were actually quite consistent with holding that the relevant kind of sentence effected an assertion. For example, those who held that to characterise an action as voluntary was to express one's willingness to hold the subject responsible for the consequences said something that no realist about the distinction between voluntary and involuntary action would have wanted to deny. Not that this has to be an objection to the expressivist's positive claim. The point is, rather, that if the positive account offered by an expressive theory nowhere goes beyond what an opponent would acknowledge as aspects of the 'pragmatics' of the relevant class of utterances, then the theoretical obligation remains to explain why it is that these pragmatic aspects actually *exhaust* the use of the relevant sentences and are not merely consequences of their possession of a genuinely assertoric role. Historically, this obligation has not, by and large, been properly met.

Second, the syntactic similarities between the sorts of 'expression' listed and what the theorists in question would have been content to regard as genuine assertions are actually far from superficial. Sentences, for instance, which, according to emotivism, are apt merely for the expression of evaluative attitudes, display all the syntactic possibilities enjoyed by descriptions of the weather. They allow, for example, a full range of tenses, and of appraisal as 'true', 'false', 'exaggerated', 'justified', and so on; they may feature embedded in the ascription of propositional attitudes; and they admit of compounding under the full range of logical operations. In connection with the last, Peter Geach argued, in an influential note, that expressive theories have no resources with which to explain the permissible occurrence of, for example, moral sentences as the antecedents of conditionals.[14]

14. Geach (1960), pp. 221–5.

If 'Stealing is wrong' serves only to express moral disapprobation, how do we construe its role in 'If stealing is wrong, encouraging people to steal is wrong also'?

Expressivism can give no answer to this question unless it is possible to construe the antecedent of such a conditional as doing something other than hypothesising its *truth*. Dummett for one has suggested that it is.[15] Each kind of sentence for which expressive theories have been proposed is used to mark the speaker's undertaking of a certain sort of commitment. Accordingly, rather than view the conditional just as a device for focusing attention on the range of circumstances in which its antecedent is true, we can see it, more generally, as a device for articulating the consequences of acceptance of the commitment that, if someone were to avow the antecedent on its own, they would undertake. For instance, the effect of the conditional at the conclusion of the preceding paragraph would be, roughly:

> If I were (to be brought to) to express a commitment to
> the wrongness of stealing, I should also (be willing to?)
> express a commitment to the wrongness of encouraging
> others to steal.[16]

Geach's point, it might be claimed, would hardly be philosophically fundamental in any case. If moral irrealism did, indeed, have absolutely no prospect of a satisfactory construal of conditionals with moral antecedents, that could scarcely be decisive. Rather, whatever case there was for moral irrealism would become potentially revisionary of our ordinary and moral linguistic practice—compare the relation between classical mathematics and the philosophical views of the intuitionists. But such radical revisionism—in effect, the proscription of all compound moral sentences—is best avoided, and Dummett's proposal, though in some respects imprecise, at least indicates a strategy for avoiding it in the present case.

15. In Dummett (1973), chap. 10.
16. *Ibid.*, pp. 251–4.

The strategy has been taken further by Simon Blackburn in connection with what he styles the general programme of *quasi-realism*.[17] This programme comes into play by way of supplement to the irrealist (for Blackburn, 'projectivist') view of some given class of statements. Quasi-realism's goal is to show how the irrealist account of the content of these statements need not be revisionary. It proceeds by attempting to supply alternative analyses of what appear, from an irrealist point of view, to be problematic modes of construction—conditionals, embeddings within propositional attitudes, even the truth predicate itself, and so on—which are to harmonise with what the irrealist wants to say about the basic statements in the class in question. In particular, therefore, the quasi-realist constructions have to proceed without any assignment of truth conditions to these basic statements.

Actually, there are a number of significant differences between Dummett's and Blackburn's proposals. Dummett's consisted essentially in calling attention to the potential utility of a conditional construction that—unlike the ordinary conditional—hypothesises not the truth of its antecedent, but its utterance with a particular recognised illocutionary force. What is contemplated is a range of conditionals with antecedents like 'if I were to be brought to ask whether P . . .', 'if I were to be brought to assert that P . . .', 'if I were to command that P . . .', and so on. The consequents of such conditionals may, then, either describe a further such utterance or may simply say something about the circumstances that would prevail if the speech act characterised in the antecedent were to be performed. This suggests, though it is not conclusive, that Dummett was tacitly viewing expressive theories as holding 'expression' to be an illocutionary operation on a thought, just as are assertion, wish, question, and command. Undoubtedly, this is one possible view. It promises perhaps the tidiest explanation of how 'expressions' fail candidacy for truth value—one directly modelled on the corresponding failure of, for instance, an indicative sentence used to express a command. Of course, if one attempts to

17. See Blackburn (1984), chap. 6, and (1986), pp. 119–41.

view 'expression' in this way, then there has to *be* an embedded thought, just as there is in the case of the command (namely, the thought whose truth it is commanded should be brought about). So, an account will be owing of what are the genuine, truth-value-bearing thoughts that are so embedded in, for instance, moral evaluation—a possible source of difficulty if the case is an example like 'Stealing is wrong', rather than 'You were wrong to steal that money'.

Whether or not this was Dummett's perception of the matter, Blackburn's seems different. If an apparent assertion is not a genuine assertion, that is, a claim that something is true, it may be a different mode of illocution of something apt to be true; but it may also be construed as a different kind of speech act altogether, no sort of operation on a thought. Blackburn's reaction to the problem of construing moral compounds, and especially conditionals with moral antecedents, is in keeping with this second conception. For Dummett, such conditionals emerge as genuine assertions. Blackburn, in contrast, has it that a conditional such as

If stealing is wrong, encouraging others to steal is wrong

is *itself* an evaluation; to wit, a positive evaluation of combining a negative evaluation of stealing with a negative evaluation of encouraging others to steal.

How do these proposals respectively cope with Geach's challenge to explain the validity of such an inference as

Stealing is wrong.
If stealing is wrong, encouraging others to steal is wrong.
So: encouraging others to steal is wrong.

On Dummett's account, the conditional premise becomes something like:

If I ever (am brought to) negatively evaluate stealing, then I also (will be willing to) negatively evaluate encouraging others to steal.

24

If that conditional is true, then if I so perform as to realise its antecedent—that is, I endorse the first premise—then it follows that I
thereby endorse, or at least that I will be willing to endorse, the
wrongness of encouraging others to steal. So, it looks as though,
modulo its inexactness, Dummett's proposal may well have the
means to validate Geach's example. One might wonder, though,
about whether the inference, even if valid as so construed, is properly
represented by Dummett's account. The gist of the second premise
ought to be not a description of a performance that I will actually (be
ready to) carry out in certain circumstances, but rather, something
normative: it is that a negative evaluation of stealing *ought* to be
accompanied by a negative evaluation of the practice of encouraging
others to steal.

In this respect, Blackburn's strategy of construing the conditional
as itself an evaluation seems superior. But what, now, does the validity
of the inference consist in—when it cannot be that the truth of the
premises guarantees that of the conclusion?[18] Anything worth calling
the validity of an inference has to reside in the inconsistency of
accepting its premises but denying its conclusion. Blackburn does
indeed speak of the 'clash of attitudes' involved in endorsing the
premises of the modus ponens example, construed as he construes it,
but in failing to endorse the conclusion. But nothing worth regarding
as *inconsistency* seems to be involved. Those who do that merely fail
to have every combination of attitudes of which they themselves
approve. That is a *moral* failing, not a logical one.[19]

---

18. That, note, still is the character of the inference when the conditional is construed in Dummett's way. The result is something on the model of:

> I hereby ask whether Q.
> If I ask whether Q, I expect an answer.
> So: I expect an answer.

19. In his excellent critical study of *Spreading the Word*, Hale (1986) notes that
Blackburn's construal of the conditional is, in any case, inapposite for examples like:

> If Jones stole that money, he should be punished.

Generally, there is no difficulty in making out a notion of inconsistency for speech acts other than assertion, provided they represent genuine modes of illocutionary force, that is, operations on a thought.

---

whose role cannot possibly be to evaluate a combination of evaluations since the antecedent is not evaluative. His ingenious proposal is, first, to refashion the account of:

> If stealing is wrong, encouraging others to steal is wrong.

as a *negative* evaluation of combining a negative evaluation of stealing with *the lack of* a negative evaluation of encouraging others to steal; and, second, to include not just evaluations, but beliefs (and presumably propositional attitudes in general) within the scope of such second-order evaluations. The conditional about Jones would then emerge as a negative evaluation of the combinations of believing that Jones stole the money but failing to approve of (positively evaluate) his punishment.

No question but that this improves Blackburn's account, and may well indicate the only viable direction for it to follow. But, notwithstanding some suggestive remarks by Hale (1986, pp. 73–4), I do not think it deflects the criticism bruited that Blackburn must misconstrue the failing of one who accepts the premises of the modus ponens example, but does not accept the conclusion. Certainly, the character of the 'inconsistency' changes: it is now a matter not of *failing* to have every combination of evaluations of which one approves, but of *actually having* a combination—a negative evaluation of stealing and the lack of a negative evaluation of encouraging others to steal—of which one *disapproves*. However, though such conduct—'doing what you boo', as Hale describes it—is naturally described as 'inconsistent', it remains that this is *moral* inconsistency: conduct that is not true to moral principle. But it is undeniable that someone who rejects Geach's inference is being, in addition, *irrational*—and this additional failing, separate from the moral one, is just as evident if he merely rejects the conditional:

> Provided that stealing is wrong, and that, if stealing is wrong,
> encouraging others to steal is wrong, then encouraging others to steal is
> wrong,

without endorsing any particular evaluation of the conjuncts in its antecedent.

A related worry (acknowledged by Hale in correspondence) is whether a projectivist who follows Hale's direction can, once having construed 'mixed' conditionals as evaluations, avoid so construing *all* conditionals. Of course, expressive theories of the conditional have their supporters, too. But there is something unhappy about being pushed towards such an account quite generally, merely by the conviction that morals are of limited objectivity.

Commands, for instance, are inconsistent just in case the thoughts are inconsistent whose truth they command be brought about; questions are inconsistent just in case the thoughts of whose truth they enquire are inconsistent; and so on. Even in these cases, the notion of inconsistency need not carry the stigma associated with assertoric case. Issuing inconsistent commands is irrational—at least if one intends that they be obeyed. But asking inconsistent questions is not. And, in any case, this seems to be, as noted, the wrong model for Blackburn's purposes. Evaluation, as he seems to conceive it, is not a mode of illocutionary force.[20]

Neither account, then, seems to cope entirely happily with the modus ponens inference. Dummett's account fails to reflect the normativity of the conditional premise; Blackburn's fails to respect the powerful prejudice that the failing of one who accepted the premises but repudiated the conclusion would not be merely moral. But there is, to my mind, a deeper cause for dissatisfaction with both approaches. What they have in common is that they see the presence of a certain kind of vocabulary—that of moral or aesthetic evaluation, for instance, or that of logical necessity and modality in general—as marking the performance of a certain kind of speech act, distinct from assertion (at least when the latter is properly regarded as the

20. Actually, and independently of the illocutionary status of evaluation, there is, of course, a notion of inconsistency for evaluations quite similar to that mooted for commands: a set of evaluations, positive and negative, is inconsistent just in case no possible world realises all the positives but avoids realising all the negatives. But this is of no obvious help in the present case. Whether the conditional is construed as originally by Blackburn, or as proposed by Hale (see note 19), one who endorses both 'Stealing is wrong' and 'If stealing is wrong, encouraging others to steal is wrong', but denies 'Encouraging others to steal is wrong', commits himself to no such inconsistent set of evaluations. There is, I have urged, a logical inconsistency in such a performance, different from both the forms of moral inconsistency that, respectively, are disclosed by the Blackburn–Hale proposals. But neither the logical inconsistency nor those types of moral inconsistency are instances of this inter-evaluational species of inconsistency. The former has essentially nothing to do with the values the subject actually accepts (compare note 19). And the latter concerns not the relations among his values, but those between his values and his conduct.

purported depiction of truth). It does not matter, now, whether the speech act in question is strictly a mode of illocutionary force or whether it is something else. In neither case are the materials at hand, it seems, for an explanation of the role of *iterated* applications of the vocabulary in question.[21] So neither proposal promises any sort of satisfactory account of the kind of applications that we seem, intelligibly enough, to be able to make of notions like logical necessity and logical possibility to statements in which such modal notions are themselves the principal operators. Such applications may not be very important in ordinary inferential contexts; but they are tremendously important in modal logic, and they are, it should be stressed, apparently intelligible. If, in contrast, affirming 'necessarily P' is some kind of projection from my inability to imagine the opposite, or marks the adoption of P as some kind of linguistic rule, or expresses my resolve to count nothing as falsification of P—or whatever the preferred expressive account is—no space seems to have been left for a construal of 'necessarily: necessarily P'.

Blackburn himself is strongly committed to the progressive character of the projectivist–quasi-realist research programme with respect to modal idiom,[22] but the point is not (merely) ad hominem. It is that modality undoubtedly raises the same kinds of problems, in this context, as does morality. There is the same kind of difficulty in seeing our judgements, modal or moral, as responses to objective features of the world. In both cases, we feel the want of a satisfactory account of the confidence that, on occasion anyway, we repose in such judgements; in both cases, philosophers have been tempted to invoke special cognitive faculties, sensitive to states of affairs of the problematic kind, as our ordinary senses are sensitive to many of the characteristics of our physical environment. In neither case has any account of this kind achieved anything but mystery. This is not to say that an irrealist account of either can be satisfactory only if it handles both equally well. But it is to suggest that the general form of an irrealist account of morals should at least be a starter in the case of modal dis-

21. The point is made in Hale (1986), pp. 78–9.
22. See, for example, Blackburn (1986), cited in note 17.

course also. There may, in the end, be good reason for rejecting the irrealist account of either or both. But we can hardly suppose that we are entertaining the strongest possible version of such an account until it is fashioned in such a way that it can be adapted to any of the areas of discourse about which an irrealist (or, more specifically, projectivist) tale may seem worth telling.

The proper response to the foregoing considerations, it seems to me, is to recognise that the step in the direction of expressive, or more generally non-assertoric accounts of those areas of discourse that, for various reasons, have inspired irrealist suspicions, is a *faux pas*. The irrealist should seek not to explain away the assertoric appearance, but to sever the connection between assertion and the realism, which he wishes to oppose. This direction has been largely passed over, no doubt, because of the intimate connection between assertion and truth: to assert a statement is to present it as true. So if moral, or modal judgements rank as assertions, we are bound to countenance, it seems, some notion of moral, or modal truth. If this seems a fatal step from a would-be irrealist point of view, it can only be because it is being assumed that where there is truth at all, realism is correct. But that is an error. Realism, even when characterised as impressionistically as above, evidently intends a conception of truth that should be understood along the line traditionally favoured by 'correspondence' theorists. What else could be the point of the play with the idea of an 'independent' reality, one that 'confers' truth values independently of our judgements? By contrast, it has yet to be understood why the notion of truth which essentially engages with that of assertion may not be the thinnest possible, merely 'disquotational' notion.

To assert a statement is to present it as true, but there need be no supposition that the notion of truth is uniform across all regions of assertoric discourse. The proper focus for the dispute between realist and irrealist tendencies in moral philosophy, the philosophy of science, the philosophy of mathematics, and elsewhere is on the notion of truth appropriate to these various kinds of statements. Actually, this is the conclusion to which Blackburn's quasi-realist programme must, if successful, lead. The goal of the quasi-realist is to explain how *all* the features of some problematic region of discourse that might inspire a realist construal of it can be harmonised with objectivism. But if this programme succeeds, and provides inter alia—as Blackburn himself anticipates—an account of what appear to be ascriptions of truth and falsity to statements in the region, then we shall wind up—running the connection between truth and assertion in the opposite direction—with a rehabilitation of the notion that such statements rank as assertions, with truth conditions, after all. Blackburn's quasi-realist thus confronts a rather obvious dilemma. Either his programme fails—in which case he does not, after all, explain how the projectivism that inspires it can satisfactorily account for the linguistic practices in question—or it succeeds, in which case it makes good all the things the projectivist started out wanting to deny: that the discourse in question is genuinely assertoric, aimed at truth, and so on. The dilemma is fatal unless what the projectivist originally wanted to maintain is actually consistent with the admission that the statements in question are, indeed, assertions, apt to be true or false in the sense, but only in the sense, that the quasi-realist explains. But if that is right, then the route through the idea that such statements are not genuinely assertoric but are 'expressive', or, one way or another, constitute some other kind of speech act, emerges as a detour. Working with that idea, and pursuing the quasi-realist programme on its basis, may help us to focus on the notion of truth that *is* appropriate to the statements in question. But once that focus is achieved, we have to drop the idea—and it hardly seems credible that only by this somewhat circuitous route can the requisite focus be gained.[23]

IV

Naturally, it is questionable whether the notion of truth can, indeed, be divided up in the manner that the foregoing considerations anticipate, and also, if it can, whether reasonably definite criteria can emerge

---

23. For pursuit of these misgivings, see the review of *Spreading the Word* in Wright (1985b).

for determining which notion is applicable within which areas of discourse. And correspondence accounts, should they prove to be the stuff of realism, have their familiar problems.[24] But, still, I think there is a programme here, and that the beginnings of some germane distinctions can be sketched.

How 'thin' can something worth regarding as a notion of truth be? We do not have a truth predicate if we merely have a device of 'disquotation', since such a device could as well be applied to utterances that are not assertions. And, it may seem, it will hardly do to say that a predicate that functions disquotationally just for assertions is a truth predicate; that account, if it is not to be circular, will require us to separate assertions from speech acts of other kinds without appeal to the notion of truth, an unpromising project. Actually, I believe the commitment to avoid circularity of this kind would be an impossible burden in the quest for an account of truth. But, in any case, one essential aspect omitted by a bare disquotational account of truth is *normativity:* truth is what assertions aim for. Now, if aiming at truth is to supply a substantial constraint on assertoric practice, an assertion's being true cannot be guaranteed simply by the assertor's taking it to be true. A constraint is substantial only if we can make sense of the idea of a misapprehension about whether or not it is satisfied, or of its being satisfied independently of any particular subject's opinion about the matter. The normativity of truth is respected by an assertoric practice only if a role is provided within that practice for the notions of ignorance, error, and improved assessment.

This, I think, is the least that must be asked. Nor is it very much. What is called for is only some *sort* of notion of a proper pedigree for an assertion, and correspondingly proper grounds for criticism of assertions. We do, indeed, practise these distinctions in all the areas of

24. Of which the foremost is probably Frege's regress argument, given in his paper 'Thoughts', in Frege (1977), pp. 3–4. See the discussion in Carruthers (1981). For a very illuminating analysis of the issues between correspondence and disquotational or 'deflationary' accounts of truth, see the contributions by Field (1986) and Forbes (1986).

discourse about which philosophers have been drawn to an irrealistic point of view. Even the sort of affective judgements—concerning what is funny, or revolting, and so on—about which almost every-body's antecedent prejudice is irrealist are allowed to be capable of being better and worse made. Judgements about what is funny, for instance, may be in bad taste, or idiosyncratic, or insincere, or just plain wrong. (There is nothing funny about what happened at Chernobyl.)

There is a connection here with Geach's point. We should have, in general, no use for conditional or disjunctive compounds of such judgements unless it was sometimes possible to appraise the truth values of the compounds independently of any knowledge of those of their constituents. Otherwise, knowledge of such a compound could never be of any practical inferential use, and its assertion would always violate Gricean 'co-operative' constraints. It is, thus, a condition of practically significant embedding of the kind Geach focused on that ignorance be possible concerning the status of the embedded statements. And ignorance is possible only if there is, indeed, a contrast in content between the claim that P is true and the claim that any particular subject assents to P—the contrast that, I have just suggested, is prerequisite for paying proper heed to the normativity of truth.

It appears, then—if I am permitted a somewhat swift conclusion—that truth, assertion, ignorance, error and significant embedding constitute a package deal. We get all of them off the ground together, or none of them. And the real significance of Geach's anti-expressivist point is that they are 'off the ground' in all the familiar cases where expressivists wanted to look away from the notion of assertion and to characterise practices in other terms. The question, then, is: What can, nevertheless, be missing? What may a region of discourse lack, even when it has all this, which may inspire doubts about its factuality?

The answer, in one unhelpful word, is 'objectivity'. I think that a number of separable ideas jostle each other here, and I have space only to advert to three of the more important. The first has to do with what I shall call the *rational command* of truth. The second concerns the distinction between (human) responses that, respectively, are and are not properly regarded as *cognitive*. The third I shall touch on at the end of this essay.

By the 'rational command' of truth, I mean the idea that truth commands the assent of any subject who has an appropriate cognitive endowment and uses it appropriately. Associated with this is the notion that belief is not an operation of the will. We do not choose our beliefs, but come to them involuntarily—though not necessarily, of course, as a result of involuntary processes—by putting ourselves at the mercy, so to speak, of our reason, our senses, any other 'cognitive receptors' we may have and the external world. Truth, then, according to this feature of the concept, is what is at the origin of the beliefs we form when we function, cognitively, as we ought.

In describing this as part of our 'concept' of truth, I mean only that it is a feature of the way we ordinarily think about truth. One of the oldest philosophical lessons is that there are other, potentially destructive elements within the notion—elements that traditional sceptical arguments exploit—that threaten to reduce the correspondence, if any, between what is true and the deliverances of our better cognitive natures to inscrutable contingency. Even prescinding from scepticism, realists in the sense of Dummett will want to insist that we can understand, for at least a significant number of kinds of statements, how their truth might altogether fail to connect with any disposition on our part to believe them, no matter how meticulous and extensive our investigation. And, in the other direction, everyone must acknowledge that what we are induced to believe by meticulous and extensive investigation may still not be the truth in any examples where no such finite investigation can encompass all the material, as it were, in which evidence of untruth might be found. Explicitly unrestricted, contingent generalisations and any statement that—like many ascriptions of dispositions—implicitly contains such a generality are the obvious instances.

One response, which would continue to allot a dominant role to the aspect of rational command, would be to move in the direction of a Peircean conception of truth: we can mean by 'truth' only that which is fated to be agreed on by all who pursue rational enquiry sufficiently far, a 'final opinion . . . independent not indeed of thought in general, but of all that is arbitrary and individual in thought'.[25] Such a conception dismisses the total or partial epistemological absolutism involved in scepticism and in Dummettian realism. And it relaxes the sense in which the truth of an unrestricted generalisation must command the assent of a rational investigator: a well-founded investigation may, indeed, mislead, but if such a generalisation is true, all rational investigators will, sooner or later, come justifiably to believe that it is.

This has been an influential construal of the notion of truth. But, insofar as some sort of preconception about the failure of certain statements to exemplify rational command is at work in the motivation for some kinds of irrealism, it is questionable whether the Peircean construct gets it quite right. For one thing, it very much *is* a philosophers' construct, building on but going a good way past anything that might plausibly be regarded as our intuitive understanding of truth. For another, the thought that only Peircean truths are true in the substantial sense we seek may seem to hold out too many hostages to fortune. If, for instance, Quine's famous thesis of the underdetermination of scientific theory by empirical data is true (fated to be agreed by all rational investigators?), then it seems that the hypotheses of such theories cannot pass the Peircean test. That would be too swift a resolution of the debate about scientific realism. Worse, any statement whose conditions of justifiable assent are a function of what else a subject believes are at risk in the same way. If whether you ought to believe a particular statement depends on what you already believe, Peircean convergence could be expected only among rational investigators who set out with the same baggage, as it were. And it has yet to be explained why their rationality alone should tend to ensure that that is so. Yet, almost all our contingent beliefs appear to be in this situation.

A Peircean can reply. The possibility adverted to is the possibility that there may be rationally incommensurable alternative systems of belief. If that is so, we can either retain the idea that one such system

25. From Peirce (1966), p. 82.

might contain the truth at the expense of the others, or we can drop the idea. To retain it is to render the connection between truth and rational enquiry utterly fortuitous. To drop it is to abandon or to relativise the notion of an accurate representation of the world. In neither case is room left for the idea that the truth is what commands the assent of an appropriately cognitively endowed, rational investigator. So the Peircean development of the notion of rational command should not be faulted on the ground that it cannot accommodate the possible consequences of the underdetermination thesis or of justificational holism. The fact is that whatever notion of truth survives for statements that fall prey to those consequences simply cannot have the feature of rational command. My own opinion is that not very much of what we are pleased to regard as factual discourse will actually fall prey to those consequences. In particular, a holistic conception of confirmation poses a global threat only if, at some level, the selection of background beliefs is unconstrained. There is no reason to suppose that this must be so, but the matter raises very large issues, which I shall not attempt to broach here.

Even so, I think the intuition of rational command should be explained along other than Peircean lines. For it is an intuition that co-exists with our inclination (however unfortunate) to allow that truth may be evidence-transcendent. So, the intuitive point is not what is true ultimately commands the assent of the rational. It is, I suggest, that what it is correct to think about any statement that is apt to be, in the appropriately substantial sense, true or false is something about which rational investigators have no option at *any given stage of investigation*. It is, more specifically, determinate of any given body of evidence whether it supports such a statement, or supports its negation, or neither. Even that is too simple. Vague statements, for instance, may nevertheless be factual. But their vagueness consists precisely in the existence of a range of cases where rational subjects may permissibly and irreducibly disagree about their status in point of justification. A similar point applies to statements, vague or not, for which the evidence is probabilistic. Different subjects may, without putting their rationality in jeopardy, have different probability thresholds, so to speak. One may require a higher probability than another before being prepared to work on the expectation that a hypothesis is true. But, so far as I can see, only in these two respects is qualification necessary. If a pair of subjects disagree about the credibility of a particular statement, and if the explanation of the disagreement concerns neither of the qualifications just noted, then either they are operating on the basis of different pools of evidence—states of information—or one (perhaps both) is misrating the evidence they share. If the states of information are different, and neither is misrating the state of information, then one state must be superior to the other: either it must contain bona fide data that the other lacks, or it must omit spurious data that the other contains. Accordingly, we may lay down the following as a criterion for the inclusion of a statement, or range of statements within the category of those apt to be true in the substantial sense—the sense which incorporates the aspects of rational command: disagreements about the status of such statements, where not attributable to vagueness or permissibly differing probability thresholds, can be explained only if fault is found with one of the protagonist's assessment of his or her data, or with the data being assessed. The data must be in some way faulty or incomplete, or, if not, must have suffered a prejudiced response.

It follows that reason to think that other kinds of explanation of disagreement are possible is reason to think that the statements disagreed about are not objective in the relevant sense, and so not apt to be substantially true or false. This is one of the primary motives that have fuelled expressive theories. It is surely, for instance, the mainspring of the thought that judgements about what is funny are not genuinely factual: none of the envisaged explanations may be appropriate in the case of a disagreement about humour—it may be, as we say, that the subjects have different 'senses of humour'. It is for the same reason that importance is attached, in the debates about moral and aesthetic realism, to the (much exaggerated) cultural variability of moral standards and the often idiosyncratic character of standards of aesthetic excellence.

It is another question, though, how one would actually set about showing that a given region of discourse failed to pass the test. A model dispute must be constructed whose explanation falls within none of the alternatives noted: it is not, that is to say, to be owing to vagueness in the statement(s) disputed about, nor to permissibly different probability thresholds, nor to faulty data—including inferential or observational error—nor to one of the subject's possession of a relatively inferior state of information, nor to a prejudiced assessment of agreed data.[26] But the question is, of course, what, for these purposes, counts as 'a state of information' or 'data'? What will tend to happen when this construction is attempted for a particular problematic class of statements—about humour, or value, or logical necessity, for instance—is that it will be relatively easy to construct a dispute that fits the bill, provided the 'data' are restricted to *other* kinds of statement whose factuality is not at issue. It is often possible, for instance, to give reasons for or against the opinion that some situation is funny; but, as just remarked, it seems perfectly conceivable that a pair of subjects may have an irreducible disagreement about such an opinion, although neither is under any misapprehension about any pertinent facts, or knows more than the other, or is somehow prejudicially over- or underrating the facts that they agree about. But this way of describing the matter explicitly takes it that the 'facts' exclude whether or not the situation in question is funny. A similar possibility obtains in the case of logical necessity.[27] And it does not seem unlikely that moral evaluations, for instance, are in a like situation, although I shall not pause here to consider the construction of an appropriate dispute.

In any such case, it is open to the realist to accept the proposed criterion but to insist that the germane data may not legitimately be

---

26. And 'dispute' here means, of course, genuine dispute. There must be no material misunderstanding.

27. For details of how such a dispute might run, see the dialogue with the Cautious Man in chapter 3 of Wright (1980). Compare Wright (1986b).

taken to exclude facts of the very species that the problematic statements apparently serve to record. The comic realist,[28] for instance,
may accommodate the model dispute that an opponent constructs by
insisting that misappraisal of the data must, indeed, be at the root of
it; it is just that the data misappraised may irreducibly concern the
humour, or lack of it, in the situation.

The *structure* of this manoeuvre is not unreasonable. Plainly, it
cannot always be the case that, for any particular class of statements
whose factuality is not disputed, they would pass the test even if we
restricted our attention to 'data' that excluded them; not all genuinely
factual disagreements have to be owing to mistakes, or ignorance, or
prejudice about other matters. But the upshot is not that the proposed
test is useless, but merely that it has a part to play only in the first
stage of a dialectic, which must now be pressed further. The test
connects failure to agree about judgements that are apt to be substantially true or false with failure of *ideal cognitive performance*.
Accordingly, the realist who responds in the way described now owes
something by way of explanation of what ideal cognitive performance might be with respect to the *sui generis* states of affairs to
which, as such a realist now contends, our judgements of humour, or
value, or modality, or whatever are responsive. We require to be told
how it is possible for us to be in touch with states of affairs of the relevant kind. What is it about them, and about us, that makes them—at
least ideally—accessible to us? It is no answer, of course, merely to
introduce a word or phrase for some putative kind of special cognitive faculty—'the sense of humour', 'conscience', 'the reason'—that is
to play the appropriate part. It is true that some of our judgements
must be, so to speak, *primitively* factual, from the point of view of the
test. But that is not to say that we have carte blanche to regard in this
way any class of judgements that would otherwise fail the test. Where
there is cognition, there must be at least the possibility of a satisfactory theoretical account of how it is accomplished.

The first preconception about a substantial notion of truth was

28. Not all realists are comic, of course.

its possession of the feature of rational command. Now we have, in effect, arrived at the second: statements are apt to be substantially true or false only if it is possible to provide a satisfactory account of the kind of cognitive powers that a mind would have to have in order to be in touch with the states of affairs that they purportedly describe.[29] But what should 'a satisfactory account' mean here? I take it that it would not be necessary to trouble ourselves with the question if it could be shown that the judgements that the realist wishes to take as expressive of special cognitive abilities could actually be satisfactorily simulated, without collusion, by a subject who had only cognitive powers that both the realist and his irrealist opponent are agreed about. Thus, if, for instance, assertibility conditions could be laid down for judgements of logical necessity that someone could recognise to obtain, whose cognitive faculties embraced only the capacity for empirical judgements and so excluded anything sensitive to logical necessity as such, it would be, on the face of it, simply a bad explanation of our handling of such judgements to view it as expressive of anything additional. *Facultates non fingendae sunt praeter necessitatem.*[30]

The irrealist, however, may not easily be able to make out such a case. This will be the situation when the ability to make acceptable, or at any rate, sincere and apparently well-understood judgements of the kind in question will depend on the subject's capacity to be *affected* in some distinctive way: to be amused, for instance, or revolted. If possessing such affective capacities is a necessary condition of full competence with the judgements in question, the irrealist's question has to be, rather, why see such affection as cognition? And the thought is, of course, that no 'satisfactory account' either of the affective response itself or of its causes can be given that will legitimate the realist's view. Contrast the sort of story that can be told about our perceptual knowledge of our immediate environment. Our theories of the nature

---

29. I try to deploy this feature of substantial truth in the context of a strategy against traditional epistemological scepticism in Wright (1985a).

30. Compare Wright (1980), chap. 23, pp. 456–60.

of matter and of the workings of our sense organs and brains are hardly complete. But we know enough to tell an elaborate story about my perception of the telephone on my desk—about the kind of object it is, and the kind of creature I am, and about why, accordingly, I am able to be aware of its being there in the way in which I am. However, we have not the slightest idea how to extend this prototype to the cases of value or humour or logical necessity. And, since that is so, it is perfectly idle to claim that, in our judgements of these various kinds, we express cognitive responses to objective states of affairs.

The likely realist reply will be to suggest that the kind of explanatory model invoked is question-begging. In insisting that the epistemology of a certain putative range of states of affairs ultimately be accounted for in terms of existing fields of natural science, the irrealist loads the dice in favour of a naturalistic ontology. The states of affairs that pass the test implicitly imposed can only be those to which natural science assigns a causal role. Accordingly, as before, it is open to the realist to claim that the suggested criterion—that a class of judgements is apt to be substantially true or false only if a satisfactory account of the (ideal) epistemology can be given—is in itself acceptable, but that it is being applied here in a tendentiously restricted way. The moral realist can urge, for instance, that just as the 'data' that figured in the statement of the first criterion should be allowed to include moral data, so a 'satisfactory account', as the notion figures in the second criterion, should be allowed to proceed by reference to a framework that includes not only natural science, but also, inter alia, moral judgement.

Does this help? Well, it might be supposed that once moral judgements themselves are allowed to be explanatorily primitive, the account of our cognition of the truth of some particular moral judgement may straightforwardly proceed by inducing the kinds of consideration that incline us to that particular judgement, namely, a moral argument based on both moral and non-moral premises. This, though, will hardly do. Such a model explanation of moral 'knowledge' would no doubt overestimate the extent to which our convictions on particular questions are principled, and would be inapplicable, besides, to at least some of the moral premises that applications of it would be likely to involve. But what is most basically wrong is that no real analogy is constructed with the perceptual case. It is not to our *knowledge* of neurophysiology and physics, for instance, that the explanation of my capacity to perceive the telephone would appeal, but to relevant hypotheses *within* those disciplines themselves. By contrast, the kind of 'explanation' of our moral knowledge, just canvassed explicitly, does appeal, not to certain moral premises, but to our knowledge of them. So it cannot provide what was being requested: an explanation of what it is about us, and about the moral realm, that makes for the possibility of cognitive relations at all.

In general, then, though it would be, I think, a fair complaint by an evaluative realist, for instance, that the original explicitly naturalistic version of the second test is unfairly loaded, the prospects for the position do not seem to become much brighter if we grant, for the sake of argument, that *moral* theory be permitted to figure in the *explanans*. Indeed, prescinding from the confusion just discussed, it is unclear what, for these purposes, moral 'theory' might be taken to be, and how it might be exploited by a more liberal style of explanation. Matters look hardly more promising for modal and comic realism, but I cannot attempt a more detailed appraisal here.

V

Blackburn writes:

> Suppose we say that we *project* an attitude or habit or other commitment which is not descriptive on to the world, when we speak and think as though there were a property of things which our sayings describe, which we can reason about, be wrong about, and so on. Projecting is what Hume refers to when he talks of 'gilding and staining all natural objects with the colours borrowed from internal sentiment', or of the mind 'spreading itself on the world'.[31]

31. Blackburn (1984), pp. 170–1.

I have spoken more often of 'irrealism' than of 'projectivism'. The latter, it seems, is best reserved for those species of irrealism that concern commitments—to borrow Blackburn's term—founded on some specific mode of 'internal sentiment' or affective phenomenology. The root projectivist notion is the Humean one that we have a tendency to seem to ourselves to find in the world qualities that, properly, are predicated of our responses to it; more specifically, that the range of our responses that we tend to talk about as though they were cognitive, apt to disclose real features of the world, is actually much broader than the range of those which really deserve to be so regarded. Projectivism is, thus, a possible and natural form for the irrealist cause to assume in the three areas—morality, modality and humour—that this discussion has mainly had in view.[32] Irrealism about scientific theory, by contrast, is not, in any version worthy of attention, projectivist. The most powerful arguments against scientific realism concern not whether any appropriately local response we have to scientific theory is cognitive—there is no such local response—but whether theoretical statements can survive the first of the two tests adumbrated: Must disagreements about scientific theory, insofar as they are not attributable to vagueness in the concepts involved, or to rationally permissible variations in standards of evi-

---

32. There are important internal differences. The relation between moral sentiment and moral judgement is much more complicated than that between amusement and judgement about what is funny. For one thing, though we may wish to allow that certain moral sentiments are natural in the sense that they are untrained, the capacity for *moral* sentiment arguably presupposes possession of moral concepts. An infant's distress at his older brother's punishment is not yet a moral response. By contrast, possession of the concept of humour is not a prerequisite for the capacity to be amused. For another, judging that a certain hypothetical state of affairs would be funny involves an element of prediction missing from the corresponding moral judgement, and is defeasible by subsequent apathetic responses in a way that moral judgement need not be. Third, both moral and modal judgements are disciplined by principle: moral sentiment, and the phenomena of conviction and unintelligibility involved, for example, in the ratification of mathematical proofs, are quite often quashed by appeal to what it is independently considered correct, morally or mathematically, to think. Humour affords a parallel to this only insofar as we moralise about it, by introducing, for example, the notion of a joke in bad taste.

dence, invariably be explicable in terms of prejudiced assessment of agreed data, or faulty data, or ignorance? Not if the underdetermination thesis is accepted. And not, perhaps, if the received wisdom is correct that the acceptability of any report of observation is invariably theoretically conditioned. For then the acceptability of any pool of data comes to depend on one's background theory. And that means that the data can exhibit the feature of rational command only if the ingredients in the background theories do. How is that to be provided for, if any data by which such theories might, in turn, be assessed will be theoretically conditioned in the same sense?[33]

In Blackburn's hands, as we have seen, projectivism starts out as an 'expressive' or non-assertoric thesis. I have suggested that this element of the view should be abandoned. The real question concerns what notion of truth is applicable to the 'projections'. The projectivist–irrealist thesis should be that only the thinnest possible notion is appropriate: we have seen, by contrast, two ways in which the notion of truth applicable to a class of commitments might, on the contrary, be 'thick'. I shall conclude by noting a potential instability in the projectivist position, and a third potentially germane distinction on the thinness–thickness scale.

The instability afflicts, paradoxically, just those cases where the projectivist line is intuitively most appealing. These are the classes of commitment that, like judgements about what is funny, seem to be most intimately associated with a well-defined kind of response, which we are already inclined to regard as affective rather than detective. The problem is that any such response can be construed as potentially detective—can be 'cognitivised', as it were—if the relevant projected 'quality' will sustain construal as a *disposition*. Suppose, for instance, that some such biconditional as this holds:

X is funny iff X is disposed to amuse many/most/normal people in many/most/normal circumstances.

33. For pursuit of this line of thought, see Wright (1986d), and chapter 4 of *Truth and Objectivity*.

There is, obviously, scope for consideration about which version of such a biconditional might be most plausible, about whether some reference to right-mindedness, or the like, might be wanted, and so on. But if *any* such biconditional construal provides the resources for a reasonably accurate descriptive account of the relevant parts of our linguistic practice, there can be no objection to the idea that judgements of humour do have the substantial truth conditions that the biconditional describes. And the relevant response—being amused—will take on cognitive status only insofar as finding oneself so affected will constitute a defeasible ground for the assertion that the right-hand side of the biconditional is realised.

A defensible form of projectivism, then, in making good the claim that a certain class of judgements is based on a response that is better not regarded as cognitive, has to interpose sufficient distance, as it were, between the judgements and the response to prevent a dispositional construal. And this will be possible only to the extent that the original projectivist image—that we make such judgements merely by way of reading back into the world features that properly belong to our response to it—is strictly misplaced. Projectivism has, therefore, a delicate balancing act to perform. If it stays too close to the image, it is liable to be undermined by a dispositional construal; if it departs too far from it, it may become unclear in what sense the response in question provides the *basis* for the relevant class of judgements, and why an argument for an irrealist view of those judgements may properly proceed from the non-cognitive character of the response. The difficulty is well illustrated, I think, by the case of moral judgements. It is prima facie very implausible to construe moral qualities as dispositions to produce moral sentiments—not least because the ascription of such a disposition does not seem to have the reason-giving force that properly belongs to a moral judgement.[34] But just for that reason, the belief that moral passion is not properly viewed as a state of cognition seems to have no very direct connection with moral irrealism.

34. But perhaps only prima facie. See the remarks on the 'Moral Sense Theory' in Smith (1986).

Consider, finally, a case where such a dispositional analysis seems attractive anyway: the case of secondary qualities.[35] Many philosophers have taken it that to be red, for instance, consists in being disposed to induce a certain kind of visual experience in the normally sighted, under normal circumstances. (I prescind from the considerations to do with trans-galactic Doppler effect, and so on.) So, we have a biconditional comparable to those mooted for 'funny' above:

> X is red iff X would be seen as red by normally
> functioning observers in normal circumstances.

Now, there is a question about how 'normality' is to be understood for the purposes of the biconditional. Suppose we understand it statistically: normally functioning observers function like most of us actually do most of the time; normal circumstances are relevantly similar to those which actually prevail most of the time. So understood, the statement on the right-hand side of the biconditional would still qualify as apt for substantial truth by both the tests earlier considered. Disagreement about such a statement might well be owing to vagueness in its constituent concepts, or to personal probability thresholds—the disputants might, for example, each have used statistical sampling techniques. But it seems impossible to understand how there could be a disagreement that could not be explained along those lines and yet owe nothing to prejudice, ignorance or misinformation. As for the second test, the sort of direction that an account of the ideal epistemology of such a judgement should take is, prima facie at least, clear. Nevertheless, to interpret the relevant notion of normality in this way is to impose a certain kind of reading on the biconditional— at least if it is held to be true a priori. In effect, we give priority to the right-hand side. What *makes* something red is how we, most of us, respond to it in the conditions that normally obtain.

---

35. The distinction I wish to use the case to illustrate is actually appreciable independently of the belief that a dispositional analysis is here appropriate, so it does not matter if the reader does not share that belief.

It is possible to elicit a third and stronger respect in which the notion of truth may be substantial if we contrast with this right-to-left reading of such a biconditional an interpretation that assigns priority, instead, to the left-hand side. Such an interpretation would see redness as property of things in themselves, connecting at best contingently with any effect induced in us under statistically normal circumstances. Accordingly, to give priority to the left-hand side of the biconditional, while retaining its a priori status, would be to impose a different interpretation on the normality provisos. The essential characteristic of a normally functioning observer will now be: one suffering from no internal impediment to the proper functioning of the capacity to *detect* red. And normal circumstances will be those in which there is no external impediment to the proper functioning of this same capacity.

I owe to Mark Johnston the suggestion of the possibility of these alternative readings of such biconditionals; he characterised them as 'projective' and 'detective', respectively.[36] I would rather reserve 'projective' and 'projectivism' in the way I have indicated. The distinction, if it can be properly elucidated, is nevertheless very important and does correspond, it seems to me, to a further aspect of our intuitive preconceptions about factuality and substantial truth. An interesting suggestion, which I suspect is not quite right, is that it also corresponds to the distinction between secondary and primary qualities. Primary qualities will sustain biconditionals for which the proper reading is detective; the biconditionals appropriate to secondary qualities, by contrast, will be properly read from right to left. However that may be, there is a distinction here—roughly, between our responses *making it true* that so-and-so is the case and their merely *reflecting* that truth—that the contrast between two ways of reading

36. In graduate classes on ethics in Princeton, spring 1986. However, the explanation of the contrast in terms of the alternative interpretations of the normality provisos demanded if the biconditional is to hold a priori is mine and may not coincide with his own preferred account. I should emphasise that I do not, at present, regard the contrast as unproblematic.

an appropriate biconditional, interpreted as holding a priori, seems to capture nicely. And this, as noted, is a distinction that comes into play for judgements that pass the tests earlier considered and are accordingly apt for truth in more than the thinnest sense. Of any such class of judgements, we can ask whether an appropriate biconditional does, indeed, hold a priori and, if so, to which side belongs the priority. If the way I introduced the distinction is appropriate, this is a question to be decided by reflection on the proper interpretation of the normality provisos. But that is not the only possible way of proceeding, and it may prove not to be best. I wish merely to suggest the thought that one important class of intuitions about objectivity—those reflected, in particular, in the attempt to draw a distinction between primary and secondary qualities—have no proper place in the disputes between realism and irrealism. Rather, when the dialectic is set up in the way I have suggested it should be, they are internal to realism.[37]

I would like to acknowledge the stimulus of conversations on these matters with Mark Johnston, David Lewis and Michael Smith, and to thank Simon Blackburn, Bob Hale, Mark Johnston and Peter Railton for extensive and very helpful comments on a previous draft.

37. Johnston wanted to commend the question whether appropriate such biconditionals for moral judgements should be read right to left as the pivotal issue for moral realism. Certainly, we need a more detailed examination of the relations among the three criteria of the capacity for substantial truth than I have been here able to attempt. But my present belief, to stress, is that the first two criteria are prior, and that the third comes into play only for judgements that satisfy them. However, that does not entail that Johnston was in error to lay emphasis on the third criterion. For the capacity to sustain the truth of *some* such biconditional may be regarded as the litmus test of whether a type of statement is apt for substantial truth at all—so, unapt for irrealism—with the first two criteria providing tests in turn—perhaps not the only tests—of this capacity. The correctness of such a view is one among a number of very interesting questions here in prospect.

PART TWO

REPLIES TO CRITICS

Academic philosophy now provides more opportunities for public engagement between authors and their critics than ever before. Within a short time after the appearance of *Truth and Objectivity* I had received invitations to respond to critical notices by Frank Jackson *(Philosophical Books)* and Timothy Williamson *(International Journal of Philosophical Studies)* as well as to field a very searching and wide-ranging set of critical observations by James van Cleve, Terence Horgan, Paul Horwich, Philip Pettit, Mark Sainsbury and Timothy Williamson, once again in a *Philosophy and Phenomenological Research* book symposium, and to confront the critical reactions of Simon Blackburn and Paul Boghossian in an Author-meets-Critics session at the 1995 Central Division Meetings of the American Philosophical Association. The resulting debate with Blackburn subsequently emerged as a more fully written-up exchange in *Mind*.

In this part of the book I include my published responses to this body of commentary. I should, naturally, have regarded it as unwise to do so unless I thought that my notes provided sufficient by way of stage-setting for the objections and observations to which they respond to make for self-contained reading. But no doubt a serious reader will want to refer, where possible, to the original commentaries to guard against any risk that I have misrepresented or undersold them. In any case I have cause to be very grateful for the thoughtful critical reactions to my work of so distinguished a group of philosophers, and I believe that my attempts to respond to them have deepened my own understanding of the dialectical possibilities and limits of a large number of the central themes in *Truth and Objectivity*. My hope is for a similar effect on readers of the present volume.

The themes of *Truth and Objectivity* revisited in this part include the 'inflationary' argument against deflationism (van Cleve, Horwich), the stability and merit of the minimalist conceptions of truth and truth-aptitude (Blackburn, Williamson), the rejection of expressivism and error theory (Blackburn, Jackson), pluralism about truth (Horwich, Jackson, Pettit, Sainsbury), the capacity of superassertibility to serve as a truth predicate (van Cleve, Horgan, Pettit, Williamson), various issues about Cognitive Command—whether its distinction from minimal truth-aptitude is stable (Boghossian, Sainsbury, Williamson), whether it is properly formulated in terms of apriority (Blackburn, Williamson) and whether it represents the weakest significant realist crux (Horgan). In addition, I attempt to respond to various misgivings about the overarching framework of *Truth and Objectivity*: to arguments (van Cleve, Williamson) that no proper truth predicate can be anything but evidentially unconstrained, to the contention (Blackburn) that the debate between realist and anti-realist should focus on different conceptions of the content of propositions in contested areas, under the aegis of a single notion of truth, and the more general suggestion (Williamson) that *Truth and Objectivity* imports unnecessary complication into the debates. The response to Blackburn gave me an opportunity to present more fully than elsewhere my misgivings about his opposed 'quasi-realist' way of looking at the issues.

3

Response to Jackson

Philosophers jealously guard traditional debates. Any attempt to redraw the boundaries of such a debate, dissolving certain entrenched constituencies thereby, is therefore bound to meet with opposition. Frank Jackson comes to the defence of the *expressivist* and *error-theoretic* constituencies in traditional realist/anti-realist debate, arguing that the attempt to marginalise them made in the first two chapters of *Truth and Objectivity* is unsuccessful.[1] However, I remain unmoved. Here I comment briefly on his remarks on expressivism and error theory in turn. Jackson is also sceptical about the pluralism concerning truth canvassed in *Truth and Objectivity*. I shall say a little about that in conclusion.

I. EXPRESSIVISM

The *Truth and Objectivity* argument against expressivism about, for example, ethical discourse has three components:

1. Jackson (1994).

(i)   Minimalism about truth—the contention that it is necessary and sufficient, in order for a predicate to qualify as a truth predicate, that it satisfy each of a basic set of platitudes about truth: that to assert is to present as true, that statements which are apt for truth have negations which are likewise, that truth is one thing, justification another, and so on.

(ii) The thesis that any *assertoric* discourse will allow the definition upon its sentences of a predicate which qualifies as a truth predicate in the light of (i).

(iii) The thesis that a discourse should be reckoned as assertoric just in case its ingredient sentences are subject to certain minimal constraints of syntax—embeddability within negation, the conditional, contexts of propositional attitude, and so on—and discipline: their use must be governed by agreed standards of warrant.

The most likely expressivist resistance to this line would involve, one would expect, argument against (i)—argument for a more robust conception of truth than minimalism allows.[2] Jackson, who likes minimalism about truth (though unenthusiastic about that title), marks out for the expressivist the option of repudiating claim (iii) instead. In company with Michael Smith and others, he argues that this is a principled option. The key to it is the platitude that assertion, when sincere, is the expression of belief.[3] For it may happen, according to

2. Thus Paul Boghossian (1990), for instance, takes it that a non-factualist view of any discourse must involve commitment to a robust conception of truth for its statements. If the non-factualist takes a minimalist (or deflationary) view of truth, then—Boghossian assumes—the statements of the discourse will qualify as truth-apt just in virtue of its assertoric shape, and the non-factualist won't have room to formulate his distinctive thesis. But this, as Jackson points out, would seem to be an oversight. One can be selective about which assertoric discourses are truth-apt while holding, for those which are, that truth is the metaphysically lightweight property which minimalism takes it to be. Minimalism about truth need not be accompanied by minimalism about truth-aptitude.

3. Cf. *Truth and Objectivity,* p. 14.

Jackson, that the indicative sentences of a discourse which meets the constraints of syntax and discipline demanded by (iii) nevertheless fail to express beliefs, because of some *further* features of the notion of belief. Just this, so the expressivist may contend, is what happens in ethics if one is prepared to be Humean about the distinction between belief and desire. On such a view, ethical sentences, for all that they meet the relevant syntactic constraints and are subject to a high degree of discipline, fail to express beliefs because the attitudes which they do express would seem to have an *intrinsically motivational* component, whereas belief, on the Humean view, does not.

This is an objection which has already received some discussion in the literature.[4] Fully to respond to it would take me further afield than it is here possible to go. Let me merely indicate the direction of what I take to be the correct response.

It would be natural to counter that Jackson's reservation is well taken only if the Humean view of belief is well taken, and that other views are competitive. A quite different conception, espoused for instance by John McDowell, would hold that a proper moral episte-mology will write the propensity to certain sorts of concern into the account of what it is to recognise moral truth.[5] But this response would miss the point of Jackson's objection. The argument of *Truth and Objectivity* was supposed to cut the ground from under the expressivist; but if Jackson is right, then, to the contrary, the expres-sivist is alive and well and locked in debate with John McDowell. The expressivist—Humean—camp may prove to lose out in that contro-versy. But—so says the objection—(iii) effectively presupposes a cer-tain outcome; so the fast-track refutation based upon it fails.

The correct response to Jackson's objection, it seems to me, is rather that he has merely hijacked the word 'belief'. Claim (iii) is not hostage, via the assertion/belief platitude, to a correct philosophical

---

4. See, for instance, the contributions by Michael Smith (twice), John Divers, Alexander Miller and Paul Horwich (1994) to the symposium on 'Expressivism and Truth'.

5. McDowell (1978). See also the discussion in Price (1988), chap. 5.

psychology of belief. Rather, *any* attitude is a belief which may be expressed by the sincere endorsement of a sentence which complies with the constraints of syntax and discipline imposed by (iii). I do not deny the right of a philosopher to insist on a more exigent sense of 'belief', in accordance with which only sentences count as belief-expressive which come out on the right side of the functional distinction, or an improved successor to the functional distinction, which the Humean view regards as central. And no doubt moral beliefs may turn out not to count as beliefs in this richer sense. But it is not belief in such a richer sense that the assertion/belief platitude concerns.

Jackson will likely respond that it is *I* who am hijacking 'belief' and subjecting it to a diluting redefinition. But the linguistic data, for what they are worth, don't support him. Ordinary intuition does not scruple to characterise a person's moral convictions as 'beliefs'; and if a belief is anything which may collaborate with a desire in the generation of a practical syllogism, then isn't

> John wishes to encourage his children to avoid wrongdoing.
> John holds that lying is wrong.
> ∴ John has reason to discourage his children from lying

a practical syllogism, and isn't 'John wishes to discourage his children from wrongdoing' the ascription of a *desire?*

This is not to undercut the debate between McDowell and the Humean, nor—as Smith suggests[6]—is it to take the anti-Humean side. Rather it is to recommend a shift in the vocabulary of that debate. The Humean's point should be that moral attitudes can qualify *only* as minimal beliefs, and lie on the wrong side of any more stringent, functional classification, in which 'belief' is reserved for more-than-minimal usage, marking the imprints of (dispassionate) cognitive engagement with the world. McDowell, by contrast, should

6. Smith et al. (1994), p. 25.

be seen as challenging any implication of a tension between passion and cognition.

Finally, let me repeat what was stressed in *Truth and Objectivity*, that none of this is supposed to *refute* expressivism.[7] Claims (i) and (iii) have the status of recommendations, offered on the basis of theoretical advantage. For the theorist who wishes, the route into expressivism via a denial of (iii) remains an option. But a theorist who takes this option because of the attractions of a Humean conception of belief accomplishes no more, I reckon, than to safeguard a distinction—if it is indeed good—which it will be open to the minimalist about belief to express in other terms; and of course the costs—in terms of the affront to common sense, the headache of 'mixed' inferences, moral modus ponens,[8] and so on—are expensive and familiar.

II. ERROR THEORY

Suppose a highly internally disciplined discourse—ethics, or pure mathematics for instance—with all the syntactic trappings of assertoric content. What are the options for a philosopher who holds that, save in vacuous cases, the beliefs expressible in the discourse are sweepingly and systematically false? Suppose, as Jackson is willing for the sake of argument to do—he clearly has reservations on both points—that the notion of superassertibility characterisable on the basis of the standards of warrant operative in the discourse will satisfy the minimal truth platitudes, and that any warrant to assert is, necessarily, warrant to regard as superassertible. Then if we may take the truth predicate operative over the discourse to be that notion of superassertibility, we have as much reason to regard any particular statement of the discourse as true as we have reason to assert it in the light of the discourse's internal standards of warrant. The error theorist would therefore seem to have just two options: to make a case

7. *Truth and Objectivity*, pp. 74–5.
8. For details of some of the accounting, see Hale (1992).

that the truth predicate that operates in the discourse is *not* that notion of superassertibility, or to argue that none—or anyway not enough—of the statements of the discourse are really assertible by its own internal standards. The latter option then embraces two further foreseeable suboptions: to disclose some incoherence in the discourse's standards of warrant, or to show that they are in fact much more demanding than they are customarily taken to be, with almost all opinion that we ordinarily take to be vindicated by them not really being so.[9]

In typical cases, the conviction of the error theorist will be that the statements of the discourse involve commitments for which the satisfaction of its standards of warrant can provide no real justification. Thus Mackie takes our moral judgements to embrace a commitment to the instantiation in the world of a certain kind of metaphysically outlandish property, something for which a good pedigree by the standards of ordinary rational moral argument provides no evidence whatever. Likewise Field takes it that pure mathematical statements typically involve reference to and quantification over abstract entities whose existence mathematical proof—or what is standardly accepted as mathematical proof—is powerless to guarantee. The commitment of such theorists, then, is to a distinction between the truth predicate which—they think—actually informs such discourses and the notion of superassertibility which may be defined upon the ordinary standards of good moral argument and mathematical proof.

This is a commitment to a certain kind of account of the meaning of the statements of a contested discourse which the initial presumption should be against, once we see that a conception of truth is to hand which will avoid the charge of massive error. For charitable interpretation dictates that we should avoid that charge if we possibly can, that is, unless best sense is made of the discourse by an account of its content which sustains a gap between truth and superassertibility. Thus a proponent of Mackie ought to show that we make best sense of moral discourse by interpreting its claims as involving com-

9. Cf. *Truth and Objectivity*, pp. 86–7.

mitment to the existence of metaphysically outlandish properties; and a proponent of Field ought to show that we make best sense of mathematical discourse not merely by construing its semantics platonistically, but by so conceiving the types of object thereby recognised that their existence is beyond mathematical proof.[10]

This form of option, and the alternative—that of arguing that none or almost none of our convictions expressed in the discourse in question actually meet its internal standards—define the space within which the error theorist has to work and, so it seems to me, make life more difficult for him than is usually recognised. Jackson, however, clearly thinks that the error theorist's life is no more difficult after *Truth and Objectivity* than before.

I have had some difficulty seeing what exactly is the focus of Jackson's disagreement here. Some clouding of the geography is occasioned by his representing Mackie as taking the second option—of denying that moral judgements really are warranted—rather than as relying upon a distinction between truth and superassertibility within ethics.[11] But Jackson proceeds to correct that impression.[12] The crux of his objection seems rather to be that

> the history of human thought provides many examples of discourses that have coherent, articulated and acknowledged standards of proper use, and yet many or most of the statements that satisfy those standards and so are assertible in this sense, are false. Sometimes, for instance, in Aristotelian and Newtonian physics, and Ptolemaic cosmology, the falsity was not known at the time when the theories and

10. Not all forms of Platonist construal would have this effect, of course.

11. 'As Wright observes, Mackie's error theory derives from his conviction that moral judgements carry the "implication of metaphysically preposterous properties". If this is right, then ethical assertions are not warrantedly assertible, for we are not warranted in believing metaphysically preposterous properties' (Jackson (1994), p. 167).

12. 'I suspect Wright will insist that this rejection misunderstands the relevant sense of warranted assertibility. What is meant is assertibility *by the standards of the discourse*' (ibid.).

discourses were first set up. Sometimes, as in ideal gas theory and in point mass models of planetary motion, the falsity was known from the beginning.[13]

These examples are uniformly wide of the mark. None of them is clearly a case of *metaphysical* error. And all are cases of theories discarded in the light of the *ordinary* standards of warrant for scientific theory—theories whose component statements, or at least those of them we have seen fit to discard, ought therefore not to be accounted as superassertible in the first place. An error-theoretic view of such examples is hardly controversial. But it does not depend on a gap between truth and superassertibility (however attractive such a gap may seem to those of scientific-realist inclination), and in any case the reminder that there are such examples changes nothing. I do not see that Jackson provides any grounds for thinking either that the options for the error theorist are not as depicted in *Truth and Objectivity,* or that it is easier, either in general or in the special case of ethics, to take up those options than was there implied.

III. A PLURALITY OF TRUTH PREDICATES?

Jackson refers to Quine's well-known thought that there are not different kinds of existence, only different kinds of existents. We should take a similar view, he urges, about truth. There are not different kinds of truth, but only systematic differences in the truth-bearers—the contents that are, or are not, true.

I suspect the impression that the pluralism canvassed in *Truth and Objectivity* is at odds with this rests on a misunderstanding. Certainly I ought not to have written, if indeed I did, in a way which suggested *ambiguity* in the word 'true'. An ambiguous term will typically allow of two (or more) quite different kinds of explanation, each determining a different extension for it. But if a truth predicate is any that sat-

13. *Ibid.,* pp. 167–8.

isfies the minimal set of platitudes—if there is no more to being a truth predicate than that—then those platitudes enshrine all that can be said about the explanation of the word, which is therefore uniform. Since, moreover, the platitudes ensure that any truth predicate for a given discourse will satisfy the Disquotational Scheme, there is no question of a pair of predicates each qualifying as a truth predicate for a given discourse yet differing in extension.[14] There are not, then, different kinds of truths as there are different kinds of seal, charge, ash, bank, quarry and report.

So wherein are supposed to consist the differences? As a parallel, consider the notion of identity. Assume for the sake of argument that, analogously to the minimalist conception of truth, identity can be characterised by the twin platitudes that everything is self-identical and that identicals share all their properties. Should we say that the *concept* of identity is therefore the same, no matter what kinds of things we consider? If we do, the claim had better be consistent with recognising that what *constitutes* identity is subject to considerable variation in tandem with the change in the kinds of objects concerned. If *a* and *b* are material objects, then their identity is constituted by spatial temporal continuity; if they are numbers, then, on Frege's famous account, their identity is constituted by the one-to-one correspondence of an associated pair of concepts; if they are the directions of a pair of lines, then their identity is constituted by those lines' being parallel; if they are persons, then their identity is constituted by—well, who can say exactly? But considerations of both psychological and bodily continuity will be paramount. Or consider the case of necessity. There is little attraction in the idea that the meaning of 'necessary' varies, according to whether it is prefixed by 'logically', or 'physically', or 'morally', and so on. But to insist on its univocity should be consistent with recognising what may harmlessly—if perhaps rather flabbily—be described as differences in the concept of necessity, depending upon whether it is logical, physical or moral necessity that we are concerned with. And these, again, are differences

14. Cf. *Truth and Objectivity*, p. 52.

in constitution, differences in what *makes for* necessity in the different kinds of case.

This talk of 'constitution' needs work, of course, but the authenticity of this general form of distinction should not be in doubt. Pluralism about truth is the contention that such a distinction may engage the concept of truth, that there need be no single discourse-invariant thing in which truth consists. Depending upon the region of discourse with which we are concerned, it may consist in superassertibility, or not; in representation of an explanatorily active state of affairs, or not; in a fact about the direction of ideal opinion, or not; and so on.

Maybe Jackson would want to disagree even with this. In any case, I feel under no pressure to disagree with his concluding suggestion that all relevant explanatory purposes in the vicinity can be served by distinctions among types of *content*. For if content is determined by truth conditions, then to recognise variety in the constitution of truth for statements in different regions of discourse *is* in effect to recognise systematic differences in the type of content possessed by such statements—just as to recognise variety in the constitution of identity for stones, people and numbers is to recognise differences in the categories of object concerned. Such differences in content will indeed suffice to reflect whatever pluralism is a going concern here; *additional* differences between kinds of truth will have no explanatory role to play. *Truth and Objectivity* does not claim otherwise.

4 Realism, Pure and Simple?
A Reply to Williamson

Timothy Williamson's searching critical study calls into question a number of concepts and claims which are important to the structure of *Truth and Objectivity*.[1] Among his contentions are

that assertoric content is not so cheap a commodity as is there suggested;

that superassertibility cannot serve as a truth predicate for any but the most limited discourses;

that the Cognitive Command constraint is open to trivialisation, being satisfied by any minimally truth-apt discourse;

that the notion of a 'discourse' is anyway ill-defined for the purposes of the pluralism about truth bruited in *Truth and Objectivity*;

that a realist should not unprotestingly accept the idea of minimalism as the default option with respect to a given region of discourse;

1. Williamson (1994b).

and, in general, that the issues about realism are better kept simple—that we do not stand to gain by trying to work within the sort of pluralistic framework which *Truth and Objectivity* recommends.

I here take the opportunity briefly to explain why, on these various matters, I continue to prefer my thoughts to Williamson's.

I. ASSERTORIC CONTENT

According to minimalism, to ascribe truth is not to ascribe a property of intrinsic metaphysical *gravitas*. Any sentence is a candidate for truth which is possessed of assertoric content; and possession of assertoric content is essentially a matter of meeting certain syntactic and disciplinary constraints—essentially, a sentence has to be capable of significant embedding within constructions such as negation, the conditional and contexts of propositional attitude; and its use must be subject to acknowledged standards of warrant. When such standards are satisfied, that will then suffice, *ceteris paribus*, to justify the claim of truth.[2]

Williamson suggests that to look at matters in this way is to risk missing a distinction—namely, that between sentences which *aspire* to assertoric content, as he puts it, and those which really achieve it. What satisfaction of the syntactic and disciplinary constraints ensures, in Williamson's view, is merely the *aspiration* to assertoric content, which aspiration may be unfulfilled nevertheless.

What necessitates such a distinction? On Williamson's view it is required to handle a sentence like 'Eldorado is crowded'—a sentence

---

2. The proviso is wanted because the best construal of the notion of truth governing a particular discourse may represent it as disconnected from the standards of warrant on which practitioners rely. Such a separation is one way of making space for error theories such as those of Mackie about ethics and Field about pure mathematics. See the remarks about fiction below.

which, 'on one respectable view', is unavailable for the making of any genuine statement since 'Eldorado' fails to refer. The example is cannily chosen, since it might be used either to highlight a difficulty posed for minimalism by recognisedly mythical and fictional discourses, or by the possibility of unwitting reference failure by practitioners of a discourse who mistakenly believe in the existence of certain objects or properties.[3] I shall say a little about both.

Discourse both within and about a fiction characteristically makes liberal use of the indicative mood, with all the syntactic variety which that subserves, and is subject to a high degree of internal discipline: there are many claims about Hamlet which are determinately correct, and many which are determinately incorrect. Ought not such statements to count, therefore, as minimally truth-apt? And is there not as much reason to regard any of them as true, therefore, as there is reason to regard it as acceptable by the standards of the fiction which it concerns?

Now certainly a minimalist might answer 'Yes' to both those questions. The result would be to enjoin an ontology of fictional characters, rather cheaply as one might think.[4] Suitable sentences featuring 'Eldorado' which are in accordance with the legend would likewise foist a reference upon that name—to a real mythical city, as it were. But I doubt if minimalism should take this line; certainly, it is not forced to. One alternative—in effect, one of the options offered to error theory in *Truth and Objectivity*[5]—would be to maintain that the truth predicate relevant to fictional discourse generally, and to Spanish legend in particular, is not the notion of superassertibility arrived at by generalisation over the standards of acceptability internal to such discourses—essentially a matter of conformity with the fiction, or legend—but involves compliance with some externally given standard; for instance, in the case in point, that it has to do with

---

3. Williamson's comparison with error-theoretic views of ethics suggests that he has the second sort of difficulty in mind.

4. This theme is pursued in Divers and Miller (1995).

5. See *Truth and Objectivity*, chap. 3, section V.

---

representation of the characteristics of a real city somewhere. The challenge posed by minimalism to the error theorist about a given region of discourse is to make out either that accepted opinion within that region hardly ever actually conforms to the standards of warrant which actually govern it, or that the notion of truth which actually informs the discourse is not superassertibility in the light of those standards. I would propose that we should take an error-theoretic view, in the latter sense, about fiction. George Eliot's fiction is of real people inhabiting a town called Middlemarch. The statements of the fiction are true or false according as there really is or is not such a town inhabited by people who are named and described as by the authoress. Warrant for such a statement, by contrast, understood in such a way as to allow George Eliot's own statements and those within the bounds of responsible interpretation of her fiction to be warranted, is a matter, broadly, of conformity with that fiction. And—what is distinctive of fiction—to have warrant in that sense is to have no reason whatever to regard such a statement as true. On such an account, there will be no pressure upon the minimalist either to countenance an 'unbearably light' ontology or to accept that, fictional discourse's satisfaction of the emphasised constraints of syntax and discipline notwithstanding, no genuinely truth-evaluable contents are dealt with therein.[6]

Alternatively, we may take Williamson's example as motivating an objection based on any view which, like that of Gareth Evans,[7] holds that failure of reference is, in the right kind of context, sufficient to divest a sentence of truth-evaluable content. On such a view, we, who mistakenly believe in the golden city of legend, may use sentences like 'Eldorado is crowded' in such a way as to respect the constraints of syntax and discipline emphasised by the minimalist, under the illusion

---

6. Similar advantages might be carried by the quite different type of proposal that fictional statement be construed as true but *elliptical,* suppressing dominant occurrences of an operator like, 'According to George Eliot's fiction, . . .' whose effect would be to create referentially opaque contexts.

7. See Evans (1982).

that we are dealing in real contents, although no genuinely assertoric content is possessed by any such sentence. And now: if an illusion of singular reference can create an illusion of assertoric content, why cannot an illusion of *predicate reference* do likewise? Cannot the case of the moral error theorist, for instance, be precisely that moral predicates, as standardly used, fail to refer to—to express—any genuine properties, and hence that moral discourse is not so much as minimally truth-apt?

This kind of view of the import of reference failure is, of course, controversial. But it would be better for the minimalist not to hold out a hostage to the outcome of that controversy. Rather, it seems to me that no damage is done to the dialectic of *Truth and Objectivity* if, at least pending resolution of such issues about reference, Williamson is granted a reference-failure-dependent distinction between genuine assertoric content and the mere aspiration to it, and it is allowed that, in cases where reference failure is an open possibility, all that is ensured by satisfaction of the constraints of syntax and discipline is possession of a kind of content indistinguishable from Williamson's mere aspiration. That there *is* nevertheless content of a sort in the relevant kind of case is indisputable. Even if 'Eldorado is crowded' actually expresses no singular thought, the sentence unquestionably has enough meaning to identify the kind of thought it aspires to express: it contains what is purportedly a singular term standing for an item of a familiar kind, understood to have certain well-understood distinguishing characteristics, and it purports to ascribe a well-understood property to that item. That is enough to ensure that tokenings of the sentence may intelligibly, if mistakenly, be believed to be true, and assessed accordingly. It is also enough to ensure that reason to suppose such a sentence true has to embrace reason to suppose that 'Eldorado' refers; and hence that the mere conformity of a particular such sentence with the legend—in circumstances where the legend is generally believed—is not sufficient to constitute a genuine warrant for the claim that the sentence is true.

This concession substantially affects the treatment neither of expressivism nor of error theory in *Truth and Objectivity.* If only reference failure stands between the aspiration to assertoric content and the real thing, then the aspiration already precludes expressivist construal, which is therefore preempted, as before, by satisfaction of the syntactical and disciplinary constraints. Nor, contrary to what Williamson implies, is life any easier for the moral error theorist. It was recognised in *Truth and Objectivity* that an error theorist might make his case precisely by arguing that little if anything of what passes as acceptable within a given discourse is, in the light of standards appropriate to it, genuinely so. The disclosure of reference failure in a discourse which repeatedly and essentially purports reference to a particular type of object or property is, of course, one way of doing that. So there is no cause for *methodological* reproach of a moral error theorist who takes just the tack that Williamson adverts to, attempting to argue that moral predicates lack reference. But it remains that in order successfully to prosecute that tack, he will have first to articulate a conception of moral properties no less clearly implicit in moral discourse than the above conception of the intended referent of 'Eldorado' is implicit in the discourse of those who believe in the legend; and then proceed to show, or anyway make it plausible, that nothing answers to that conception. And there's the rub. There is no doubt about the ontological commitments of one who subscribes to the Eldorado legend. But it is quite another thing to disclose a commitment, in ordinary moral thought and argument, to properties sufficiently metaphysically outlandish to facilitate the second part of the error theorist's task. In any case, it will be made neither easier nor harder to do so if one corollary of success will be that moral discourse presents only an illusion of genuinely assertoric content.

II. Truth and Superassertibility

Can superassertibility—the property of being warranted by some state of information and then remaining warranted no matter how that state of information is enlarged upon or improved—function as a truth predicate? Williamson is sceptical. For suppose, for *reductio*, that truth and superassertibility coincide within a discourse D, and let q be a statement of that discourse, and (*) the statement

> q and no one ever has warrant for q.

By the hypothesised coincidence, and the Disquotational Scheme, we have that

> (*) is superassertible if and only if q and no one ever has warrant for q.

It follows that if (*) is not superassertible, then

> Not (q and no one ever has warrant for q).

Since (*) cannot be superassertible, the latter may be detached, whence, by classical logic:

> If q, then someone sometime has a warrant for q.

But this result is surely unacceptable: q may be any statement of D and there can be no a priori guarantee that all the truths of D will sometime be warranted.

This reasoning, as Williamson notes, has affinities with Fitch's so-called paradox[8] and might be challenged in some of the ways familiar from the discussion of that paradox. For instance, the broad strategy of Dorothy Edgington's discussion of Fitch might be adapted to challenge Williamson's claim that (*) is not superassertible.[9] Williamson reasons that (*) can be superassertible

> only if some state of information provides a warrant to assert that: q and no-one ever has a warrant to assert that q. But a warrant to assert

8. Fitch (1963).
9. Edgington (1985).

that conjunction is impossible, for it would involve a warrant to assert the first conjunct, that q, and the existence of such a warrant is contradicted by the second conjunct, that no-one ever has a warrant to assert that q.[10]

Now strictly, this reasoning is good only if the existence of a warrant is the same thing as somebody sometime having that warrant. If the existence of a warrant is held to consist, rather, in its *availability* to one who prosecutes an appropriate channel of investigation, then a warrant can exist which no one will ever actually have. It would be fair to reply that that distinction cannot help so long as it is accepted that no one can simultaneously be warranted in believing both q and that no one will ever have a warrant for q.[11] For in that case no such warrant could be reckoned to be so much as available. But—the Edgington-type point—we have to ask after the range of the quantifier 'no one' in (*)'s second conjunct. Whatever it is, it is consistent with each of the subjects who fall within it always lacking warrant for q that there should be *another* subject who has warrant both for q and for the perennial ignorance on the matter of each of the subjects in the former range. Of course, such a subject will not be able to *express* that for which he has warrant by a tokening of the sentence, 'q and no one ever has warrant for q'. But that is owing to the, in effect, indexicality of the quantifier. It is familiar that justification for a tokening of an indexical sentence may be possible only for someone in whose mouth the claim thereby made would need to be reexpressed. (Consider a tokening of 'I am the leftmost', uttered by the leftmost child in a row of immobilised, blindfolded children.) Where indexical sentences are concerned, superassertibility, like truth, has to

---

10. Williamson (1994b), p. 138.

11. The contrary supposition, that someone could be in position justifiably to accept a claim of the form, 'P and no one will ever have a warrant for P', has points of affinity with Moore's Paradox—'P and I do not believe that P'—though the latter, as usually presented, concerns assertion rather than belief, and makes no explicit play with warrant.

be construed as a property of specific tokenings; and it is a property which belongs to a tokening in virtue of the claim made thereby.[12]

A distinct reservation about Williamson's argument would concern its reliance on classical logic at the final stage. Williamson explicitly signals this reliance, but observes in a footnote that I myself have been critical of attempts to resolve Fitch's paradox by recourse to intuitionistic logic.[13] He means his readers to conclude, presumably, that I could have no consistent quarrel with the use of classical logic in the present context. In fact, however, *Truth and Objectivity* explicitly argues[14] that classical logic must be a casualty in any region of discourse where truth is held to be epistemically constrained but it is acknowledged that not all issues are guaranteed to be (weakly) decidable.[15] This was, moreover, explicitly signalled as a change of heart. Since superassertibility is evidentially constrained, any discourse for which truth is held to be constituted by superassertibility, and which is rich enough to express the premises for Williamson's argument must—if sentences like (*) are not effectively (weakly) decidable—be one for which classical logic has been rejected. In that case, even prescinding from the previous concern, the final step in the argument would be undermined.

The most basic concern, however, about Williamson's adaptation of Fitch is that it merely ignores provisos which are explicit in *Truth*

---

12. Williamson has objected to me in correspondence that to read quantifiers indexically in this way, and thereby to associate them rigidly with a particular domain, is to abrogate the means for any but a contradictory reading of a sentence like 'There is no one who could have been born in the Cretaceous Age, but someone might have been.' I agree that there should be a way of hearing such a sentence which calls for non-rigid construal of its second quantifier. But it seems doubtful that such a construal is ever needed except within the scope of a modal operator; and in particular it is unclear what it would come to in the case of a quantifier with dominant scope, like the 'no one' in the example we are concerned with.

13. Williamson (1994b), p. 144, n. 11.

14. See *Truth and Objectivity*, chap. 2, section III.

15. A proposition is weakly decidable just in case at least *defeasible* evidence is available to decide between it and its negation.

and Objectivity. It is explicitly acknowledged that superassertibility cannot do duty as a truth predicate for any discourse and which truth can be convincingly argued to be epistemically unconstrained. *If* Williamson is right that there can be no such thing as a warrant for any sentence of the type of (*), then the truth of any such sentence transcends all possible evidence, and cannot accordingly be modelled by superassertibility. What was claimed is that superassertibility will serve as a model for the truth predicate—that is, an extensionally adequate construal of it—for any discourse all of whose truths are knowable. If (*) is a sentence which cannot be warranted, then no such discourse will contain a sentence of that ilk. There is therefore no thesis in *Truth and Objectivity* with which Williamson's argument, even if sound, engages. Williamson will be likely to reply that any worthwhile discourse will surely embrace the means for discussion of which of its sentences are, have been, or will be warranted; and that the concession that no discourse containing the resources for the construction of a sentence like (*) can allow construal of its truth predicate as superassertibility is therefore tantamount to the concession that superassertibility can do justice to truth only in highly artificial, restricted circumstances. But that is wrong. When we envisage the possibility of different outcomes to the realist/anti-realist debates about, for instance, morals, mathematics and comedy, we are concerned with the status of commitments distinctive of those areas of discourse in a sense in which—for moral, mathematical and comic 'P' respectively—someone who asserts 'No one will ever have a warrant for P' need *not* have undertaken a moral, mathematical or comic commitment.

III.   An Attempt to Trivialise Cognitive Command

A discourse exerts Cognitive Command just in case it is a priori that disagreements formulated within it, where not attributable to vagueness, of any of a variety of kinds,[16] will involve some form of cogni-

16. For details, see *Truth and Objectivity,* pp. 143 ff.

tive shortcoming. I argued that a discourse's meeting this condition is necessary if we are to think of it as apt to *represent* in a more-than-minimal sense, and that minimally truth-apt discourses can fail to meet the condition. The latter claim has proved to provoke suspicion.[17] Williamson argues, in effect, that it can be sustained only by making out a more refined sense of 'cognitive shortcoming' than anything explained in *Truth and Objectivity,* and that it is unclear along what lines such an explanation might run.

In the book, my strategy to ward off trivialisation was to try to show how the ascription of Cognitive Command to a discourse is something that cannot be undertaken lightly, but, even after the minimal truth-aptitude of a discourse is agreed, demands serious philosophical work: either a case must be made for semantic (Dummettian) realism for the discourse in question, or some form of intuitional epistemology must be postulated for statements of the discourse, or for others which must come into dispute if a disagreement within the discourse is to be rationally sustained. In Williamson's view, this attempt fails. It fails because a very simple line of thought directly delivers the conclusion, that cognitive shortcoming must be involved in any dispute within a minimally truth-apt discourse, without further philosophical obligation. As Williamson expresses the matter:

> Suppose that my opinion 'Rhubarb is disgusting' and your opinion 'Rhubarb is delicious' are both true. Then, by the disquotational property of minimal truth, rhubarb is disgusting and rhubarb is delicious. That, however, is impossible; . . . it follows that our opinions are not both true. Thus it seems to be a priori that our difference of opinion does involve something which may properly be regarded as a cognitive shortcoming.[18]

17. In addition to Williamson, Mark Sainsbury (1996) has expressed doubts on this score. The remarks that follow bear on a doubt generated in discussion of the book by philosophers at Ohio State University and communicated to me by Stewart Shapiro.

18. Williamson (1994b), p. 140.

Are matters so simple? How exactly does the assurance emerge that one of the protagonists in the rhubarb dispute is coming cognitively short? Certainly, not both opinions can be true. But it would seem necessary, if cognitive shortcoming is to be implicated in the dispute, that one protagonist in particular (or of course both) be guilty of it. Williamson therefore needs to be able to conclude that either one or the other of the opinions involved must be determinately untrue. And it is a *classical* step to that from the lemma that not both are true.[19] Bivalence—or at least determinacy as between truth and untruth—is needed to justify such a step. Such principles may be viewed as question-begging in a context in which, could we but get a decent grip on the notion, it may be right to think in terms of the possibility of there being 'no fact of the matter'.

Let us try, on Williamson's behalf, a variant, equally simple line of argument, free of distinctively classical moves. Put up, for *reductio*, the hypothesis that the dispute about rhubarb involves no cognitive shortcoming; and suppose that my opinion is merely that rhubarb is not disgusting. And now suppose:

> (1) Rhubarb is disgusting.

Then:

> (2) I am guilty of cognitive shortcoming (since I hold that it isn't disgusting).

Therefore:

> (3) It is not the case that rhubarb is disgusting (from (1) and the hypothesis).

Hence:

19. The step, precisely, from 'not (A & B)' to 'not A ∨ not B'.

(4) Williamson is guilty of cognitive shortcoming (since he holds that rhubarb is disgusting).

But that again contradicts the original hypothesis, that no one is guilty of cognitive shortcoming, which is therefore false.

Anyone inclined to draw the conclusion that Williamson is right, and that cognitive shortcoming must indeed be involved in any dispute within a minimally truth-apt region of thought, ought to reflect that a perfectly parallel argument could be run concerning a conflict of opinion about a borderline case of some *vague* concept, say a shade of colour on the borderline between red and purple. Intuitively, part of what is meant by the idea that the borderline between red and purple is vague is precisely that there are shades of colour in that region about which neither verdict, 'red' nor 'purple', is *mandated,* though either is *permissible.* It follows that about such a shade you and I may permissibly disagree about the merit of the verdict, 'purple'. The conclusion is utterly unwelcome that one of us has to be in error. But the line of argument just illustrated looks to railroad that conclusion through.

What is going wrong?[20] Even in a case where no particular verdict is mandated, to the extent that a verdict, say 'purple', is permissible,

---

20. Williamson, who favours the 'epistemic' view of vagueness (see his contribution to the symposium, 'Vagueness and Ignorance' in Williamson (1992a)), will not feel obliged to think that anything is wrong. But the charge that Cognitive Command is open to trivialisation is not, presumably, intended to depend upon that view. In correspondence, Williamson has argued that the 'utterly unwelcome' conclusion about disputes over borderline cases ought actually to be accepted—at least if it is a cognitive shortcoming to believe what one does not know. For since one can presumably know only what is definitely the case, and since neither disputed opinion will be definitely true of a borderline case, neither opinion can constitute knowledge.

This is not the place to attempt a detailed treatment of the issues raised by this line of thought. I will merely say

(i) that there seems to me to be little to recommend the principle that only known opinion avoids cognitive shortcoming;

(ii) that there is *something* to recommend the idea that, when a particular view of a borderline case is permissible, so is the claim of that view to amount to knowledge;

to that extent the *consequences* of that verdict have to be reckoned permissible too. But if the shade is purple, then someone who thinks otherwise is guilty of cognitive shortcoming. So if it is permissible to regard the shade as purple, it must also be permissible to think that cognitive shortcoming is involved in the dispute. That is perfectly in accord with the immediate conclusion of the *reductio,* whose effect is to enforce denial of the hypothesis that no cognitive shortcoming is involved. But Cognitive Command, remember, requires *more* than permissibility for the claim that cognitive shortcoming is involved: it requires an *a priori mandate* for that claim. And that has not been made out. Or rather: such a mandate is forthcoming only if we grant a double negation elimination step on the immediate conclusion of the *reductio,* and so rely on classical logic once again. There's nothing wrong with the argument about the rhubarb dispute—as far as it goes. The point is rather that the conclusion falls short of what is necessary to justify Williamson's suspicion.

Concerning a dispute about a borderline case nothing is more natural than to affirm that nobody need be wrong. But we must *not* affirm that. For if nobody is wrong, then since it follows from A's opinion, that p, that B's opinion, that not-p, is wrong, A has to be wrong—contrary to hypothesis. To take indeterminacy seriously is to recognise that for a shade to lie on the borderline between red and purple is for it to enjoy a status consistent *both* with its being red *and* with its being purple—not a third kind of status, inconsistent with both. To take it that it may be determinately the case—hence mandated—that no cognitive shortcoming is involved in a conflict of opinion about such a case is implicitly inconsistent with the recognition that this is the nature of indeterminacy.

(iii)   that the same thought speaks at least for the *permissibility* of the characterisation, 'definitely F' of borderline cases of F (and hence speaks against the idea that it is mandatory to characterise such cases as 'not definitely F and not definitely not F');

(iv)   finally, that the intuition that borderline cases may permissibly be viewed in conflicting ways seems to me, by comparison with views on these other matters, relatively robust.

That, at any rate, is the view which I would favour of the border-line cases spawned by semantic vagueness. And what I am suggesting is that discourses in which Cognitive Command fails involve indeterminacy of a structurally similar sort—only not generated, of course, by semantic vagueness. Each protagonist in the dispute about rhubarb is committed to regarding the other as guilty of cognitive shortcoming; and the view of each protagonist is permissible. But to take it that the determinately correct view is that no shortcoming is involved in that dispute, is to take it that those views are *not* permissible. So that hypothesis is indeed at fault, and has to be rejected. The point, however, is that to reject the hypothesis is not to saddle the aesthetics of food with Cognitive Command. It has not been shown to be a priori that cognitive shortcoming has to be involved in such a dispute; what has been shown is only that there can be no mandate for the claim that *no* shortcoming is involved. That is exactly as it should be if conflicting opinions are permissible.

What Williamson's simple train of thought, reworked in this way, brings out is that care is necessary in the description of what is involved in a discourse's failure of Cognitive Command—more care, no doubt, than I consistently exercised in *Truth and Objectivity*. What remains (plausibly) true is that it is not a priori that a dispute about whether or not rhubarb is disgusting has to involve cognitive shortcoming. But that's not to say that it may be right to suppose that no shortcoming is involved. For if it were right, then neither protagonist—each of whom is committed to shortcoming on the part of the other—can be right, so each is guilty of cognitive shortcoming after all. The contrast between discourses which exert Cognitive Command and the merely minimally truth-apt is a contrast between those wherein disagreements must, subject to the other conditions, be ascribed to cognitive shortcoming and those which make possible disagreements for which such an ascription is not mandated.

The foregoing outlines moves available to a defender of distance between minimal truth-aptitude and Cognitive Command who continues to work with the thin notion whereby the holding of an untrue opinion is sufficient for cognitive shortcoming. Williamson, as noted, believes that a satisfactory response to his objection will have to work with a more substantial notion, and is sceptical whether anything suitable is available. It is therefore important to note that in the right circumstances the thin notion becomes itself rather more substantial than he seems to recognise. What occasions the thin notion is the desire that Cognitive Command should catch discourses for which we think of truth as evidentially unconstrained. The motivating kind of case is illustrated by the dispute, outlined in the latter half of chapter 4 of *Truth and Objectivity*, in which two scientific theorists arrive at conflicting theoretical opinions via the internally blameless prosecution of good scientific method. If we think ourselves entitled to the view that there must be facts of the matter which one, or both, are misrepresenting, then the capacity of the Cognitive Command constraint to put controls on the notion of 'representation', understood in a fashion congenial to the realist, demands that cognitive shortcoming be involved in such a dispute; so there is no option but to say that the mere holding of an untrue opinion suffices, in such a case, for cognitive shortcoming. Obviously matters change, however, if we are concerned with statements whose truth or untruth cannot, we conceive, lie beyond detection. In such cases the holding of an untrue opinion ensures something more, namely either that optimal means for determination of the truth status of the statement in question have not been implemented, or that they have been misimplemented. And in such a case there will therefore be some fact about the way a subject has arrived at an errant view such that one who happened to know of that fact would have grounds for reservation about the errant view *independently* of any self-standing opinion on the matter concerned.[21] Such a notion is actually pointed to in a number of passages in *Truth and Objectivity*, though Williamson does not discuss them.[22]

In any area of discourse, therefore—like, plausibly, the aesthetics of rhubarb—where we pretend to no conception of how truth and

21. Note that this is not to say that there has always to be an effective way of finding such a fact in any case where one exists.

22. See, for instance, *Truth and Objectivity*, p. 103.

untruth might altogether lie beyond our recognition, the claim that someone is holding an untrue opinion, and is thereby guilty of cognitive shortcoming, must be held to imply some in principle *independently appreciable* shortcoming in the grounding of that opinion. That is the claim that it takes 'substantial philosophy', of the kind mapped out on one main branch of the tree of alternatives explored in *Truth and Objectivity*, to make good. And it is something which a minimalist about the comic, or the aesthetics of rhubarb, will believe it is impossible to make good.

IV. DISCOURSES, DEFAULT VIEWS AND KEEPING LIFE SIMPLE

Anyone who regards the debate between realist and anti-realist not as a single overarching metaphysical struggle but as the union of various local debates, so that the realist might conceivably win in the mathematical case, for instance, but lose in the moral, will want to go along with the idea of a plurality of discourses with respect to which local realist and anti-realist views can be brought into opposition. Williamson does not challenge that exactly. But he is resistant to the idea that such debates need not exhibit a common structure, whereby the realist about a given discourse is always represented as making essentially the same kind of claim; and more resistant still to the suggestion that anti-realism—minimalism—might be the default view. And above all, he is totally out of sympathy with the idea that a variety of truth predicates may be characteristic of different discourses. I finish this essay by briefly responding to these ideas in reverse order.

I believe Williamson misunderstands the pluralism about truth canvassed in *Truth and Objectivity*. Here is a passage typical of the sort of reservation he has:

Suppose that the discourses D1 and D2 are both conducted in English ... let 'A1' and 'A2' be declarative sentences in D1 and D2 respectively. Thus 'either A1 or A2' is also a declarative sentence of English. Some notion of truth is applicable to both the disjunction and its disjuncts, for otherwise the platitude that 'either A1 or A2' is true if and only if either 'A1' is true or 'A2' is true, would be vitiated by equivocation. Thus at least one notion of truth is applicable to both 'A1' and 'A2', and to longer sentences in which they are embedded.[23]

This is an illustration of the more general point that

> A natural language is strongly unified in syntax and semantics. Any finite set of its words can be combined together within the unity of a sentence. The notion of truth must respect and reflect this integrity. Truths are many; truth is one.[24]

The pluralism suggested in *Truth and Objectivity* is not in tension with this. And I ought not to have written, if indeed I anywhere do, in a way which suggested the postulation of *ambiguity* in the word 'true'. An ambiguous term typically needs two or more explanations, each determining a different extension for it. For the minimalist, however, a truth predicate is any that satisfies the minimal set of platitudes: those platitudes enshrine all that can be said by way of explanation of the meaning of the word, which is therefore *uniform*. Since, moreover,—as Williamson himself emphasises[25]—a truth predicate for a given discourse will satisfy the Disquotational Scheme, there is no question of a pair of predicates each qualifying as a truth predicate for a given discourse yet differing in extension. 'True' is not ambiguous as are 'stage', 'tear', and 'still'.

The variety which truth predicates in different discourses may nevertheless exhibit may be illustrated by a parallel with identity. In one sense the concept of identity does not vary as we consider different ranges of individuals, but is sustained by uniform inferential links, grounded in the twin platitudes that everything is self-identical and that identicals share all their properties. Nevertheless what *consti-*

---

23. Williamson (1994b), p. 141.
24. *Ibid.*
25. *Ibid.*, p. 135. Cf. *Truth and Objectivity*, p. 52.

tutes identity is subject to considerable variation as we vary the kinds of objects with which we are concerned. The identity of material objects is arguably constituted by spatio-temporal continuity; identity and distinctness among numbers, on Frege's famous account, is dictated by relations of one–one correspondence among associated concepts; the directions of lines are identified and distinguished by relations of parallelism between lines; and it is, notoriously, very difficult to say what constitutes identity for persons, though considerations of bodily and psychological continuity call the shots.

The notion of 'constitution' applied here could no doubt be usefully clarified, but I see no reason to question the authenticity of the general idea that the instantiation of a certain concept may be constituted in different ways, depending upon the kind of instantiators concerned. That at any rate is the contention of pluralism about truth. There is no single discourse-invariant thing in which truth consists. Depending upon the region of discourse with which we are concerned, it may consist in superassertibility, or not; in representation of explanatorily active states of affairs, or not; in a fact about the direction of ideal opinion, or not; and so on. That is to ascribe a species of diversity to the concept; but it is not of a kind to generate the sort of problem about the interpretation of the truth predicate when discourses mingle which Williamson alleges.

Of course, it would be consistent to accept that truth has a variable constitution, sometimes amounting to something congenial to the realist, sometimes not, without according default priority to anti-realism. Williamson begs leave to doubt that there is any good reason for such a view of the priorities, complaining that

> [u]nfortunately, Wright doesn't make it clear why it is more 'unassuming' to assume that the truth predicate has no intuitively realist extra features than to assume that it has no intuitively anti-realist features (nor why we may need to make either assumption prior to investigation).[26]

26. *Ibid.*, p. 136. See *Truth and Objectivity*, p. 174, for one statement of the idea that he is reacting against.

This remark would be fitting, it seems to me, if a merely minimally truth-apt discourse represented a neutral zone, about which neither a realist nor an anti-realist view would be appropriate, and if both realist and anti-realist had to substantiate their views by pointing to *additional* features which discourses might possess. But with one exception, that is not the way of it. The exception—the case where an intuitive anti-realism might feed upon the demonstration of a positive feature—is that of Euthryphronic discourses, wherein the extension of the truth predicate is (partially) best-opinion determined. But in each of the other cases I distinguished—Evidence Transcendence, Cognitive Command, and Wide Cosmological Role—the anti-realist contention is of a property *missing,* and is carried in train by the contention that the discourse in question is *merely* minimally truth-apt. That has the following effect. If we are agreed that a certain discourse is minimally truth-apt, and have so far carried out no investigation as to how it fares in the light of the various cruces, then we ought not so far, in our thought about truth and objectivity for the discourse in question, fall into any assumption inconsistent with the eventuality that it prove *merely* minimally truth-apt. If the justifiability of an anti-realist view depended upon the discourse's possession of *further* 'anti-realism relevant' features, then a kind of neutralism would be the default stance. But because that is not so, the distinction between neutralism and anti-realism effectively collapses.

That is not to say that the default assumption should be that subsequent investigation will turn out negatively, from a realist point of view. Williamson would be right to complain about that. The point is merely the obvious one that, given only the datum of minimal truth-aptitude, the conservative strategy will be to make no assumption about the kind of content possessed by the discourse, and the constitution of truth within it, which is not justified by that datum. So we will avoid thinking about such things in any of the ways evoked by standard realist imagery. We will thereby be default anti-realists—not in the sense that we assume that subsequent investigation will go the anti-realist's way, but in the sense that nothing in our practice of the discourse, nor in the conceptions of truth and objectivity for it which we can so far justifiably profess, will change if that proves to be so.

Williamson concludes his study on a note of scepticism about whether what he views as 'the proliferation of complexity' effected by *Truth and Objectivity* best serves the consideration of this set of issues. Insofar as this doubt is generated by his convictions that truth has to be construed as uniform, and that key distinctions such as that between minimal truth-aptitude and Cognitive Command have not been made out, then it is addressed by the preceding remarks, assuming that they are sound. But it seems to me that even one utterly sceptical about the specific proposals of *Truth and Objectivity* should mistrust the direction of Williamson's remarks here. The classical forms for opposition between realist and anti-realist—in particular, the expressivist, error-theoretic and Dummettian paradigms—demonstrably fail us when we use any one of them to attempt to construct a satisfying *übersicht* of realist and anti-realist disputes in all the areas in which they arise. Whether or not *Truth and Objectivity* takes useful initial steps, nothing seems to be more certain in this area than that these debates exhibit an intrinsic variety and that we can only make their clarification and conduct unnecessarily difficult by assuming otherwise.

I am indebted to Bob Hale, Stewart Shapiro and Timothy Williamson for correspondence and discussion.

5

Responses to Commentators: Van Cleve, Horwich, Pettit, Horgan, Sainsbury, Williamson

I. ON THE INSTABILITY OF CLASSICAL DEFLATIONISM

The 'inflationary' argument of chapter 1 of *Truth and Objectivity*—the argument that the classical deflationary conception of truth must, on its own assumptions, inflate into something more substantial—is puzzled over by James van Cleve and, unsurprisingly, roundly rejected by Paul Horwich. Van Cleve wonders about the precise role in the argument of the normativity of the truth predicate, and wonders what exactly it is about deflationism, in contrast with minimalism, which puts it in tension with the existence of distinct norms of truth and warranted assertibility. Horwich too complains that the argument is structurally unclear and unconvincing, charging that it turns on a *non sequitur* and that even if it could engage the traditional form of deflationism which holds that truth is not a property, it would pass by the version of the position which he himself has defended at length. And he too is puzzled about the role of normativity in the inflationary argument, since he thinks that those aspects of the truth predicate which reflect its normativity may straightforwardly be accounted for by appeal to the Equivalence Schema (or, presumably, the Disquotational Scheme). I first offer some remarks by way of clarification, hoping thereby to speak to van Cleve's queries, and then respond to Horwich's objections.

Classical deflationism is the view that there is no legitimate subject matter for the debates between correspondence theorists, coherence theorists, pragmatists (at least, the ones who intend to say something about what truth should be held to consist in) and those philosophers who, like Frege, hold that truth is a substantial, though indefinable characteristic of the items—be they sentences, propositions, or attitudes—which have it. For the classical deflationist, these misbegotten debates arise because of a misunderstanding of the role of the truth predicate: it functions as an adjective, so one naturally expects its function to be to ascribe a property. But that is not its function, and there is no such property. Its real function is as a device of *endorsement*. In general, such endorsement can be achieved, without using any special device, just by asserting, or assenting to a particular proposition (say). The need for the truth predicate arises only because endorsement can sometimes be indefinite ('Something he said is true'), or generalised ('Everything he said is true'), and because we sometimes may wish to endorse a proposition by name ('The Axiom of Constructibility is true') without specification of its content.

That this is the central point of our having the word 'true' is emphasised by Horwich.[1] And while he officially disclaims the contention that truth is not a property,[2] this does not in fact mark any significant divergence between his position and that of classical deflationism, since in allowing truth to be a property, he means only to acknowledge that the syntactic role of 'true'—as determined by how best it is formalised in order to recover the validity of certain intuitive inferences containing it—is that of a predicate. It remains that, like the classical deflationist, Horwich still intends to deny that there is any proper philosophical question about what fits a proposition to be characterised as 'true', any legitimate general question

1. See Horwich (1998a), pp. 2–3.
2. *Ibid.*, p. 38.

concerning in what the truth of a proposition consists. And against those who think otherwise, he wants to set the standard deflationist idea that there is essentially no more to the truth predicate than the role imposed upon it by the Disquotational Scheme—or, on his own account, by the counterpart Equivalence Schema for propositions.

My inflationary argument is to the effect that this is an incoherent package. More specifically, the argument contends that any predicate whose role is (all but) fully characterised by the Disquotational Scheme (or the Equivalence Schema) cannot be a predicate about which the philosophical question, wherein consists a sentence's satisfaction of it, is misguided in the way in which the classical deflationist and Horwich agree in supposing. In other words, to think of the truth predicate as explained via the Disquotational Scheme is to leave no room for the idea that it is *merely* a device of endorsement. There has to be something in which being true consists, even if, as it may be, Frege was right that nothing analytically illuminating can be said about what that is.

The argument proceeds by two lemmas. The first is about normativity. It is argued that any predicate which is explained by stipulating that it is to be subject to the Disquotational Scheme will function normatively over assertion/acceptance of the range of sentences for which it is thereby defined, and will indeed coincide in normative force with warranted acceptance/assertibility for those sentences: that is, to have reason to think that the predicate applies to a sentence will be to have a warrant for accepting that sentence; and to have a warrant for accepting the sentence will be to have reason to think the predicate applies.

Now, if a predicate functions normatively over a given practice—that is, if moves within the practice can be justified by reason to think that the predicate qualifies them, and if refraining from or, where appropriate, cancelling them can be justified by reason to think that it does not—then there are just two possibilities. One is that the predicate in question serves to record a norm that is peculiar and distinctive to it. The other is that it is a device whereby one may indirectly signal moves' satisfaction of *other* norms, characteristically expressed in other words. What would the second option come to when the practice in question is the making and acceptance of statements? The practice is unquestionably highly normatively constrained. If 'true' is not to mark a distinctive, *sui generis* norm, then what remain are the context-sensitive standards of acceptability which we can lump under the catch-all term 'warrant'. So the second option comes to the thought that 'true' is a device for registering the acceptability of a statement by those standards—for registering the possession of warrants. But this proposal is ruled out by the second lemma of the inflationary argument, that 'true' and 'warranted' are liable to diverge in extension over any discourse which allows the possibility of neutral states of information—states of information which, for a particular statement, warrant neither its assertion nor its denial. And this potential extensional divergence is, again, shown to be a consequence directly of the Disquotational Scheme. (I take it as obvious that a predicate cannot simply be a device for registering the acceptability of a particular move in the light of a certain norm, φ, if it may properly be applied in circumstances where the predicate which actually expresses that norm fails to apply or conversely.)

The upshot is accordingly that any theorist who holds that the Disquotational Scheme (or the Equivalence Schema) is explanatory of the truth predicate is committed to the first option: the truth predicate has to be associated with a distinctive kind of critical or commendatory claim—there is a way in which a statement can be in, or out of order which is not the same as its being warranted or not, and which it is the role of 'true' to mark. The question is whether that reflection can sit well with deflationism. My contention is that it cannot.

Notice, though, that the issue is *not* whether the truth predicate's possession of this role can be fully accounted for just by appeal to the Disquotational Scheme. Horwich tends to write as though in order to show that some aspect of the use of 'true' poses no difficulty for his views, it suffices to indicate how the Disquotational Scheme (or in his case the Equivalence Schema) contains the resources to explain that particular aspect. But that's an *ignoratio elenchi*. The whole point of the inflationary argument is that that does *not* suffice—that to suppose that 'true' is explained by the Disquotational Scheme is *already* to suppose something inconsistent with the official deflationist line on 'true'. That what we might call the *sui generis normativity* of 'true' follows from the role the deflationist assigns to the Disquotational Scheme is the whole point of the argument. It has no tendency to show that the point is harmless to deflationism.

Still, what makes it *not* harmless? Well, once it is recognised that, as I expressed the matter a moment ago, there is a way in which a statement can be in or out of order independently of whether or not it is warranted, I do not see how it could fail to be reckoned a real property of a statement that it was or was not so in order, nor how the question could be deflected: In what does being in order, or out of order, in that kind of way, consist? Once it is granted that the role of 'true' is to mark a particular kind of achievement, or failing, on the part of a statement, distinct from being warranted or not, there has to be a place for the question: What does such an achievement, or failing, amount to? The question may have no very illuminating answer in general, but that, if so, would tend to corroborate Frege's indefinabilist realism about truth, rather than deflationism. In brief: if a term registers a distinctive norm over a practice, the presumption has to be that there will be something in which a move's compliance or noncompliance with that norm will consist. And whichever state it occupies, that will then be a real characteristic—property—of the move. It is mere word-spinning to deny it.

Now there is, to be sure—though I did not remark on this in *Truth and Objectivity*—an assumption made in this line of thought. It might be contended that what, strictly, has been shown is only that, if the truth predicate is explained via the Disquotational Scheme, then a use is imposed upon it which *calls for* a norm over the making and acceptance of statements distinct from warrant. It is another question whether there *really is* such a norm—whether there really is such a way for a statement to be in, or out of order. It is one thing, in other words, for an expression to be used in the making of a distinctive kind of normative judgement; it's quite another matter for there to be such a thing as a bearer's *really deserving* a judgement of that kind. An error theorist about ethics, for example, may readily grant that ethical terms are used normatively—are used to applaud, and censure, particular episodes of conduct, for instance. But he will deny nevertheless that there are any real characteristics by its possession of which an episode of conduct may qualify for such appraisal.

This, however, need not delay us. The deflationist cannot intend any counterpart of this line of thought. He is not an error theorist about truth. For he will be quite content to allow that all manner of statements *really are true*—when the right circumstances obtain: 'Grass is green', for instance, really is true just when grass is green; 'Snow is white' really is true just when snow is white, and so on. For the deflationist, there is, for each meaningful statement—or at least, for each with an objective subject matter—an objective condition under which the word 'true' is rightly applied to it. So he can take no refuge in error theory.[3] It is this objectivism about the conditions of rightful application of 'true' to particular statements, coupled with the distinctive normativity of the predicate, which enforces the recognition that there really is such a thing as a statement's complying or failing to comply with the norm of truth. The advertised inflation is thereby accomplished.[4]

---

3. Or, for that matter, in expressivism. The context, ' "P" is true', if governed by the Disquotational Scheme, has all the features required to qualify for assertoric content, at least by the lights of the minimalism concerning that notion advocated in *Truth and Objectivity*. Indeed, Strawson's 'performatory' theory of truth was one of the principal targets of the classic argument in Geach (1969).

4. Van Cleve wonders what if any stand I would take on the issue whether instances of the Disquotational Scheme are *contingent* truths. I am not sure that I need to take a view, though it might ring oddly to some ears if someone, be they minimalist or not, who viewed the Disquotational Scheme as among the determinants of the concept of truth, were to accept the contingency of instances of it. Still, I think it clear they are contingent, for a simple reason—'Grass is green' might have had a different meaning, and thus been true in a grassless world, for instance—but that contingency for this reason is consistent with instances of the Disquotational Scheme being *a priori*, in a suitably relaxed sense which would allow apriority to any truth available to reflection on meanings alone.

Someone who conceded, for these reasons, that truth is a real property would so far still be at liberty to question whether the property in question is ever in common between different statements. If it were not, that might save one remaining deflationary thesis—the emptiness of the classical debates about the constitution of truth. A deflationist, that is, could now grant that her traditional account of the role and purpose of 'true' is misguided but still insist that the traditional debates are bad since they overlook that truth is, so to speak, *nothing which true statements share*: the truth of 'Snow is white', for instance, consists in snow's being white, whereas that of 'Grass is green' consists in grass' being green, and so on.

This thought is challenged at pp. 29–31 of *Truth and Objectivity*, where it is observed that one who accepts the Disquotational Scheme as explanatory of 'true' must also allow that truth admits of a uniform characterisation (the principle there called DS*). But let me here say a little more. The consideration that truth is, in the way illustrated, constituted differently for different statements is actually a very bad reason for thinking that it is not a uniform property. The pattern illustrated is a commonplace. Many properties are such that their satisfaction conditions vary as a function of variation in the character of a potential subject. Consider, for example, 'has fulfilled his educational potential'. What it takes to instantiate this will depend on other aspects of the nature of the individual concerned; yet that ought to be consistent with there being a clear sense in which it expresses the same property in all cases, which may yet be open to an illuminating general account. In general, how x has to be in order to be F can depend in part on how it is with x, and vary accordingly, without any motive being provided thereby for regarding it as an error to try to provide some illuminating general account of a condition which being F involves satisfying. *Of course* what statements have to do in order to be true varies: for their meanings vary and truth value is a function of meaning. But it would be an egregious *non sequitur* to infer that there is no one condition which, modulo their meaning, their being true consists in satisfying.

To conclude this section, let me take the opportunity to counter a response to the inflationary argument offered by Ian Rumfitt.[5] Rumfitt maintains that the divergence in the behaviour of 'true' and 'assertible' constituted by the former's compliance with the Negation Equivalence:

'Not P' is true ↔ Not: 'P' is true,

while the corresponding

'Not P' is assertible ↔ Not: 'P' is assertible,

fails, right to left, in any discourse which permits neutral states of information, may straightforwardly be accommodated in a fashion entirely consonant with the 'spirit' of deflationism, without admission of a distinctive norm of truth, if the deflationist is prepared to allow primitive norms of *warranted denial* to operate alongside those of warranted assertion. Rather, that is, than restrict his distinctive deflationary claims to the word 'true', the deflationist should contend

> that 'is true' and 'is not true' function purely as devices for endorsing *and rejecting* assertions, beliefs and so on . . . and which therefore register no norms distinct from justified assertibility *and justified deniability* (Rumfitt (1995), p. 103; compare *Truth and Objectivity*, p. 30).

How would this help with the Negation Equivalence? Rumfitt is not entirely explicit, but the point may seem clear enough. Since denying a statement is asserting its negation, a primitive warrant—an *antiwarrant* is Rumfitt's term—for the denial of 'P', registered by a sentence of the form, ' "P" is not true' or, equivalently, 'Not: "P" is true', will be *eo ipso* a warrant for asserting 'Not P', so—via the Disquotational Scheme—for asserting ' "Not P" is true'. So the validity of the Negation Equivalence, right to left, is easily explained, while

5. Rumfitt (1995).

the invalidity of the corresponding principle for assertibility is secured, as before, by the possibility of states of information in which one has neither warrant nor anti-warrant for P.

What, though, about the result of negating both halves of the Negation Equivalence:

'Not P' is not true ↔ Not: 'P' is not true.

Now the effect of the proposal, that the role of 'is not true' is to register the presence of an anti-warrant, is merely to reinstate a form of the original difficulty. For the principle

'Not P' is anti-warranted ↔ Not: 'P' is anti-warranted,

is no less unacceptable if neutral states of information are possible than is

'Not P' is assertible ↔ Not: 'P' is assertible.

In short, for any discourse in which neutral states of information are a possibility, the Disquotational Scheme imposes a potential extensional divergence both between 'is true' and 'is assertible' *and* between 'is not true' and 'is anti-warranted'. Rumfitt's proposal that the deflationist should recognise anti-warrant as primitive—whatever its independent problems and interest—thus provides no counter whatever to the inflationary argument.

II. SUPERASSERTIBILITY AND RELATED MATTERS

Van Cleve, Horgan and Pettit are each unpersuaded of the credentials of superassertibility to serve as a truth predicate. Here I review their doubts in turn.

Van Cleve suggests, to begin with, that the biconditional—what I termed the Negation Equivalence—derived from the Disquotational Scheme, which enjoins the potential extensional divergence of truth and assertibility, namely,

'Not P' is true if and only if 'P' is not true,

is already inconsistent with any evidentially constrained conception of truth—superassertibility being, of course, an evidentially constrained notion—since, he takes it, the right-to-left ingredient must surely be disallowed in such cases.

I'm not sure why he thinks so. If truth is evidentially constrained, then, certainly, the failure of a statement to meet the constraint—whatever exact shape the latter takes—will be sufficient for its untruth, and hence, moving across the biconditional, sufficient for the truth of its negation. And this implication will no doubt be uncongenial to one of realist inclination, for whom the possibility will seem evident that a suitably selected statement might be true even though no evidence for or against it is available in principle. But of course *that* possibility will not be at all evident to one who thinks of truth as evidentially constrained. Van Cleve writes as though there is here a difficulty which should be appreciated even on a Dummettian anti-realist perspective. Unfortunately, he does not say enough to make it clear what the difficulty is. In section III of chapter 2 of *Truth and Objectivity*, I argued that the correct response to the Negation Equivalence for such an anti-realist is to see it as imposing on the concept of negation generally an analogue of that feature of intuitionistic mathematical negation which has it that a proof of the unprovability of a statement is a proof of the negation of that statement. So far as I can see, van Cleve says nothing to disturb the stability of that response. To be sure, it involves revising ordinary habits of thought and speech involving negation. Dummettian anti-realism is a revisionary doctrine.

Van Cleve has, however, a more specific argument about superassertibility in particular. He reasons as follows. By the failure of the Negation Equivalence, right to left, for warrant (because of the possibility of neutral states of information), we have (this is van Cleve's notation):

(i) $-(WP \rightarrow W-P)$.

We also have that superassertibility implies warrant:

(ii) $SP \rightarrow WP$.

It therefore follows that superassertibility, too, cannot subserve the right-to-left direction of the Negation Equivalence; that is, that we have:

(iii) $-(SP \rightarrow SP)$

For otherwise we could pass from $-WP$ to $-SP$, via (ii) and thereby to $S-P$, and thereby—substituting 'not P' for 'P' in (ii)—to $W-P$, contrary to hypothesis. Since it is granted that the Negation Equivalence must hold for any truth predicate, it follows that superassertibility isn't one, just provided we are concerned with a discourse which allows of neutral states of information and no matter what its other properties.

This fallacious reasoning is the product of an insufficiently articulate symbolism. Warrant is relative to a state of information. For a particular subject matter to allow of neutral states of information is for it not to be the case that any possible state of information which fails to warrant a particular statement concerning that subject matter thereby warrants the negation of that statement. So, letting 'I' range over possible states of information, we may represent the failure of the Negation Equivalence for warrant like this:

(i)′ $-((\forall I)(-W_I P \rightarrow W_I -P))$.

By contrast, the sense in which superassertibility implicates warrant is only that if a statement is superassertible, then it is warranted in some state of information:

(ii)′ $SP \to (\exists I)\, W_I P$.

If we now essay the purported reductio of $-SP \to S-P$, it works out like this:

(1)	$-SP \to S-P$	assumption for reductio
(2)	$-(\exists I)W_I P \to -SP$	from (ii)′
(3)	$-(\exists I)W_I P \to S-P$	from (1) and (2)
(4)	$S-P \to (\exists I)\, W_I-P$	'$-P$' for 'P' in (ii)′
(5)	$-(\exists I)W_I P \to (\exists I)W_I-P$	from (3) and (4)

Line (5) is what, in van Cleve's notation, is represented as inconsistent with (i)—the failure of the Negation Equivalence for warrant. But of course it is not so inconsistent. What line (5) says is that the unattainability of any state of information warranting P suffices for the existence of a state of information warranting not P. Since the former is something for which it must be possible, at least in principle, to accumulate inductive grounds, and since those grounds will be—in the presence of an account of negation of the kind which, as just argued, a proponent of an evidentially constrained conception of truth must give in any case—grounds for the negation of P, this consequence is entirely valid in the relevant setting. And it is in no way inconsistent with the possibility of the neutral states of information, as affirmed by (i)′.

If superassertibility is to be defensible as a truth predicate, whether globally or locally, then it must, globally or locally, satisfy the minimal platitudes. Van Cleve next worries about a turn taken by my discussion of the claim of superassertibility to satisfy the Equivalence Schema.[6] The relevant principle is

(E^s) It is superassertible that P if and only if P

and what bothers van Cleve is my suggestion that what may seem to be the obvious kind of counterexamples to the necessity of that

6. *Truth and Objectivity*, pp. 51–2.

biconditional—namely, instances of 'P' which, we might think, could be true even though no stable justification of them is attainable—would be question-begging. My point was simply that in order to appreciate how such a case—Goldbach's Conjecture, perhaps—might provide for the truth of the right-hand side of E^s while falsifying the left-hand side, we need to be using an evidentially unconstrained notion of truth to begin with, which is therefore already recognised as distinct from superassertibility. We have not shown that superassertibility fails to satisfy the platitudes if, in order to construct a purported counterexample, we need to invoke a notion of truth for the relevant range of statements which is *already* distinguished from superassertibility. In order relevantly to counter-exemplify E^s, we need instead to produce a case where one side, but not the other, is *superassertible*.

If I read him right, van Cleve isn't quite sure whether to cry 'foul' here or not. So he contents himself with an argument that, if the point is not a foul, then theories of truth, consistently adhered to, may be very difficult to refute—at least in a way mutually acceptable to the disputants. I am not sure that that is quite the right conclusion to draw, so a little comment may be useful.

First, I want to insist that there is no foul. The minimalist about truth holds that, to the extent that the concept is determinate, it is fixed by the minimal platitudes—a range of basic, a priori principles. So van Cleve is offering in effect what Michael Smith, following through on an idea original to Frank Ramsey and developed by Carnap, David Lewis, Frank Jackson and others, has called a 'network analysis' of the concept.[7] Consider a putatively comprehensive enumeration of those platitudes, from which all occurrences of the word 'true' are omitted and replaced by a variable. Then the gist of the network analysis is that a truth concept is any which is, a priori, a satisfier of the open sentence—call it the *network condition*—which conjoins each ingredient sentence in this enumeration. Clearly, it must

7. See Michael Smith (1994), esp. chap. 2.

be a constraint on this kind of approach that the network condition not be permitted to retain residual occurrences of the definiendum. If not, then, first, the result will be circular in the way that any analysis is which makes essential use of the very term being analysed; and, second, in cases where we are characterising a *role* which may have a number of distinct satisfiers, we run the risk of barring perfectly good candidates by, in effect, distorting the import of the network condition through reading certain of its ingredient conjuncts in terms of other—perhaps, on their own terms, perfectly good—candidates.

That said, I think what follows is not that theories of truth, however bizarre, may now be much more difficult to refute than perhaps they ought to be, but only that their refutation may have to look elsewhere than to the way they handle themselves in relation to the basic platitudes. And indeed theories of truth have, of course, more to do than to conserve a priori principles involving the notion. They have also to succeed in characterising something which may plausibly be taken to be normative over the (relevant local) practice of statement-making and belief-formation, and they have to answer to, though not necessarily be perfectly congruent with, our antecedent ideas about the extension of the notion. The oracular view of truth proposed in van Cleve's example, however well or badly it fares in the matter of platitude-conservation, and however difficult a staunch adherent of it might be to refute on his own terms, is certain to do very badly when it comes to making sense of the assertoric practices of ordinary folk to whom that conception has never occurred, and of the range of statements which they are prepared to allow to be true or to be at least possibly true.

I turn now to a misunderstanding. Terence Horgan, in section III of his comments, attributes to me an across-the-board identification of truth with superassertibility. Likewise, Philip Pettit takes it to be my view that superassertibility is at least an across-the-board satisfier of all the minimal platitudes—so that if the truth predicate in some particular discourse is best *not* interpreted as superassertibility, it will be for reasons independent of the constraints imposed on truth predicates by those basic platitudes. Neither of these is my view. I do indeed canvass the global identification of truth and superassertibility as one way of interpreting the import of Dummettian anti-realism; but *Truth and Objectivity* does not argue for Dummettian anti-realism as a global thesis and is concerned, to the contrary, to advance a framework in which it might coherently be espoused locally, without commitment to a similar view about other areas of thought.[8] To be sure, the view Pettit ascribes to me, that superassertibility is always a satisfier of the platitudes for truth but may be ruled out as an interpretation of the truth predicate in certain areas on other grounds, is consistent with this qualification. But that is a position which would demand that truth and superassertibility were everywhere necessarily co-extensive, since otherwise the Equivalence Schema for superassertibility, Eˢ above, could not hold a priori.[9] In general, realism about a given discourse may well, depending upon its exact form, entail that superassertibility is *not* there a satisfier of the basic platitudes. So I want to distance myself from Pettit's description of me as 'forced to think of realists as saying that what identifies a suitable truth-property for any discourse is the common platitudes plus something else: plus some other discourse-specific principles'.[10]

Horgan doubts that there is a plausible case for identifying truth with superassertibility anywhere. He takes it as evident that the extensions of the two concepts fail to coincide in cases like his example concerning the population of Tennessee in 5000 B.C.; and even where there is a, perhaps necessary, coincidence, he takes it that the modes of evaluation implicated in the two concepts are quite different: superassertibility is an epistemic norm, truth is not. It would be quite unfair to complain that he does not, in his necessarily very brief remarks, provide any argument for the latter, unqualified claim. The question is how someone who thought of truth in ethics, say—or perhaps in philosophy,—along broadly superassertibilist lines, with the

---

8. I am not, in saying this, now formally withdrawing any sympathy for the global view. But it is important to understand that the programme of *Truth and Objectivity* is not hostage to such sympathy's being justified.

9. Cf. *Truth and Objectivity*, p. 53.

10. Pettit (1996), p. 887.

true identified as that which survives the most careful and well-informed disputation, would be handicapped in the prosecution of those discourses. Horgan's view must be, it seems to me, that there would have to be a handicap. For if there need be none, if such a mis-understanding could be operationally quite idle, it is going to be a very nice question in what its being a *mis*understanding could consist. As for the particular case of statements concerning the past, I think all, including myself, who have felt some sympathy with Dummettian anti-realism have been prepared to grant that they surely provide one of the most fraught areas for the semantic anti-realist thesis. I do not think that the debate is by any means closed, though here is certainly not the place to try to take it further. But I repeat that the global iden-tifiability of truth with superassertibility is not a thesis defended in *Truth and Objectivity*.

Pettit has a more radical misgiving about superassertibility, writing that he is not convinced 'that superassertibility is defined for every discourse, so that some statements there are superassertible, others not'.[11] The characterisation is a little misleading, since the way he goes on to develop the worry makes it clear that it is not about whether superassertibility is well defined, but about whether it has a *non-empty extension* in ordinary discourses—whether there really are any superassertible statements. He first sketches the doubt for proba-bility statements, then extends it to any statements based on inductive warrant, and finally argues a related point for comic discourse.

To begin with, does any possible warrant that we could have meet the condition required for the superassertibility of the statement that a particular coin is fair (that is, that the probability of its landing heads is close to a half)? Pettit answers:

> I don't think so . . . Even in a world subject to the actual physical laws, it is always going to be possible for [a substantial series of trials corrob-orating the fairness of the coin] to be followed by a freak sequence— say, a long run of heads—that would deprive [that series] of its war-ranting force.[12]

11. *Ibid.*, p. 888.
12. *Ibid.*

Moreover,

> [t]he lesson of the example clearly extends to all claims that are based
> on inductive warrants; with any warrant for such a claim a freak run of
> observations would undermine it. Superassertibility does not seem to
> be satisfied, then, for the discourses associated with such claims.[13]

I find it hard to see the force of this. In order for it to be superassertible that the coin is fair, there has to be some state of information which warrants that claim and which continues to do so no matter how enlarged upon or improved. The immediate conclusion, then, if a favourable initial series of trials goes on to be swamped by a freakish run, is only that the favourable initial series does not *per se* provide for a superassertibility-conferring state of information. That is still consistent with the claim about the fairness of the coin *being* superassertible. Pettit seems, moreover, to think it sufficient for his point that, no matter how extended the favourable series, a subsequent freak sequence is always *possible*. Not so: to claim superassertibility for the proposition that the coin is fair is only to claim that there is some sequence of trials which supports that claim and which is such that, *as a matter of fact,* any enlarged sequence will continue to support it. There is no denial that a freakish subsequent run is possible. On the contrary, the claim of fairness is defeasible: the possibility of defeat by a larger sequence of trials is admitted all along.[14]

Actually, so far from providing a problem case, it seems to me that probability discourse is an especially attractive candidate for superassertibilist construal. For consider what it would be for *no* particular

---

13. *Ibid.*

14. The reader should be reminded that the range of the states-of-information quantifier in the characterisation of superassertibility does not comprise all merely possible states of information—if it did, Pettit's point would be entirely just—nor is it restricted to actually occurring such states. Rather it comprises an intermediate set: the *actually accessible* states of information—states of information which this world, *constituted as it is,* would generate in a suitably receptive, investigating subject.

numerical probability statement, even a very approximated one, to be superassertible. That would mean that, no matter which such statement we took, any series of trials which more or less corroborated it would be but a proper initial segment of a larger series in which that corroboration was lost. What could it mean in such a predicament to say that there *was* a determinate probability associated with, say, a particular coin's turning up heads—in what could consist the fact that such a statement was *true*?

For his third type of example, that of comic discourse, Pettit argues rather differently. He takes it that the funny is what would amuse people meeting certain standard conditions of normality—people who 'are not lunatics that would laugh at anything, for example, nor melancholics that would laugh at nothing'. His thought is then—I take it—that the best type of ground we could have for the claim that a particular joke, say, is funny would be evidence of a positive comic response from normal folk. And his objection is that if—as he believes—the satisfaction of normality conditions does not lend itself to superassertibility, then neither in consequence will claims about what is funny.

However, closer scrutiny of the worry would seem to disclose essentially the same misunderstanding as before. Pettit's idea about normality is, approximately, that the conditions under which I give a comic verdict are normal just when there is nothing about them which, in the event that my verdict clashes with that of others, would be received (by somehow idealised judges?) as sufficient reason to discount my verdict. This is a condition which, in the nature of the case, cannot be guaranteed to obtain:

> [L]ater discrepancies [may always lead us] to indict any present circumstances as having been faulty and misleading in some way. And so under this approach no warrant for the claim that a joke is funny is such that it would survive any arbitrarily close scrutiny or any arbitrarily extensive information.[15]

15. Pettit (1996), p. 889.

But again, the conclusion is unwarranted. The lack of guarantee that conditions are normal implicates merely an epistemic possibility. Lack of superassertibility for that claim, by contrast, would demand that the possibility obtained.

III. ALETHIC PLURALISM

As remarked earlier, one who takes the minimalist line about truth, that the concept is fixed by a set of basic platitudes about it, ought to be open to the possibility, prior to any demonstration of categoricity, that it may prove to have a variety of models, as it were. It is a central contention of *Truth and Objectivity* that the notion of truth is in just this situation. For instance, the core platitudes may consistently be supplemented both by the supposition that all truths are knowable and by the supposition that some truths are quite beyond evidence. Under the former, superassertibility may be shown to be a model of truth; under the latter, it is not, and truth will presumably require interpretation in terms of some form of robust correspondence. It is a key suggestion of the book that this potential plurality reflects the distinctions that are relevant to realism/anti-realism debate: that the justification of a broadly realist or anti-realist view of a given discourse turns on the character of the local truth predicate.

A key thesis but, it would seem, one of the more contentious. Three commentators—Horwich, Pettit and Sainsbury—are expressly negative about it, though each allows that the broader framework of the book, and particularly the suggestion that there is no single, simple crux between realism and anti-realism but a variety of relevant considerations, could survive the reinstatement of the usual monism about truth.

I am happy to accept the last point—indeed, it is in effect acknowledged in *Truth and Objectivity* when I allow in the first chapter that the deflationary conception would serve the project were it not for its internal difficulties.[16] I maintain, nevertheless, that a pluralist view of

16. *Truth and Objectivity,* pp. 12–13.

truth, properly understood, is correct—and ought to seem less controversial than *Truth and Objectivity* perhaps allowed it to seem. In particular, the understanding of pluralism rejected by Sainsbury and Pettit is nothing that I want it to maintain.

I have already had the opportunity for additional remarks on this matter,[17] so here I shall be brisk. Briefly, I am very content to accept Sainsbury's 'friendly emendation' as a clarification. The contention of *Truth and Objectivity* is not that 'true' is ambiguous, that it means different things as applied within different regions of discourse. On the contrary, the concept admits of a uniform characterisation wherever it is applied—the characterisation given by the minimal platitudes, which determine everything that is *essential* to the concept of truth. Parallel contentions would be that everything essential to the concept of identity is determined by the principles that it is reflexive and a congruence for an arbitrary property, and that everything essential to the concept of existence—to take Sainsbury's own example—is determined by its being subject to the standard rules for the introduction and elimination of the existential quantifier. The form of pluralism for which space is allowed by this overarching uniformity is one of, roughly, *variable realisation*. What constitutes the existence of a number may be very different from what constitutes the existence of a material object. The identity of persons is generally held to call for a special account, contrasting with that appropriate to the identity of material continuants generally. And what constitutes truth in ethics may be quite different from what constitutes truth in theoretical physics.

This pluralism seems hardly distinguishable from the view expressed by Pettit in the following admirable passage:

> Under the envisaged scenario, there remains only one sort of truth: that which is defined by the platitudes-satisfying role. It is just that what truth involves in one area—what realises the appropriate role—may be

17. See Wright (1994b) (this volume Essay 3). Also pp. 213–16 of Wright (1995c) (this volume Essay 8).

different from what it involves in another. The difference between what truth involves in the different areas will be explained by reference to the different subject-matters: the different truth-conditions, and the different truth-makers, in each discourse.[18]

I have to accept that *Truth and Objectivity* should have done more to explain the view being proposed. At any rate, I do not think I have any real quarrel with either Pettit or Sainsbury on this matter—except to demur at Pettit's retention of the term 'monism' for the broad position on which we agree. (Would someone who knew that either of two quite different physical constitutions can be involved in a substance's being jade helpfully describe herself as taking a 'monistic' view of jade?)

Horwich's criticisms are a different matter. Good deflationist that he is, he is in no position to accept pluralism about truth, even so qualified. Truth cannot admit of variable realisation if, as for the deflationist, there is nothing substantial in which it *ever* consists. For deflationism, pluralism will seem merely to compound the errors of its more traditional antagonists. However, it should be clear that Horwich's suggestion that the pluralist idiom of *Truth and Objectivity* is merely a matter of 'unorthodox terminology', a 'cheap pluralism' generated by an 'idiosyncratic' decision to regard as truth predicates expressions for concepts which merely have some points of analogy with truth, is a serious misrepresentation. It is not a mere terminolog-

---

18. Pettit (1996), p. 886. Compare Sainsbury:

In the case of 'exist' the obvious move is to take a minimalist line about its content, so that it is topic-neutral, fit to be appended to any kind of designator, and then tackle the questions about what is involved in the existence (thus minimally and uniformly understood) of different kinds of things. Wright's position is surely analogous: he takes a minimalist line about truth, equipping himself with a notion which ought to be usable, in the mouths of philosophers of many persuasions, with respect to a wide variety of sentences. The questions to be tackled are questions about what is involved in the truth (thus minimally and uniformly understood) of sentences of different kinds. (Sainsbury (1996), p. 900)

ical decision to call 'superassertibility' a truth predicate—in areas where it behaves like one—but a substantial thesis, involving substantial contentions concerning the appropriateness of a 'network'-type account of truth, the right things to count as basic platitudes in this particular case, and the behaviour of 'superassertibility' in the discourse in question. It is, rather, Horwich himself who engages in terminological legislation when he insists that nothing should count as a truth predicate unless its satisfaction of the Disquotational Scheme may be appreciated non-inferentially.[19]

Horwich charges me with the 'more serious mistake, going beyond terminological naivety', of supposing that

> just because certain general facts about truth (i.e. general facts articulated by means of the truth-predicate) vary from one domain to another, there must be various concepts of truth or, perhaps, various concepts that constitute truth. We don't suppose that the concept of *left*, or the property constituting *leftness*, undergo a transatlantic shift in virtue of the variating in driving laws; we characterise that variation with a single concept and refer to a single property.[20]

I hope there is no instance of that transition in *Truth and Objectivity*. I do not, of course, suppose that if different things are true of truth in different areas of discourse, that suffices for differences between the local concepts of truth, or between what constitutes their instantiation. What I do suppose is that the *particular* differences marked by the various realism-relevant cruces distinguished in *Truth and Objectivity* sustain the idea that truth is variably constituted in discourses which respectively pass or fail the associated tests; that there is, for instance, every point in thinking of truth as constituted differently in discourses where it respectively can and cannot be interpreted as superassertibility, or in discourses where the Correspondence Platitude

19. Horwich (1996), p. 880.
20. *Ibid.*, p. 881.

respectively has or lacks the additional substance associated with the cruces of Cognitive Command and Wide Cosmological Role. I do not see that Horwich says anything to disturb this.[21]

21. Perhaps I could here take the chance to correct an error, noted by Horwich, in the presentation of an argument—not, I think, *pace* Horwich, in the argument itself—concerning superassertibility at *Truth and Objectivity*, p. 59. The issue there concerns the status of the Equivalence Schema for superassertibility:

(E^s) It is superassertible that P if and only if P

and the argument offered is to show that, on the assumptions that we are concerned only with epistemically accessible matters—in particular, that each such statement in the range of 'P' satisfies

P $\leftrightarrow$ P is knowable

—and that what is knowable is superassertible, the supposition of counter-examples,

P and P is not superassertible

or

P is superassertible and Not P

to either of the ingredient conditionals in E^s gives rise to contradiction. Showing this in the second case involves appeal to the commutativity of superassertibility and negation as propositional operators (effectively, a version of the Negation Equivalence for superassertibility), one half of which—the direction

Not (P is superassertible) $\rightarrow$ Superassertible (not P)

—is established on the stated assumptions. However, it is actually the other direction,

Superassertible (not P) $\rightarrow$ Not (P is superassertible)

which is wanted for the immediate purpose; and this is not discussed. True, I refer to the authority for the relevant step as provided by the 'commutativity lemma', so may be presumed—at least by a charitable reader—to have had something more than a one-way conditional in mind! It remains that the half of the lemma wanted for the immediate purpose is not proved, and that the half that is proved is not to the immediate purpose.

The unsatisfactory state of the presentation at p. 59, first pointed out to me by Christopher Gauker and, independently, by Bernhard Weiss, seems to have been the result of a less than properly attentive compression of the relevant discussion in the

IV. COGNITIVE COMMAND

Outside professional philosophical circles it would pass for the merest common sense that there is a distinction between discourses in which disputes may answer to no real 'fact of the matter' and discourses whose subject matter is substantial enough to guarantee the correctness, or incorrectness, of a contested claim. *Truth and Objectivity* proposes the exertion of Cognitive Command as a necessary condition for a discourse to fall in the latter camp. The idea is, roughly—though I nowhere put it quite this way in the book—that the presence of a real 'fact of the matter' must impinge on the range of admissible explanations of a dispute, since one or another antagonist will have to have been imperfectly appreciative of it. Assuming that each has a cognitive endowment sufficient, in the best case, for the appreciation of such matters, the implication has to be that one or other has employed this endowment in a less than fully satisfactory way—something worth describing as a 'cognitive shortcoming' has to be involved.

This simple line of thought needs to be complicated to allow for the role that vagueness, of one or another kind, may play in the generation of disputes. But we don't need to engage that complication now. It also assumes that the putative fact of the matter is within the cognitive reach of the disputants. But if it is not—if it is a potentially evidence-transcendent fact—then that will suffice in any case for the involvement of cognitive shortcoming in the dispute, since the best cognitive efforts of the disputants will then perforce come short. (That may sound sophistical but it isn't: the limitations of our cognitive powers are quite properly regarded as shortcomings.)

---

second Waynflete lecture, in which the two halves of the 'commutativity lemma' were addressed separately. The needed half,

Superassertible (not P) → Not (P is superassertible)

is equivalent to the inconsistency of 'P is superassertible' and 'Not P is superassertible', and is therefore uncontentious so long any two states of information are conceived as mutually accessible.

It is vital to the project of *Truth and Objectivity* that a discourse can be minimally truth-apt and yet fail this condition, so that there is no a priori guarantee that disputes within it have to implicate cognitive shortcoming (or else be excusable by vagueness). However, the immediate effect of the formulation given is only to tie the common-sensical distinction to the notion of cognitive shortcoming; no control has yet been imposed on the responsible application of the latter, and there is accordingly nothing to stop an awkward customer—whom I called the 'trivialising theorist'—from admitting the tie but then deflating the concept of the cognitive to the point where whatever propensities—the sense of humour, or of the ridiculous, or of the disgusting—are at work in a particular discourse count as fully cognitive, and clashes between them accordingly as cognitive shortcomings. If this move cannot be prevented, then the contrast between minimal truth-aptitude and Cognitive Command is lost.

One response would be to seek the needed control by attempting a direct, independent account of what should qualify an opinion-forming faculty as cognitive. But, first, that looks a dauntingly difficult task and, second, it is hard to see how the story could proceed without *prior* verdicts about the factuality or otherwise of the opinions which the faculty in question enabled one to form. My suggestion in *Truth and Objectivity* was, instead, that this mistakes the onus of proof. The trivialising theorist should be made to face up to his responsibilities. To think of the subject matter of a particular discourse as exerting Cognitive Command is to enter into certain quite definite theoretical obligations which are not to be lightly undertaken.

We can cut short the long story given on pp. 48–56 of *Truth and Objectivity* by focusing on the case where the disputed matter is agreed on all hands not to be evidence-transcendent, where the opinions of the antagonists are not inference-based, and where the dispute can be confined to the immediate issue and need ramify into no other subject matter. Disputes about comedy can and often do meet each of these three conditions. To suppose that cognitive shortcoming is at work in such a dispute is to be committed, I suggested, to a *sui generis epistemology*—to the idea that opinions on the relevant subject matter are generated, in basic cases, by the operation of a special faculty which is directly receptive to the kind of state of affairs in question. And in that case, there had better be a story to be told about how the faculty works, about what its operations consist in and how it is keyed to the relevant subject matter. Moreover, I suggested this story must be at the service of the *best* explanation of our practice of the discourse and especially of cases of non-collusive agreement in opinions expressed within it. Since a best explanation will need, naturally, to be both detailed and convincing in detail, this is not an obligation which can be met by mere 'trivialisation' of the concept of the cognitive.

Mark Sainsbury doubts that the trivialising theorist can be shaken off so easily. He contends, first, that their very disagreement commits each antagonist to regarding the other as in error; second, that in terms of an appropriately 'lean' concept of a faculty—'an inner state which systematically, for some range of impinging inputs, disposes a subject to respond in a certain way'—each must accordingly regard the other as the victim of a less than perfectly functioning faculty; and, third, that it cannot be right to refuse to qualify such a faculty as 'cognitive' just on the ground that we cannot foresee any account of the detail of its workings. Perhaps such reserve would be justified if, as assumed in my discussion, the relevant faculty would have to be *sui generis*—a faculty which, as Sainsbury rightly describes my intent, 'if its output is best characterised as judgements in an area of discourse for which the concept ϕ is distinctive, has inputs best described in terms of the impingement of the property ϕ'. But, he contends, not every intuitional faculty—one whose output is non-inferential opinion—is *sui generis* in that sense, and in many cases we rightly regard such intuitional faculties as cognitive without any detailed conception of their working.[22]

---

22. Sainsbury's objection should be contrasted with a rather different form of attempted destabilisation of the minimal truth-aptitude/Cognitive Command boundary, which also exploits the thought that the mere existence of a disagreement is in tension with the idea of an absence of shortcoming on either side. This other line of thought (put forward in Williamson (1994b) and, in a related form, in Shapiro and

The nub of Sainsbury's objection comes, I'm taking it, with the last consideration—the availability, to the trivialising theorist, of the paradigm of intuitional cognitive faculties which are not *sui generis* and whose status as cognitive needs no vindication by the provision of a detailed account of their operations. Now, I do not feel compelled to dispute the first part of this: the claim that when a range of opinions are formed otherwise than by inference, it is not necessary, in order for the faculties involved in their formation to rank as cognitive, that they be *sui generis*—that they involve direct receptivity to 'impingements' best characterised in terms of the concepts distinctive of opinion in that range. In Sainsbury's view, it is not required, for instance, of someone who wishes to make a case that the sense of humour should count as cognitive, that they show that it should be conceived as working on inputs best described in terms of the impingement of the properties of being funny or unfunny. He offers the counterexamples of chicken-sexing, and the detection by taste of the region of origin of a wine. Neither case is, I think, completely clear-cut. It might be contested whether a wine-taster's abilities are entirely non-inferential, since he presumably needs experience of the various resonances of odour and taste associated with different regions. And even if chicken-sexers need have no idea how they do it, and little if anything to say about what perceptible features of the chicks they are responding to, I do not know whether, in mastering the skill, a period

---

Taschek (1996)), argues that since I am committed, merely by my acceptance of P, into holding that you, who accept that not P, are guilty of shortcoming, it follows, under the hypothesis that our dispute involves no shortcoming, that I cannot be right in accepting P; but then *I* am guilty of shortcoming!—contrary to hypothesis. Accordingly—as Williamson's version of the objection runs—the idea that a disagreement might involve no *cognitive* shortcoming (contrast: mere shortcoming) must demand a special account of what a cognitive shortcoming is—a demand which *Truth and Objectivity* accordingly had no business in trying to finesse. I have discussed this version of the objection elsewhere (this volume Essay 4) and respond in detail to the Shapiro–Taschek version (which purports to demonstrate that minimal truth-aptitude plus Epistemic Constraint ensures Cognitive Command) in Essay 15 below. I mention these arguments only to signal that I am taking Sainsbury's point to be distinct.

is necessary when they subject their intuitive inclinations to independent corroboration. If it is, then maybe their magical-seeming opinions have an inferential component too. But let Sainsbury be granted that these are genuinely intuitional examples. In neither case, anyway, ought we to be thinking in terms of a *sui generis* capacity: ordinary perceptual capacities and training seemingly suffice.

What is not clear to me, even so, is why Sainsbury thinks that examples of this structure reinstate the threat of trivialisation, rather than merely calling for refinement of the argument in *Truth and Objectivity*. If we are content, in advance of any detailed conception of how they work, to regard the relevant faculties of chicken-sexers as cognitive, it is because they are at the service of reliable detection of facts which can be routinely if less spectacularly detected by other methods involving only what are unquestionably cognitive abilities. So too with the detection of origins of wines, if that is indeed a non-inferential ability. In short, if we are sometimes content, even in the absence of any detail about their operation, to regard intuitional but non-*sui-generis* opinion-forming faculties as cognitive, it is because all the evidence is that they are keyed to states of affairs which we *already* conceive as open to cognition in other, less spectacular ways. And this in turn makes us confident that an account of the detail must be possible, even at a stage when we lack any inkling in what terms it might proceed. What follows is that the cognitive status of an ability, like the sense of humour, could indeed in principle be defended, without supplying the detail called for under a *sui generis* conception of it, by assimilating its operation to the kind of case Sainsbury calls attention to. But that is a far cry from allowing that cognitive status may be bestowed merely by trivialisation, without work. The relevant ability will have to be shown to be *reliable*, and that will demand an antecedent case that the relevant subject matter is detectable by others of our faculties, in a different way. So there is still a substantial explanatory obligation. Moreover, since this obligation clearly cannot be met by recourse to 'Sainsburyan'—intuitional but non-*sui-generis*—faculties indefinitely, the space of alternatives for fulfilling it must, sooner or later, be confined to *sui generis* and to inferential abilities, when the discussion can assume the course followed in *Truth and Objectivity*.

Sainsbury's worry was that Cognitive Command is too easy a constraint. Williamson expresses the opposite concern. As the constraint is motivated in my book, the exertion of Cognitive Command by a discourse is a matter of the *content* of its ingredient statements, determined by their being fitted for the representation of self-standing states of affairs. It is thus to be *a priori* that (modulo the appropriate proviso about vagueness) cognitive shortcoming be involved in disputes about them. Williamson contends that to demand apriority here is to set an impossibly high standard. A similar difficulty, he contends, afflicts the way I draw the Euthyphro Contrast, demanding of Euthyphronic discourses, again, that it be a priori that best opinion, appropriate substantially accounted for, co-varies with the facts. In Williamson's view, this requirement 'condemns the anti realist to defeat in almost every case'.

The assumption of *Truth and Objectivity* is that the objectivity of a discourse, as reflected in its status with respect to Cognitive Command or the Euthyphro Contrast, is a matter which is available to purely conceptual reflection. But Williamson's contrasting view, it appears, is that it cannot be a priori which of human beings' characteristic forms of shared response are keyed to real features of the world and which are not. He writes:

> But how could a stone age man, by conceptual reflection, have refuted the speculation that colour was as fundamental a property of things as shape, causally responsible for best opinion about it and not supervenient on other physical properties?[23]

Likewise—I imagine he would say—it is surely open to empirical investigation whether the best account of the aetiology of our comic responses, and of the degree of community in them which we exhibit, will see them as keyed to certain 'fundamental' properties of the pre-

23. Williamson (1996c), p. 906.

vailing circumstances and hence as the output of a means of detection of those properties. We may indeed be quite sure that this is not so. But this certainty, rather than a priori, is a product of long-term acclimatisation to the kinds of explanatory paradigm that have proved fruitful in physical science.

This is about as profound a disagreement with the programme of *Truth and Objectivity* as it is possible to have. A proper response to it would need to confront a much more developed statement of the opposing point of view than Williamson had the opportunity to present on this occasion. Here I will mention just two relevant matters. First, Williamson's picture, that we have to approach the question of the objectivity of a discourse with our minds open to *empirical* possibilities of finding, or failing to find the ontology—of comic or moral properties, for instance—which it distinctively calls for, begs an alternative determination of the objectivity of the discourse in which the relevant empirical questions, and the answers to them, might be expressed. In particular, if natural science is to be able to teach us whether colours, or comic, or aesthetic, or moral qualities are real, we had better have settled in advance on the objectivity of the relevant parts of natural scientific discourse. How does Williamson envisage this settlement's being reached? Is there any alternative to thinking of science's (putative) credentials in this matter as earned a priori? If there is none, what are the cruces which, a priori, it satisfies—what relation do they bear to those explored in *Truth and Objectivity*?

Second, I do not see that it is any implication of the account I proposed of the Euthyphro Contrast that a clear-headed stone-age user of colour vocabulary—if colour is indeed Euthyphronic—could have refuted a priori the speculation that colour is a fundamental, causally explanatory property of things. For one thing, a supporter of that proposal has no evident reason to insist that the status of a range of predicates—as Euthyphronic, or as natural kind terms, or as neither—has to be a matter of determinate intention within a particular linguistic community. But, more importantly, I am not in any case persuaded that, by treating the extensions of a range of expressions as partially determined by our best opinions, we thereby foreclose on the option, should empirical findings render it convenient, of treating them as standing for explanatorily unified kinds. This is the matter which is, in effect, under consideration on pp. 128–32 of *Truth and Objectivity,* though I cannot enlarge on that discussion here. Suffice it to say that, in my view, the contrast between natural kind terms and Euthyphronic ones emerges not in any barrier to our regarding the latter as denoting real kinds, but rather in there being no barrier to their continued use, in good faith, should it prove that they do not.

Truth and Objectivity contains a conjecture—we might call it the Cognitive Command hypothesis—that satisfaction of this constraint represents the *weakest* realism-relevant property that a discourse can enjoy over and above the characteristics involved in minimal truth-aptitude. Now, Horgan is unhappy with the epistemic flavour of most of the cruces in the *Truth and Objectivity* framework, and so finds the Cognitive Command constraint objectionable on that account. But he also thinks that, when the epistemic constraints are supplanted by, as he would prefer, semantic ones, in particular with what he terms the constraint of *tightness,* then an intermediate crux does indeed emerge, so that the Cognitive Command conjecture fails. The tightness of the semantic norms operative over a given discourse requires, roughly, that the correctness of its claims is settled just by their content and the world, in a way that is to 'preclude any role for an individual's attitudes, preferences, or any other such idiosyncrasy as a permissible factor'. And it would seem, so he suggests, to be a possibility that a discourse could be tight in this way and yet fail of Cognitive Command since disputants—about some theoretical scientific matter, for instance—may disagree

> about the net import of the evidence in question. . . . Often enough, the various parties to [such a] dispute seem to concur about what the relevant evidence is and why, but then they part company about the right assessment of where this evidence points, on balance. Often enough, the core disagreement evidently stems not from someone's exhibiting a cognitive deficit, but from differing standards of epistemic assessment.[24]

24. Horgan (1996), p. 896.

Horgan is well aware, of course, that this possibility—of disputants differing in the weight they attach to an agreed body of relevant evidence—would pose no problem to the Cognitive Command conjecture if how much weight ought to be attached to a particular body of evidence were a fully objective matter. But he points out, reasonably enough, that that is not something which the formulation of the Cognitive Command constraint can simply take for granted.

But nor did it. The fullest discussion of the constraint explicitly caters for the possibility of permissible variations in what I called 'personal thresholds of evidence'.[25] This is one of three kinds of vagueness—the others being vagueness in the content of the disputed claim, or in its conditions of its acceptability—intended collectively to exhaust the range of cases where the absence of cognitive shortcoming in a dispute need not reflect adversely on the objectivity of the disputed subject matter. It would be unreasonable to complain that, in the limited space at its disposal, Horgan does not make his notion of tightness completely clear. But I wonder whether, rather than representing a crux intermediate between minimal truth-aptitude and Cognitive Command, the notion he has in mind is not exactly what is explicated by Cognitive Command, once the provision for the third form of vagueness is given its proper due.

V. On the General Framework

I have offered no proof that the general framework of my book—minimalism about truth and truth-aptitude, and pluralism about the ways to elucidate and argue for or against realist intuitions—represents the best way to look at these matters. The plausibility of its claims will depend partly on the extent to which my suggestions seem to make sense of actual debates, partly on the operational advantages that minimalism provides over other anti-realist paradigms, but ultimately on the outcome of the sort of critical discussion so usefully illustrated

25. *Truth and Objectivity,* pp. 144 ff.

by my present commentators. Since philosophers are notoriously conservative when it comes to entrenched ways of thinking about old
problems, I find it extremely gratifying that four of the six featured in
this essay seem to be broadly hospitable to the general reorientation I
propose. Horwich, for instance, has no major disagreement with the
programme of *Truth and Objectivity*, demurring only in that he
thinks his own form of deflationism can provide the necessary philosophy of truth and truth-aptitude, and in being uneasy about my tying
the effect of the various realism-relevant cruces to a pluralism about
truth. Sainsbury does not really disagree—I think—with the pluralism
about truth and, excepting his reservations about the substance of the
Cognitive Command constraint, is otherwise broadly sympathetic.[26]
Horgan emphasises his attraction to the 'generic conception', although
he has misgivings about the epistemic character of three of the particular constraints on which I focus (the exception being Wide Cosmological Role). And Pettit, too, is broadly sympathetic. Admittedly, he
prefers to view the issue between realist and anti-realist as concerning
what he calls the 'free-standingness' of the truth conditions of statements in a contested discourse, and he lists a variety of marks, prima
facie distinct from my realism-relevant cruces, by which such free-
standingness may be gauged.[27] But I see no serious differences here.
As we have seen, Pettit, like Sainsbury, is not really antagonistic to
alethic pluralism, as I want it to be understood. Moreover, the second
and fourth (and perhaps also the third) of his marks would appear to
be implicated in Cognitive Command, while the fifth and sixth connect with the issues to do with the Euthyphro Contrast and with the
potential Evidence Transcendence of truth. In any case, the catalogue
of cruces in *Truth and Objectivity* made no claim to be comprehen-

26. Though were he right about the trivialisability of Cognitive Command, that
would of course necessitate quite extensive changes in the argument of the book.

27. Pettit's marks, each a property of the truth conditions of the statements in a
particular discourse, or a condition on (our knowledge of) their satisfaction, are six:
irreducibility, non-relativity, public availability, independence of fiat, bivalence, no
infallibility. See Pettit (1996), pp. 884–5.

sive; that others should seek to define cognate or complementary distinctions is a reaction I hoped to encourage.

It is different with van Cleve and Williamson. Each canvasses a line of argument which, if sustained, would completely subvert the contrast between a discourse's being minimally truth-apt and its satisfying further realism-relevant constraints, and thereby altogether block the programme of the book. I close this essay by briefly commenting on these two lines of argument, though not in the detail they deserve.

Suppose P is a statement belonging to a minimally truth-apt discourse and hence subject to standards of warranted assertibility. Williamson contends that, in order to be in possession of warrant to assert a particular statement, it is not enough that a speaker has evidence making it highly probable. Warrant for an assertion demands *knowledge*:

> For example, if I bought one of n tickets in a lottery, the fact that its chance of winning is only 1/n does not entitle me to say that it will not win, no matter how large n is. Even if, to no-one's surprise, my ticket does not win, you can justly criticise my assertion by saying, 'but you didn't *know* that it would not win'.[28]

However, knowledge—Williamson continues—demands *reliability*. And one is reliably right that P

> only if, in all cases that could easily arise and that one could easily fail to discriminate from the given case, it is true that P. Reliability demands a margin for error.[29]

The thought, I take it, is that to know that P in a particular case, I have to be reliable in my judgements, whether or not P is true, across a range of cases. And if there were cases which I could easily fail to discriminate from a case where I rightly take P to be true but in which P would not be true, I would not be so reliable. It is therefore built

28. Williamson (1996c), pp. 907–8.
29. *Ibid.*

into the concept of knowledge that if one knows that P in a given case, then P must also be true in any such relevantly similar case. But of course, as Williamson observes, the cost of supposing that one could know that P in all such cases would be to set up a Sorites paradox. In any discourse, therefore, which allows of assertible, and hence knowable statements, but which deals in imperceptibly variable or easily mutually mistakable states of affairs, truth will have to outrun knowability, and hence assertibility. So minimal truth-aptitude incorporates, in and of itself, a potential for evidence-transcendent truth, and the whole framework of *Truth and Objectivity* is consequently undermined: if we are dealing with a discourse involving genuinely assertible contents, then we are likely to be dealing with contents for which Dummettian realism is the appropriate view. The only avenue for anti-realist intuition will be the denial of genuine assertibility.

Williamson doubtless realises that the twin premises of this rather unexpected line of argument are too controversial to allow it to be convincing without a great deal of further development.[30] The lottery example is meant to trigger the intuition that one who makes an assertion will, in normal circumstances, be taken to have laid claim to knowledge of its truth. Speaking for myself, I do not find that intuition terribly strong. There are many contexts—medical diagnosis, weather forecasting, ordinary psychology, history, economics, plant ecology, and so on—in which we conceive the primary business to be the making and reception of reliable claims, but where to claim knowledge, strictly so regarded, of the truth of such claims would often, even usually, seem inflated. But consideration of controls on the practice of *assertion* is anyway beside the point: the material notion of warranted assertion—that which goes with minimal truth-aptitude—is simply the exterior counterpart of warranted *belief* and there is, prima facie, no plausibility whatever in the suggestion that possession of sufficient reason to believe a proposition demands noth-

---

30. He has fuller discussions elsewhere. The knowing–asserting link is argued for in Williamson (1996d). For knowledge and margins for error, see Williamson (1992b) and (1994a), chap. 8.

ing less than knowledge of it. The long tradition in epistemology of distinguishing between knowledge and reasonable belief may indeed be misguided; but if it is, it will demand a very substantial argument to show it.

Williamson's second premise, that knowledge demands a margin of error, is only prima facie less controversial than the first. Note, to begin with, that it must be in jeopardy for discourses which qualify as *Euthyphronic*—at least according to the kind of understanding of that idea proposed in *Truth and Objectivity*. Presumably, one who knowingly arrives at a *best* opinion about some Euthyphronic matter—by the standards spelled out by the antecedent conditions in an appropriate provisional equation—will thereby know of its truth. It follows that an opinion cannot count as best unless in agreement with other opinions about the same matter formed under conditions which are otherwise likewise best. For suppose, as seems likely enough to occur, that a pair of visually normal, fully competent subjects, reacting to a Sorites series of colour patches under seemingly optimal conditions, and so forth, diverge in their inclinations at some point about whether or not a particular patch can still justifiably be described as red: if both verdicts can rank as best, then the Euthyphronist about colour will be forced into allowing inconsistent claims about that particular patch to stand. So it is built into the position that there may be a *last* case in such a series which a subject knows to be red—a last case where his judgement meets all the conditions of a best opinion, including that of consensus with other judges operating under the remaining conditions of optimality—followed immediately by a first patch where the claim to knowledge lapses because the consensus amongst otherwise best judges breaks down.[31] And these two patches may, of course, be indistinguishable from—or, anyway, easily mistaken for—each other.

Notice that a reservation of this kind about Williamson's principle—that P must be true in any case sufficiently closely similar

---

31. The response to the Sorites paradox for colour implicit in this thought is further elaborated in section VII of Wright (1987a).

to a case in which it is known to be true—will not apply only to discourses which qualify as Euthyphronic by the rather demanding conditions proposed in *Truth and Objectivity*. Consider any minimally truth-apt discourse which fails to exert Cognitive Command. There may be no knowing whether or not a disputed claim in such a discourse is true. But there would seem to be no point in denying the title 'knowledge' to an opinion which enjoyed consensus among all the practitioners of such discourse when it depends upon no collateral misapprehension and is not independently open to question. Yet such an impeccable consensus would, it is very likely, break down abruptly in the course of a series of marginal transformations of the consensual case.

There is, indeed, a different kind of misgiving about Williamson's principle which could be felt even by one utterly out of sympathy with the ideas of *Truth and Objectivity*. The idea is unquestionably appealing that knowledge requires reliability. But reliability over *what range of cases?* Why, in order for my opinion that P in particular circumstances, C, to pass this test, is it necessary that I be a reliable judge about P in *other* kinds of circumstances, however apparently similar or easily confused with C? The idea is, presumably, that if I were prone to error about other such cases, I would be bound to be unreliable in any circumstances easily confused with them, as C are by hypothesis. But that's just an empirical assumption. And the kind of local reliability it precludes may be readily envisaged. Consider an instrument—a digital speedometer on a car, say—whose function is to register, using a finite range of possible outputs, inputs of continuously variable magnitude within a finitely bounded range. Such a device may be so constructed that, when functioning properly, it gives a specific reading—say '10 mph'—whenever the input corresponds to anything within some fixed margin of that particular road speed, but sometimes gives the same reading to inputs outside that range, depending on what reading it was giving before, on whether the car is accelerating or decelerating, and so on. The reading '10 mph' would thus be reliable over one range of cases, and unreliable over another, notwithstanding the fact that some of the latter would approximate some of the former as closely as you like, so that the differences between them would certainly lie within the threshold of sensitivity of the device, whatever it was.[32] I can see no conceptual objection to the idea that a device might have this pattern of responses. And if, for example, the device was a human being, and its responses judgements, I can see no objection to the suggestion that its correct responses in the good cases—the analogues of the inputs within the specified margin of a road speed of ten miles an hour—ought, at least as far as considerations of reliability are concerned, to count as knowledge. Again, it is no obstacle to this thought that the difference between some of the good cases and some of the others will be indiscriminable to such a judging subject. There is nothing conceptually absurd in the idea that a subject may have different patterns of response to presentations which are very similar, or even indiscriminable to him. Indiscriminability is one thing; identity of causal powers is another.

Van Cleve argues in the final section of his remarks that for a discourse to contain minimally truth-apt claims is for it to contain claims apt for *realist* truth—that any truth predicate complying with the Equivalence Schema will be resistant to all the classical anti-realist interpretations of truth. At this point he does not have superassertibility in mind—having already disposed of its alethic pretensions, he considers, by the considerations reviewed above in section II of this essay—but is thinking instead of proposals like that which Hilary Putnam once made (on van Cleve's understanding),[33] and traditional forms of coherence theory, which involve proposing an analysis of truth in terms of subjunctive conditionals. For Putnam, the relevant

32. There is an issue, of course, about how exactly to interpret the idea of such a device's having a sensitivity threshold. For more on this kind of example, see *ibid.*, section III.

33. The locus classicus, of course, is Putnam (1981), chap. 3. Putnam himself later renounced epistemic conceptions of truth. See, for instance, his Dewey Lectures (Putnam (1994a), pp. 503, 510–1). The matter is discussed in detail in Essay 11 in this volume.

conditional would be something like: 'If epistemically ideal circumstances were to obtain, we would judge that P'. For the type of coherence theory explicitly addressed by van Cleve, the relevant conditional would be, in his formulation, 'If there were a controlled, coherent and comprehensive set of beliefs, the proposition that P would belong to it'.

The problem van Cleve has in mind is presented by an intriguing argument of Alvin Plantinga's going back some twenty years.[34] Here is (a modest simplification of) Plantinga's argument in outline: assume any purported analysis of truth of the form

$$P \text{ is true} \leftrightarrow Q \mathbin{\Box\!\!\rightarrow} Z(P)$$

where Q is an idealising hypothesis, Z(. . .) is any condition on propositions—for instance, being judged to be true by the ideally rational and informed thinkers whose existence is hypothesised by Q, or cohering with the maximally coherent set of beliefs whose existence is hypothesised by Q, and so on—and $\Box\!\!\rightarrow$ expresses the subjunctive conditional. Since this is an analysis, it presumably holds in necessitated form:

(i) Necessarily: (P is true $\leftrightarrow$ (Q $\Box\!\!\rightarrow$ Z(P)))

Now suppose

(ii) Possibly (Q & Not Z(Q))

Then, by the Equivalence Schema,

(iii) Possibly (Q is true & (Q & Not Z(Q)))

But (iii) contradicts (i), which therefore entails

(iv) Not possibly (Q & Not Z(Q))

34. Plantinga (1982).

So

    (v)   Necessarily $(Q \rightarrow Z(Q))$

A strict implication ought to be sufficient for a subjunctive conditional, so

    (vi) $Q \mathrel{\square\!\!\rightarrow} Z(Q)$

So, from (i),

    (vii)   Q is true

So, by the Equivalence Schema again,

    (viii)   Q

The upshot is, it seems, that Putnam must accept that conditions are *already* 'epistemically ideal', and that a coherence theorist must accept that there already is a controlled, comprehensive and coherent set of beliefs.[35]

Obviously this is absurd. Note, however, that the reasoning in no way depends upon what is offered being an *analysis,* but will go thorough for any suggested equivalent of 'P is true' of the appropriate form. So a *realist* who accepted that, while not an analysis of truth, there is a necessary biconditional link between 'P is true' and some subjunctive conditional about the beliefs of a suitably idealised subject—perhaps because the idealisation would ensure that the thinker in question would *track* all truth—is on the face of it put in difficulties too. What, then, if we take Q as: 'There is a unique omniscient being'—one who believes all truths and no falsehoods—and Z(. . .)

---

35. Notice that Plantinga's reasoning after line (vi) depends on a biconditional principle and thus cannot engage an anti-realist who proposes merely a one-way evidential constraint on truth rather than an analysis.

as: '. . . would be believed by the unique omniscient being'? Are not the true propositions exactly those which would be believed by such a being? If so, we have another instance of (i), and Plantinga's argument, if good, apparently lends itself to a proof of the existence of the Christian God, or at least of a being possessing His traditional epistemic powers. (Plantinga himself might welcome that finding; but not, surely, by this route.)

In fact, of course, we are here running foul of a version of the Conditional Fallacy.[36] No subjunctive conditional can be strictly equivalent to a categorical proposition if the realisation of its antecedent cannot be guaranteed not to impinge on the truth value of that proposition. So an instance of (i) has a chance of being correct only if P and Q are independent. If there were an omniscient being, He would indeed believe exactly the truths. But it cannot be correct to represent the purport of that by something of the form of (i) if we want both 'there is an omniscient being' and its negation to be admissible substituends for P. If the range of P is to be unrestricted, then the claim must be, rather, that an omniscient being would believe all and only the truths *that would then obtain;* not (i), but the corresponding

$$\text{Necessarily: } (Q \mathbin{\square\!\!\rightarrow} (P \text{ is true} \leftrightarrow Z(P)))$$

is what is wanted.[37]

The obvious next question is: Why should not a supporter of (putative) Putnam make the same adjustment? This is to ask what the cost to such a philosopher would be if what were proposed were not

(P1) Necessarily: a proposition is true if and only if, were conditions epistemically ideal, it would be believed

36. The term originates in Shope (1978).

37. This will all be very familiar to a reader who is *au courant* with the move from 'Basic Equations' to 'Provisional Biconditionals'; cf. *Truth and Objectivity,* pp. 117–20.

but

> (P2) Necessarily: if conditions were epistemically ideal,
> then the true propositions would be all and only those
> which were believed.

The matter needs a fuller discussion than I can embark on here. But I do not think it is clear that there would be *any* significant cost. Note to begin with that (P2) is still inconsistent with the conception of truth and truth-conferrers beloved of Putnam's ('metaphysical') realist antagonist, for whom it can be no necessity, even under the very best epistemic conditions, that the truth is available. So much is implicit in the idea that an ideal empirical theory can be false. To be sure, (P2) would, even so, still fail to capture the intention of a proponent of (P1) if it was fair to summarise its gist as being that, under the conditions depicted by its antecedent, the truth *would be* evidentially constrained—so leaving room for the thought that, *as things are,* it is not. But note in that connection that the intended interpretation of the obtaining of ideal conditions invoked by (P1) always had to be that it would occasion *no disturbance* in the actual distribution of truth values among propositions—it was to be their *actual truth values* that would be available to us under epistemically ideal conditions. If there is indeed an interpretation of what it would be for conditions to be epistemically ideal which can honour that requirement, it is available to condition the reading of (P2) as well. Of course, it was just on that point that (P1) foundered—when applied to the very proposition that conditions are not epistemically ideal. That, and anything entailing it, would, we know, have different truth values if the antecedent of (P2) were true. So (P2) fails to impose an epistemic constraint on the truth conditions of that family of propositions. But it is not clear that any serious limitation of the generality of the anti-realist thesis has to be occasioned by that: that conditions are not epistemically ideal is something we know now! In short: if (P1) would do what is wanted of it up to the point where it trips over the Conditional Fallacy, then there is no obvious candidate for an evidence-transcendent truth that slips past (P2).

I continue to think that, by invoking 'epistemically ideal' conditions, the discussion in *Reason, Truth and History* idealised assertibility in the wrong direction—contrast the turn taken by the idealisation involved in superassertibility. But there seems to me to be every chance that the essence of the *Reason, Truth and History* proposal— as, rightly or wrongly, commonly interpreted—can at least be stabilised against Plantinga's argument.[38]

I am very grateful to my commentators for the work they have expended in generating so interesting a set of critical reactions. Thanks also to Alvin Plantinga for a stimulating electronic exchange on the matters of the last section, and to Bob Hale and John Skorupski for helpful discussion of many of the other points raised.

38. Plantinga's argument has not received the same degree of attention as another purported short way with Evidential Constraint—the argument, originally due to Fitch (1963) that to restrict the truths to what it is possible to know must have the unwelcome consequence that they are restricted to what is actually known. I must defer to another occasion the question whether, if the anti-realist may indeed meet Plantinga's objection by retreating to something akin to (P2), a response to Fitch might be made by essentially the same manoeuvre. (The matter is discussed in Essay 11 in this volume.)

6

Comrades against Quietism

Simon Blackburn would like to turn what he views as the prevailing tide of metaphysical opinion—the 'pragmatist', 'internal realist', 'minimalist', 'deflationist', or 'quietist' tide of what he nicely describes as the 'denial of differences, the celebration of the seamless web of language, the soothing away of distinction'.[1] While a little unsure of my welcome—and doubtful, actually, how strong the current against us really is—I am happy to join him in the water. *Truth and Objectivity* is dedicated to explaining and making good the kinds of distinction which are rejected by the trend Blackburn deplores. The whole project of the book is the cartography of what he terms 'contour'— the characterisation of dimensions in which different areas of our thought and discourse might vary and, by so varying, give point to 'realist' and 'anti-realist' thoughts about them.

Blackburn acknowledges this (if maybe a little grudgingly). However, he claims a 'more contoured' vision of the metaphysical landscape

---

1. Blackburn (1998b), p. 157. Blackburn's paper elaborates his remarks made at an Author-meets-Critics session on my *Truth and Objectivity* held at the Central Division Meetings of the American Philosophical Association at Chicago in April 1995.

than mine. I think the image misrepresents our main differences. For while—although contesting some of the details—he broadly applauds the contrasts emphasised in my book, it is not as if there are then *additional* discriminations which he would have me make. His complaint seems to be not that I draw too few distinctions, but that I draw the *wrong* distinctions—or mischaracterise distinctions which we agree should be made. For instance, he wants to prevent the territory traditionally occupied by expressivist anti-realist proposals from being swallowed up by the minimalism about truth and truth-aptitude advanced in *Truth and Objectivity,* to reserve space for the idea that the 'propositional surface' of moral language, or conditionals, or talk of probabilities, for instance, may serve to mask the real nature of what is happening in discourses of those kinds. Yet while he regards expressivism, broadly construed, as giving an account of the workings of certain discourses alternative and preferable to the proposal that they are 'qualified by no interesting feature serving to give point to an intuitive realism about [them]—that [they deploy] minimally truth-apt contents and that is the whole of the matter',[2] there do not seem to be other cases where he regards the minimalist proposal as doing better justice to anti-realist intuition than expressivism can. Blackburn thus rejects rather than complicates—that is, adds an additional contour line to—the *Truth and Objectivity* characterisation of a basic anti-realism.[3] Likewise he rejects rather than complicates the suggestion that realism-relevant distinctions may be assisted by the framework of

2. See *Truth and Objectivity,* p. 142.

3. He seems to be saying as much himself in his note 5: 'Myself I doubt whether the issue of whether disagreement illustrates a cognitive defect—i.e. whether a discourse exerts Cognitive Command—can be pursued except via the very considerations that suggest expressivism. For instance, to decide whether ground-floor modal or moral disagreement illustrates a cognitive defect somewhere would require discovering whether, instead, it is better seen as indicating a failure of imagination, or sympathy, or of practical or intellectual policy'. His suggestion, in other words, is that a discourse's failure of Cognitive Command can be expected to lead us straight to considerations which suggest an expressivist—rather than minimalist—account of it.

a pluralism about truth. In general, the issue between us is not how many the distinctions are, or how deep they go, but how they should be drawn.

It is a familiar phenomenon in activist politics that disagreements among closely related factions are often more intensely felt than disagreements with more radically opposed ideas, and are often pursued under the accusation of insufficiency of distance from the latter. This bickering works against political credibility, and I suspect that the proponents of metaphysical contour run a similar risk. Still, an effective opposition to the 'soothing away of distinction' has to come equipped with the correct distinctions. So it is worth trying to get these matters right. Hence, while I appreciate Blackburn's support on many issues, not least in his apposite remarks about Richard Rorty's criticisms of my work,[4] I concentrate in what follows on our more significant points of theoretical disagreement and on certain misrepresentations (mainly of what he says I said about Wittgenstein) and apparent misunderstandings (mainly in connection with semantic minimalism and its threatened globalisation).

I

I begin with a thumbnail sketch of how contour is meant to emerge in *Truth and Objectivity*. One thing which I think has encouraged Blackburn's 'more contoured than thou' self-impression is my use of 'minimalism' and its cognates—terms which he associates with the quietist opposition. So perhaps it merits emphasis that the minimalism proposed in *Truth and Objectivity* is merely a combination of specific views about what qualifies a predicate as a truth predicate and about what suffices for a discourse to be truth-apt. It involves nothing deflationary about metaphysics in general or the realism debates in particular. The combination may, as far as it goes, be congenial to quietism,

4. In Rorty (1995).

but it is a major point of the argument of *Truth and Objectivity* that these views about truth and truth-aptitude do *not* imply quietism and are, to the contrary, at the service of resistance to it.

The minimalist view about *truth,* in briefest summary, is that it is necessary and sufficient, in order for a predicate to qualify as a truth predicate, that it satisfy each of a basic set of platitudes about truth: for instance, that to assert is to present as true, that statements which are apt for truth have negations which are likewise, that truth is one thing, justification is another, and so on. Minimalism about *truth-aptitude,* likewise hastily summarised, comprises the twin contentions

(i) that any discourse dealing in assertoric contents will allow the definition upon its sentences of a predicate which qualifies as a truth predicate in the light of the minimalist proposal about truth; and

(ii) that a discourse should be reckoned to deal in such contents just in case its ingredient sentences are subject to certain minimal constraints of syntax—embeddability within negation, the conditional, contexts of propositional attitude, and so on—and discipline: their use must be governed by agreed standards of warrant.

With each of these minimalisms in place, almost all the areas which have traditionally provoked realist/anti-realist debate—ethics, aesthetics, intentional psychology, mathematics, theoretical science, and so on—will turn out to traffic in truth-apt contents, which moreover, when the disciplinary standards proper to the discourse are satisfied, we are going to be entitled to claim to be true. So two traditional forms of anti-realism are immediately under pressure: classical *expressivism*—the denial that a target discourse, although possessed of 'propositional surface', really deals in truth-apt contents—is not going to be an option; and the *error theorist,* like John Mackie on ethics or Hartry Field on mathematics, though not out of the game straight away, will have his work cut out to make the charge of global error stick—typically, he'll have to point out some shortfall between the standards of warrant that actually inform the discourse in question and the notion of truth that actually applies therein.

As the last remark implies, minimalism about truth, as I conceive it, in contrast with the deflationary conception of truth which I believe it should supersede, is not committed to the idea that what is involved in truth has to be uniform across all areas of our thought. Any truth predicate, in whatever area, will satisfy the minimal platitudes—that's what *makes* it a truth predicate. But the truth predicates in different areas of thought may in addition exhibit differences—differences in, broadly speaking, the kind of circumstance that constitutes their applying, when they apply—which help to fill out and render discussible realist and anti-realist oppositions. That is where the hope of contour surfaces within the framework of the two minimalisms. *Truth and Objectivity* tries to show how that hope might be realised in a variety of different ways.

This potential pluralism about truth seems to have been misunderstood in some quarters. But I do not think it ought to seem too shocking a notion. If it does shock, it may be because it is being received as the suggestion of a kind of ambiguity in the word 'true'. But that's not the point at all. An ambiguous term typically admits of two (or more) quite different kinds of explanation, each of which determines a different extension for it. But if a truth predicate is any that satisfies the minimal set of platitudes—if there's no more to being a truth predicate than that—then all that can be said by way of explanation of the word 'true' is enshrined in those platitudes, which explanation is therefore *uniform*. In addition, since the platitudes will certainly be chosen so as to ensure that any truth predicate satisfies the Disquotational Scheme, there won't be any possibility of a pair of predicates each qualifying as a truth predicate for a single discourse and yet differing in their extension within it.

The kind of plurality that's envisaged may be brought out by a comparison with identity. Minimally, identity can be characterised as that relation which is universally reflexive and a congruence for an arbitrary property. To that extent, the concept of identity is uniform across varying kinds of object. But that uniformity had better be consistent with our recognising that what *constitutes* identity is subject to considerable variation depending on the kinds of objects concerned. The identity of material objects is constituted by spatial and temporal continuity; for cardinal numbers, according to Frege's famous proposal, identity is constituted by the one–one correspondence of an associated pair of concepts; for the directions of a pair of straight lines, identity is constituted by those lines' being parallel; and for persons, identity is constituted by—well, it's notoriously difficult to say, but the case is different to each of the preceding. Identity, one might thus say, is *formally* uniform, but may vary *in constitution* as we consider different potential identicals. Clearly there is space for a similar contention about truth: truth is formally uniform—in the sense determined by satisfaction of the platitudes—but its constitution may vary depending on the type of statement and subject matter concerned.

This is the space that, by pointing to the various cruces—Cognitive Command, Wide Cosmological Role, the Euthyphro Contrast, and so on—discussed in *Truth and Objectivity,* I was trying to fill. Platitudinously, truth is always correspondence to fact. But what correspondence to fact is may vary, in realism-relevant ways, if the notion of correspondence carries the connotation of substantial representation which the Cognitive Command constraint tries to control, or if the facts concerned have the robustness of Wide Cosmological Role. Likewise, if truth in some discourse is—or might as well be taken to be—superassertibility, then, for that area, we must surrender the idea of truth as a matter of fit with external states of affairs of which enduring satisfaction of that discourse's internal disciplinary constraints is merely a symptom, or marker.

II

Blackburn regards the combination of the two minimalisms, about truth and about truth-aptitude respectively, as 'a much more strange view than it might seem at first sight'. His principal objection is that the combination sets up a tension with what is evidently possible, 'that there should be norms of acceptance and rejection of utterances of indicative sentences which exist for other reasons than that those sentences have truth conditions'.[5] Among the kinds of sentences which, he suggests, minimalism should countenance as minimally truth-apt, but whose use is manifestly governed by non-truth-connected norms, are Austinian performatives, like promises, christenings, and so on, sentences uttered or written in the course of fiction, and metaphors.

These particular three examples raise many issues which it would be impractical to attempt to treat here.[6] However, Blackburn's own brisk discussion neglects two considerations which, once noted, make it rather implausible, I think, that a detailed discussion of such cases would uncover any serious difficulties for the minimalist proposal. The first is simply that to hold that a region of discourse deals in minimally truth-apt contents involves—of course—absolutely no commitment to the view that the *only* norms governing indicative utterances within it are ones connected with truth. No one is going to deny that the assertion of a truth-apt sentence may be open to criticism for all kinds of reasons besides a failure to be true. Minimalism is perfectly comfortable with this, and puts no obstacles before a philosopher who, for whatever reason, regards the taxonomy of the non-truth-connected norms operative over particular indicative utterances, or the attitudinal psychology involved in operating them, as of special importance. Let him draw what distinctions and note what differences he will. Nothing in the minimalist view of truth and truth-aptitude stands in the way of the idea that, in making an assertion, one may be doing many other things in tandem so that one's utterance may be subject to other norms of appraisal besides those which govern assertion, and the attitudinal psychology which underlies it may be correspondingly complicated and involve a lot more than just belief.

5. Blackburn (1998b), p. 159.
6. I say a little more about the case of fiction in Wright (1994a) (this volume Essay 4).

Second—and perhaps a little less obvious—the minimalist proposal is only concerned with when it is right to think of discourses as trafficking in truth-apt contents. *Truth and Objectivity* could usefully have placed more emphasis upon the point that a positive verdict about a particular discourse in that respect is—contrary to what Blackburn assumes—by no means a commitment to the view that the standard use of (all) its indicative sentences is to *assert* those contents. The most salient cases where the two come apart are indeed precisely the performatives: utterances like 'I name this ship the *Marie Celeste*' or 'With this ring I thee wed' are certainly associated with truth-apt contents—that is why they are available for embedding in conditionals, propositional attitude constructions, and so on—but their role is, or so one would think, not to assert such contents but to *realise* them—bring about their truth.

Similar distinctions could be applied to the treatment of both fiction and metaphor. Indeed, as I read Davidson's well-known discussion of the latter, that is exactly what he, for one, did propose: 'metaphorising', his idea was, should be seen as a distinctive form of speech act—an operation upon a truth-apt content contrasting with the simple assertion of it.[7] (That would explain why the obvious literal inappropriateness of most metaphors is not an objection to them.) A strategically similar proposal about fiction might have it that in fictional contexts the distinctive such operation is *pretended assertion*—where such an utterance is no more a real assertion than a stage murder is a murder—but that what is pretendedly asserted is, likewise, a straightforwardly truth-apt content (though one which, if it involves fictional names, may fail of truth, it is open to us to hold, through reference failure).

I am not here endorsing these particular suggestions. My point is simply that minimalism is no commitment to the idea that any simple indicative utterance associated with a particular truth-apt content has to be thought of as the assertion of that content: again, something quite different may be happening, and the attitudinal psychology

7. See Davidson (1978).

associated with the performance may be non-doxastic in consequence. Blackburn writes as though minimalism had to be inhospitable to the thought that 'commitment in some areas is not a simple matter of belief, but more to do with endorsement of invitations to think of things in a certain light (metaphors), movements of thought (conditionals), the successful evocation of moods and emotions (poetry), or movements from representation to motivation (ethics)'. Well, if there is merit in any of those suggestions, it can surely be brought out by their development in one of the two ways pointed to: by pragmatic and psychological considerations viewed as supplementary to a basic assertoric account of the sentences which express the 'commitments' in question, or by viewing those sentences as the bearers of truth-apt contents which it is, however, not their standard use to assert. Either way, minimalism should be able comfortably to accommodate the relevant development.[8]

8. The foregoing brings out that it is important to distinguish two broad forms of expressivist proposal. One—what I have called classical expressivism—holds that no truth-evaluable contents are expressed by, for example, any ethical sentences. This is the view that is squeezed out by minimalism. But a second form of proposal, just urged to be consistent with minimalism, would be not that the relevant discourse does not deal in truth-evaluable contents at all, but that the characteristic use of its (simple) indicative sentences is, rather, not to assert such contents. This second form of claim seems to be exactly what is wanted in the service of some traditional expressivist views—for instance, in order to give the best run for its money to the kind of non-assertoric thesis about avowals (certain first-person psychological ascriptions) sometimes thought to have been proposed by the later Wittgenstein. For more on this, see Wright (1997). But I doubt that it should seem terribly attractive to those drawn towards ethical expressivism. The effect would be that even if 'Stealing is wrong' were not itself typically used to make an assertion, it would be reckoned to be associated with a content which was nevertheless in principle *apt* for assertion, which could be hypothesised to be true, presented as the antecedent of a conditional, reasoned from, and so on. So questions would have to be allowed about what kind of content that was, what it would be to be justified in taking it to be true, and so on—questions whose principled avoidance was precisely one of the attractions of classical ethical expressivism.

III

En passant, Blackburn throws in his lot with those critics, like Frank Jackson, Graham Oppy and Michael Smith, who have objected—'tellingly', in Blackburn's view—that the position taken in *Truth and Objectivity* depends upon focusing only on a selection of the platitudes concerning the notions of truth and assertion, and ignoring in particular equally platitudinous connections of those notions with *belief*.[9] The thought is, familiarly, that one may be forced to look below the propositional surface of, for example, ethical discourse if one takes it as a platitude that assertion is the profession of belief but also accepts, with Hume, that no belief can be, in and of itself, a motivational state and regards it as clear that whatever is professed by an ethical 'assertion', it is such a motivational state.

This is again a line of thought which warrants a more elaborate discussion than I can venture here.[10] It might seem that the only clean way to dispose of the objection would be to controvert one of the latter two claims: to argue directly that certain kinds of belief are intrinsically motivational after all,[11] or that the attitudes expressed by sincere ethical claims are, appearances notwithstanding, not *intrinsically* motivational.[12] To accept a challenge to pursue those issues, however, would be to acknowledge that the minimalism of *Truth and Objectivity* is hostage to such unfinished business. And that I do not acknowledge (even if either hostage might well be redeemed). The correct response is rather that, insofar as the questions whether a belief can be, in and of itself, a motivational state, and whether the states professed by ethical utterances are indeed intrinsically motivational, are taken to be open and philosophically substantial, to that extent it is simply *not* a platitude that the assertion of any minimally

9. See Jackson, Oppy and Smith (1994).

10. I discuss it further in Wright (1994b) (this volume Essay 3).

11. This is a view often taken to be defended by John McDowell; see McDowell (1978).

12. Michael Smith himself eventually takes such a view in Smith (1994).

truth-apt content is a profession of belief. Or rather: for one who accepts that those issues are open, *belief* is not the notion in terms of which to articulate the platitude which lurks in the vicinity. However, we can easily find an alternative expression by taking over for the purpose a term to which Blackburn conveniently—and rather revealingly—often has recourse: *commitment*. For Blackburn's 'commitments' are typically expressed by indicative sentences; they may be argued for and against, reasoned to and from, accepted, doubted and entertained. So the notion ought to give us all we need. The relevant platitude is thus, in effect, that the assertion of a minimally truth-apt content is the profession of a commitment. Since Blackburn's view is that only some commitments are really *beliefs*, he therefore owes an account, which I do not know that he has anywhere attempted to provide, of what is distinctive of the narrower class. The minimalist, however, has no reason to reject out of hand the suggestion that such a worthwhile distinction may exist, and can with good grace accept Blackburn's annexure of the term 'belief' to the narrower class, if it exists, as a conceivably well-motivated linguistic reform. We can wait and see how well motivated it is. It remains that ordinary practice does not scruple to use 'belief' where Blackburn prefers his term of art and that it is only with the more generous notion that there is the platitudinous connection with assertion which this line of objection wholly misguidedly seeks to exploit.

IV

Blackburn's second principal disagreement with the framework of *Truth and Objectivity* concerns the *location* of the contour. For Blackburn, the relevant plurality is not among ways in which truth may be constituted in different regions of discourse, but among the *bearers* of truth—the realism-relevant distinctions are to be made by seeking out variety among kinds of *propositions*. Thus Blackburn's 'quasi-realist' about ethics who is also realist about, say, theoretical physics holds not that their respective truth predicates differ: that truth in ethics, say, is broadly a matter of superassertibility while truth in physics is a matter of relation to robust external matters—a relation of which enduring satisfaction of best empirical-theoretic methodology is at best an indicator—but rather that there is a key distinction between ethical and theoretical-physical propositions, a distinction which can peacefully coexist with their both being satisfiers of some *uniform* notion of truth.

That *sounds* like it could be a real theoretical contrast. But on closer inspection there are difficulties in seeing how it could be stable; and I doubt in any case if it gets to the heart of our differences. The problem is to understand what *kind* of distinctions among types of proposition, of the sort that Blackburn wants to draw, might be constitutive of realist/anti-realist contrasts yet go unreflected by systematic differences in what makes for their *truth*. If the suggestion that ethics and theoretical physics traffic in different kinds of proposition is to be anything germane to the respective causes of anti-realism about ethics and realism about theoretical physics, for example, then it surely has to import the idea that the two kinds of proposition relate in different ways to the real world (that is, the austere physical, non-intentional, non-modal, value-free world which, in Blackburn's implicit underlying metaphysical picture, acts as a boundary on all genuine literal description). In brief, using Blackburn's shorthand, I don't see how he can avoid saying that the truth of a q-proposition is a very different kind of circumstance to the truth of a d-proposition. Yet once that point is acknowledged, it is hard to see how the insistence that a uniform truth predicate applies to propositions of both kinds can be intelligible except under the aegis of something very close to the minimalism about truth canvassed in *Truth and Objectivity*.

The converse direction of implication is also plausible. If Blackburn's preferred form of distinction at the level of propositions—the 'Ramsey option', as he calls it—seems to demand reflection by distinctions in what the truth of his various kinds of proposition consists in, it also seems clear that someone who accepts the *Truth and Objectivity* framework can agree that a discourse's stalling at or surmounting the cruces of Cognitive Command, Wide Cosmological Role, and so on should be expected to have implications for the kind of contents—the propositions—in which it deals.

Thus this particular alleged difference between Blackburn and myself seems fugitive to me: it simply isn't clear what the 'Ramsey option' really comes to—not if it has to be something antithetical to the proposals of *Truth and Objectivity*.

V

In my view, the real—most significant—contrasts between the ways Blackburn and I respectively like to view these matters concern not the vehicle of realist/anti-realist contrast—kinds of truth versus kinds of propositions—but our respective conceptions of what can be taken for granted and what needs to be explained. On my view, truth-aptitude is relatively easily earned; and once a discourse is recognised as truth-apt, the default view should be that claims to truth within it are justified by satisfaction of its proper standards of warrant. (To stress: that's the *default* view—it can be defeated by, inter alia, enforcing a contrast between truth and superassertibility within the discourse in question.) For Blackburn, on the other hand, those of our discourses—including comedy, ethics, aesthetics, probability—which possess propositional surface collectively overfill the Cup of Reality. And it is his unspoken assumption that it is only in so far as a discourse serves to depict what is within the Cup of Reality that its propositional surface may be regarded as unproblematic. So Blackburn finds a *standing puzzle about the presence of propositional surface in a wide range of discourses*—all those, so the breadth Blackburn likes to assign to the quasi-realist programme would suggest, which are not depictive of the fully physical, non-intentional, non-modal, value-free World—and a standing philosophical obligation to construct some kind of response to that puzzle. From this standpoint, *Truth and Objectivity* will seem guilty of an egregious oversight: to someone working within its framework, a wide sweep of deep philosophical problems, in Blackburn's view, is simply invisible.

Now, I think that in the course of the development of this outlook since the publication of *Spreading the Word*[13] it has become increasingly unclear what it would be to *address* the alleged puzzles which thus provide the *raison d'être* of the quasi-realist programme—puzzles of propositional surface supposedly extending beyond its proper home. Consider the idea that ethical discourse, for instance, is not genuinely descriptive, and hence that its propositional surface is problematical. For someone so convinced, a natural response might be to wonder whether the propositional surface is not au fond *incidental*—whether ethical thought, *qua* ethical, could in principle receive clothing of a quite different kind. That suggestion has the merit of relative clarity of direction, and it is indeed the form which Blackburn was at first content to give to his proposal. The resulting programme is the familiar—and technically interesting—one of trying to show how ethical thought, diagnosed as expressive of attitude, for example, rather than descriptive of the world, could in principle assume a non-propositional shape without compromise of any of our ethical activity—including, par excellence, ethical *reasoning*—and how a propositional structure might then be harmlessly, if misleadingly, superimposed upon it, as a *façon de parler*. This was the programme canvassed in *Spreading the Word* and pursued elsewhere, albeit with significant modifications.[14] But it has become clear that it founders on seemingly decisive difficulties concerning the interpretation of the conditional.[15] Recently, apparently in recognition of such more technical difficulties, Blackburn has tended to soften the quasi-realist brief: rather than show, for example, how the propositional surface of moral discourse might be consistent with its lacking truth-apt content, the quasi-realist is now charged merely to explain, without recourse to the idea of representation of moral fact, how the emergence of moral thinking in propositional shape is *intelligible*. More generally, philosophy is somehow to

---

13. Blackburn (1984).

14. See *ibid.*, chap. 6. For a different tack, see Blackburn (1988).

15. See Hale (1986). For revised criticisms in the light of later suggestions of Blackburn's, see Hale (1992).

explain the presence of propositional surface in regions where—it is somehow given—there is some incongruity about it, in ways that precisely do *not* presuppose or have to make good the claim that our thinking in these regions could proceed in its entirety without the assumption of propositional surface. But it is hereabouts that I, at least, begin to lose my sense of what the project is about. To sympathise with it, you have to have a feel for (something like) the question: '*How come* moral discourse, for example, possesses the syntax and discipline distinctive of minimal truth-aptitude in Wright's sense?' But that's a question which it seems we might make something of only if we knew of another—non-propositional—surface that ethical discourse, *qua* ethical, might wear. And that is just what we cannot know unless the original form of Blackburn's proposal can—improbably—succeed.

Blackburn assumes that propositional surface is a philosophically straightforward phenomenon only in areas where we are in the business of literal description of the world, and his project is to explain how other discourses may still intelligibly and justifiably wear such a surface. The assumption betrays a bipartite interplay which drives all Blackburn's work on these issues: the interplay between the thought that realism about a discourse is best explicated as the conviction that it is *literally descriptive*—deals in real representational propositions, as it were—and the idea that, at least as a first approximation, literal descriptiveness is a matter of possession of propositional surface. If both these notions are allowed to stand unqualified, then of course realism threatens a cheap victory wherever there is propositional surface—and the anti-realist about a particular region is left with no option but to try to make out how propositional surface is there inappropriate—so that a quite different way of talking would be preferable. Blackburn's conservative alternative seeks to avoid this by qualifying the second component: propositional surface may sometimes be explained in a way that disconnects it from genuine descriptive function (from traffic in real propositions and the expression of genuinely representational states). Now I of course applaud the project of trying to explain how propositional surface may be disengaged from realist commitment. That is exactly what the minimalism of *Truth and Objectivity* is about. The complaint I have been making is that I do not know what such an explanation might consist in if it has simultaneously somehow to vindicate—to *exculpate*—the propositional surface.[16] But in any case I regard the first component in the interplay as unfortunate. It *cannot* be a theoretically happy starting point to think of realism in terms of literal descriptiveness—for it is merely common sense that comic discourse literally describes matters of comedy, moral discourse literally describes moral matters, and likewise for any propositionally surfaced discourse where anti-realism ought to be an option. 'Literally descriptive' is itself open to more or less deflationary interpretations. The metaphysical hypostasis of the 'real proposition' (or 'genuinely representational state') implicit in Blackburn's conception of realism is something which needs to be explained and justified—not a notion on which to place a theoretical load from the outset.

In general, crucial questions are begged by the quasi-realist starting point. Even if there were an intelligible and necessary explanatory task for quasi-realism to take on—a task which *Truth and Objectivity* would lead us to shirk—the work could start only *after* we had made a distinction between cases where realism is acceptable, and propositional surface consequently unproblematic, and cases where neither is so. So it is presupposed that we already know what realism *is*—what it is to take a realist view of an area of thought, how such a view might be justified and what it would be to avoid it. These are issues which are evidently at the heart of the metaphysical question, not things to take a stance on before starting work. That is the most fun-

---

16. At least not once the *Spreading the Word* paradigm is discarded—the paradigm of showing how an expressivist interpretation can be supplied for an indicative discourse which is conservative of all the inferential and other moves facilitated by its propositional clothing. (It is another matter, of course, whether that clothing would thereby automatically be shown to be inessential—a harmless superimposition. The question would still have to arise why the expressive reinterpretation, rather than a face-value propositional interpretation, was the better reflection of the real nature of the discourse.)

damental reason why I prefer my way of looking at the matter to Blackburn's. You cannot so much as motivate the quasi-realist programme in any particular region of thought without a prior decision about what *real*—not 'quasi-'—realism consists in, and why it is inappropriate in that region. Those are exactly the kind of questions which *Truth and Objectivity* is intended to help us address.

VI

Blackburn is keen to confound those quietists who would like to cite Wittgenstein's sponsorship—indeed he would like to make Wittgenstein out as effectively a pioneer of quasi-realism instead![17] So he understandably plays up the passages, which are abundant in Wittgenstein's writings from his middle period onwards, in which, despite the propositional surface of species of commitment, Wittgenstein raises questions about the felicity of notions like 'description' and 'fact', and proposes assimilations to, or comparisons with, non-assertoric modes of utterance. Ethics, mathematics, modal claims, avowals, and the 'hinge propositions' of *On Certainty* all come in for this kind of treatment. As Blackburn reminds us, Wittgenstein was tempted to take as a motto for the *Philosophical Investigations* Kent's line in *King Lear*: 'I'll teach you differences'.[18] And at *Investigations* §304 we are urged to 'make a radical break with the idea that language always functions in one way, always serves the same purpose: to convey thoughts—which may be about houses, pains, good and evil, or anything else you please'. 'Language', as it occurs in that passage, will presumably bear interpretation as something like: discourse of propositional surface.

The fact is, however, that, these tendencies notwithstanding, Wittgenstein is never prepared to wonder about the *propriety* of our generosity with propositional surface—the generosity that sets up the

17. In this connection, compare the remarks on pp. 6 and 7 of Blackburn (1993).
18. He didn't, however. Why not?

alleged quasi-realist puzzles. Readers will recall the gist of *Investigations* §136 and surrounding sections: propositions are what *we call* propositions and we call something a proposition 'when *in our language* [Wittgenstein's own emphasis] we apply the calculus of truth functions to it'—that is, propositions are what *we* submit to the discipline of sentential logic. If we suppose that Wittgenstein thought that there was a robust, relatively sharp distinction between areas where propositional surface goes along with genuine literal description and areas where it serves, rather, to mask other kinds of linguistic activity—kinds of activity which are only misleadingly given a propositional surface—then it's going to be hard to avoid saying that there is a tension in Wittgenstein's thinking here which he simply didn't resolve. Perhaps it can be resolved by a quasi-realist rehabilitation of propositional surface in the dodgy cases—whatever exactly that might consist in—but it ought to be a source of discomfort to Blackburn's interpretation that Wittgenstein seems nowhere to appreciate that such a rehabilitative programme is required. He *finds no puzzle* in our generosity with propositional surface. And he applies no criticism to it. He merely cautions us against letting it cause us to overlook differences. Section 135 contains, indeed, an explicit comparison between the concept of proposition and Wittgenstein's favourite example of a diversity-encompassing concept, the concept *game*. The analogue of the quasi-realist thought, applied to the other term in that comparison, would be that underlying our generosity with the concept game is a distinction between cases where the application is most appropriate—cases where, such is the general nature of the activity involved, we are concerned with games in the truest sense—and cases where there is a prima facie tension between the actual nature of the activity involved and its classification as a game. But of course the whole point of family resemblance concepts, as Wittgenstein conceives them, is that they work in a way which subverts any such contrast. There is no truest sense of 'game'.

It may well seem that Wittgenstein's thinking actually squares much better with the programme of *Truth and Objectivity* than it does with quasi-realism! We begin by recognising, in a spirit of tolerance, our customary generosity with propositional surface. That's the whole point of the minimalist conceptions of truth and truth-aptitude. But then, rather than go quietist, we look for the differences that propositional surface may mask. My formulations of Cognitive Command, Wide Cosmological Role, and so on are attempts to say what at least some such interesting differences may be. But I don't want to overplay the point. Wittgenstein is going to notice differences with a view to undercutting the appeal of certain metaphysical pictures—Platonism in mathematics, for instance. Whereas the distinctions in *Truth and Objectivity* are offered in an explicitly theoretical spirit which it may well be expected he would have deplored.

I don't want to spend much longer on this—the three pages at the start of chapter 6 of *Truth and Objectivity* to which Blackburn is reacting are not really very important to the development of that chapter—but it needs to be said that his remarks seriously misrepresent their gist, partly as a result of what appears to be deliberately selective quotation. He quotes my suggestion that you have to overlook a distinction in order to find an *obvious* inconsistency between the passages where Wittgenstein seems to want to look past propositional surface and the passages on which the quietist interpretation draws. His comparing mathematical statements to commands, for instance, might be read as having the purpose of persuading us to deny that mathematical statements are genuine propositions—and then you have the obvious inconsistency with, for example, *Investigations* §136—but it might also be intended in a fashion which is inimical to the idea of any general distinction between cases where propositional surface goes along with real propositionhood, as it were, and cases where it does not—'to suggest', as I put it, 'that there is not the clean distinction to be made between genuinely truth-apt contents and "merely grammatical" assertions which the expressivist needs to work with'. Blackburn cuts the quote off there, ignores the occurrence of 'clean' and then dryly remarks,

[s]o one would expect evidence of Wittgenstein saying, in effect, that he has had us fooled all along. We thought he was teaching differences,

but really he was subverting the differences he seemed to bring up. All along he was warning us against thinking of mathematics in terms of rules, thinking that the difference between description and expression of attitude was important . . . there are no such differences! His motto is I'll teach you samenesses![19]

Well, it is a nice joke. But the sentence immediately after the end of the passage Blackburn quoted continues:

Rather, the 'merely grammatical' notions are the only *general* notions of truth and assertoric content which we have, and beyond them lies only a plethora of differences

—note that: *differences*—

which we need to notice and describe. A philosophical picture of what's going on in a discourse may of course be motivated by overlooking differences between it and others. So there will be space for appraisal of such pictures. But there's no space for debate about the applicability of metaphysically hypostatised notions of truth and assertoric content; and differences which merely call a philosophical picture into question must not be credited with a bearing on the very integrity of the language game concerned.[20]

VII

The primary concern of chapter 6 of *Truth and Objectivity* is with the line of thought—it doesn't much matter whether Wittgenstein himself ever had anything like it—which sees some form of irrealism about content as the proper conclusion of Wittgenstein's discussion of following a rule, and then wonders how such a conclusion can be prevented from ramifying into an irrealism about everything. This seems

19. Blackburn (1998b), p. 165.
20. *Truth and Objectivity,* pp. 203–4.

to me by far the most interesting extant argument for quietism; but how best to formulate it, and whether it succeeds, are still unresolved questions.

The leading question considered in chapter 6 is whether, if minimalism about semantic discourse is accepted—if all talk about the semantics of linguistic expressions is regarded as merely minimally truth-apt and as satisfying no further realism-relevant condition—the same conclusion follows for all assertoric discourse. Two arguments purporting to enforce an affirmative answer are distinguished and discussed. There is what I called the *Intuitive Version,* and there is a distinct argument due to Paul Boghossian and first bruited in his article on the rule-following considerations.[21]

That the latter proves resistable ought not to be allowed to obscure the contribution Boghossian's discussion makes to this difficult question. Blackburn remarks that 'Wright himself is not now persuaded by [Boghossian's] argument, for complex reasons that I'm not sure bear on its major infirmities'. The suggestion that this is something on which I have changed my mind gives cause for concern. It makes me suspect that Blackburn himself may have paid insufficient attention to the distinction between the Intuitive Version and Boghossian's argument. This would also explain some of his, as they seem to me, continuingly unsatisfactory remarks about the role of semantic descent.

To elaborate. Boghossian's argument, recall, works with robust—that is, non-minimal, non-deflationary—notions of truth and truth-conditionality, and takes it that the semantic minimalist (his 'non-factualist') will consequently be committed to:

(i) For any sentence S and propositional content P, 'S has the truth condition that P' is not truth-conditional.

A minimalist about truth and truth-aptitude should not worry about this formulation. (There is no good objection to restricting the word

---

21. Boghossian (1989a).

'true' to statements meeting some realism-importing condition, reserving, say, 'correct' for the minimalist notion.) The argument then proceeds through two steps:

(ii) For any S and P, it's not the case that 'S has the truth condition that P' is true

—a seemingly evident consequence of (i) since only a sentence with the truth condition can be true, presumably. So

(iii) For any S and P, it's not the case that S has the truth condition that P,

which follows from (ii) by disquotation.

The first point I want to stress—yet again[22]—is that despite the fact that its conclusion is metalinguistic, this argument is already *complete*. You have established global minimalism when you have shown that no matter what declarative *sentence* S you consider, S is not apt for robust truth as characterised a moment ago, that is, meets no realism-importing condition. *There is no need to descend* to a claim about the status of the judgement that S expresses; we have already said all we need to say about the status of that judgement by showing—purportedly—that the sentence which expresses it is not apt for robust truth. As we shall see, matters stand quite differently with the Intuitive Version—there, a semantic descent is indeed essential if the global minimalist conclusion is to ensue. But that is just the respect in which the arguments differ, and which Blackburn seems stubbornly to miss.

What is wrong with Boghossian's argument? The 'complex reasons' for rejecting it which Blackburn feels may not go to the 'heart of its infirmities' are easily enough summarised. The first worry to have is about the step of disquotation. Surely the conditional

If P, then 'P' is true

22. It was stressed at *Truth and Objectivity*, p. 222; see in particular note 16 on that page.

cannot remain acceptable if 'P' may be not a truth-apt but a merely correctness-apt sentence? And if it is not acceptable, then neither is the contraposition on it which Boghossian's step from (ii) to (iii) depends on.

That is the thought that Blackburn himself is expressing when he says 'Once truth is sorted you cannot infer that "not P" from "S expresses P" and "S is not trued" '. So why the additional complexity in my discussion that is not to his taste? Well, because matters are not actually quite so simple. The response assumes that ' "P" is true' will be incorrect, or even false, if 'P' is merely correctness-apt. But what if we stipulated differently? What if we stipulated that ' "P" is true' is *correct* (though not true) when 'P' is correct, and allowed that a conditional is correct if it has a correct antecedent and consequent? Unless there's some further objection to that proposal, the disquotational step can stand.

That is the reason why I took the trouble—entered into the unwelcome complexity necessary—to show that, if we did accept that proposal, the bump would come up elsewhere in the carpet. Specifically, either we lose the conditional

'P' is true → 'P' has a truth condition,

in which case we lose the earlier step from Boghossian's (i) to (ii) or ' "P" has a truth condition' ceases to be a satisfactory way of expressing realism about (the subject matter) of 'P' (since it can be *correctly* affirmed of a sentence, 'P', which is merely correctness-apt). In that second case, Boghossian's premise (i) ceases to capture the position under consideration.

Blackburn himself proposes to scotch Boghossian's argument by means of a dilemma. If we go the Ramsey route, distinguishing kinds of proposition, but retaining a single notion of truth, then propositions about content, even though 'soft' as viewed by the minimalist, *will* have truth conditions—in the only sense of 'truth conditions' in town—and Boghossian's (i) will once again be a misrepresentation of the irrealist–minimalist view. If on the other hand, we go the way that Blackburn does not recommend, distinguishing minimalist and robust truth predicates, then the objection he wants to make is the one that I just mentioned—the one that needs the additional complexity that he didn't give it.

Concerning the first horn, I'm not sure, for the reason I mooted earlier, that the 'Ramsey route' is a distinct and stable option. It is clear, however, that even if it is, there could be no good objection to the introduction of a term 'true' to mark the condition of 'hard' propositions which are true in the Blackburn–Ramsey uniform sense (whatever that is), while once again reserving 'correct' as the corresponding epithet of 'soft' propositions. This would not be to invent a difference where Blackburn and Ramsey see none, but would merely be, as it were, an inflection on the truth predicate, comparable to ordinary gender inflections (as when 'grandfather' and 'grandmother' are used as inflections on 'grandparent'). After a similar trick on 'is truth-conditional' and its cognates, no soft proposition could be acceptably described as 'truth-conditional'—compare: 'Agnes is not a grandfather'. So we could then reinstate Boghossian's (i) as a satisfactory formulation of the semantic minimalist view, for all Blackburn could say to the contrary, and run the argument exactly as before.

Moral: it is *not* the 'major infirmity' of Boghossian's argument that, in its selection of premise (i), it ignores the Ramsey option. Even if that option exists in the form Blackburn likes to think, and even if we choose it, we will have to do more than reject the premise of Boghossian's argument—specifically, we will have to pursue the issues on the second horn of Blackburn's dilemma—if we are to see the argument for the fallacy it is.

VIII

Finally to the Intuitive Version of the argument to global minimalism. This goes via the apparent platitude that whether or not a statement is true is a function of its content and the state of the world in relevant respects. The thought is then: if matters of content somehow go soft after Wittgenstein's discussion of rule-following, then so will all matters which functionally depend upon them, including, therefore, matters of statements' truth. But if all matters of truth are soft, then everything is soft.

Here, unlike in Boghossian's argument, there is indeed an essential play with semantic descent. It comes in the last step. It is one thing to have the conclusion that claims of the form, ' "P" is true', are soft, but quite another matter to go minimalist about the corresponding claims that P.

In his remarks, Blackburn misconstrues a passage in which I was expounding the general gist of this argument as evidence that I myself accept the semantic descent. In fact, I think the issue is fraught. That is why I discussed it in some detail. The worry is whether any apparent increment of objectivity, secured by the semantic descent, could be more than an artefact of creative accounting. If the judgement whether or not 'P' is true is made a soft judgement—whatever that means—by dependence on an appraisal of the content of the sentence 'P', well, isn't it likewise the case that *all* our judgements, at both object- and meta-linguistic levels, go through an appraisal of content?

Of course that remark only gestures at a concern which, in the chapter, I tried to render more discussable and explicit. Agreeably, Blackburn takes the worry very seriously, and thinks it may help us to assuage it if we make a comparison with what he calls the 'Gestalt switch' involved in the movement from third-personal to first-personal perspectives on the indeterminacy of radical translation. Our language, that is, may allow of alternative interpretations, even by best interpretative method, but the first-personal perspective—our ordinary thinking about what we ourselves mean by particular expressions—does not see the multiple possibilities. In much the same way, if I understand Blackburn's suggestion, we look straight past the involvement of language in our appraisal of object-linguistic claims.

Now, I am not very clear how it would help if this interesting suggestion were right. But in any case, and at the risk of seeming ungrateful, I close by noting what seems to be a conclusive objection to it. Even granting that the indeterminacy of radical interpretation—or if you prefer, the inscrutability of reference—is a fact, it's not so much, it seems to me, that the possibilities of multiple interpretation are somehow passed over when one takes the first-personal perspective as that they are not, from that perspective, so much as *coherently formulable*. It is not that I am ordinarily somehow blind, or anyway persistently inattentive to the possibility that 'Cat' in my idiolect denotes undetached cat parts, say, rather than cats: I am thinking in my idiolect when that putative possibility is articulated, and I rightly dismiss it on *purely disquotational grounds*. There is no question but that 'Cat' in my idiolect denotes cats, since that claim is itself formulated in my idiolect. By contrast, there seems to be no parallel difficulty in contemplating the thought that, in appraising the judgement that cats are vertebrates, my first move is inevitably an appreciation of the content of the very words I just used. Thus the sense, if any, in which that move is invisible to me—and how such invisibility would help with the threat of creeping minimalism—are not illumined by Blackburn's parallel.

PART THREE

ETHICS

Moral discourse provides a prime location for the application and testing of a metaphysics of objectivity and of realism and its oppositions. On the one hand, the question of the status of moral thought in these respects is one of the oldest of philosophical questions. On the other, particular metaphysical proposals have to stand the test of how plausible and illuminating an account they can generate of a status of moral thought. The two essays in this part begin to explore the bearing on morals of the metaphysical framework of *Truth and Objectivity*.

Essay 7 is my inaugural address to the Joint Session of the Mind Association and Aristotelian Society held at St. Andrews in 1988. It was written in reaction to an idea which had come into prominence in the 1980s, that an illuminating comparison might be made between moral qualities and secondary qualities in Locke's sense—qualities such as colour, taste and smell. The comparison seemed attractive, to those who promoted it, because of the plausible mix of subjectivity and objectivity which, if sustained, it might grant to moral discourse: moral claims might profess to state matters of fact in whatever way and to whatever degree the colour of the sky or the smell of roses might be regarded as matters of fact, but while having the same kind of dependence on human modes of sensibility and affect. The initial focus of my essay is on John McDowell's version of the secondary quality proposal, according to which we should think of moral quality as open to a kind of *perceptual* receptivity, as colour is open to reception by our visual systems. I argue that while this view has the resources to resist a number of objections which critics at the time—notably, Blackburn, Dancy and McGinn—levelled against it, there is an inherent implausibility in the idea that moral judgement is based upon a distinctive form of moral experience and that a robust analogy between moral qualities and secondary qualities had therefore better prescind from the latters' characteristic dependence on a single mode of human sensory experience. What remains is then the broad suggestion that moral qualities, like the secondary qualities, are judgement-dependent in the sense that takes centre stage in the Euthyphro Contrast: that we should think of the extensions of moral qualities not as tracked by best moral opinion but as constitutively dependent upon it, just as the extension of the colour red depends constitutively upon the judgements based, in the best circumstances, on the kinds of colour experience undergone by normal human beings, in contrast to the independence of human experience, at least as normally conceived, of Lockean primary qualities like shape, number and mass.

The principal claim of the essay is that this comparison is flawed by a fatal disanalogy: that what makes a judgement about, say, colour best—the conditions which our best judgements meet—can be explained in a fashion independent of the details of the extension of colour properties, whereas any plausible account of what makes a moral opinion best must make ineliminable reference to the moral competence of the judge—which competence can only be understood in terms of a disposition to make correct moral judgements. The relationship, in the moral case, between an opinion's being best and its being correct accordingly emerges as conceptually analogous to that which obtains in the case of primary qualities, rather than secondary ones. But the conception of moral qualities as primary involves the very hyper-objectification of them which provided the basis for John

Mackie's criticisms of ethical realism, and to which the secondary quality comparison was supposed to provide a sensible alternative.

Essay 8 was specially written for a conference of the same title organised by Brad Hooker at Reading in 1994. It aims at a concise statement of how someone sympathetic to the general framework of *Truth and Objectivity* should view the debates about ethical realism in the then-recent literature. It accordingly argues that ethical anti-realism ought not, as in its expressivist and error-theoretic incarnations, embrace the denial that moral judgements are so much as true; that the issue concerns, rather, how truth in ethics ought to be conceived; that moral anti-realism should be the contention that moral truth be conceived as a kind of superassertibility—of enduring satisfaction of standards of moral acceptability—and that moral realism accordingly owes a contrasting conception of moral truth as *fit* or *representation* of certain self-standing, discourse-independent states of affairs. The essay then sketches how the debate might be joined under the aegis of this broad conception of its proper content, and a prima facie case is made that—by the constraints both of Cognitive Command and of Width of Cosmological Role—the realist will probably fare badly in it. It is urged, however—and this is perhaps the most important point in the discussion, if it is correct—that the prospect of defeat for moral realism, so conceived, is not significant. What has really been prized by those philosophers who have wanted to be moral realists is not the possibility of moral truth as realistically conceived, but a certain kind of objectivity of moral judgement: the objectivity which would be ensured if there were an intrinsic dynamic towards convergence in moral thinking itself, and if the direction of this convergence were, by standards imminent to moral thought, towards improvement. The existence of such a dynamic would be quite consistent with moral discourse's being merely minimally truth-apt. But whether, or how much, of human moral thinking contains the seeds of such convergence is something that moral philosophy seems to be some considerable distance from resolving.

7   Moral Values, Projection and Secondary Qualities

I

A recently popular strategy among supporters of moral realism relies on a comparison between concepts of moral evaluation and the kind of quality—determinate qualities of colour, taste, texture, sound, and so on—which Locke characterised as *secondary* (in contrast to shape, extension, solidity, motion and number, which he of course dignified as *primary*).[1] Prima facie it is apt to seem an odd sort of strategy. Locke himself wrote:

> The ideas of primary qualities of bodies are resemblances of them, and their patterns do really exist in the bodies themselves, but the ideas produced in us by the secondary qualities have no resemblance of them at

---

1. See preeminently McDowell (1981) and (1985); Wiggins (1987c), esp. section 6, and (1987b), esp. section 5. There are glimmerings of the comparison in Putnam (1981), pp. 145–7. The notion of moral virtue as a perceptual capacity receives a sophisticated presentation in McDowell (1978).

The comparison is criticised in Blackburn (1985a). Other critical discussions include Dancy (1986) and McGinn (1983), chap. 8.

all. There is nothing like our ideas [of secondary qualities] existing in the bodies themselves.[2]

Locke's own conception of the distinction between primary and secondary qualities thus incorporated an 'error theory' of the latter: the thought that nothing really is as secondary quality experience represents it as being. So it would be natural to expect that it would be an *opponent* of moral realism who would find most use for substantial analogies between moral evaluatives and secondary quality predicates. Hume, indeed, in a famous passage[3] puts the (purported) analogy to just such use:

> [W]hen you pronounce any action or character to be vicious, you mean nothing, but that from the constitution of your nature you have a feeling or sentiment of blame from the contemplation of it. Vice and virtue, therefore, may be compared to sounds, colours, heat and cold, which according to modern philosophy, are not qualities in objects but perceptions in the mind.[4]

It is one thing, however, to think that Locke's distinction marks a correct and fundamental contrast between two types of predication which we make of material objects, but another to think that, properly drawn, it is a distinction which is inevitably disadvantageous to the secondary side, so to speak, that secondary quality ascription emerges not merely as, in some interesting sense, subjective but as somehow *tainted* with subjectivity, deficient in objectivity. Those who sight a potential defence of moral realism in the comparison with secondary qualities reject the deflationary aspect of Locke's own conception.[5]

I share the conviction that when the element of subjectivity is properly located, it poses no threat to the objectivity of secondary quality ascription or to the idea that an object's secondary qualities constitute

2. Locke (1969), p. 69.
3. Cf. McGinn (1983), p. 145.
4. Hume (1967), p. 469.
5. See McDowell (1985), sections 2 and 3.

material for cognition, in a proper sense of that term. And it would be surprising, at the least, if secondary qualities sustained *no* interesting analogies with evaluative predicates—the notion of an 'interesting analogy' is, after all, pretty elastic. The question is whether such analogies as there are indicate a cogent line of defence for moral realism; specifically, whether subjectivity enters our moral evaluations in a manner comparable to its role in our judgements of secondary qualities and thus, on the view of the latter which I accept, in a fashion benign for the prospect of a form of moral realism whose essential claims are the objectivity of moral judgement and its cognitive character. In this essay I argue that when sufficient care is taken with the distinction between primary and secondary qualities to allow the demands of the comparison between the latter and moral predicates to emerge in the clearest light, it also emerges that the comparison is flawed at the crucial point; indeed, that an argument for moral realism based on the comparison is no less misconceived than the corresponding argument *against* moral realism suggested by the passage from Hume.[6]

II

McDowell writes:

> A secondary quality is a property the ascription of which to an object is not adequately understood except as true, if it is true, in virtue of the object's disposition to present a certain sort of perceptual appearance: specifically, an appearance characterisable by using a word for the property itself to say how the object perceptually appears.[7]

6. Here I side with McGinn (1983), and disagree with Dancy who regards the primary/secondary distinction as itself altogether untrustworthy; see Dancy (1986), pp. 185–7. But I do not find McGinn's own criticisms of the comparison convincing; and I do not think that the six points of disanalogy outlined in Blackburn (1985a), pp. 13–15) decisively defeat the comparison either. See section II below.

7. McDowell (1985), p. 111.

And later:

> Secondary qualities are qualities not adequately conceivable except in terms of certain subjective states, and thus subjective themselves in a sense that characterisation defines.[8]

By contrast,

> a primary quality would be objective in the sense that what it is for something to have it can be adequately understood otherwise than in terms of dispositions to give rise to subjective states.[9]

These remarks, unsupplemented, provide a very lean counterpart of Locke's conception of the distinction. There is no mention of the idea of primary qualities as essential to any adequate conception of material body;[10] gone is the distinctively Lockean idea that, whereas our ideas of primary qualities may be thought of as faithful to material objects as they are in themselves, there is no sense in the idea of a resemblance between our idea of an object's colour and the object itself;[11] and unmentioned is what Bennett calls Locke's Causal Thesis—the idea that primary qualities provide a causal-explanatory base for secondary qualities.[12] But the remarks are, as McDowell notes,[13] faithful to an element in Locke's discussion—the idea of secondary qualities as powers or dispositions—and suggest, clearly enough as it may seem, what sort of analogy with evaluative predicates may be being proposed. Colours, tastes, sounds, smells and textures are proper objects of our five respective senses. If we think of secondary qualities in the broadly dispositional way canvassed by McDowell, then we have to think of the colour, for example, of an object as

8. *Ibid.,* p. 113.
9. *Ibid.*
10. See, e.g., Locke (1969), Essay II, 8, 9, p. 67.
11. *Ibid.,* II, 8, 15.
12. *Ibid.,* II, 8, 22; see Bennett (1971), chap. 4, section 22.
13. McDowell (1985), p. 112.

consisting in a disposition to induce a certain sort of visual experience which, *ceteris paribus,* constitutes a perception of that very quality. And some, including McDowell, who have wanted to defend—at least up to a point—an analogy between moral and secondary qualities, seem to have had it in mind to recommend precisely the transportation of this combination to the moral case: the claim is to be that our faculty of moral judgement may illuminatingly be thought of as a *perceptual* capacity with moral qualities as its proper objects. The moral quality of a situation is to be thought of, broadly, as a disposition to induce a certain sort of distinctive experience, the having of which will count, *ceteris paribus,* as the perception of that very quality.[14]

14. It is this combination of ideas which is a principal cause of Dancy's disquiet both with a dispositional account of secondary qualities and with the analogy. See Dancy (1986), pp. 174, 181 ff. He writes:

We may well wonder whether our experience really does represent objects to us as having these dispositions, and suppose instead that however dispositional our understanding of them may be, still our experience of them is non-dispositional. Can we take seriously the way in which colour appears to us, which seems to me at least to be stubbornly non-dispositional, if we insist that the right account of the 'distinctively phenomenal' nature which colour is represented as having is to be understood as its being (or existing in virtue of) a disposition to present a certain sort of appearance.

The worry is: If redness *is* a dispositional property, should not experience as of something red—an experience which *represents* an object as red—represent it (as, in Dancy's view, it does not) as possessing the relevant disposition? Well, not if the representational content of an experience is a function of the concepts which the subject is actually able to bring to bear upon it, and if it is possible to grasp the concept red without *realising* that it is a concept of a dispositional property. I find it plausible that properly describing the representational content of an experience does generate a substitutionally highly opaque context in that way—one opaque with respect to the substitution of analytical equivalents (which, incidentally, a dispositional construal of secondary qualities need not represent itself as supplying). But if it does not, Dancy's objection fails in any case. For then there is no objection to construing the representational content of an experience as of something red in accordance with the dispositional account of redness even if, like Dancy, the subject is reluctant to accept such a

It needs to be recognised that the resources of this general view of the semantics and epistemology of moral judgement are much more considerable than one might at first be tempted to think. In particular, I do not think that someone drawn to it need be at a loss for (at least the beginnings of) replies to any of the four most powerful-seeming objections that are typically levelled against it.[15] These concern, respectively, the supervenience of the moral quality of a situation upon its non-moral characteristics; the intrinsically reason-giving character of moral characteristics; one kind of unacceptable relativity which such a construal of moral characteristics is thought to impose; and the failure of the view to provide any space for certain things which strike us as evident possibilities in the case of moral judgement but have no counterpart in the case of secondary quality ascription—for instance, that particular dominant trends in moral evaluation may be morally mistaken, and that other cultures may disagree with us dramatically about the extension of moral predicates. I shall briefly indicate how, as it seems to me, these lines of criticism may perhaps be met—I claim no originality for some of what I shall say—before indicating a fifth criticism which, I think, the proposal can meet only by somewhat refashioning itself.

I shall not comment here on the general difficulty which Simon Blackburn has argued is posed for moral realism by the supervenience of moral upon non-moral qualities.[16] Our question is rather what, if any, difficulty specific to the defence of moral realism which feeds on the proposed analogy between moral and secondary qualities is presented by supervenience. It is of course true that the kind of super-

---

construal. Or better: any objection has to be an *independent* objection to the dispositional construal—it cannot simply rest on the subject's reluctance.

Dancy's worry is effectively criticised, on rather different grounds, by C. Hookway in his contribution to the same symposium. See Hookway (1986), esp. section III.

15. See Blackburn (1985a), pp. 13–15; McGinn (1983), pp. 150–5.

16. See Blackburn (1971) and (1985b); see also Blackburn (1984), pp. 182–7. Blackburn's argument is criticised in McFetridge (1985) and in Noonan (1987). See also Klagge (1987); Wright (1985b), pp. 315–18.

venience displayed by moral qualities is quite different from anything exhibited by secondary qualities.[17] Differences in colour are, as a matter of scientific fact, and perhaps must be, as a matter of metaphysical necessity, associated with underlying physical differences. But someone who believes that two situations deserve differing moral verdicts is *obliged to believe* that they possess certain non-moral differences too if that person is to qualify as morally competent, whereas the metaphysical error—if any—involved in believing that colour ascriptions can 'hang loose' from physical constitution need not impugn someone's competence to appraise colour. But why is this a difficulty? Well, the point about competence, further specified, is that one who returns differing moral evaluations of two situations is required, on pain of moral incompetence, not merely to believe that there are further non-moral differences between them, but to have some story to tell about what those differences are. And the differing evaluations can be justified only if this story is. Whereas if the dispositional-cum-perceptual conception of moral qualities were correct, it ought to be justification enough merely to find oneself differently morally affected by the two situations and with no reason to suppose that one is functioning abnormally in any relevant respect.

But this does not seem a convincing objection. The secondary quality proposal is (or ought to be) that we should think of moral qualities, like colours, and so on, as dispositions to induce certain sorts of perceptual effect in *appropriately receptive subjects*. That comparison, as far as it goes, provides no reason for thinking that every kind of constraint which operates on the notion of appropriate receptivity in the moral case will be mirrored by something in the case of secondary qualities. Accordingly, it is open to a proponent of the analogy to supplement the proposal by insisting on a difference: it is a criterion for subjects' being appropriately receptive in the moral case that they be disposed to record moral differences only where they believe that they have noticed non-moral ones; in the case of Lockean secondary qualities, by contrast, the account of what it is for a subject to be

17. As remarked in Blackburn (1985a), pp. 13–14.

appropriately receptive has no analogue of that and should proceed along other lines.

The second objection is well expressed by Blackburn:

> It is up to a subject whether he cares about any particular secondary property in any way. If morality consisted in the perception of qualities, there would be a theoretical space for a culture which perceived the properties perfectly, but paid no attention to them. But however it is precisely fixed, the practical nature of morality is clearly intrinsic to it, and there is not this theoretical space.[18]

This is apt to seem a powerful consideration. On reflection, though, it is perhaps a little *too* powerful. For what the point engages is not the specific idea of moral states of affairs as susceptible to a kind of perception but, quite generally, the idea of moral *belief*. Blackburn's thought would have been as plausible, in just the same kind of way, had it been:

> Believing that a certain state of affairs is one thing and caring about it is another. It is up to a subject whether he cares about any particular state of affairs which he believes to obtain. If morality consisted in the formation and possession of moral beliefs, there would be a theoretical space for a culture which substantially shared our moral beliefs, while failing to share our moral concerns. But however it is precisely fixed, the practical nature of morality is clearly intrinsic to it, and there is not this theoretical space.

There is, of course, a tradition of opposition to moral realism which does precisely dispute whether moral assertions constitute genuine statements, apt to be true or false, believed or disbelieved. I myself think that this is probably not a good direction—and certainly not the only direction—for the opposition to take.[19] To grant that notions of truth and falsity, and thereby belief and disbelief, can engage with

18. *Ibid.*, p. 15.
19. See Wright (1988b).

moral contents is no concession to moral realism at all; the question is what the notion of truth *comes to* in the moral case—and whether, in particular, it can carry the significance which moral realism requires. But however that may be, it should be clear that the original objection is simply question-begging. If there are moral states of affairs which may be believed, or even perceived, to obtain, then they will be, of their very nature, states of affairs to know of which is to acquire certain concerns and certain potential reasons for action. Moral perception, if there is such a thing, will precisely *be* perception of a cause for concern.[20]

The third objection—that the analogy with secondary qualities imposes an unwelcome moral relativism[21]—likewise does not depend essentially on the play with the idea of moral perception, but could be brought against any view which held that moral qualities should be construed dispositionally, in terms of their effects on our moral opinions. Simply, the objection runs, the effect which something is disposed to have on us will depend on, and may vary with, *our* condition no less than that of the object. So if some practice stops having a certain sort of moral effect on us—not because of any change in its manner, circumstances, or other effects but because *we* change—then a dispositional account of moral qualities has no option, according to the objection, but to construe that as a change in the moral status of the practice, even if our preferred description of the case would invoke the ideas of improved or deteriorated moral discrimination. But this, like the first objection, overlooks the fact that there will be, in any full dispositional account of moral qualities, constraints imposed on the *kind* of subject on which they are disposed to work their distinctive effects. It will be by their characteristic effects on 'appropriately receptive' subjects that moral qualities are dispositionally identified; and only, therefore, by reference to changes in the responses of *such* subjects that changes in moral status may be defined.

20. The thought is elaborated in McDowell (1978), esp. pp. 18–25.
21. See, e.g., Blackburn (1981), pp. 174–5, and (1985a), p. 14; cf. McGinn (1983), p. 150.

And, once again, it may well be a criterion for subjects being appropriately receptive—whether distinct subjects or the same subject at different times—that they do not differ in their moral evaluation of a practice or act unless holding differing beliefs about circumstances, manner, or other effects, and so on. Of course, a proponent of the dispositional view still has the task of saying *what* 'appropriate receptivity' is. But that's another matter.[22]

The fourth objection is that there's no sense to be made of the idea of our being in extensive error about which things are characterised by some particular secondary quality. But we do want to make space for the idea that moral error has been widespread in the past—concerning the status of slavery, for instance—and is still so in the present. Similarly, and for the same reason, no sense is to be made of the idea of widespread disagreement between cultures about the application of secondary qualities; the appearance of such disagreement would be regarded, rather, as ground, for example, for suspecting a mistranslation. Whereas extensive disagreements between

---

22. It is worth remarking that, contrary to Blackburn's and McGinn's suggestion (Blackburn (1981), pp. 174–5, and (1985a), p. 14; McGinn (1983), pp. 9–11), at least some secondary qualities—according to our ordinary understanding of them—would call for similar refinement in a dispositional construal of them. We do not, for instance, believe that, were we all to become colour blind, red and green things would change in colour, preferring to describe such a situation as one in which we should lose the capacity to make a distinction which is there anyway, whether we draw it or not. Here 'appropriately receptive' means something like: having powers of colour discrimination which human beings *actually* typically enjoy. And the occurrences of 'actually' in the subjunctive conditionals which we would formulate to specify explicitly the dispositions in which colour (putatively) consisted would function rigidly, securing reference to what is as a matter of fact the typical visual constitution of human beings. The point is made, in effect, in Hookway (1986), p. 194. The defence in Wiggins (1987b), pp. 206–7, of the sort of proposal with which we are concerned relies on an exactly analogous play with the idea of our *actual* moral propensities, both in response to the charge of implied relativism and in response to the fourth objection, mentioned above, about to be discussed. The resources afforded by 'actually' in the context of these concerns were originally pointed out in Davies and Humberstone (1980), pp. 22–5.

cultures on moral matters do occur—or so it is often thought—and would anyway be perfectly intelligible even if they did not. The differences are undeniable. But, once again, we can discern at least the shape of an explanation of them which would be consistent with a construal of moral qualities as, like secondary qualities, dispositions to induce certain sorts of (perceptual) effects. The differences will be seen as originating, once again, in the conditions for 'appropriate receptivity', and in disanalogies between them in the two kinds of case. If the function of my visual system is on a par with what is actually typical of human kind, then I count as appropriately receptive for the experience of colour. So there is bound to be a difficulty about the idea of our collectively falling into extensive error in our judgement of colour *provided* enough of us are involved to ensure that some at least are possessed of typical visual function, and the purported errors are sufficiently extensive to ensure that not all can be explained in the various ways in which we do explain the kind of illusions of colour which can afflict the normally sighted. And there is going to be just the same kind of difficulty about supposing another culture to have fallen into sufficiently extensive error in their judgements of colour, provided we have sufficient reason to think that they are employing concepts of colour which we also recognise.

In the moral case, by contrast, appropriate receptivity may differ from what suffices in the case of colour precisely by involving some explicit distance from what is typical of moral responses in our culture, or in another. Wiggins speaks of our 'actual *propensities*' (my italics) of moral judgement in order to mark exactly such a contrast.[23] In both cases, colour and moral value, what count are our *best* responses. But there is no reason to think that best performance may come, in the moral case, as effortlessly or as frequently as in the case of colour. Judgements which accord with our deepest moral propensities may substantially diverge from those which we are actually disposed to make. The objection simply passes over this contrast and the possibility that there may be ways of making it out which are not

23. See note 22 above.

forced, in the end, to gloss our deepest propensities for moral judgement as though they *keep track* of independently constituted moral
values (and so surrender the analogy with secondary qualities). What
is necessary is that the process of due moral deliberation and the
achievement of refinement of moral sensibility be made out to have its
own internal, self-contained and ultimately self-stabilising dynamic
founded in human nature.[24] The attempt to make out this idea may,
of course, founder. My point is only that there is evident conceptual
space within the broad constraints imposed by the secondary quality
analogy for the attempt.

III

Nevertheless I do not think that the strictly *perceptual* aspect of the
proposal is happy. Of course, it is harmless to think of value as 'perceived', if that means no more than: correctly judged. The extra,
which is not harmless, is the idea of moral judgement as possessing
a distinctive phenomenology, as encompassing a distinctive kind of
experience(s) or distinctive kinds of other psychological effect. How
should such effects be modelled? Since it is of the essence of valuing to
care, one way or another, it is tempting to think of them as emotional.
But such emotion seems to be a *consequence* of valuing certain things
rather than part of the process of coming to do so. The latter can be
and often is a dispassionate process. Whereas the analogy would
require that we think of the caring emotion as standing to the value in
the cognitive mode in which the experience of red stands to the
colour. Not only that, but it seems to me very moot whether there is

24. The development of the position in Wiggins (1987b), p. 203, and (1987d),
pp. 160–1, is compounded by his willingness to allow an element of cultural relativity
at the foundations of the process, as it were; to accept that the basic propensities
which constitute the dynamic may themselves be constituted not just by human nature
but by culture-dependent or otherwise variable factors. This residual relativism, not to
be defused by play with rigidification, is at risk, it seems to me, of falling to the fourth
objection. What can it make of the idea of transcultural moral disputes?

anyway any distinctive mode of *moral* emotional concern, identified purely phenomenologically and distinguishable from what we feel for other kinds of values. Virtue is satisfied when one is concerned for the right reasons about the right kinds of thing: it is not necessary also to feel a particular *timbre* of concern.

But there is, to my mind at least, a more basic point. If our experience of secondary qualities provides a model of anything, then it is of a notion of experience which is, up to a point at least, *raw*. It is true that there is in anyone's experience a delicate interplay between its manifest character and their concepts and understanding. It seems right to say that there is a difference between seeing the duck and rabbit aspects in Jastrow's 'duck-rabbit' which is not exhausted simply by the capacity to interpret it (publicly) in the two appropriately different ways, but is possible nonetheless only to a subject who has the conceptual resources which the two interpretations would call for. That is, there is an *experience* available here which depends on a subject's possession of certain concepts but is more than simply the exercise of those concepts. Likewise, if you overhear an exchange in a language with which you are just a little familiar though not enough to understand the exchange, there are likely to be sounds and audible structures which are salient to you and which would simply not have been part of the manifest content of the experience had the language been totally unfamiliar. The point is quite general. It is not merely what we are able to say or judge about it but the experience itself— what actually registers in consciousness—which depends, in some measure, on the concepts we bring to bear. The point remains: if our experience of secondary qualities is to be the model, then not *everything* in the manifest character of an experience can be seen as owed to concepts brought to bear. We explain a baby's starting at a sudden noise by thinking of him as subject to certain sorts of auditory phenomenological effect; but no concept ascription is involved.

What I doubt is whether we can find anything of sufficient rawness in the phenomenology of moral judgement to give the notion of 'moral experience' any serious work to do. The question is whether there are modes of experience which should properly count as moral but which would be possible for a normal human subject who possessed as yet no moral concepts. It is hardly a completely perspicuous question, but it is also hard to see what motive there could be for returning a positive answer. Very small children, to whom we should hesitate to ascribe any concept of humour, will laugh at grimaces and other forms of clowning, and may harmlessly be described as finding them funny. What would be comparable, preconceptual finding of moral value? Suppose such a child is distressed by the sight of a jockey whipping his horse. Should that count as a primitive sentiment of moral disapprobation? It should be obvious that the question is underdetermined. Perhaps the child is frightened by the thundering of the horse's hooves, or the jockey's mask, or feels himself threatened. What is necessary, if the sentiment is to count as moral, is that its cause be conceived *by the child* in a certain way, and that its causality be dependent on its being so conceived. It has to be the horse's presumed distress, conceived as such, and even perhaps some conception of the mercenary motives for its affliction, which causes the child's distress. So the suggestion is that there is no basis for describing an affective response as moral unless the subject gives evidence of the conceptual resources which would suffice to explain it as such. The question, however, is less whether that suggestion is an adequate reflection of the manner in which we are actually prepared to classify responses as moral or not, than whether anything essential to a sound moral psychology would be lost if it were.

These are sketchy remarks on a complex and subtle matter. But I think I may be excused their sketchiness if I am right to suppose that, odd as it may at first seem, we can indeed surrender the notion of moral experience—of any kind of distinctive affective phenomenology associated with moral judgement—without surrendering the insight, if there is one, which the comparison between moral and secondary qualities is supposed to involve. That insight is thought to consist in an explanation which, following the prototype of secondary qualities when their situation is properly understood, harmonises the subjectivity of moral judgement with moral realism. I shall argue that secondary qualities do indeed provide a prototype for such harmony, and may be seen to do so even when, somewhat artificially, our distinctive modes of response to their instances are construed not as the having of certain sorts of experiences but as the formation of certain sorts of appropriate belief. If this is right, then the alleged insight should be capable of surviving the construal of our moral responses as essentially—and as I should prefer—the formation of beliefs with moral content (*ergo*, beliefs whose formation is analytically tied to a disposition to certain sorts of practical concern).

IV

We can start with the widely accepted[25] and familiar[26] *basic equation*[27] for 'red':

> x is red ↔ for any S: if S were perceptually normal and were to encounter x in perceptually normal conditions, S would experience x as red.

25. For instance, in Peacocke (1983), p. 28; Evans (1980), p. 98; Sellars (1963), p. 142. Of course the wording varies slightly. (It is interesting, to anticipate the terms of my discussion below, that Sellars explains what he regards as the necessary truth of the basic equation by interpreting it in terms of *conduciveness*—see Sellars (1963), p. 147—thus missing, if I am right, the most distinctive feature of 'red' which reflecting on the basic equation may lead one to recognise.)

26. But, perhaps not quite so familiarly, flawed. A construal of the truth conditions of any type of statement, P, in terms of a conditional: if R, then S, always holds out a potential hostage to fortune—at least if the conditional has contrary-to-fact import—insofar as its accuracy will depend on whether realisation of R might somehow impinge on the state of affairs conferring truth (or falsity) on P. And this hostage is not redeemed in the present case. The reason is that our conception of colour allows the possibility that, for example, bringing about perceptually normal conditions—irradiating an object with the appropriate quality of light—may affect its colour. Aetiolated plants slowly resume normal production of chlorophyll when restored to daylight. Suppose they greened up almost instantaneously. Then the counterfactual 'If a perceptually normal S were to encounter one of these plants in perceptually normal conditions,

How would we need to modify this in order to produce something plausible when 'would believe x to be red' replaces 'would experience x as red'? Well, what might explain S's failure to believe that x is red despite experiencing it as red? A lack of the conceptual wherewithal to form beliefs about colour; or failure to be appropriately attentive to the experience of x as red; or failure to realise that the object of this experience is x; or, despite being perceptually normal, S might be prey to some ulterior cognitive dysfunction which prevented formation of the appropriate belief; or S might have some doubt about whether the conditions of observation and/or his/her own perceptual function were indeed normal, so about whether it was possible to rely on the experience of x as red—(or have some doubt, for that matter, about any of the immediately preceding conditions just added). So we need to consider something like:

> *Red*
> x is red ↔ for any S: if S knows which object x is, and knowingly observes it in plain view in normal perceptual conditions; and is fully attentive to this observation; and is perceptually normal and is prey to no other cognitive

---

he would experience it as green' would be true of the sickly white plant while it was in the dark.

Properly respecting this point would complicate the ensuing discussion but would *not* essentially affect its conclusions. What it shows is that the basic equation needs to be replaced by a *provisional biconditional*:

> For any S: if S were perceptually normal and x were presented to S
> under perceptually normal conditions, then (S would experience x as red
> if and only if x was red).

And the general form of distinction which, as I shall suggest, the contrast between primary and secondary qualities may exhibit can be drawn, *mutatis mutandis,* as effectively by consideration of provisional biconditionals as by consideration of basic equations. Accordingly, and for reasons of space, I have elected to proceed without engaging this complication.

27. The term is Mark Johnston's.

dysfunction; and is free of doubt about the satisfaction of any of these conditions—*then* if S forms a belief about x's colour, that belief will be that x is red.

This is plausible enough to be going on with. But how, when we find it plausible, are we understanding its two uses of the notion of normality? We have a choice. The idea of normal function in a particular system, for instance, is ambiguous between that of *proper* function for such a system and that of *typical* or *usual* function—function in a manner which is statistically normal within the relevant class of systems. Now, it is part of our concept of a human visual system's functioning properly—functioning as it ought—that it functions in a fashion conducive to the correct appraisal of colour. 'Normal perceptual conditions' may similarly be glossed as: conditions which are conducive to the visual appraisal of (inter alia) colour.[28] The first interpretation of normality is, accordingly, what I shall call the *conduciveness interpretation*. Under the conduciveness interpretation, *Red* does not merely hold true; it holds true a priori.

What of the second, broadly statistical interpretation of normality? It would, I think, subserve the correctness of *Red* if we glossed the notion of normal perceptual function as: perceptual function of a kind which is actually typical of human beings.[29] But it will not do so to gloss 'normal perceptual circumstances'. The conditions which actually usually prevail during winter in Spitzbergen, for instance, or in a normal photographic darkroom, are not suited for colour appraisal. A good description of conditions which are, optimally, so suited would be: conditions of illumination like those which actually typically obtain at noon on a cloudy summer's day out of doors and out of shadow. Even here 'typically' is required because such conditions

---

28. Cf. note 25 above.

29. Where 'actually' is understood as securing rigidity, so preempting the implication that a change in the typical function of our visual systems—as a result of disease, perhaps—would command, via *Red,* a change in the extension of 'Red'. Cf. note 22 above.

---

are sometimes disturbed by solar eclipses, nuclear explosions, dust storms and volcanic discharges. So there is still an element of statisticality. But notice: when both uses of the notion of normality are so interpreted, in broadly statistical terms, *Red* continues not merely to hold true but to hold true a priori. For our knowledge that typical visual functioning and conditions of illumination like those I just broadly statistically characterised are conducive for the appraisal of colour is not a posteriori knowledge. This consideration will be crucial in what follows.

Almost everyone who writes on the bearing of the primary/secondary distinction on moral evaluation contrasts colour with shape. With shape, as with colour, there is a plausible form of basic equation; for instance,

> x is square ↔ for any S: if S is perceptually normal and
> encounters x in perceptually normal conditions, S will
> experience x as square.

This, though, is much less perspicuous than the original basic equation for 'red'. What is it to experience x as square? If it involves that x should *look square,* that is, present a square appearance,[30] then— even if normality is interpreted as conduciveness—the biconditional is untrue. For a square surface may, depending on its size and relative orientation, look trapezoid, for instance, to a particular subject, even though their visual system is functioning in every respect conducive to the competent registration of shape and the conditions of observation are perfectly conducive to such proper function. Not only that. If a square surface is characterised as one enclosing exactly four equal angles whose four sides are exactly equal in length, then squareness simply isn't visually *salient:* there is, actually, no such thing as a visual system's functioning in a fashion conducive to the competent registration of squareness. It will be, experientially, all the same to the subject whether the perceived object is square or merely approximately so.

30. Contrast with this: look *as if it is* square; or: look as a square object would look.

Bearing these nuisances in mind, what form should a plausible doxastic generalisation of the basic equation take? Something close to the following would seem to be appropriate:

> *Approximately Square*
> x is approximately square ↔ for any S: if S knows which object x is, and knowingly observes it in plain view from a sufficient variety of positions in normal perceptual conditions, and is fully attentive to these observations, and is perceptually normal and is prey to no other cognitive dysfunction, and is free of doubt about the satisfaction of any of these conditions—*then* if S forms a belief about x's shape, that belief will be that x is approximately square.

This is not beyond objection even if normality is interpreted as conduciveness.[31] But it does not seem unlikely that it could be tightened so as to result in something a priori true, with normality so understood.

Part of the reason why that does not seem unlikely is because conditions which are *conducive* for the (visual) appraisal of shape are going to have to be conditions under which the shape of an object is *stable* through the positional reorientations which a proper judgement about its shape will involve. And it is clear that any substantial elaboration of *Approximately Square*—an elaboration which tries to say what, substantially, conduciveness, of subjects and circumstances, here consists in—has somehow to retain the force of this stability proviso on its right-hand side if it is to retain plausibility. But it seems extremely doubtful whether that can be done by any kind of statistical construal of the notion of normal perceptual conditions. Some objects, after all, just do very often vary in (approximate) shape over short intervals, irrespective of what else is true of the conditions in which, if they are, they are being observed. So a substantial elaboration of the right-hand side of *Approximately Square* is going to have

31. S might, for example, lacking the concept *square*, but possessing that of *quadrilateral*, form the belief that x is a quadrilateral.

to add, it seems, some condition stipulating x's (relative) stability in shape through the period of S's observations.

That consideration establishes a crucial disanalogy with colour. It may or may not be possible so to refine *Approximately Square* that it expresses something a priori true and at the same time gives a sub-stantial account—in contrast to mere play with the idea of conducive-ness—of what it takes for a subject's belief to 'track' (approximate) shape. But even if this can be done, the resulting biconditional will lack a feature possessed by *Red*. Each biconditional takes the form

> P ↔ for any S: S operates under conditions C → (S forms a
> germane belief → that belief is that P).

In the case of *Red*, interpreted along the substantial, partly statistical lines which I began to sketch, satisfaction of the relevant conditions C is something which is *logically independent of any truths concerning the application of colour concepts* (and could indeed—a stronger point—be appraised, in a particular case, by someone whose vision was monochromatic and who possessed no colour concepts at all). That fact, coupled with the apriority of *Red,* so interpreted, puts us in position to make a proposal about 'red' which it is not open to us to make about 'approximately square'. The proposal is that the beliefs, if any, which we (would) have formed, or will or would form, under the relevant C-conditions, *serve to determine the extension* of the concept red. And this claim is to be understood by contrast with the thought that such beliefs *keep track* of an extension which is inde-pendently determined. It is open to us to make this proposal because *Red* retains its apriority when substantially, partly statistically inter-preted and because there is no candidate account in the offing of what *else* might determine the extension of 'red' if our best—approximately C-conditioned—beliefs do not do so. But it would not be possible to make this proposal if, among the relevant C-conditions, there were some whose satisfaction depended on the extension of 'red' as deter-mined independently. And it is an analogue of just that characteristic which the needed proviso about stability in shape would introduce into an appropriately substantial elucidation of *Approximately Square,* even if the result were still an a priori truth.

There is a further point. The apriority of the relevant biconditional is, of course, essential to the idea that our best beliefs determine the extension of the truth predicate among relevant classes of statements. For if a biconditional dependence between two classes of judgement is a posteriori, we obviously have no option but to think of the circumstances which respectively determine whether members of each class are true as distinct. So we can drive the sketched disanalogy home by reflecting that, even with a proviso about stability in shape added, there is little or no prospect—to put the point cautiously—of a substantial elucidation of *Approximately Square* which is also an a priori truth. To see this, reflect that 'x is approximately square' also sustains a different kind of biconditional, namely,

> x is approximately square ↔ if the four sides and four
> interior angles of x were to be correctly measured, and no
> change were to take place in the shape or size of x during
> the process, then the sides would be determined to be
> approximately equal in length, and the angles would be
> determined to be approximate right angles.

This biconditional—call it the *canonical biconditional*—holds true a priori. So a substantial elucidation of *Approximately Square,* even if it incorporates a condition about stability in shape, can hold true a priori only if the result of biconditionally linking its right-hand side with the right-hand side of the canonical biconditional likewise holds true a priori. Now, the right-hand side of such a substantial elucidation is going to be something on the model of:

> For any S: if S knows which object x is, and knowingly
> observes it in plain view from a sufficient variety of
> positions in normal [to be substantially, perhaps partly
> statistically, elucidated] perceptual conditions, and is fully
> attentive to these observations, throughout which x is

stable in shape; and if S is perceptually normal [to be substantially elucidated] and is prey to no other cognitive dysfunction, and is free of doubt about the satisfaction of any of these conditions—*then* if S forms a belief about x's shape, that belief will be that x is approximately square.

But it is hard to see how the biconditional connection of anything along these lines with the right-hand side of the canonical biconditional could result in an a priori truth. For, bluntly, it is not a priori true, but merely a deep fact of experience, that our (best) judgements of approximate shape, made on the basis of predominantly visual observations, usually 'pan out' when appraised in accordance with more refined operational techniques, where such are appropriate, of the kind the canonical biconditional illustrates. It is not a priori that the world in which we actually live allows reliable perceptual appraisal of approximate shape—is not, for example, a world in which the paths travelled by photons are subject to grossly distorting forces.

What conclusions do I mean these reflections to suggest? Principally, that the most significant form of distinction for our purposes which is illustrated by primary and secondary qualities is as follows. The extension of the truth predicate among statements which ascribe primary qualities is determined not by our best opinions but independently of them; this is a consequence of the consideration that biconditionals of the kind illustrated, whose left-hand sides ascribe primary qualities and whose right-hand sides attempt to articulate, in substantial terms, what it takes in order for there to be an assurance that a subject's opinion about the left-hand side will be correct, (i) are likely to need conditions on the pedigree of that opinion whose satisfaction presupposes facts about the extension of the very (determinable) primary quality in question, and (ii) are—so long as they really do say what the conditions in question should be, and do not merely stipulate that they have to be 'conducive'—at best a posteriori truths. By contrast, our best opinions about the extension of the truth predicate among ascriptions of secondary qualities *are* what most fundamentally determine that extension. And this is a consequence of the considerations (i) that appropriate a priori true biconditionals can be constructed whose descriptions of what constitutes an appropriate pedigree for the opinions in question is both substantial and such that its satisfaction is independent of the extension of the secondary quality in question; and (ii) that no rival accounts are available of what *other* factors might determine the extensions of such qualities, of which the apriority of such biconditionals is a derivable consequence—there is, in other words, no explaining away the credentials of our best opinions about the extension of a secondary quality to play an extension-determining role.[32]

This 'conclusion' really only has the status of a hypothesis. For we have considered no instances of the primary/secondary distinction besides shape and colour (though that is no sin in the context of our present concerns, since these examples have dominated the literature in which the suggestion of an analogy between value and secondary qualities has been mooted and discussed) and, even here, there are complications and details with which I have no space to attempt to engage. But I believe enough may have been said to give the hypothesis

---

32. Perhaps it is superfluous to remark that no overdetermination would be introduced by endorsing this conception of the secondary alongside the idea that being red, for example, is a matter of physical constitution; for our best opinions about what is red simultaneously determine what—if any—type of determinate physical constitution red things share.

Incidentally I do not, in offering this account of the primary/secondary distinction as the most significant for our purposes, mean to turn my back on the pioneering exegesis in Bennett (1965) and (1971), chap. 4. Bennett brings out that an affliction corresponding to a primary quality as colour-blindness stands to colour would so compromise the operations of a sufferer as to open to question whether they should be thought of as perceiving the material world at all (the example he discusses is size, but see the observations on *number* in Craig (1975), pp. 22 ff)—in effect, that, in contrast with colour-blindness, there is no such thing as being insensitive to the distinctions within some determinable primary quality but otherwise perceptually competent. I am inclined to accept that there is a correct and important distinction to be drawn along these lines—though I daresay Bennett would demur at the formulation just given. It is a nice question, which I cannot pursue here, what the relation is between the distinction proposed by Bennett and that offered in the text.

some plausibility. If it is right, then we have the prospect of a satisfying account of what is subjective and what is objective in secondary quality ascription, and of how the element of subjectivity is compatible with objectivity. Secondary quality ascription is subjective because it is, ultimately, *we human beings,* equipped with the capacity for the range of experiences which we actually have, who, by our responses under optimum conditions, determine which such ascriptions are true. It is objective because facts about which such ascriptions *are* true inherit exactly the 'hardness', or 'bruteness', possessed by facts about what we believe and facts about the character—whether or not optimum—of the conditions under which our beliefs are formed. Of course, this will not satisfy a philosopher who independently has worries about the objectivity of the psychological. But ascriptions of colour, for instance, can—if *Red* indeed be interpreted substantially so as to hold a priori—at least inherit whatever objectivity does belong to the psychological and to the other non-psychological conditions that feature on the right-hand side of *Red.*

There is every prospect of other exemplifications of this form of distinction. I believe that the proper construal of first-person authority for intentional and sensational states, for instance, may well prove to be that they are, in effect, 'secondary': that subjects' best judgements fix the extension of the truth predicate among ascriptions of belief, desire and feeling to them.[33] The question is, do ascriptions of moral quality provide another illustration?

V

What would a corresponding biconditional for a particular moral judgement look like? Suppose P is 'That remark of Jones' was culpably insensitive'. Then an (unavoidably cumbersome) first-shot would be

---

33. So the principal epistemological error of the Cartesian philosophy of mind would be that it mistakes the psychological subject's extension-determining role for a kind of superlatively sure detection.

Moral
P ↔ for any S: if S scrutinises the motives, consequences
and, for Jones, foreseeable consequences in the context of
the remark; and does this in a fashion which involves no
error concerning non-moral fact or logic, and embraces all
morally relevant considerations; and if S gives all this the
fullest attention, and so is victim to no error or oversight
concerning any relevant aspect of his/her deliberation; and
if S is a morally suitable subject—accepts the right moral
principles, or has the right moral intuitions or sentiments,
or whatever; and if S has no doubt about the satisfaction
in any of these conditions, *then* if S forms a moral
evaluation of Jones' remark,[34] that evaluation will be
that P.

The clumsiness of *Moral* is due partly to the fact that what is at stake
is a judgement about a particular action, and partly to the need to
ensure that S keeps track of all germane non-moral matters. But it is
not, perhaps, so unwieldy that we cannot fix ideas. First, it is, plausibly, a good candidate for (refinement into) an a priori truth. Second,
its C-conditions are not, as they stand, wholly unsubstantially specified. We are told, for instance, that a proper appraisal of Jones'
remark will have to involve scrutiny of its motives and foreseeable
effects, and the bringing to bear of appropriate moral principles or
sentiments. However, it is by no means clear how a substantial
account should proceed of S's 'moral suitability'—an account which
distances itself from 'whatever it takes to form correct moral opinion', and tries to say substantially what it does take. Thus, third and
crucial, the evident prima facie analogy is not with *Red* but with *Approximately Square,* when amended to include a condition of stability

---

34. Here it is tempting to think that the other conditions ensure that S *will* form
such an evaluation, since they stipulate that he/she possesses the appropriate concepts
and concerns. However that may be, it seemed better to conserve the pattern illustrated by *Red* and *Approximately Square.*

in shape. So amended, the point was, the satisfaction of the C-conditions in *Approximately Square* was not independent of the extension of shape concepts. In like fashion, the satisfaction of the C-conditions in *Moral* is not independent of the extension of moral concepts—S's moral suitability, in particular, is itself, presumably, a matter for moral judgement.

The matter needs fuller examination, but here I can only record the belief that the last will be a feature of any plausible such biconditional for the moral case—certainly of any which plausibly holds a priori. And if that is right, then here is where the analogy between moral and secondary qualities most fundamentally breaks down: proper pedigree for visual appraisals of colour is a matter of meeting conditions whose satisfaction in a particular case does not directly depend on what the extension of colour predicates is; proper pedigree for moral judgements, by contrast, is a matter of meeting conditions the satisfaction of some of which is, irreducibly, a moral question.

Two things follow if *Moral* is, in the relevant respect, typical of the best that can be done. First, moral qualities are not like secondary qualities in the crucial respect: the extension of the truth predicate among ascriptions of moral quality may not be thought of as determined by our best beliefs—or, at least, the case for thinking otherwise would have to be a different one.[35] The reason, as with judgements of approximate shape, is because whether such a belief is *best* depends on antecedent truths concerning shape/moral status. Second, and for that reason, judgements of moral quality cannot *inherit* objectivity in the way in which, as we saw, judgements of secondary quality can. They cannot do so because the inheritance can only be from the psychological and from the other kinds of C-condition in a relevant biconditional. And, in the moral case, some of the other C-conditions will themselves be moral. So the mix of subjectivity and objectivity is simply not as in the case of secondary qualities. The comparison is misconceived, and can only encourage a misconceived confidence in the objectivity of morals.

35. This is not a rhetorical qualification. See note 37 below.

VI

We should not conclude that any such confidence is misconceived. Of course the foregoing considerations, as far as they go, should be welcome to those who favour a projective view of moral judgement, as well as those who, like the late John Mackie, view moral discourse as incorporating an error. But the error would not be that the phenomenology of moral discourse erroneously contrives to represent moral quality as if it were 'out there'—whether or not that is true—but that a correct analysis of the *ideal epistemology* of moral judgement, as disclosed in a full refinement of something like *Moral*, will, precisely, represent moral qualities *as if they were primary*—which, I believe, error theorists, projectivists and objectivists who argue for an analogy with secondary qualities are correct in holding that they cannot be.[36] Projectivists, for their part, can be expected to take satisfaction from the thought that the presence of irreducibly moral conditions in any plausible account of the pedigree of best moral judgement is just what you would expect if such 'judgements' were no more than dignifications of non-cognitive sentiment and the notion of cognitive pedigree was here, at bottom, a sham. But either of these responses would be a premature reaction, it seems to me, to our findings.

If the principal lesson is that the kind of objectivity possessed by ascriptions of secondary qualities cannot be secured for ascriptions of moral quality by the same route, and if—as I accept—there is no realist capital to be made from a comparison with primary qualities

---

36. For two basic reasons. First, how an object is in respect of its primary qualities essentially has effects of other kinds, both on cognitive subjects and on objects of other sorts, than being cognised to be so. But moral qualities, for all but those who would propose naturalistic reductions of them, lack this diversity of interactive role. Second, the epistemology of primary qualities *is* interactive; precisely because their application is determined independently of our best opinions, there is a story to tell about what fits us to detect their application—what it is about them and us which makes it possible, when it is possible, for fact and opinion to coincide. And again, failing some naturalistic reduction, we have, I think, no inkling of how such a story concerning our appraisal of moral value might run.

either, an argument against moral realism ensues only if objectivity would demand the aptness of one comparison or the other. But the *self-containment* of moral epistemology—the circumstance that judging that a moral judgement has a proper pedigree will involve moral judgement—has at least a prima facie analogue in mathematical judgement[37]—something whose fundamentally anthropocentric character, if that is the right sort of view of it to take, ought to be consistent with its enjoyment of a fairly robust species of objectivity. So that may yet be the more illuminating tradition of comparison to explore—if a comparison is wanted at all.[38]

My thanks to Simon Blackburn, Bob Hale and Michael Smith for helpful advice. This essay, even though it is critical of the principal positive suggestion about the construal of moral judgements which he then wanted to make, owes much to Mark Johnston's graduate classes on ethics at Princeton in spring 1986.

37. The right-hand-side conditions on S in a basic equation for '$17 \times 32 = 544$' would have, for instance, to involve reference to S's performance of an appropriate error-free calculation.

38. Locke himself participates in the tradition—see, for example, Locke (1969), essay III, 11, 16 (omitted in the Selby-Bigge edition). But, as always, the crucial question concerns in what precise respects the comparison is to be entertained. There is a debate in the literature about whether mathematics passes the 'best explanation' test of objectivity—whether reference to mathematical facts needs to feature in the best explanation of our mathematical beliefs—in a fashion which may illuminate the case for moral judgement. See Williams (1985), chap. 8; Wiggins (1987d), section 7; review of Williams in McDowell (1986), section 3. The point of my suggestion, however, is to advert not to that debate but to the question whether there is a case, quite different from what is available in the case of secondary qualities, for holding that our best mathematical judgements determine, rather than reflect, the extension of the truth predicate among mathematical propositions. This conception, and its opposition to the idea of a determinate mathematical reality constituted independently of our best cognitive efforts—the essence of Platonism—is at the heart of the intuitionists' philosophy of mathematics, underlying their rejection both of the actual infinite and of any proof-transcendent notion of mathematical truth. The matter is pursued in detail in Divers and Miller (1999). The idea that moral truth is similarly *constructive* is as attractive as any secular conception of morality; but the question how best it might be substantiated is very open.

8

Truth in Ethics

The tradition of anti-realist thought about ethics—manifest in the desire to make some sort of disadvantageous comparison, in point of its objectivity or the reality of the states of affairs with which it deals, between moral discourse and, say, the discourses of mathematics and physical science—is no doubt as old as moral philosophy itself. In modern times the anti-realist tendency has typically cast itself as a denial that moral statements are *true*. And this denial has in turn taken two quite different shapes. Some, like John Mackie, have been willing to grant that moral discourse has all the semantical features necessary to aim at truth—that it trades in genuine assertions, apt to be true or false as literally construed—but that it sweepingly and systematically fails in that aim.[1] It does so because the truth of its statements would call for items of a metaphysically outlandish sort—queer, intrinsically reason-giving properties, for which our best science can find no explanatory use and which seem to promise no hope of reduction to the properties it does use. But this view contrasts sharply

---

1. Mackie (1977).

with an idea of Hume, befriended by A. J. Ayer and R. M. Hare and more recently developed by Simon Blackburn and Alan Gibbard, that although moral discourse wears a surface of assertoric content, its *deep* syntax is different—that it provides a medium not for the depiction of facts but rather for the expression of *attitudes*.[2] According to this expressivist form of moral anti-realism, both moral realism and its error-theoretic opposition are guilty of a mistake comparable to the assumption of a truth condition for an indicative sentence which is actually being used to express a rule, or an order.

That these tendencies have had distinguished adherents and are of long standing ought not to blind us to how unlikely it is that either can serve a satisfactory moral philosophy. The Mackie view allows that a moral thinker quests for truth, and uses a discourse which, at least as far as its semantics is concerned, is fitted to that project. But the world lets the moral thinker down; there are no real moral properties out there, no moral facts. The great discomfort with such a view is that, unless more is said, it simply relegates moral discourse to bad faith. Whatever we may once have thought, as soon as philosophy has taught us that the world is unsuited to confer truth on any of our claims about what is right, or wrong, or obligatory, and so on, the reasonable response ought surely to be to forgo making any such claims. That wouldn't be to forgo the right to any form of moral sentiment, I suppose. But it would, apparently, be to forgo any conception of a *proper basis* for such sentiment—to forgo the point of reasoned appreciation and debate about what is moral, and of criticism of others' opinions about it. Such consequences are surely calamitous. If it is of the essence of moral judgement to aim at the truth, and if philosophy teaches us that there is no moral truth to hit, how are we supposed to take ourselves seriously in thinking the way

2. The *loci classici* of modern ethical expressivism are of course the famous 'Critique of Ethics and Theology' offered in chapter 6 of Ayer (1936); and Hare (1952). An invaluable précis of Hare's current views is provided by his 'Universal Prescriptivism', chapter 40 of Singer (1991). Chapter 6, 'Evaluations, Projections and Quasi-realism', of Blackburn (1984) remains the best introduction to his view; Alan Gibbard's ideas are developed systematically in Gibbard (1990).

we do about any issue which we regard as of major moral importance? How can opinions which cool philosophical reflection teaches are no better than superstition be rationally permitted to constrain one's actions in the way that moral opinions distinctively do?

One form of response to this kind of difficulty which has found favour with error theorists generally is to seek to disclose some other purpose for the discourse in question, some norm of appraisal *besides* truth, at which its statements can be seen as aimed and which they can satisfy. Hartry Field's nominalist play with the idea of *conservativeness* in pure mathematics precisely represents an attempt at such a strategy.[3] In Field's view, pure mathematical statements are typically literally false—since their truth would call for metaphysically outlandish objects of various kinds—but we may rationally endorse them nevertheless because their falsity does not compromise their *inferential utility:* when adjoined to metaphysically pukka, non-outlandish statements of whatever sort, they allow for the derivation only of consequences that independently follow from those statements (which makes them harmless) and typically greatly facilitate the construction of such derivations (which makes them useful).

But this strategy, transposed to the moral case, would invite what seems to me a very good question: If, among the welter of falsehoods which we enunciate in moral discourse, there is a good distinction to be drawn between those which are acceptable in the light of some such subsidiary norm and those which are not—a distinction which actually informs ordinary discussion and criticism of moral claims—then why insist on construing *truth* for moral discourse in terms which motivate a charge of global error, rather than explicate it in terms of the satisfaction of the putative subsidiary norm, whatever it is? The question may have a good answer. The error theorist may be able to argue that the superstition that he finds in ordinary moral thought goes too deep to permit any construction of moral truth which avoids it to be acceptable as an account of *moral* truth. But I do not know of promising argument in that direction.

3. Field (1980) and (1989).

The prospects for a satisfying moral expressivism seem to me to be equally doubtful. Moral discourse is *disciplined* to a very great degree. Acceptable moral opinion is not just a matter of what feels comfortable, but has to survive appraisal by quite refined and complicated standards. Moral argument can be difficult and its conclusions unobvious. But to whatever extent such generally acknowledged underlying standards inform the appraisal of particular moral judgements and argument, to that extent the claim that moral discourse is not genuinely assertoric but serves merely as a medium for the expression of attitude will seem unmotivated in contradistinction to the idea that the truth predicate which applies within it is some sort of construct out of the relevant species of discipline. And the force of this complaint is greatly enhanced, so it seems to me—though I do not pretend to a command of all the most recent expressivist manoeuvres—by the fact that we do not seem yet to have been provided with any clear and workable idea of how to construe discourses which exhibit all the overt syntactic trappings of assertion—negation, the conditional construction, embedding within propositional attitudes, hypothesis and inference and so on—in such a way that the contents involved are not assertoric but are presented with illocutionary force of quite a different kind, apt to the expression of attitude.

It's worth briefly illustrating this with reference to a well-known proposal of Simon Blackburn's.[4] Consider the following sample argument:

> *Premise* 1: Stealing is wrong.
> *Premise* 2: If stealing is wrong, conniving at stealing is wrong.
> ∴ *Conclusion:* Conniving at stealing is wrong.

This is a moral modus ponens—a very simple, valid piece of moral reasoning. What account can the expressivist offer of its validity? Well, if moral statements are not strictly speaking assertions, then the major premise 2 cannot be an assertion either—you cannot make an

---

4. See Blackburn (1984), chap. 6.

assertion by yoking non-assertoric clauses together with a binary con-
nective; indeed, the ordinary conditional cannot be so much as gram-
matically applied to an antecedent that is not assertoric. So what is
the logical form of premise 2? All the expressivist can offer, it seems, is
that it is the expression of a complex attitude—a *conditional* attitude:
roughly, to affirm 2 is to endorse taking a negative moral attitude
towards conniving at stealing if a negative moral attitude is taken
towards stealing itself.

Now the striking effect of this—essentially Blackburn's—construal
of the content of the two premises is that there will be at the worst a
moral failing on the part of one who accepts them but fails to possess
the attitude which would be expressed by an endorsement of the conclusion. If I disapprove of stealing, and applaud disapproval of conniving on the part of anyone who disapproves of stealing, yet do not
myself disapprove of conniving, then I merely fail to have an attitude
of which, were I to have it, I would, in the circumstances, approve. I
fail to live up to my values, if you like. That is a lapse; but it is not the
grotesque lapse of rationality that ought to be involved in a failure to
accept the stated conclusion on the part of one who accepts the premises 1 and 2. If the expressivist doesn't have the resources to find the
more grotesque, rational failing, that's a sure sign there's something
wrong with the account.

Expressivists, including Blackburn, have had other proposals to
make about this particular type of difficulty, of course. But one
inclined to an intuitive anti-realism about morals—to the kind of disadvantageous comparison that I mentioned—ought to worry about a
direction of development of his basic intuition which holds out so
substantial a hostage to syntactico-reconstructive fortune. And if
expressivism grinds to a stop on this type of difficulty, can it really be
that only error theory—the classification of morality as superstition—
can provide a vehicle for the anti-realist?

That will certainly be the situation if to concede truth to moral
statements is to concede realism. In that case the only anti-realist
options must involve the denial of truth, either because moral statements are not so much as truth-apt or because, though truth-apt, they

are largely false. But what we want, of course, is a way of casting the anti-realist intuition which is consistent with the integrity of moral discourse and argument, and which allows us take a moral point of view with a clean intellectual conscience. Conversely, it doesn't seem as though the failings of error theory and expressivism should count as establishing realism by elimination. So there had better be another shape for ethical anti-realism to take. But what shape?

II

Here is one proposal. We need to win through to a conception of truth which allows us to grant truth-aptitude, and indeed truth, to responsible judgements within a given discourse without thereby conceding a realist view of it. Such a view will hold that to ascribe truth to a statement need not be to ascribe a property of intrinsic metaphysical *gravitas,* that any sentence is a candidate for truth which is possessed of assertoric content, and that possession of assertoric content is essentially a matter of meeting certain syntactic and disciplinary constraints—essentially, sentences are assertoric which are capable of significant embedding within constructions such as negation, the conditional, and in contexts of propositional attitude, and whose use is subject to acknowledged standards of warrant. When such standards are satisfied that will then suffice, other things being equal, defeasibly to justify the claim that the sentence in question is true.

Now there is, of course, on the market a long-standing conception of truth which accomplishes all this—so-called *deflationary* conception, according to which 'true' may indeed significantly be predicated of all sentences in the catchment just outlined, without heavyweight metaphysical commitment, precisely because the word does not express a real property at all but is only a device of *endorsement*—a device we need only because we sometimes want to endorse a statement given by a noun phrase, like 'Riemann's Hypothesis' or 'what he just said', which does not specify its content, or because we want to endorse whole batches of statements at once ('Most of what he said is true'). But the deflationary conception will not serve our present purpose. I have argued elsewhere[5] that to accept that a truth predicate can be defined upon any discourse which counts as assertoric in the sense we are concerned with, and that any such predicate must be governed by the Disquotational Scheme:

'p' is true if and only if p

enforces the recognition (i) that the word will record a norm governing assertion and belief-formation which is distinct from assertibility—that is, warrant by whatever standards inform the discourse in question—and (ii) that its compliance or non-compliance with *this* norm can hardly fail to be reckoned to be a substantial property of a statement. I won't rehearse the considerations that drive that conclusion now. What I want to dwell on for a minute is how it might be possible for the anti-realist to grant that moral discourse may be truth-apt, and to allow—as the error theorist cannot—that ordinary good grounds for a particular moral opinion are indeed grounds for taking it to be true, while retaining room for conceiving of truth as a substantial property and so avoiding deflationism.

Consider a parallel with the concept of identity. In one sense the notion of identity is invariant as we consider different ranges of individuals. Its invariance is sustained by uniform inferential links, grounded in the twin platitudes that everything is self-identical and that identicals share all their properties. Nevertheless, what *constitutes* identity is subject to considerable variation as we vary the kind of objects with which we are concerned. Thus the identity of material objects is arguably constituted by spatio-temporal continuity; identity and distinctness among numbers, on the other hand, according to Frege's famous account, are dictated by relations of one–one correspondence among associated concepts; the shapes of plane figures are identified and distinguished by relations of geometrical similarity among them; identity among directions of lines is constituted by

5. See *Truth and Objectivity*, chap. 1, section III.

relations of parallelism between lines; and it is notoriously elusive what constitutes identity for persons, though considerations of bodily and psychological continuity call the shots.

The notion of 'constitution' here invoked could no doubt be usefully clarified, but I see no reason to question the authenticity of the general idea that the instantiation of a certain concept may be constituted in different ways, depending on the kind of instantiators concerned. So: identity is one concept, but what constitutes the identity of a with b may vary, depending on the type of individual a and b are. Evidently there is space for a corresponding contention about truth. There need be no single, discourse-invariant thing in which truth consists. Depending on the type of statement with which we are concerned, the constitution of truth may sometimes reside in factors congenial to an intuitive realism, sometimes not.

I should emphasise, lest there be any misunderstanding, that the pluralism I am canvassing would not involve the idea that 'true' is ambiguous, any more than a corresponding conclusion is invited about 'is identical to'. An ambiguous term typically needs a variety of explanations, each determining a different extension for it. But if we can make out the parallel with identity, we will succeed in disclosing a basic set of principles—corresponding to the reflexivity and unrestricted congruence of identity—which will govern the concept of truth in all areas of discourse. These principles will enshrine all that can be said in general about the explanation of the word, and to that extent its meaning will be uniform. Moreover, one such principle will certainly be the Disquotational Scheme, which will ensure that any pair of predicates each of which qualifies as a truth predicate for a given discourse will have to coincide in extension. 'True', therefore, cannot be ambiguous as are 'stage', 'still' and 'rush'.

What might be the principles which such a view of truth could call upon to play the analogous role to reflexivity and unrestricted congruence in the case of identity? Well, one such will certainly be the Disquotational Scheme, on which traditional deflationism more or less exclusively focuses. But lurking behind the Disquotational Scheme is the more fundamental thesis that to assert is to present as true. Other relevant principles would be:

That to every truth-apt content corresponds a truth-apt negation;
That a content is true just in case it corresponds to the facts, depicts
  things as they are, and so on;
That truth and justification are distinct;
That truth is absolute—there is no being more or less true;
That truth is stable—if a content is ever true, it always is.

Arguable further additions would concern the connections between truth and transformations of tense and other indexicals, and principles concerning other connectives besides negation. The controlling thought remains that to be a truth predicate is merely to satisfy a set of very general, very intuitive a priori laws—in effect, the platitudes noted and their kin.

Investigation discloses that any discourse which is assertoric in the sense we are concerned with—a discourse meeting the basic disciplinary and syntactic constraints outlined—will allow the definition upon it of a predicate which satisfies all these platitudes about truth.[6] Since, according to the view proposed, there is no more to an expression's being a truth predicate than its satisfaction of those platitudes, there will accordingly be no room left for the expressivist view that, appearances to the contrary, such a discourse does not really deal in truth-apt contents.[7] Equally, since the Disquotational Scheme will control the truth predicate in question, reason to accept any statement of

6. For synopsis of the relevant considerations, see *ibid.*, chap. 2, section I, and chap. 3, section I.

7. This claim has proved to seem too swift to some, who have urged that it should be consistent with a discourse's sustaining a predicate which satisfies all the platitudes noted that it fail to provide a medium for the expression of *belief*—conceived, *à la* Hume, as, unlike both desire and, for example, ethical attitude, an intrinsically unmotivational state. Since it is plausibly also a platitude that beliefs are what sincere assertions express, it would follow that the assertoric character of moral discourse in particular is not so easily secured. The issue is usefully debated in the contributions by Michael Smith (twice), John Divers and Alexander Miller, and Paul Horwich to the symposium on 'Expressivism and Truth' in Smith et al. (1994). The objection is also pressed by Frank Jackson in his review of *Truth and Objectivity* in Jackson (1994). I respond in the same number of that journal, pp. 169–75.

the discourse in question will be reason to regard it as true, and there will be no space for the sort of metaphysical rift between truth and justification by ordinary standards which is the error theorist's stock-in-trade.

III

That, then, is the outline of an approach that might provide what we want: a perspective on truth and truth-aptitude which will allow the moral anti-realist to grant that moral discourse enjoys both without jettison of the idea that truth is a real property. But I have merely sketched a shape. What needs to be indicated now, pursuing the analogy with identity, are counterparts of the ways in which identity can be variously constituted among varying kinds of identicals, some ways of being true being more, and some less congenial to intuitive realist and anti-realist inclination.

Consider any type of opinion for which we feel we can pretend to no conception of how truth might lie beyond human recognition in principle. Opinion about what is and isn't funny would seem to provide one example. Disagreement in such opinions may of course be intractable in principle, but in such a case we shall hesitate to regard either conflicting opinion as true. What seems to make no sense is the idea of a situation's being determinate in comic quality, as it were, although human beings are simply not empowered, even in principle, to recognise that quality. By contrast, many would be comfortable with the idea that in some areas of enquiry the connection between prosecution of best method and getting at the truth is, at bottom, 'serendipitous', so that, for example, the internally blameless prosecution of best scientific method by theorists with somewhat different starting points may lead to the generation of incompatible but rationally incommensurable scientific theories.

Some forms of realist construal of the content of moral judgements—those which see moral truth as grounded in the will of God, for example, or as a potentially incalculable function of social utility—would have the effect of placing morality in the latter camp. But many would feel that there is little, if any, more sense than in the case of comedy to be given to the idea that moral quality may in principle outreach the efforts of an ordinarily receptive, careful moral thinker. Now one very important consideration—which needs substantiation in detail which I cannot provide now—is that when a region of thought has that feature—namely, that no clear sense can be attached to the idea that it provides means for the expression of truths which human beings are constitutionally incapable of recognising—then the concept I have elsewhere given the somewhat ungainly title of *superassertibility* will effectively function as a truth predicate: that is, superassertibility will validate the basic platitudes about truth which, according to the approach I have outlined, are constitutive of the notion.[8]

Superassertibility, as the term suggests, is a construction out of ordinary assertibility. Ordinary assertibility is relative to a state of information: it is as assessed in a particular informational context that statements are or are not assertible. Superassertibility, by contrast, is an absolute notion: a statement is superassertible if it is assertible in some state of information and then remains so no matter how that state of information is enlarged upon or improved.

It is instructive to compare superassertibility with the conception of truth, also constructed out of assertibility, favoured by some of the American pragmatists. C. S. Peirce conceived of truth as what is assertible—justified—at some ideal limit of enquiry, when all relevant information is in. Superassertibility, by contrast, avoids play with arguably mythical limits: it is a matter of enduring assertibility under an ideally prosecuted, indefinitely continuing investigation, rather than of assertibility attained when such an investigation is somehow completed.

I suspect that some, though probably not all, of the criticisms frequently levelled at the claims of the Peircian notion to amount to a concept of truth could have been deflected if pragmatists had worked

---

8. See *Truth and Objectivity,* chap. 2, sections V and esp. VI.

with superassertibility instead. But however that may be, it should be clear that any assertoric discourse, disciplined by acknowledged standards of acceptability for its statements, must allow the definition on the back of those standards of a species of superassertibility: it will be a matter of justification in the light of those standards in a particular context, and of the survival of that justification, no matter how much additional relevant information is accrued. There is therefore the option, for those who are content to think of morals as analogous to comedy in the relevant respect, of thinking of moral truth as a kind of superassertibility: the morally true is that which can be morally justified and which then retains that justification no matter how refined or extensive an additional consideration is given to the matter.

Moral superassertibility, so described, is vague and highly abstract. But the important thing about it comes across even at this level of characterisation—namely, that it is a *language-game internal* notion, as it were. Superassertibility is a projection of whatever internal discipline informs a discourse (and such discipline there has to be if we are dealing in genuine contents). To think of a discourse as dealing with truth-apt contents, accordingly, need involve, when truth is conceived as superassertibility, no work for a type of idea which is absolutely central to traditional realist thinking: the idea of *correspondence,* of representation of real, external states of affairs. When truth is so conceived, various relations between truth and superassertibility will be possible. The superassertibility of a statement may be *explained* by its being true (if our standards of acceptability track the truth) or the two concepts may diverge an extension (if they do not). But there will be no *identity*. One basic form of opposition between realist and antirealist views of a discourse will be between those who think of the truth of a statement as constituted in some substantial relation of fit or representation—the traditional imagery of the mirror—and those who conceive, or might as well conceive, of truth as superassertibility, as durable satisfaction of the discourse's internal disciplinary constraints.

Before developing that a little, let me pause to note how the looseness of the notion of moral superassertibility, as so far characterised, immediately allows an important fragmentation within the anti-realist camp. Moral truth, for the anti-realist, will be durable justifiability in the light of the standards that discipline ordinary moral thinking. But which standards are those? There is nothing in the proposal to preempt all belief in moral progress—belief in the possibility of a gradual refinement of moral thinking and of a gradual convergence in moral points of view, stabilised by the standards that are the very products of that refinement. But that optimistic conception contrasts with two possible others. Some will be tempted to view the detail of the discipline to which moral thinking is subjected as essentially *local*—to a culture, or a nation, or a period, or an age group—and will want to deny that moral thinking embodies any intrinsic dynamic towards convergence across widely differing standpoints. The discipline is real enough, on this view, but it is essentially a parochial form of discipline and it is merely a sociological question how far the parish can be made to extend. Finally, and less optimistic still, there is space for the *irrealist* or nihilist view that the whole notion of the discipline to which moral discourse is subject is a sort of charade, an illusion comparable to that which, in Wittgenstein's view, conditions the idea that there could be a language fit for the description of sensations conceived as Cartesian private objects. (Such a view of morals seems evidently to fly in the face of the social facts. I mention it only to indicate how the general map of the issues which I am proposing does leave a corner for the irrealist to try to occupy.)

Reverting to the issue of realism, there may seem to be a tension between the suggestion that the hallmark of a realist conception of truth is its implication of the notion of representation, or fit, and the inclusion, among the set of basic platitudes constitutive of any truth predicate, of one to the effect that to be true is to correspond to the facts. It is crucial to see that this is not really a difficulty. It is indeed a platitude that a statement is true if and only if it corresponds to the facts. But it is so only insofar as we understand a statement's correspondence to fact to involve no more than that matters stand as it affirms. For reflect that if 'p' says that p, then matters will stand as 'p' affirms if and only if p. Since by the Disquotational Scheme, 'p' is true if and only if p, it follows that matters stand as 'p' affirms just in case 'p' is true—essentially the Correspondence Platitude. What this simple argument brings out, however, is not that there is no alternative to a realist conception of truth—that realism is built into the core of the notion—but rather that the phraseology of correspondence may embody much less of a metaphysical commitment than realism supposes. Correspondence phraseology—and all the paraphrases of it that we are likely to think of—are co-licensed, as it were, with talk of truth. But since, as just illustrated, the Correspondence Platitude is a *derived* platitude, it follows that such talk need have no more content than flows into it, so to speak, from the parent platitudes that license that derivation. On the surface, the Correspondence Platitude takes us from a predicate, 'true', to a relation, and lays it down as necessary and sufficient for the predicate to apply to a statement that the latter bears that relation to a suitably designated object-term. I suggest that the question for the realist has to be whether our understanding of what it is for this relation to obtain has, in the case of any particular discourse, *more* to it than can be derived from the co-permissibility of the claim that it obtains with the claim that a relevant statement is true, and the co-permissibility of the latter with the claim that the statement is assertible. *That* much understanding is what is bestowed by the derivability of the Correspondence Platitude from the minimal platitudes concerning any truth predicate. The realist—one who holds to a contrast between a representational conception of truth, so to say, and superassertibility, and maintains that it is the former which operates in a favoured region of discourse—owes us some additional substance to his talk of 'representation', 'correspondence' and 'facts', which the Correspondence Platitude, as a mere platitude, is insufficient to ensure.

Naturally, there can only be two places to look for such additional substance. One is the relational term—the idea of representation, or correspondence. Here the quest will be for some additional aspect to our understanding of the relational term, exceeding anything imposed by its liaison with the minimal platitudes, which somehow gives a point to realist intuition in the area of discourse in question. The other course is to work on the object-term—*the facts*—and, once again, to try to show how we are committed, in that area, to a more robust conception of them than is entrained merely by the ubiquitous permission to gloss 'is true' as 'corresponds to the facts'.

In the space remaining, I try rapidly to indicate how some quite familiar considerations from the debates concerning moral realism slot neatly into this perspective, tending to show—if they are correct—that the would-be moral realist cannot live up to the demands of the kind of robustly representational conception of truth by which I am proposing that realism generally should define itself. Then, in conclusion, I offer some brief, necessarily inadequate reflections about why, as it seems to me at least, the failure of moral realism would not have to be a matter of concern.

IV

The thought of a realist—unless he is pessimistic enough to think that what is true in the relevant region of discourse is altogether beyond our ken—is that responsibly to practise in that region is to enter into a kind of representational mode of cognitive function, comparable in relevant respects to, say, taking a photograph or making a wax impression of a key. Certain matters stand thus and so independently of us—compare the photographed scene and the contours of the key. We engage in a certain process, to wit, we put ourselves at the mercy, so to speak, of the standards of appraisal appropriate to the discourse in question—compare taking the snapshot or impressing the key on the wax—and the result is to leave an imprint in our minds which, in the best case, appropriately matches the independently standing state of affairs.

Philosophers, most notably the early Wittgenstein and J. L. Austin, have of course tried to be much more definite about this type of conception.[9] But even vaguely so presented, it does have certain quite

9. The *locus classicus* for Austin's view, of course, is Austin (1950).

definite obligations. If we take photographs of the *same* scene which somehow turn out to represent it in incompatible ways, there has to have been some kind of shortcoming in the function of one of the cameras or in the way it was used. If the wax impressions we take of a single key turn out to be of such a shape that no one key can fit them both, then again there has to have been some fault in the way we went about it or in the materials used. The price you pay for taking the idea of representation in the serious way the realist wants to take it is that when subjects' representations prove to conflict, then (prescinding from certain necessary qualifications, mainly to do with vagueness, which I won't elaborate now) there has to have been something amiss with the way they were arrived at or with their vehicle—the wax, the camera, or the thinker. Accordingly, one obligation of the moral realist will be to hold, and therefore to justify holding, that moral disagreements, since they involve a clash of what purport to be substantial representations, have to involve defects of process or materials: at least one of the protagonists has to be guilty of a deficiency in the way he arrives at his view, or to be somehow constitutionally unfit.

That is an obligation imposed by an attempt to imbue the notion of representation, or correspondence, with a more full-blooded content than it derives from the Correspondence Platitude. The second obligation derives from the correlative attempt to find additional substance in 'the facts' to which true statements correspond. Broadly, it ought to be possible to justify conceiving of such facts as just as robust and independent of the practice of the discourse in which we supposedly aim to represent them as are the photographed scene and the impressed key. What would that involve?

What needs to be shown is that the relevant beliefs are exactly an *epiphenomenon*—that they are, as it were, driven by the facts. And it is hard to see how that might be shown except by showing how the primary phenomena—the states of affairs such beliefs allegedly represent—display other forms of impact upon and interaction within the wider world than are involved in their connections with the epiphenomena. It is unclear how to think about the matter except along these broad lines.

The second obligation on the realist is therefore exactly the dual of an alleged obligation that an influential debate—I'm thinking of that involving Harman, Wiggins and the so-called Cornell Realists—has pivoted around.[10] That debate involves a challenge to the realist to explain how moral states of affairs contribute to the best explanation of moral beliefs. What I am urging that the realist had better be able to do, by contrast, is to explain how moral states of affairs contribute to the explanation of things *other than* moral beliefs.

Of course, the two areas of obligation need more refined presentation and discussion. But enough has maybe been said to indicate why the ante-post betting might favour the anti-realist. As far as the first obligation is concerned, it is of course evident that moral disagreements can be and frequently are attributable to confused thinking, factual ignorance and sheer prejudice. But the obligation imposed by a robust reading of the notion of representation is to show that deficiency *has* to be involved in the generation of any such dispute (prescinding from the irrelevant case of vagueness). Any student of morality who has come to feel, therefore, that a substantial body of the principles that inform our ordinary moral thought are essentially contestable, and that no rational or cognitive deficiency is needed to sustain the clashes on things like sexual morality, the value of individual freedom, the moral status of animals and the ethics of suicide and mercy-killing, which are freely exemplified within and across cultures, won't give much for the realist's chances.

As far as the second obligation is concerned, we have to ask: Of the obtaining of what states of affairs might the obtaining of moral states of affairs contribute towards the explanation? Much of the detail of the debate about the best explanation of moral belief to which I alluded is of course relevant to this question. But without going

10. See Harman (1977), chapter 1 of which is reprinted as Harman (1988). David Wiggins' principal contributions to the debate are Essay 4 of Wiggins (1987a), and Wiggins (1990–1). The leading 'Cornell Realist' is Nicholas Sturgeon. See in particular Sturgeon (1985). Sturgeon's debate with Harman is continued in a further exchange in Gillespie (1986), pp. 57–78.

into that, it is difficult to see that matters can in the end turn out very satisfactorily from a realist point of view. What is there that is so strictly because such-and-such a *moral* state of affairs obtains—a state of affairs, say, of the general form: such-and-such circumstances impose such-and-such an obligation upon an agent who meets certain conditions?

By way of comparison, consider the state of affairs of a pond's being frozen over. Reference to the ice-covering on the pond can contribute towards explaining at least four distinct kinds of thing:

1. Someone's perceiving, and hence believing, that the pond is frozen
2. The tendency of the goldfish to cluster towards the bottom of the pond
3. Someone's slipping and falling when stepping onto the surface
4. The tendency of a Celsius thermometer to read zero when placed on the surface

The ice-covering on the pond can be ascribed, that is, each of four kinds of consequence: cognitive effects; effects on sentient, but non-conceptual creatures; effects on us as physically interactive agents; and certain brute effects on inanimate matter. By contrast, although some philosophers have made a case that moral facts can contribute towards the explanation of agents' moral beliefs, the kind of fact about obligation cited would seem unfit to play any part in the *direct*—that is, propositional attitude-unmediated explanation—of any effects of the latter three sorts: it is hard to think of anything which is true of sentient but non-conceptual creatures, or of mobile organisms, or of inanimate matter, which is true because such a moral fact obtains and in whose explanation it is unnecessary to advert to anyone's appreciation of that moral fact.[11]

11. The limitation gestured at here is meant to be a priori: it is not that moral facts are merely accidentally lazy, as it were. Accidental laziness would not be enough to create a tension with the robustness of moral facts.

V

Naturally, these reflections ought to leave unmoved a realist who conceives that morality is backed by some sort of external sanction, either on traditional theological lines or because some naturalistic reconstruction of moral fact is proposed. But it seems to me that there would be some unclarity at this point about the motives of a moral realist who, as a way of maintaining the line, proposed to *seek* some such reconstruction. For what should a sensible moral realist want which cannot be incorporated in the kind of anti-realism which, viewing truth as a real property, grants the truth-aptitude of moral discourse and allows that responsible moral opinion may justifiably claim to be true?

Such an anti-realism discounts any suggestion that moral discourse is beset by systematic error, or is merely the sheepish expression of emotion masked by the wolfish syntax of genuine judgement. As earlier noted, it can also be hospitable, merely *qua* anti-realism, to the idea that the sensibilities on which moral discourse is founded are capable of *improvement*—that morals can undergo significant development and, by dint of our efforts, the story of our moral development can unfold better than it might otherwise have done. It is true the anti-realist will have to grant that such ideas of progress or deterioration are ones which we can have use for only from *within* a committed moral point of view; that any refinement of which our moral sensibilities are capable can only be a matter of the approaching of a certain equilibrium as appraised by the exercise of those very sensibilities. And making out that there is indeed such a dynamic towards equilibrium in moral thought will need a lot of sensitive work. But suppose that project cannot succeed, and our moral thinking is at bottom the irreducibly parochial affair that relativists have urged it is; then I cannot see that there would be much consolation in the realist's belief in real moral states of affairs which, accordingly, some moral cultures—and it could as well be ours—are presumably doomed to miss.

For the moral anti-realist, there will be no defensible analogue of the scientific realist's thought that the real progress of science is measured by the extent to which our theories represent a reality whose nature owes nothing to our natures or the standards that inform our conception of responsible discourse about it. It will not be possible to regard the disciplined formation of a moral view as a seriously representational mode of function, or as a form of activity in which we respond to states of affairs which, precisely because they are at the service of the explanation of other things, can be put to serious work in explaining the course assumed by these responses. But my point has been that those concessions need not enforce the dilemma: either exile ethics from the realm of truth or dilute the concept of truth to the point of vacuity. So: what is so alarming about the prospect of moral anti-realism?

There may be a *psychological* problem: a tendency to cease to *identify* with those of one's opinions which philosophy discloses to lack an external sanction—to suffer a loss of moral problems, as it were. But I do not think that a clear-headed moral anti-realist ought for one moment to feel impelled to a general moral tolerance. Such a tolerance accepts that no differences of moral opinion need involve anything worthy of criticism. But while the anti-realist will have to accept that such differences need involve nothing worth regarding as *cognitive* shortcoming—as deficiency in representation, substantially conceived—the ordinary view will remain available that shortcoming may nevertheless often be involved, albeit an irreducibly *moral* shortcoming, a type of failing which can be appreciated only from a committed moral point of view.

In general—I guess the point is obvious enough—the immediate price of anti-realism about morals is merely that the gravity of moral judgement will lack an external sanction. When one is asked, 'Why bother to try to arrive at correct moral opinion?', the only available answer will be: because such an opinion informs *better* conduct—better, that is, from a moral point of view. The value of moral truth will thus be an instrumental, moral value. It is common to think that there are, by contrast, intrinsic, general values associated with pure discovery, understanding and knowledge of the real world. Properly to characterise and to understand such values seems to me to be a very difficult task. In any case, for the moral anti-realist, that kind of value cannot attach to moral truth. But I think it has seemed important that it should only because of the tendency of philosophers to suppose that there is nothing for truth to be that is not associated with value of that sort.

'What more could a sensible moral realist want?' What those whose intuitive inclination is to moral realism really want, I suggest, is not truth as representation—realism as properly understood—but a certain kind of objectivity in moral appraisal: ideally, precisely that a tendency towards convergence in the conception of what is morally important and how much importance it has, be indeed intrinsic to moral thinking itself. How much, and what kinds of moral appraisal may indeed contain the seeds of such convergence seems to me a great—perhaps the greatest—unresolved question in moral philosophy. My argument has been that the question has nothing to do with moral realism, but arises within the anti-realist camp.

This essay is a lightly edited version of what I presented at the Reading conference of the same name. Readers of *Truth and Objectivity* may experience what Quine once called a sense of *déjà lu,* for the paper is in essentials merely a collation of some of the thoughts about ethics that featured in that book along the way.

Thanks to questioners at the Reading conference and at the presentation of this material as a public lecture at the University of Kansas in October 1994.

PART FOUR

TRUTH

The four essays collected together in this part pursue a range of issues concerning truth and truth conditions. Some complement and extend the development of the minimalist conception of truth and truth-aptitude defended in *Truth and Objectivity*, and all are variously concerned with the general metaphysics of truth: the battle between correspondence, coherence, pragmatist and deflationary conceptions of truth.

Essay 9 is a critical study of Ralph Walker's searching critique of coherence conceptions of truth in Walker (1989). Many philosophy students nowadays are taught to associate coherentism with various forms of outmoded idealist metaphysics. The central contention of Walker's book is that it is actually the upshot of perennially powerful philosophical pressures and lives on, in disguised form, in contemporary anti-realist conceptions of truth and meaning, as well as in the communitarian ideas about objectivity and meaning proposed by recently influential interpretations of the later Wittgenstein. Walker argues, however, that these recent trends, no less than the views of the nineteenth- and early-twentieth-century idealists, can be made to succumb to one very general form of objection, versions of which, with minor variations, are put forward throughout his book. It is this contention that provides the focal point of my essay.

The objection, very approximately, is that—whatever exactly 'coherence' is taken to mean—coherence within a system of propositions has no prospect of constituting a distinguishing feature of the truths unless we first demarcate with *which* propositions, as a base class, coherence is to count. Truths to the effect that a particular proposition is a member of this base class (for instance, are among those which we *believe*) are then argued to lie beyond the reach of the account. My discussion develops three distinct versions of this objection, one epistemological and two metaphysical. I argue that the real upshot of the better of the two metaphysical objections is that coherentism, as an entirely general account of the constitution of truth, has no resources to explain contingency (a result, to be sure, that would have been perfectly congenial to those idealist metaphysicians who held that all contingency was illusion!). However, Walker's attempts to spotlight a similar form of structural difficulty in the proposals of modern anti-realists and Wittgensteinians are argued to be unsuccessful.

Essay 10 grew out of a lecture given at the Goethe University in Frankfurt in the spring of 1996 and offers further development of the views about truth and aptitude for truth outlined in the first two chapters of *Truth and Objectivity*. Its point of departure is the classic early-twentieth-century debate between correspondence, coherence and pragmatist conceptions of truth. That debate, I argue, is most fruitfully seen not as concerning the proper analysis of the concept of truth but as focused upon the metaphysical structure of truth: on what, if any, kind of property or relation truth is, with the varieties of deflationary conception that came rather later thus constituting a kind of error-theoretic view of the metaphysical question. The argument against deflationary conceptions of truth given in chapter 1 of *Truth and Objectivity* is deepened and extended in this essay, and (drawing on the discussion of Walker's 'master argument' in Essay 9) a case is made that both intrinsicist and coherentist conceptions of truth can alike provide no satisfactory account of contingent truth. It follows that, if some single, comprehensive metaphysics of truth is to be given, it must exemplify the broad pattern, favoured by correspondence accounts, of construing truth as a relation between propositions (or whatever the bearers of truth value are taken to be) and non-propositional reality.

Against this conclusion, however, the essay sets the pluralist perspective of *Truth and Objectivity* and amplifies it. Thus, while the concept of truth is indeed, in a deflationary spirit, regarded as fixed by a set of basic a priori principles (including, but by no means exhausted by, the Disquotational Scheme), it is allowed that this concept may present different properties in different regions of discourse, and that the varying character of such properties may connect importantly with the debates between realism and anti-realism. This approach has affinities to the conception of philosophical analysis in the neo-Ramseyan style pursued by writers such as David Lewis, Frank Jackson and Michael Smith. The difference is that there is no presumption that the open 'Ramsey sentences' allow of just a single satisfier. Two appendices illustrate respectively how coherence (for arithmetical discourse) and superassertibility (for discourses meeting certain special constraints) may discharge the role of truth. (I believe that the second appendix improves, in certain respects, on the parallel discussion in *Truth and Objectivity*.)

Essay 11 was written for a Festschrift for Hilary Putnam though, after extensive delays, eventually published in the *Journal of Philosophy*. It focuses on the fourth realism-relevant crux distinguished in *Truth and Objectivity*, though hardly discussed there: namely, the construal of truth, globally or locally, as evidence transcendent. The issues are pursued through the lens of Putnam's reversion in his Dewey Lectures (Putnam 1994a) to what he calls a 'common-sense' or 'natural' realism, after his 'internalist' period through the 1970s and early 1980s—which in turn had represented a reaction to the hard-line realism featured in his earliest work. Putnam's internalist phase saw him mounting a series of attacks on a position he labelled 'metaphysical' realism and espousing an evidentially constrained conception of truth, although the exact nature of the intended constraint never received definitive expression. The main preoccupation of Essay 11 is with how this key aspect of Putnam's internalism might best be (or have been) interpreted.

The question is not rendered academic by Putnam's subsequent recantation. That recantation is marked by Putnam's wanting to allow certain—what he now regards as commonsensical—examples of potentially evidence-transcendent truth while avoiding the cognitive alienation implicit in metaphysical realism (and so endorsing, for instance, a direct realist philosophy of perception). The essay makes a case that when an internalist constraint upon truth is formulated in the most resilient way—so as to be capable of withstanding well-known objections of Alvin Plantinga and F. B. Fitch—it can sit quite comfortably alongside many of these 'common-sense' examples of Evidence Transcendence and indeed provides for a natural expression of direct realism. So there is encouragement for the view that, whatever his own impression of the matter, many features of Putnam's most recent reviews represent not a rejection of the middle-period internalism, but a further working out of the implications and possibilities of the (somewhat relaxed) form of evidential constraint on truth which that outlook is most usefully seen as involving.

As the closing sections of Essay 11 emphasise, this perspective does not accommodate all aspects of the realist views that Putnam now accepts. In particular it cannot accommodate ways in which, as he now seems prepared to allow, ideal empirical theories may be undetectably false. Yet earlier, this admission was regarded as a cardinal tenet not of common sense but of *metaphysical* realism. The essay concludes with, in effect, a challenge to Putnam to explain why these aspects of his 'natural realism of the common man' do not involve slipping back into a wolfish—metaphysical—realist outlook, even if disguised in sheepish rhetoric. Putnam (2001) has responded to this challenge, charging that the treatment given to the Fitch paradox by my moderate form of internal realism may be extended to cover the kind of truths transcending the evidence and methods of empirical theory which it seems to him commonsensical to admit; and that this admission is distinguished from the excesses of metaphysical realism by the feature that the potential Evidence Transcendence involved is actually part of the *content* of the empirical theories in question. The previously unpublished postscript to Essay 11 takes up these allegations.

Essay 12 consists of the first two sections of a larger paper (Wright 2001a) written for Michael P. Lynch's edited anthology on truth (Lynch 2001), followed by a previously unpublished discussion of one aspect of Robert Brandom's recent work. The effect of the combination is to give another—perhaps improved—expression to the anti-deflationist argument of *Truth and Objectivity*. The essence of that argument is that deflationism fails an explanatory obligation: specifically, that it is in no position to explain aspects of our practice which betray the subjection of assertion, and of belief-formation, to a norm of correctness other than assertibility, while yet being committed—by principles it makes central to its own account—to recognising those aspects. The operation of a distinct such norm is what underwrites the contrast between the claims that P (or that P is true) and that P is assertible, so that it follows that if the anti-deflationary argument is sustained, then deflationism is likewise in difficulty with the very distinction between the content of an arbitrary assertion and the content of a claim that it is assertible. Now it is exactly this distinction which, for his own non-deflationist reasons, Brandom in his 'Objectivity and the Normative Fine Structure of Rationality' (Brandom (2000)) hopes to reconstruct without taking the notion of truth as primitive, just by appeal to the operation of norms of entitlement and commitment. An earlier version of his paper was originally presented at a symposium at the central divisional meetings of the American Philosophical Association at Pittsburgh in 1997. The second part of Essay 12 consists of a lightly edited version of my comments on that occasion. If their thrust is correct, then Brandom's manoeuvres hold out no prospect of assistance to the deflationist.

9

Truth as Coherence

I

If, *pace* deflationism, truth is a genuine property at all, then the choices are between viewing it as conferred on a proposition—or whatever one takes the primary bearers of truth value to be—by the relations it bears to things which are not (in the typical case) themselves propositions, and viewing it as conferred on a proposition by the relations it sustains to other propositions.[1] Any view of the latter kind may be regarded as a coherence theory, though particular proposals may naturally vary considerably in their conception of 'coherence'—in the inter-propositional relations which they take to count.

Such conceptions of truth are nowadays widely regarded as belonging with the various idealisms which flourished in nineteenth-century German and British philosophy, and as having perished with their progenitors—indeed, as open to decisive refutation by the simple counter-arguments standardly trotted out in metaphysics textbooks. To be sure, there are some who have suggested otherwise. Paul

---

1. Since it cannot—at least in the case of contingencies—be an intrinsic property.

Horwich,[2] for instance, has alleged that the writings of Michael Dummett and Hilary Putnam in effect 'resurrect' the coherence theory of truth—a claim with which I am concerned below. Ralph Walker also takes this view.[3] Indeed, a leading thesis of his book is that coherentism, so far from being merely a knockabout by-product of fanciful forms of idealism, is actually the natural outcome of perennially powerful forms of philosophical pressure, of currents of thought which continue to draw the attention and respect of contemporary philosophers. So far, moreover, from succumbing to the standard textbook arguments, it has the resources straightforwardly to see them off.

Walker is, however, no proponent of coherentism. On the contrary, all such views *do* admit, he argues, of a decisive refutation—a line of argument I call the *Master Objection,* applications of which, with local variations, liberally pepper his discussion. And if this is so, then it follows, of course, that there must be error either in the ideas which pressure towards coherentism or in the view that coherentism is ultimately an apt response to those ideas.

In Walker's diagnosis, the most interesting of these sources of pressure are three. First, coherentism is naturally seen as offering an escape from Cartesian scepticism. If truth is conferred not by relations between our thought and a potentially inscrutable reality, but is constituted *within* our thoughts, then there may seem no scope for scepticism of the *malin genie* type—so no scope for doubt that the world as it really is might altogether belie our conception of it. Second, Walker agrees with Horwich that certain modern forms of verificationism do indeed involve a commitment to some form of coherentism, as does— third—the anthropocentrism about concepts, similarities and rules prefigured in Kant but firmly associated in modern philosophy with the later Wittgenstein.

It is the second and third contentions which give Walker's treatment especial potential importance. He regards coherentism, plausi-

2. Horwich (1998a), p. 9.
3. Walker (1989). Subsequent references in this essay are to this book unless otherwise stated.

bly enough, as ultimately a futile response to Cartesian scepticism, since doubts of the *malin genie* sort ought to be allowed to get a grip with respect to our apprehension of the conceptual relationships among our thoughts, if they are allowed to get a grip at all. But the lines of argument leading to coherentism from anti-realism, and from the ideas of the later Wittgenstein, he views as well taken. If that is right, and if the relevant forms of the Master Objection are cogent, then Walker's discussion in effect demonstrates that truth cannot lucidly be thought of as an epistemically constrained property, after the fashion of Dummett and Putnam, and that the entire thrust of Wittgenstein's ideas on rules, at least as Walker interprets it, is mistaken. There remains only the option—apart from the deflationist conception which Walker passes over in silence—of conceiving of the truth of a proposition as constituted in 'some kind of correspondence with a reality independent of what may be believed about it' (p. 3): a radically non-epistemic conception of truth consisting in fit with facts that 'obtain in their own right and independently of us, of our classifications, and of our agreements' (p. 144). Indeed this highly realist characterisation of the correspondence theory is Walker's preferred account from the start.

This is philosophical high-rolling, and the focus of what follows will be on whether Walker really succeeds in bagging the pot. Both the Master Objection itself, and the coherentist impetus putatively internal to semantical anti-realism (internal realism) and to Walker's Wittgenstein's thinking about rules, will bear a more detailed consideration than he gives them. In the next section I distinguish three versions of the Master Objection, one epistemological, the other two constitutive. In section III I argue that Walker ought to have seen that a proper accommodation with the Master Objection must itself generate the resources whereby Dummett and Putnam can avoid coherentism—so that Walker's own arguments show, in effect, that an epistemically constrained conception of truth need not be coherentist. Sections IV and V, respectively, argue that the version of the Master Objection which Walker brings against his Wittgenstein succeeds only in the presence of an unsupported and implausible assumption, and that his treatment provides no explanation why a structurally similar objection does not succeed against the correspondence theory which Walker favours. Finally section VI will contend that the version of the Master Objection which *does* tell against the form of coherentism which Walker erects in response to the 'textbook' objections, is inapplicable to his Wittgenstein.

II

The Master Objection is purportedly fatal to the prospects of any pure version of the coherence theory of truth and many impure versions.[4] (Pure versions hold that all truth consists in coherence; impure versions that some does.) It emerges from one of the textbook objections: the 'Bishop Stubbs' objection, first lodged by Russell,[5] that

> coherence as the definition of truth fails because there is no proof that there can be only one coherent system.[6]

4. See pp. 97, 99–101, 143–5, 157, 162, 178–9, 192–3, 199, 207, 210–11.
5. Russell (1906–7), pp. 33–4:

[T]he objection to the coherence theory lies in this, that it presupposes a more usual meaning of truth and falsehood in constructing its coherent whole, and this more usual meaning, though indispensable to the theory, cannot be explained by means of the theory. The proposition, 'Bishop Stubbs was hanged for murder' is, we are told, not coherent with the whole of truth or with experience. But that means, when we examine it, that something is *known* which is inconsistent with this proposition. Thus what is inconsistent with the proposition must be something *true;* it may be perfectly possible to construct a coherent whole of false propositions in which 'Bishop Stubbs was hanged for murder' would find a place. In a word, the partial truths of which the whole of truth is composed must be such propositions as would commonly be called true, not such as would commonly be called false; there is no explanation, on the coherence theory, of the distinction commonly expressed by the words *true* and *false,* and no evidence that a system of false propositions might not, as in a good novel, be just as coherent as the system which is the whole of truth.

6. Russell (1912), p. 122. Cf. Walker (1989), pp. 3, 25.

Why exactly is that consideration an objection? Because if coherence is so understood that virtually any (non-self-contradictory) proposition can indeed participate in *some* sufficiently large, coherent system of propositions, then the coherence theory cannot distinguish true propositions from false ones. More specifically, it cannot explain why a principle like

If P is true, not P is not true

should hold. But so basic a principle is absolutely constitutive of our understanding of truth and should be a direct consequence of any correct account of the concept.

One foreseeable coherentist response to this, surprisingly not considered by Walker, would be that there is indeed no guarantee that global, mutually incompatible but internally coherent systems of propositions do not exist, and that truth should accordingly be conceived as *relative to a system*. No absolute truth or falsity therefore exists; there *is* no general distinction to be drawn between true and false beliefs without reference to what else is believed; and principles like the above hold only *within* rather than across systems. I shall say no more now about this relativistic response, except to remark that, for a reason to emerge much later, it doesn't actually matter that Walker omits to respond to it.[7]

The Master Objection engages a different form of response whereby, rather than go relativist, the coherence theorist *privileges* some particular set of beliefs, B, defining truth as coherence within a system in which each member of B is an element. (Here 'belief' means: something we actually believe, or would believe under conditions the theorist will specify.) Walker seems to take it as clear that privileging will dispose of the Bishop Stubbs objection as stated. But actually whether it will—whether it will ensure that the uniqueness of truth is a *consequence* of the account of truth—will obviously depend on

7. See note 15 below.

how 'coherence' is further characterised. For some possible readings of 'coherence'—mere consistency, for example—it may still be that the coherence of the B-based system can survive the addition either of P or of not P individually.[8]

In addition, it is not, contrary to Walker's suggestion, immediately clear why the privileging response demands invocation of *belief:* presumably it suffices, in order to respond to the immediate objection in this kind of way, to specify a self-coherent base class of propositions coherence with which is to be the mark of truth. It is not a priori evident why this base class has to be defined by reference to what we do or would believe.[9]

In any case, the key to the Master Objection is the thought that the coherence theorist who makes the privileging manoeuvre cannot account for the *status* of the beliefs which make up the privileged base. Here is a typical passage:

> The objection is that in the last resort no such theory can give an adequate account of what it is for a proposition to be believed, and hence to be a candidate for determining what the coherent system is. For it is essential that the coherent system be a system of beliefs, and not just a system of propositions in the abstract. There is no difficulty in generating plenty of rival alternative systems of propositions. (p. 210)

Likewise:

> The difficulty is that [Hegel] cannot possibly hold that something's *being a belief* is not independent of its being . . . believed to be such, because the regress to which this would give rise *would* be vicious . . .

8. In fact, it is worth emphasising that there is in Walker's book almost no discussion of what 'coherence' might most plausibly be taken to cover. The discussion of the theory, and the development of the objections to it, both proceed almost entirely in structural terms. (Of course this ensures that his conclusions will be of very general scope, just so long as they are soundly drawn.)

9. In places Walker seems to consider and reject this thought, but his stated reason ('propositions in the abstract are hardly to be distinguished from the facts that the correspondence theorist invokes' p. 4; cf. also p. 210, quoted below) is not very clear.

[I]f P's being a belief depends upon its being believed to be a belief, and that upon its being believed to be believed to be a belief, there is nothing to constitute any proposition a belief to start with. [We cannot unproblematically know] that certain things are believed if to know that P is a belief is to know that 'P is a belief' coheres with the rational system [and] to know that it coheres with the rational system is to know that it coheres with certain propositions which are not only rational but believed. (pp. 99–100)

It seems quite clear that Walker is on to something. But what exactly does the objection come to? I think there is actually more than one objection which may naturally be read into his formulations, and that Walker does not clearly separate them.

The Epistemological Objection

This is perhaps the most salient line of thought in the second passage quoted above. Generalised to apply not just to the invocation of belief which Walker envisages but to all forms of the privileging response, it is roughly as follows: a proposition's having a certain property (truth) cannot be operationally defined in terms of its bearing a relation R (coherence) to some specified class of propositions B if its doing so depends on which propositions are members of B and if that can only be decided by determining whether or not propositions stating that other propositions are/are not members of B themselves bear R to B. Even if coherence is as clearly characterised as you like, still, you cannot tell whether P is true if telling demands you know what is in B and if, in order to know of any particular proposition Q whether or not it is in B, you must first determine whether 'Q is a member of B' coheres with B. If such a definition is to be useable, then plainly the membership of B has to be determinable independently.

This line of thought is manifestly cogent.[10] A corollary worth

---

10. I do not know if it quite coincides in detail with the version of the Master Objection which Walker brings against the coherence theory of knowledge. The interested reader should study pp. 178–84.

observing is that someone who takes *all* truth to consist in coherence cannot regard coherence as the sole *criterion* of truth. To repeat: if the *only* way of telling whether a proposition is true is to determine its coherence with some base class of propositions, then you need first to know what's in that class, that is, which propositions about the membership of that class are true; but in order to know that, you must—if coherence is the sole test of truth—determine *their* coherence with B; which you cannot do unless you *already* know what is in B.[11] At the least then, the epistemological objection discloses that the pure coherence theorist owes an account of how truth can be recognised *other than* by testing for coherence. Moreover she will need to show, of course, that the needed supplementary criterion, which will not involve directly testing for coherence, is nevertheless a detector of

11. Reader's familiar with Boghossian (1989b) may find this reasoning reminiscent of the proof offered there (pp. 9–10) that psychological self-knowledge cannot, at least on any internalist conception of justification, be purely *inferential*. Boghossian observes, in essentials, that since acquiring an inferential justification for P involves recognising that P may justifiably be inferred from propositions which one already justifiably accepts, a distinct item of self-knowledge—that one accepts those propositions—is presupposed in any case when P concerns one's own psychology; and this item cannot in general also have been acquired inferentially or no end of discrete items of self-knowledge would be presupposed by any inferential justification of such a P. Does this point exhibit the same structure as the epistemological version of the Master Objection if, say, 'may justifiably be inferred from' replaces 'coheres with'?

Not quite. The predicament for a purely coherentist epistemology (of everything) which would be strictly parallel to that which Boghossian finds for a purely inferential epistemology of self-knowledge would be if the knowledge that coherence with a particular set of propositions sufficed for truth could be acquired only by determining *their* coherence with an ulterior set of propositions already known to be such that coherence with them sufficed for truth. But the predicament actually disclosed by the epistemological version of the Master Objection is one not of a regress but of a *circle* of presupposition: you cannot verify what's in B without assessing the coherence of certain propositions with B; and you cannot do that without first knowing what's in B.

The taxonomy of ways in which model epistemologies can self-destruct is interesting. Certainly, the contrast between regressiveness and circularity is not exhaustive nor, always, very sharp. But here is not the place to pursue it further.

coherence—since that is what truth, putatively, is. One would not expect providing such a criterion to be the work of a weekend.

Walker, though, manifestly does not intend a merely epistemological objection. An explanatorily circular definition may still *correctly,* even if uselessly, characterise its definiendum. Walker's intention is to show, more, that truth cannot everywhere *consist* in coherence: not merely that there is an operational circularity in such a characterisation but that it is demonstrably unsustainable, that the fact of my believing P—P's being a member of B—*cannot be constituted* by the participation of the proposition that I believe P in a coherent system founded upon B. More generally, the facts which determine the base class invoked by the privileging response cannot be constituted by the participation of the propositions which record them in a coherent system founded upon that very base class.

It might seem, before we go any further, that whatever argument might be produced for this constitutive claim, the coherence theorist could take it in stride, since her theory offers an account of the *truth of propositions,* not of the *obtaining of facts/states of affairs.* Its concern is with the truth of the proposition that I believe P, not with the circumstance of my believing P, and it might therefore allow that (the fact of) P's being a member of B cannot consist in the participation of the proposition that P is a member of B in a coherent system founded upon B while continuing to adhere to the coherence account of the truth of the proposition that P is a member of B.

But this would seem a hopeless tack, for at least two reasons. First, once a robust distinction is drawn between the obtaining of the fact and the truth of the proposition, it seems there can be no obstacle to an account of the truth conditions of the proposition which identifies their satisfaction with the obtaining of the fact—so that a coherence theorist who took this line would effectively presuppose all the materials necessary for a competing, correspondence conception of truth: namely, one whereby truth is conferred by the obtaining of facts, and the obtaining of facts is not constituted by coherence among propositions.

Second, the prospects for so robust a distinction in any case look very unlikely. Worlds in which the proposition that I believe that P is true are, necessarily, all and only the worlds in which I believe that P. How then can the first circumstance be constituted by relations among propositions while the second requires a quite different kind of analysis? Walker nowhere explicitly argues for the assumption he needs at this point. But I think he is entitled to take it that a coherence account of truth must perforce be, *eo ipso,* a coherence account of the obtaining of states of affairs, and hence that my believing P—P's being a member of B—must be conceived, on a pure coherence account, in terms of the coherence, within an appropriate system, of the proposition that I do.

The Constitutive Objection: First Version

Well and good. What is wrong, then, with the contention that P's being a member of the base, B, is constituted by the coherence of the proposition that P is a member of B with the members of B? Why cannot the truth of claims about membership in the base itself be constituted by the coherence with the base, or lack of coherence with the base, of those very same claims?

The countervailing thought is that the existence of a determinate fact of the matter, whether decidable or not, about whether a proposition coheres with some set of propositions requires that membership in that set be determined independently—independently, that is, of the answers to questions about propositions' coherence with that same set. According to the coherence theory, however, the question whether the proposition that P is a member of B coheres with B is *identical to* the question whether P is a member of B; and the membership of B cannot accordingly be conceived as determined independently of questions of coherence with that very set. So, according to the countervailing thought, the subclass of questions about coherence with B which effectively concern the membership of B are all alike indeterminate. And in that case there *is* no determinate B; so no such thing as determinate coherence with it; so no such thing as truth.

Is this reasoning compelling? Readers of Walker who share my experience will find it strangely difficult to be sure. But one thing is clear: the point, if good at all, would seem to have nothing especially to do with coherence, or truth, in particular but to be *structural*: it applies, if at all, then to any characterisation—any putative account of a concept—which postulates a certain kind of interdependence. What, more precisely, is in question is whether any non-vacuous characterisation of a concept can be given just by determining that the values of a specified function on its instances are to bear some further specified relation to those very instances—the range of items supposedly characterised.

To help fix the rather abstract issue, consider a putative definition of a set:

(D) $x \in T$ iff $R(F(x), T)$

—the members of T are all and only the things which when taken as the arguments of a specified function, F, yield a value which bears a specified relation R to T itself. In the instance of (D) which preoccupies us, T is B, R is coherence, x an arbitrary proposition, and $F(x)$ is the proposition that $x \in B$. And the objection is that, no matter how well defined R and F may be in a particular instance, the naked impredicativity of (D) will have the effect not merely that we cannot *tell* which set T is but that there *is* no particular set which T is—that (D) introduces no sufficiently determinate condition to constitute any fact of the matter.

Let R be, for instance, '. . . has exactly as many members as some member of . . .' and let F be the identity function. In that case the gist of (D) is that all and only sets with exactly as many members as a member of T are members of T. Is there, accordingly, so far any fact of the matter whether, for instance, $\{\Lambda\}$ is a member of T?

It is tempting to think that there cannot be, on grounds somewhat as follows. $\{\Lambda\}$ qualifies just in case T contains at least one singleton— either $\{\Lambda\}$ itself or something else. But no matter what other singleton we consider, no more definite an answer would seem to have been provided for: it will qualify just in case T contains at least one singleton—that is all that can be said. So no determination *has* been provided for the case of {Λ}, nor therefore for the case of any other singleton. Since the same will hold for all n-membered sets, no matter what value is given to n, we should conclude that (D), under this interpretation, does not define a set at all.

But closer inspection shows that this attempt to bring home the putative indeterminacy of (D) misfires. Indeed, instances of (D) can exert a surprising degree of constraint on the candidates to be T. Suppose, for *reductio,* that T contains some non-empty set a; then it contains every set of like cardinality to a. But *every* set is, on standard set-existence assumptions, a member of some set of like cardinality to a, no matter what a's cardinality may be. So the *union* of the members of T must be the universal set. In any set theory, therefore, in which, as is standard, there is no universal set but every set has a union, T cannot contain any non-empty a; in particular it cannot contain {Λ}. Rather it must itself be either Λ or {Λ}. And if— as is natural—we so understand 'x has exactly as many members as some member of y' that it can be true only if y is non-empty, then this reasoning establishes, on standard set-theoretic assumptions, that T is {Λ}.

So much, then, for any thought we might have had that no instance of the structure of (D) can pick out a determinate set. Where does that leave the objection? Needing, I would suggest, some sort of distinction between a condition which merely *uniquely characterises* a set, or property, and a *strict definition* of it. What we have just noted is that an instance of (D) may indeed express a condition which is *true* of just one set. But its doing so is a situation whose intelligibility depends upon the availability of *some other,* more basic characterisation of the set so described—for instance, 'the set whose sole member is the empty set' in the actual example. In *The Varieties of Reference,* Gareth Evans introduced the idea of the 'fundamental ground of difference' of an object—the condition which strictly defines it, which individuates it from all objects of the same kind in a fashion appropriate to objects of that kind.[12] It would seem that this, or something close to it, is the notion needed to make good the basic intuition which drives the present version of the constitutive objection. The thought should be that while (the extension of) a property may satisfy an instance of (D), no property can have an extension whose *fundamental ground of difference* is given by a condition of that structure. A theorist who so characterises a property that the last word, as it were, on the individuation of its instances is such a condition, has accordingly either mischaracterised it or betrayed that there is no determinate property to be concerned with in the first place.

If this is where the objection eventually goes, then clearly it is going to take further work on Evans's idea to clinch it. But the basic thought is apt to remain impressive. The claim is not that it cannot be *true* that the members of some basic set of beliefs, B, are all and only the propositions P for which the proposition, that P is a member of B, coheres with that very set. The claim is rather that this cannot be the *fundamental ground of difference* of B. Yet for the pure coherence theorist who follows the privileging strategy,

P is a member of B iff Coheres (the proposition that P is a member of B, B)

is the last word on whether or not P is in the base (is a belief, or whatever)—there is nothing else for the fact that P ∈ B to consist in *except* the coherence of the proposition that P ∈ B with the base. The theorist must therefore face the conclusion: either he has mischaracterised what the truth of propositions of that form consists in, or there is no determinate property of being a member of the base (being a belief or

12. 'For any object whatever, then, there is what may be called the fundamental ground of difference of that object (at a time). This will be a specific answer to the question, "What differentiates that object from others?" of the kind appropriate to objects of that sort. For example, the fundamental ground of difference of the number three is being the third number in the series of numbers . . .' (Evans (1982), p. 107).

whatever). On the former alternative, the coherence conception is abandoned. On the latter, there can be no fact of the matter whether or not any particular P is in the base; and the fabric of truth, conceived as coherence with the base, collapses.

The Constitutive Objection: Second Version

Some of the things Walker says suggest a third version of the Master Objection. Start again with the Bishop Stubbs objection: suppose we have two large, mutually incompatible but internally coherent systems of propositions, S^+ and $S^\#$, founded respectively on a pair of incompatible bases, B^+ and $B^\#$. Then there is no clear reason why for each P^+ and $P^\#$ in the respective bases, S^+ and $S^\#$ should not be augmented, without loss of coherence, by a proposition to the effect that P^+, or $P^\#$ respectively is believed. Plainly that does not suffice to make it true that either base captures any of our *actual* beliefs; and supposing we are consistent, it cannot be true that both do. So the coherence theorist owes an account of what *would* suffice to make it the case that S^+, for instance, is based on beliefs we actually hold while $S^\#$ is not.

But what feature can he possibly advert to? If the fact that the constituents of B^+ are among our actual beliefs is to be constituted by relations of coherence among those propositions and other elements of S^+, why do not the corresponding relations accomplish—contrary to the hypothesis of the overall consistency of our beliefs—the same for the propositions in $B^\#$? But if the fact that the constituents of B^+ are among our actual beliefs is *not* to be constituted by relations of coherence among those propositions and other elements of S^+, then how—consistently with a pure coherence account—can the fact be constituted at all? Doesn't some *extrinsic* consideration have to be invoked, independent of the internal relations within either of the systems, and isn't it impossible for a pure coherence account to acknowledge any such consideration? I'll return to this.

It is not clear to me which (if either) of these constitutive forms of objection better corresponds to Walker's principal intent. But in any case, since neither makes any specific assumptions about the nature of 'coherence', what each shows, if cogent, is that no attempt to analyse the truth of a proposition in terms of its relations to some designated class of propositions can satisfactorily handle truths of the form:

P is a member of the designated class

—can satisfactorily handle the individuation of the converse domain of the intended relation(s).[13]

III

As remarked, Walker discerns a commitment to a coherence account of truth in the semantical anti-realism canvassed in Dummett's writings and in the 'internal realism' advocated by Putnam. Is he right to do so?

I do not think so. No doubt there is an intuitive realism which belongs with the correspondence conception of truth—a realism which conceives of our thought in confrontation with an independent, objective world, something almost entirely not of our making, possessing a host of determinate features which may pass forever unremarked by human consciousness. The conception of truth which goes with this picture is that it is constituted by *fit* between our beliefs and the characteristics of this independent, determinate reality. *One* way, it is true, of making the 'independence' of the world more concrete is to hold that it may be determinate in ways that are thinkable and describable but for human beings, limited as we are, forever

---

13. If (privileging) coherence theories cannot cope with the terms of the favoured relation, do they do better with the relation itself? Certainly, the matter looks likely to be equally fraught. Can the coherence of P with some class of propositions itself be held to consist in the coherence of the proposition that P so coheres with the same, or a different class of propositions? Can facts about coherence themselves be constituted by the relations of coherence sustained by the propositions which state them? It is a surprising omission in Walker's discussion that he nowhere considers what kind of account views of this general kind might be able to offer about the truth conditions of propositions to the effect that the favoured relation obtains.

unknowable. To hold, contrary to Putnam and Dummett, that truth may transcend evidence, is therefore a natural gloss on the root idea of realism, that truth is conferred by states of affairs which are independent of us. What is not obvious is that a rejection of Evidence Transcendence must therefore ramify backwards into a denial of the root conception, a denial that truth is a matter of fit with an independent world.

To be sure, the root conception is very vague and needs some kind of elaboration if it is to be so much as discussable. But it is plausible—indeed, it might seem quite evident—that the best interpretation of the anti-realist arguments given by Dummett and Putnam will see them not as offering a corrective to this general conception of the nature of truth, but rather as imposing a condition on the elements in the domain of the truth relation; that is, a condition which must be satisfied if such elements—statements or beliefs—are to be *fitted* for truth. Rather than view these philosophers as rejecting the very idea of truth as correspondence, as something conferred from outwith our scheme of belief, one natural—I should have thought the most natural—interpretation of Dummett's and Putnam's cardinal thought is precisely that it is only when truth is conceived as *essentially recognisable*—only when truth is so construed that the truth of a statement must, at least in principle, allow corroboration by evidence—that we can *make sense* of the idea of a correspondence with fact. Before a content can correspond to fact, it must be apt so to correspond—must be a content of a certain, potentially *representational* kind. The basic contention of the semantical anti-realist–internal realist is, for various reasons, that statements qualify as possessing such content only when it is a priori that their being true, if they are, assures the availability of grounds for affirming that they are true.

This is not Walker's view on the matter. Does he disclose any cogent reason for discarding it and branding the anti-realist a 'closet coherentist'? The most explicit statement of his reasons is this:

> According to the anti-realist this idea of verification-transcendent truth is a myth. The idea of verification-transcendent truth is just the idea of

truth that the correspondence theory makes use of. In rejecting it, the anti-realist adopts the alternative view, that truth is not independent of our capacity to find out about it, or in other words to have beliefs about it—beliefs that are warranted in their context.

What does it mean to say that a belief is warranted in its context? The context may consist of other beliefs which support it, or of perceptual circumstances, or both. With many beliefs, like the belief that it is cold or that there is a table before me, it is natural to feel that it is the perceptual circumstances that warrant them. But for the anti-realist the fact that such-and-such perceptual circumstances obtain cannot itself be independent of our recognition of it, any more than any other fact can be independent of our recognition. Hence even where a belief is warranted by something perceptual, it is still in effect another belief that warrants it; and this means that we have on our hands a pure form of the coherence theory of truth. Beliefs must fit in appropriately with other beliefs which are themselves warranted in the same fashion, through coherence; and so far as it makes sense to talk of truth at all, truth is a matter of what we can in this fashion recognise as true. (pp. 35–6)

There seem to be two ingredient claims here: that warrantedness in context is a matter of coherence with other beliefs held in that context, and that the anti-realist will so conceive the relations between truth and warrantedness that the same must go for his conception of truth. However, the second is of no concern to us—interesting though the relations between warrantedness and anti-realist conceptions of truth may be—unless the first is true. Does Walker *himself* think it is true?

Well, there is something very peculiar about his argument if so, since the epistemological version of the Master Objection has presumably already disposed of the idea that all warrant can be a matter of coherence. In any case, a simple dilemma arises:

(i) While the anti-realist has controversial views about the role of the notion of warranted acceptability, the notion itself is common currency. If the epistemological version of the

Master Objection succeeds in showing that it cannot every-where be construed intra-doxastically, in terms of coherence, then even an anti-realist who proposes to *identify* truth with (an idealised form of) warranted acceptability should not be seen as proposing a coherence account of truth, since there is no viable coherence account of warranted acceptability.

(ii) If, on the other hand, the Master Objection fails against a coherence account of warranted acceptability, then it fails against that version of the coherence theory of truth which identifies truth with (idealised) warranted acceptability. And in that case the whole architecture of Walker's book collapses.

Walker's view has therefore to be not that warrantedness is a mat-ter of coherence, but that *anti-realism* at least—in the teeth of the epistemological Master Objection—has to take it so. That indeed would seem to be the gist of this passage within the quote above:

> [F]or the anti-realist the fact that such-and-such perceptual circum-stances obtain cannot itself be independent of our recognition of it, any more than any other fact can be independent of our recognition. Hence even where a belief is warranted by something perceptual, it is still in effect another belief that warrants it.

But that should surely carry no conviction. To see why, ask what con-ception of warrantedness Walker himself would find congenial. Well, the epistemological version of the Master Objection shows that the justifiability of a belief cannot always be construed in terms of its coherence with a received class of beliefs since that account is power-less to handle the justifiability of beliefs—second-order beliefs—iden-tifying the membership of that class. Nevertheless such second-order beliefs presumably can be—indeed, usually are—fully justified. Since Walker views the (constitutive versions of the) Master Objection as imposing a correspondence conception of the truth of such beliefs, can he do better than an account of their justification which takes very seriously the idea that we are normally non-inferentially aware of what we believe—that is, non-inferentially aware of the facts to which our second-order beliefs correspond?

Now, if that is the general direction his account of second-order belief should take, then there is evident scope for a parallel, non-coherentist account of the justification conditions of beliefs about our *experience*—about how things perceptually seem to us. But on such an account, and counting experience as 'something perceptual', it will not be true that

> even where a belief is warranted by something perceptual, it is still in effect another belief that warrants it.

Beliefs about the way the world *seems*, like those about what beliefs one holds, may serve to determine a framework within which justification may, for all that has been said to the contrary, be analysed in terms of coherence. But such beliefs must *themselves* allow of justification in quite other, non-coherentist terms.

In brief: Walker must, for the sake of mere consistency with his own arguments, offer a non-coherentist account of the justifiability of our second-order beliefs. And he offers no reason—indeed, there *is* no clear reason—why such an account, whatever its detail, would not naturally extend to our beliefs concerning our perceptual experience. Yet nothing in the account, so extended, would be inconsistent with the idea that

> the fact that such-and-such perceptual circumstances obtain cannot itself be independent of our recognition of it

—nothing in the account would be inconsistent, that is, with the idea that the character of one's perceptual experience is something which is essentially available to consciousness. If Walker is taking it that the anti-realist must mean *more* than that by 'not independent of our recognition', then he is making an unsupported, question-begging assumption. If, on the other hand, that is all the anti-realist need mean, then Walker is guilty of a *non sequitur* and his own arguments contain the germ of the resources to absolve the anti-realist from the charge of coherentism about warrant.

IV

Walker attempts to deploy the Master Objection against what he takes to be the central gist of Wittgenstein's discussion of rule-following—the denial that a fact can obtain 'in its own right and independently of us, of our classifications, and of our agreements'.[14] Walker's claim is not exactly that, by this anthropocentralisation, as it were, of facts, Wittgenstein lumbers himself with a pure coherence theory of truth, but rather that he places himself in a position in which his handling of the relations between the concepts of community agreement and warrant involves a similar structural impasse to that besetting pure coherentism.

This contention is not as clearly developed as its importance demands. Walker presents it as follows:

> Wittgenstein builds much—indeed everything—upon our agreement in judgement. That we agree is something that is, very commonly, warrantedly assertible. Whenever a judgement is warrantedly assertible it is the agreement of the community that makes it so; so it is the agreement of the community, and nothing else, that makes it warrantedly assertible that the community agrees. This is not circular, because the

14. Pp. 143–5. He is notably rather less concerned with the accuracy of his attributions in Wittgenstein's case than with others of the philosophers, especially Kant, who loom prominently in his book, writing (p. 124) of the view he intends to consider that 'It is enough that it is a position which is interesting in its own right, and which has gained considerable currency in recent years under Wittgenstein's name'. Another reviewer (Candlish (1990)), deploring this tendency in Wittgensteinian commentary, has suggested that 'Crispinstein' would be as good a name as 'Kripkenstein' (and either better than 'Wittgenstein'?) for the author whom Walker is actually addressing. However that may be, I shall limit myself in what follows to the force of Walker's arguments against the position which, whether Wittgenstein's or not, whether interesting or not, he intends to address.

content of the second agreement is different from the content of the first: it is an agreement to the effect that the first agreement obtains. But it gives rise to a regress. Agreement was said to provide the standard; but the standard for the claim that agreement occurs is a further agreement; and the standard for the claim that that obtains is agreement once again. This means that there is no standard, for the regress is vicious in the same way as the regress that arose for Hegel's theory . . .

. . . Wittgenstein's position differs from Hegel's in that he is concerned with the agreement of the community rather than with the beliefs of the Absolute, but that can clearly make no relevant difference to the regress. It differs also in that he considers not that the agreement guarantees truth, but that it licenses warranted assertibility. But this makes no relevant difference either. For P to be warrantedly assertible is for it to be agreed that it is; for it to be agreed that P is warrantedly assertible is for it to be warrantedly assertible that it is agreed that P is warrantedly assertible; for this to be warrantedly assertible in its turn is for it to be agreed that it is. This is not a harmless regress, like the trivial one generated by the fact that if P is true, it is true that P is true, because it means that once again we have only a series of propositions, and there is nothing to make any of them warrantedly assertible to start with. We can easily generate a set of propositions including 'Bishop Stubbs was hanged for murder', 'It is warrantedly assertible that Bishop Stubbs was hanged for murder', 'It is agreed that it is warrantedly assertible that Bishop Stubbs was hanged for murder', 'It is warrantedly assertible that it is agreed that it is warrantedly assertible that Bishop Stubbs was hanged for murder', and so on. What is needed to break out of the regress is that at some stage the agreement should be a *fact*: a fact that obtains in its own right and independently of us, of our classifications, and of our agreements. But it is just this that the [Wittgenstein's] theory will not let us have. (pp. 143–4)

To help get a focus on this, consider first a position which Walker would doubtless acknowledge to be a mere parody of Wittgenstein's view: the notion that truth is *constituted* by communal consensus. So the proposal is

(i)   P is true iff there is a communal consensus that P.

The question to which this directly gives rise is: What constitutes the satisfaction of the condition on the right-hand side? In what does the obtaining of a communal consensus that P consist? Well, given that whatever constitutes a communal consensus that P is what constitutes the truth of the proposition that there is a communal consensus that P, the inevitable shape of the account—all the consensualist can offer—would seem to be that

(ii)   There is a communal consensus that P iff there is a communal consensus that there is a communal consensus that P

and an infinite regress ensues. This of course offends the intuitive thought that there might be a communal consensus on some matter without anyone's having considered whether there is. But that objection, impressive or not, is not the Master Objection. The salient point is rather that (ii) may be recast as an instance of (D) above:

(D)$x \in$ T iff R($F(x)$, T),

when T is to be the set of propositions on which there is communal consensus, $F(x)$ is the proposition that there is a communal consensus that x, and R is set membership. And the ensuing objection is, recall, not that no set can satisfy such a condition but that no set can be *strictly defined* by—have its 'fundamental ground of difference' given by—such a condition. Yet that is just what a proponent of the crude consensualist conception of truth is apparently committed to denying. For all there is to constitute the membership of the set of propositions on which there is consensus is . . . consensus. The theorist, so runs the objection, thereby clumsily abrogates the resources necessary for the existence of a determinate T—a determinate class of propositions about which there is communal consensus—in the first place, and his proposed account of truth collapses. Again, *nota bene*, it does not follow that (i) is not true. But it does follow that the existence of a communal consensus that P cannot in general be that in virtue of which the truth of P *consists*.

Has Walker's Wittgenstein blundered into essentially this difficulty? He (Walker's Wittgenstein) appears to hold that if not all facts, then at least facts about warranted assertibility are constituted by consensus, that is, that

W(P) iff A[W(P)]

with the regress as outlined in the second quoted paragraph above then proceeding to

A[W(P)] iff W(A[W(P)])
W(A[W(P)]) iff A[W(A[W(P)])]

and so on, where each biconditional is to read as making a *constitutive* claim, right-to-left. Now Walker himself does not quite develop matters this way, but reflect that since such constitutive claims are presumably transitive, we may strike out the first element in each odd-numbered component in the regress, as it were, and simplify to a series of transitions of the form:

A[W(. . .)] iff A[W(A[W(. . .)])]

which merely iterates applications of the compound operator, 'A[W(. . .)]'. So taking T as the set of propositions such that A[W(P)], *F*(x) as the proposition that A[W(x)], and R as set membership, we are once again presented with an instance of the schema D. Accordingly, if that constitutes the theorist's last word on the membership of the set in question, then, according to the first constitutive version of the Master Objection, he has no right to the idea that there *is* any determinate range of propositions such that A[W(P)], nor therefore—by the first equivalence in the regress—to the idea that there is any determinate range of propositions which are warrantedly assertible.

The 'communitisation' of the notion of assertoric warrant thus results in its abrogation.

I take it that this is the essential structure of Walker's (rather cleverly conceived) objection to his Wittgenstein. It turns, in effect, on spotting that even a restricted consensualism will fall within the scope of the argument against the crude generalised version, provided the states of affairs falling within the restriction include facts concerning consensus about those very states of affairs.

Notice, however, a crucial point: that Walker gets that effect in the case in question by making an assumption he does not explicitly signal. In order to run the regress we need to suppose not merely that facts about warranted assertibility are constituted by consensus—that it is our agreement that makes a proposition warrantedly assertible—but more, and conversely, that facts about consensus are constituted by the warranted assertibility of their obtaining—that it is the warranted assertibility of the claim that consensus obtains that makes it so. This is not an equivalent but the *dual*—A[P] iff W(A[P])—of the first biconditional in the regress; and without it, so far as I can see, there is no proceeding to the second.

I do not know whether this is just a slip—whether Walker has simply run together 'W(P) iff A[W(P)]' and 'A[P] iff W(A[P])'—or whether he thinks the latter is something to which Wittgenstein is independently committed. But in any case there are cogent intuitive objections to both its ingredient conditionals. Against the right-to-left component, there is no evident reason why impressive evidence for the existence of a consensus about P might not be misleading. And against the left-to-right, one should object that while a consensus ought normally to be detectable—so that it is likely for a wide class of circumstances that if A[P], then W(A[P])—it can hardly be a priori that the implementation of whatever process it takes to warrant the claim that a consensus exists would not materially interfere with the opinions of the participants, destroying the very consensus there would otherwise have been. (Opinion polls?!) So the idea that the truth of the left-hand side must be *constituted* by that of an appropriate instance of the right-hand side has no plausibility whatever. Maybe Walker thinks his Wittgenstein is in no position to endorse either of these objections. But if so, his reasons do not emerge at all clearly. And if the regress does not get started, there is no need to invoke a 'de-anthropocentralised' notion of fact to stop it.

V

It does not seem, then, that Walker has successfully deployed the Master Objection against the 'Wittgensteinian' ideas he is concerned to rebut. But we can in any case no longer defer consideration of a more general misgiving about the version—the first constitutive version—of the Master Objection just now in play. Walker several times contrasts the regresses disclosed in his various applications of the Master Objection with the 'harmless' or 'trivial' regresses involved in the very concept of truth and in the correspondence theory. (See, for example, pp. 99, 144.) And of course it is vital that there be a contrast if the objection is to discriminate against the range of proposals to which Walker applies it and in favour of the correspondence conception which he favours. But it is questionable whether this putative 'harmlessness' has been well enough thought through.

What prevents someone's running the first constitutive version of the Master Objection against the contention that

(iii)   P is true iff P corresponds to the facts

taken not as a platitude but as the battle-cry of the correspondence theory, a claim about the constitution of truth? Can't we exactly parallel what happened earlier? As with the consensualist account, (i) above, the immediate question to which (iii) gives rise is: What constitutes the satisfaction of the condition on the right-hand side? In what does P's corresponding to the facts consist? And now, given that whatever constitutes P's corresponding to the facts is what constitutes the truth of the proposition that P corresponds to the facts, all, it may be charged, the correspondence account can ultimately offer is that

> (iv)   P corresponds to the facts iff that P corresponds to
>   the facts, corresponds to the facts

and an infinite regress ensues—though a harmless one in Walker's view. But why? Clearly (iv), like (ii), may be recast as an instance of (D):

> (D) $x \in T$ iff $R(F(x), T)$

when T is to be the set of propositions which correspond to the facts, $F(x)$ is the proposition that x corresponds to the facts, and R is set membership. And the objection, remember, is that no set can be *defined* by—have its membership *constituted* by—such a condition. Yet what can the correspondence theorist ultimately offer as constituting the membership of the set of propositions which correspond to fact other than the correspondence to fact, or otherwise, of propositions to the effect that the former correspond to fact? So why doesn't he too 'clumsily abrogate the resources necessary for the existence of a determinate T'—a determinate class of propositions which correspond to fact—and thereby ensure the collapse of *his* proposed account of truth? Once again, the point is not that (iii) cannot be true but rather—if the parallel conclusion about consensualism was good—that P's correspondence to fact cannot in general be that in virtue of which the truth of P *consists*.

A challenge of this shape may evidently be issued to *any* proposed characterisation of truth of the form

> P is true iff $F(P)$

as soon as we press the question: What is it for the condition, $F(P)$, to be met? For since whatever constitutes P's meeting condition $F(\dots)$ is the same as what constitutes the truth of the proposition that $F(P)$, the answer is inevitable that $F(P)$ is satisfied just in case $F(F(P))$. It may thus be argued that the outlined challenge of the Master Objection to the crude consensualist account of truth is really no more than a version of a point which applies to *all* purported analyses of truth, and therefore carries no punch against consensualism, or coherentism, or any other account in particular. The proper conclusion is rather that there can *be* no statement of what constitutes the truth of a proposition—and that truth is accordingly indefinable, just as Frege thought.

What is the correct perspective? Does this line of thought effectively explode the first constitutive version of the Master Objection? On reflection, everything depends upon the *status* of the instances of (D)

$$x \in T \text{ iff } R(F(x), T)$$

which the correspondence and coherence theorists are respectively committed to. The Master Objection has it that while a set, T, can satisfy such a condition, it cannot be *fundamentally* defined thereby— that it must be constituted by some, more basic individuative condition from which its satisfaction of the instance of (D) follows. The correspondence theorist must therefore maintain that while

(iv)   P corresponds to the facts iff that P corresponds to the facts

is (of course) a correct thesis, its right-to-left ingredient is not a *constitutive* claim. If P corresponds to fact, its doing so does not *consist* in the correspondence to fact of the proposition that it does so. Rather, I suppose, it is the other way about: the correspondence to fact of a proposition is constituted by the fact to which it corresponds. By contrast, a proponent of Walker's objection must contend, the right-to-left ingredient of the instance of (D) which a 'privileging' version of the coherence theory must endorse—that P is a member of the base class, B, just in case the proposition that it is so coheres with the members of B—*must* be viewed as making a constitutive claim, since—for the pure coherentist, at any rate—facts in general can be constituted by nothing other than relations of coherence among propositions.

The ground for the last claim offered earlier, recall, was in effect that since, for the pure coherentist, the truth of any proposition P *is* constituted by its relations of coherence to other propositions, denial of the same for the fact that P would have the effect that P might be constituted as a truth independently of the fact that P—which is (i) absurd and (ii) allows 'the facts' just the kind of autonomy which is congenial to the correspondence conception. If that thought is good, and if the correspondence theorist can make out that the direction of constitution, as it were, in (iv) is the reverse, then this general misgiving about the first constitutive version of the Master Objection can be allayed.

But this is really to do no more than describe the *shape* of a response to the misgiving—we have not broached the question of how to explain and justify the presupposed idea of asymmetries of constitution between a priori equivalents. It is a weakness of Walker's book that the need to do so goes apparently unheeded. Until enough of an account is offered to make good the relevant disanalogy between the coherence and correspondence accounts, the force of the first constitutive version of the Master Objection must be viewed as unproven. I shall not pursue the matter further here.

VI

Does Walker do better against his Wittgenstein if we interpret his point in terms of the second constitutive version of the Master Objection? That objection was that distinct, internally coherent systems of propositions are possible, matching each other in articulation and detail and each founded upon a base class. Each may include, for each proposition in its base, a proposition to the effect that that proposition is in the base—is believed, or whatever the base characteristic is. The challenge to the coherence theorist was then to explain what would make it the case that one such system was actually *ours;* and the contention of the objection was that no satisfactory answer could proceed in terms of the raw materials on which the coherence theory of truth is founded, since what is to be characterised is an *extrinsic* property of the system—a property which may vary independently of what additions are or are not coherent with the two systems.

I am inclined to think *this* objection is already compelling. Perhaps the cleanest way of seeing its force is to reflect that coherence, however exactly the theorist might attempt to explain it further, is going to be a matter of the *internal* relations of the propositions in a system— and hence will not vary as a matter of contingency. How then can the truth conditions of *any* contingent proposition be captured by a claim of the form,

P coheres with S?

Well, only if 'S' is non-rigid—only if the reference of 'S' is allowed to vary. But the case we are concerned with is one where the reference of 'S' is *fixed*: we are asking what makes it the case, or not the case, that *this particular* S is ours? The only form of answer the theorist has at his disposal is in terms of the coherence, or otherwise, of certain propositions with this specified S. And no such answer can possibly be adequate since it will be accounting for a contingency—the detail of our beliefs—in terms of non-contingent relationships between S and the propositions it moots.[15]

However, this way of developing the objection will not engage Walker's Wittgenstein, or indeed crude consensualism, since those views do not see warranted assertibility, or truth, as constituted in the internal relations within a system of propositions but in external facts about consensus. No doubt we can, as Walker says, easily

generate a set of propositions including 'Bishop Stubbs was hanged for murder', 'It is warrantedly assertible that Bishop Stubbs was hanged

15. As the reader will see, this way of presenting matters bites against the relativist response to the original Bishop Stubbs objection which we bracketed earlier. Let it be that no absolute truth exists; still the relativist-coherentist has the task of explaining what it is for it to be true, relative to our system no doubt, that it, rather than an internally coherent competitor, is actually the system we accept. It is clear that his relativism in no way assists the prospects of a satisfactory response.

for murder', 'It is agreed that it is warrantedly assertible that Bishop Stubbs was hanged for murder', 'It is warrantedly assertible that it is agreed that it is warrantedly assertible that Bishop Stubbs was hanged for murder', and so on (p. 144)

but the question is what precise difficulty for his Wittgenstein is supposed to be posed by the constructibility of such a set—why should one who holds that facts about warranted assertibility are constituted in consensus have implicitly surrendered any entitlement to the idea that all those propositions are *false?* Walker asserts that

what is needed to break out of the regress is that at some stage the agreement should be a *fact:* a fact that obtains in its own right and independently of us, of our classifications, and of our agreements. (p. 144)

And certainly his Wittgenstein denies that any fact is wholly independent 'of us, of our classifications, and of our agreements'. But whatever exactly that denial amounts to, it surely need not involve repudiation of the whole idea of truth as conferred by correspondence to fact. The issue rather concerns what the Wittgensteinian views as a muddled hyper-objectification of the idea of correspondence to fact. Why shouldn't a properly modest version of it serve the thought, that each of the propositions in Walker's regress is false, just as well as Walker's preferred realist version?

10

∠

Truth:
A Traditional Debate
Reviewed

I

Every student of English-speaking analytical metaphysics is taught that the early-twentieth-century philosophical debate about truth confronted the correspondence theory, supported by Russell, Moore, the early Wittgenstein and, later, J. L. Austin, with the coherence theory advocated by the British idealists.[1] Sometimes the pragmatist conception of truth deriving from Dewey, William James and C. S. Peirce is regarded as a third player. And as befits a debate at the dawn of analytical philosophy, the matter in dispute is normally taken to have been the proper analysis of the concept.

No doubt this conception nicely explains some of the characteristic turns taken in the debate. Analysis, as traditionally conceived, has to

---

1. Two *loci classici* of coherentism are H. H. Joachim (1906) and F. H. Bradley (1914). Ralph Walker has argued that coherentism is implicit also in the forms of anti-realism canvassed by Michael Dummett and Hilary Putnam (at least, the Hilary Putnam of *Reason, Truth and History*). See Ralph Walker (1989). Myself I doubt this—for further discussion, see my critical study of Walker's book in Wright (1995b).

consist in the provision of illuminating conceptual equivalences; and illumination will depend, according to the standard rules of play, on the *analysans'* utilising only concepts which, in the best case, are in some way prior to and independent of the notion being analysed—or, if that's too much to ask, then concepts which at least permit of some form of explication which does not in turn take one straight back to that notion. Thus if it is proposed, in this spirit, that truth is correspondence to external fact, it will be possible for a critic both to grant the *correctness* of the proposal and to reject it nevertheless—because, it may be contended, it fails to comply with the conditions on an illuminating *analysis*. In particular, it will be an obligation on an analysis of truth in terms of correspondence that it be possible to supply appropriate independent explications of the notions of 'correspondence' and 'fact', and it is exactly here, of course, that many of the traditional difficulties for the correspondence proposal have been located. Likewise, if we propose to analyse truth in terms of coherence, or on broadly pragmatist lines, we must be prepared to allow that any and every occurrence of 'true' as applied to what the analysis recognises to be its primary bearers—sentences, or propositions, or whatever—may be replaced, without change of meaning,[2] by an expression of the preferred analysans. And, again, many of the knots into which critics have tied proposals of these kinds depend upon exploitation of this constraint. As recently as 1982, for instance, Alvin Plantinga observed that if 'true' just means: *would be believed by cognitively ideal subjects operating under cognitively ideal conditions,* then there seems to be no prospect of recovering, without paradox, an account of the content of the thought: it is true that conditions are not cognitively ideal.[3]

2. How this constraint may be made to consist with the requirement that analysis be illuminating is, of course, the heart of Moore's Paradox of Analysis. But the sort of objection about to be noted need read no more into sameness of content than sameness of truth conditions.

3. Plantinga (1982). Plantinga's point also engages certain formulations of the coherence theory. For instance to suppose that 'true' means: *would be believed by a subject who had arrived at a maximally coherent and comprehensive set of beliefs,* is

Truth: A Traditional Debate Reviewed

When the debate is all about the analysis of the concept of truth, then at least two other kinds of position have to be possible—and, historically, they have indeed been occupied. One is the indefinabilist view adopted by Frege: that truth allows of *no* analysis, because it is too simple, or primitive, or because any notions involved in a formulation which is at least correct will rapidly bring one back to truth, so compromising illumination. Frege held this view for reasons whose cogency is a matter of dispute but the apparent paucity of successful analyses of *anything* in analytical philosophy, and the inchoate and uneasy state of the methodology of analysis itself, must encourage the thought that this negative stance will not easily be dismissed.[4] Quite different—and rather more interesting—is the proposal that correspondence, coherentist, pragmatist and even indefinabilist conceptions of truth all err in their common conviction that 'true' presents a substantial characteristic at all. This is the deflationist tradition, which is usually thought to have originated in Ramsey, was defended in rather different ways by Ayer and Strawson, and which survives in contemporary writers such as Paul Horwich and Hartry Field.[5] According to deflationism, there simply isn't anything which truth, in general, *is*. It is a misconstrual of the role of the adjective 'true' to see it as expressing the concept of a substantial characteristic of which one of the traditional accounts might provide a correct analysis, or which might allow of no correct analysis. Those who think otherwise

---

again implicitly to surrender the means to construe the truth of the thought: no one holds a maximally coherent and comprehensive set of beliefs. The problem is a special case of the so-called Conditional Fallacy: any analysis in terms of subjunctive conditionals is potentially in trouble if its intended range comprises statements which are incompatible with the protases of the relevant conditionals.

4. For discussion, see Peter Carruthers (1981). See also the useful account in Ralph Walker's survey article, "Theories of Truth", in Walker (1997), esp. section 6.

5. Horwich (1998a) provides a detailed defence of the deflationary tradition and a useful bibliography of its literature. While Field (1986) eventually suggests that there are purposes for which a correspondence conception is needed, his more recent (1994) takes a more committed deflationary line.

are missing the point that the role of a significant adjective doesn't have to be to ascribe a genuine property.

My first principal point is that, notwithstanding the fact that it rationalises many of the moves made, and doubtless reflects therefore the intentions of many of the protagonists, the conception of the traditional debate about truth as centred upon reductive analysis of the concept is not best fitted to generate the most fruitful interpretation of it. To see this, suppose for the sake of argument that the indefinabilists are right: that 'true'—like, say, 'red'—admits of no illuminating conceptual breakdown. It is striking that philosophical discussion of colour has hardly been silenced by the corresponding point about the concept *red* or basic colour concepts generally. The contention that there is, as Locke thought, an interesting distinction between primary and secondary qualities of objects and that red is a secondary quality; the contention that whether an object is red is, in some way, a 'response-dependent' matter, or more generally that there is some form of implicit relativity in the idea of an object's being red; the contention that red is, on the contrary, a non-relational property of objects or, more specifically, that red things form a natural kind; even the 'error-theoretic' view that a complete inventory of characteristics found in the real world would contain no mention of the colours—all these views, and an acknowledgement of the interest of the debates to which they contribute, are consistent with recognition of the indefinability of colour concepts. So, consistently with its indefinability—if it is indefinable—a similar range of issues can be expected to arise in connection with truth. 'True'—even when taken, in the broad sense which interests us, as a predicate of content-bearing things—is predicated of a variety of items: beliefs, thoughts, propositions, token utterances of type sentences. But whatever such items we have in mind, we can ask whether one of them being true is in any way an *implicitly relational* matter—and if so, what are the terms of the relation; whether it is a *response-dependent* matter, or in any other way dependent on subjectivity or a point of view; whether there is indeed nothing generally in which the truth of such an item consists—

whether an inventory of all the properties to be found in the world would include mention of *no such thing as truth*.

Indeed, such issues arise for any putative characteristic, Φ. Should we (ontologists) take Φ seriously at all, or is some sort of error-theoretic or deflationary view appropriate? If we do take it seriously, should we think of the situation of an item's being Φ as purely a matter of how it is intrinsically with that item, or are we rather dealing with some form of relation? Is an item's being Φ an objective matter (and what does it mean to say so)? These are analytic-philosophical issues par excellence, but their resolution need not await—and might not be settled by—the provision of a correct conceptual analysis.

II

Suppose we discard the analysis-centred conception of the traditional debate and look at it instead in the way suggested by the foregoing reflections. Clearly the deflationary option remains in play, holding that truth is not a genuine characteristic of anything—that it would find no place in an inventory of what is real. The other views all allow the reality of truth but differ about its *structure*, or in respects relevant to the broad question of objectivity. Correspondence theory holds that truth is a relational characteristic whose terms are respectively propositions—to pick one among the possibilities[6]—and *non-propositional items*—facts, or states of affairs—in an independent world.[7] The proposal thus bears both on structure and, so proposers of correspondence intend, on objectivity too. Coherence theory agrees about the relationality of truth, but disagrees about the terms of the relation: on this type of view, the truth of a proposition consists not in a relation to something non-propositional, but in its participation in a

---

6. Sentences, token utterances, statements, beliefs and thoughts are some among the other content-bearing items which we ordinarily think of as apt for truth.

7. Excepting, of course, the case where a proposition is itself about propositions.

system, meeting certain conditions, whose other participants are likewise propositions—so ultimately in relations to those other propositions. This is again, in the first instance, a view about the structure of truth, but it was intended by its original proponents to provide a vehicle for their idealism. And pragmatism—the view that truth is, broadly, a matter of operational success of some kind—while making no clear suggestion about structure (though there may be commitments in this direction once the relevant dimensions of success are clarified), stands in opposition to the correspondence theorists' thoughts about objectivity without—intentionally anyway—implying anything like such idealism.

Let's focus for the time being on the question of structure, and return later to some of the issues connected with pragmatism. We may chart the possibilities in a tree, shown in the following figure:

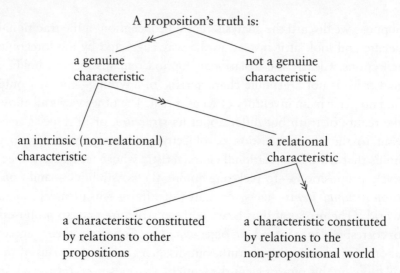

Essentially, then, just four structural proposals are possible: deflationism, intrinsicism and the two forms of relationalism, coherentism and correspondence. I think it's fair to say that this conception of correspondence, shorn of any further analytical or explanatory obligations, comes across as highly commonsensical. In general, we'd want to think both that there is a real distinction marked by the classification of some propositions as true and others as false, and that it is a distinction which cannot generally be understood without reference to things which are not themselves propositions, so cannot be understood in intrinsicist or coherentist terms.

This piece of common sense is not to be confused with the idea that, understood one way, correspondence is nothing more than a platitude. The platitude is that predications of 'true' may always harmlessly be glossed in terms of correspondence to fact, telling it like it is, and so on. These paraphrases incorporate no substantial commitment about the structure of truth any more than the paraphrasability of 'she did it for John' by 'she did it on John's behalf' involves a commitment to the view that altruistic action is really a three-term relation. By contrast, the ordinary, commonsensical conception of the kind of thing a proposition's truth is involves exactly the structural commitments associated with the feathered path on the above tree.

It will be a second main contention of this essay that there is no stable alternative to allowing at least some scope to this commonsensical conception.

III

In order to make good that contention, we need to see that each of the three alternatives gives rise to intractable problems.

Intrinsicism is the easiest case to deal with. Fix attention on the case of contingent truths. If its truth value were an intrinsic—but contingent—property of a particular proposition, then no contingent change in any other object should entail change in the proposition in that particular respect. That's an instance of a quite general principle. The mass, for instance, of a given body is a contingent but intrinsic property of that body only if no contingent change in any other object would entail change in that object's mass. By contrast, a property—for instance, being a grandfather—is essentially relational, even if expressed by what looks like a semantically simple predicate, if change in other objects may entail that a particular object sheds or acquires that property. By this simple test, truth is, manifestly, not an intrinsic property. For the truth value of any contingent proposition must co-vary with hypothetical changes in the characteristics of things it concerns—so that a hypothetical change, for instance, in the location of my coffee cup may entail an alteration in the truth value of the proposition that there is no coffee cup on my desk, even though that proposition and the particular coffee cup in question are quite distinct existences. To be sure, this line of thought creates no difficulty for the idea that the truth value of a *necessary* proposition might be an intrinsic property. So, indeed, it may be. But clearly intrinsicism cannot handle the general run of contingent cases.[8]

It might be rejoined that the canvassed account of the contrast between intrinsic and relational properties is incorrect or circular. For a property F may be an intrinsic characteristic of an object and yet its loss, say, may still be entailed by change in another object provided that latter change is permitted to be in *non-intrinsic respects*. For instance, if G is a ('Cambridge') property possessed by any object just in case *a* has intrinsic characteristic F, then any other object's losing G will entail that *a* has lost F. This observation is, however, beside the point. All the objection to intrinsicism needs is that the account be correct, not that it be explanatory. If it is at least granted that F is an intrinsic property of *a* just in case no *intrinsic* change in any other object can entail change in *a* in that respect, it will follow as before that truth cannot be an intrinsic property of any proposition whose content is that another object has some particular intrinsic but contingent property.

IV

It is a rather more complicated business to elicit what is fundamentally unsatisfactory about the deflationary conception of truth. The difficulties here are owing partly to the point that deflationism is more of a

8. I do not know that anyone has ever seriously proposed an intrinsicist conception of truth quite generally.

'tendency' than a definite philosophical position, and different deflationists display differences of formulation and emphasis which make it
hard to see what may be essential and what optional in their views.
There are, however, a number of characteristic, interrelated claims:

(i)   that there is no property of truth which is an
       appropriate object of philosophical attention:
       something which we might try to analyse, or in
       whose structure we might be interested, or which
       might give rise to issues about objectivity. Contrary
       to the presupposition both of the traditional debate
       and of its revision canvassed above, there is *nothing*
       in which the truth of a proposition, for example,
       consists. 'True' expresses no real property.[9]

That negative contention is then characteristically augmented by a
variety of considerations about the meaning or positive function of
the word 'true', for instance:

(ii)   that, as applied to sentences, 'true' is just the device
       of *disquotation*—a device for affirming at the
       metalinguistic level (by locutions of the form: 'p' is
       true) exactly what can be affirmed at the object-
       language level by an assertoric use of 'p';

(iii) that the Disquotational Scheme

       'p' is true if and only if p

---

9. Horwich is more guarded on this than many writers in the deflationist tradition.
But although he seems unwilling expressly to deny that truth is a property, it is not, he
contends, a 'complex property'—not 'an ingredient of reality whose underlying
essence will, it is hoped, one day be revealed by philosophical or scientific analysis'
(Horwich (1998a), p. 2). Thus there is, for Horwich, nothing to say about what truth
really consists in; no real question for correspondence and coherence accounts, for
example, to address themselves to.

(or if the primary grammar of 'true' is considered to be that of an operator on (or predicable of) propositions, the Equivalence Schema

It is true that p/that p is true if and only if p)

is (all but) a complete explanation of the meaning of 'true';

(iv) that 'true' is just a device of endorsement—we only have any use for such a predicate because we sometimes choose to endorse propositions indirectly, without specifying their content ('The sixth sentence of *Remarks on the Foundations of Mathematics* IV, §3 is true' or 'Fermat's Last Theorem has turned out to be true') and sometimes want to endorse whole batches of propositions at once ('Almost everything Richard Rorty says is true'). In other kinds of case we can dispense with the word altogether.

Deflationism has been subjected to a variety of criticisms: for instance, that its characteristic lionisation of the Disquotational Scheme is in tension with the manifest unacceptability of that principle when vagueness or other phenomena leading to failures of bivalence are operative;[10] that it is inconsistent with a truth-conditional conception of meaning or more generally with the semantic role of truth;[11] that it cannot accommodate the idea of scientific progress; most generally, that it violates our intuitions about correspondence, about truth as bestowed by fit with an external, objective world.[12] Here I shall rehearse an argument I have given elsewhere to the effect that deflationism is internally unstable.[13] Specifically, there is a contradiction

10. This criticism is first lodged, I believe, in Dummett (1959a).

11. This claim too is advanced in *ibid*.

12. All these directions of criticism are usefully referenced and reviewed in Horwich (1998a).

13. See chapter 1 of *Truth and Objectivity*.

between the kind of account of the function of 'true' which deflation-ists broadly want to give and the contention that the concept of truth, properly understood, is not the concept of a genuine, substantial property.

Let us focus, for ease of exposition, on 'true' as predicable of propositions, and on the positive deflationist contention that, in its most basic use, the word is essentially a device of endorsement which, except in cases where the content of the proposition endorsed is not explicitly given, or where quantification over propositions is involved, may be dispensed with altogether in favour of a simple assertion of the proposition characterised as 'true'.

It is hardly deniable that 'true' does have this kind of function and that its uses may often be paraphrased away without materially affecting the content of what is said. The issue is rather whether the point can carry the intended deflationary implications. And the crucial question for that issue is: What is it to *endorse* a proposition? Endorsement generally involves an element of recommendation, or approval of an item as meeting a certain standard. That's what I'm doing when, for example, in helping my child choose an ice cream I point at the pistachio and say 'That's a nice one'. What kind of commendation is involved in the case of 'true'? Plausibly, that if I affirm a proposition's truth, I'm recommending its acceptance, commending it as meeting a certain doxastic standard, as it were. In this way, affirmations of truth—and likewise denials of truth—are normative claims. To endorse a proposition as true is to affirm that it is acceptable as a belief or statement; to deny that a proposition is true is to affirm that it is correspondingly unacceptable.

To be sure, nothing in that should impress as immediately uncomfortable for deflationism. No deflationist has wanted, or ought to have wanted, to deny that believing and statement-making are normatively constrained activities—activities governed by standards, non-compliance with which opens a thinker to criticism. However, once that is accepted, the question has to be confronted of what the relevant standards are. In particular, if 'true' is essentially just a device of endorsement, then in using it I am saying that a proposition is in good shape as far as certain relevant norms are concerned. What, for deflationism, are those norms?—What does 'good shape' here consist in?

Believing and stating are, naturally, subject to rather different norms. In very many contexts, justification for a belief is insufficient to confer justification for its public expression, partly because assertion is socially constrained—the public expression of a fully justified belief may give offence, or bore people, and so on—and partly because complex principles of conversational implication make it possible to encourage false beliefs in an audience by the judicious selection and assertion of fully justified ones.[14] However, if one wanted to criticise an assertion on this type of broadly social or pragmatic ground, one wouldn't do so by denying its truth. So, as a first approximation, it seems the deflationist should say that the use of 'true' in the basic kind of case is to endorse a proposition as *epistemically justified,* or to endorse an utterance as acceptable just insofar as the epistemic justification of the proposition it expresses is concerned.

In any case, what the deflationist clearly *cannot* allow is that 'true', when used to endorse, has the function of commending a proposition for its satisfaction of *some distinctive norm* which contrasts with epistemic justification and which only 'true' and equivalents serve to mark. For if there were a distinctive such norm, it could hardly fail to be reckoned a genuine property of a proposition that it did, or did not comply with it. And if the norm in question were uniquely associated with 'true' and its cognates, that would be as much as to allow that there was a special property of *truth*—at which point the deflationary game would have been given away. So for the deflationist, it appears, the basic use of 'true' has to be to signal a proposition's compliance with norms whose proper characterisation will not proceed in terms of equivalents of 'true'. If it is propositions, rather than utterances, that we are concerned with, epistemic justification would then seem to be the only plausible candidate.[15]

14. The classic treatment of the phenomenon is, of course, Grice (1989).

15. This would be less than a commitment to the idea that 'true' *means* epistemically justified. There is a distinction between holding that a word expresses no property but is used to commend items for their possession of a certain property and holding that it expresses that very property.

It would follow that the basic use of 'not true' should be to signal a proposition's *non*-compliance with relevant norms of epistemic justification. But if that were so, there should in general be nothing to choose between the denial that a proposition is true and the denial that it is justified. And not only does that misrepresent the ordinary usage of the terms, it is inconsistent with principles to which deflationism itself is committed, and which are, indeed, at the heart of the deflationary account: the Disquotational Scheme and its analogue for propositions, the Equivalence Schema.

I'll illustrate the relevant point as it flows from the latter. The schema provides that, for an arbitrary proposition p,

It is true that p ↔ p

If we substitute 'not p' for 'p' at both occurrences, we have

It is true that not p ↔ not p

while if we negate both sides, we derive

It is not true that p ↔ not p

And from the latter two principles, via transitivity of the biconditional, we have

It is not true that p if and only if it is true that not p

In brief: the Equivalence Schema entails, given only the most basic assumptions about its scope and about the logic of negation, that truth and negation commute as prefixes. Manifestly, this is not true in general of warrant and negation: there is, in general, no sound inference from

It is not the case that p is warranted

to

It is the case that not p is warranted

This pattern of inference cannot be sustained in any case where the correctness of its premise is owing to the *neutrality* of our state of information—to the fact that we have no evidence bearing either on p or its negation.

The Equivalence Schema itself, then, is a commitment to repudiating the idea that '. . . is not true' is a device for denying that a proposition complies with norms of warrant/justification—for if it were such a device, it ought not to commute with negation. But what other account can deflationism offer of what the denial of truth amounts to, given its express contention that '. . . is true' is merely a device of endorsement, so a device for affirming a proposition's compliance with some norm or other, and given that the only norms on the board—in a context in which the existence of any self-standing norm of truth has been rejected—are justificatory ones?[16]

16. There is scope for some skirmishing. Ian Rumfitt has responded that the divergence in the behaviour of 'true' and 'assertible' just noted may straightforwardly be accommodated in a fashion entirely consonant with the purposes of deflationism, without admission of a distinctive norm of truth, provided the deflationist is prepared to allow primitive norms of *warranted denial* to operate alongside those of warranted assertion (Rumfitt (1995)). Rather, that is, than restrict his distinctive deflationary claims to the word 'true', the deflationist should contend 'that "is true" and "is not true" function purely as devices for endorsing *and rejecting* assertions, beliefs and so on . . . and which therefore register no norms distinct from justified assertibility *and justified deniability*' (*ibid.*, p. 103; compare *Truth and Objectivity*, p. 30). How would this help to explain the commutativity of truth and negation? Rumfitt is not entirely explicit, but the point may seem clear enough. Since denying a statement is asserting its negation, a primitive warrant—an *anti-warrant* is Rumfitt's term—for the denial of p, registered by a claim of the form, it is not true that p, will be *eo ipso* a warrant for asserting the negation of p, so—via the Disquotational Scheme—for asserting that it is true that not p. So the problematical direction of commutativity is secured, while the invalidity of the corresponding principle for assertibility is vouchsafed, as before, by the possibility of states of information in which one has neither warrant nor anti-warrant for p.

However the problem recurs. Consider again the problematical equivalence,

It is not true that p if and only if it is true that not p

and the result of negating both its sides:

It is not not true that p if and only if it is not true that not p

In fact, it's intuitively perfectly evident that the use of 'true' *is* tied to a norm—to a way in which acceptance of a proposition may be in good, or bad, standing—quite separate from the question of its justification in the light of the acceptor's state of information. An acceptance that grass is green, that is, may be open to censure if there is no warrant for accepting that grass is green; but it is in bad standing in quite another way if, warranted or not, it is actually not the case that grass is green. Correspondingly it is in good standing, in one way, just if accepted on the basis of sufficient justification, whether or not grass is green; but it is in good standing in another way if, irrespective of what justification may be possessed by the acceptor, grass is actually green. The concept of truth is a concept of a way a proposition may or may not be in good standing which precisely *contrasts* with its justificatory status at any particular time. That is the point which we've elicited from the Equivalence Schema. But it is independently evident, and any satisfactory philosophy of truth has to respect it.

There is no hope, then, for a deflationary account of truth which allows, or is anyway committed to the idea that 'true', in its most basic use, is a device for endorsing propositions as complying with other norms. A device of endorsement it may be, at least in the basic case. But the concept of the associated norm is of something *sui generis*.

Can the deflationist regroup? What the foregoing forces is an admission that, for each particular proposition, we have the concept of

---

Supposing that the role of '(is) not true' were merely to register the presence of an anti-warrant, there seems no way of shirking the transition to

It is not anti-warranted that p if and only if it is anti-warranted that not p

But that, of course, is no less unacceptable when neutral states of information are possible than is

It is not warranted that p if and only if it is warranted that not p

In short, for any discourse in which neutral states of information are a possibility, the Equivalence Schema imposes a contrast both between 'is true' and 'is assertible', *and* between 'is not true' and 'is anti-warranted'. Rumfitt's proposal that the deflationist should recognise anti-warrant as primitive—whatever its independent interest—is thus of no assistance with her present difficulty.

a norm which is distinct from warrant and is flagged by the word 'true'. And once it is allowed that the role of 'true' is to mark a particular kind of achievement, or failing, on the part of a proposition, contrasting with its being warranted or not, there will have to be decent sense in the question: What does such an achievement, or failing, amount to? To be sure, that is a question which may turn out to admit of no very illuminating or non-trivial answer—but if so, that would tend to be a point in favour of Frege's indefinabilism, rather than deflationism. If a term registers a distinctive norm over a practice, the presumption ought to be that there will be something in which a move's compliance or non-compliance with that norm will consist. And whichever status it has, that will then be a real characteristic of the move. So what room does deflationism have for manoeuvre?

There are two possibilities. First, it might be contended that all, strictly, that has been noted—has been shown to follow from the Equivalence Schema—is that 'true' is so used as to *call for*—express— a norm over the acceptance of propositions which is distinct from warrant. It's quite another matter whether there *really is* such a norm—whether there really is such a way for a proposition to be in, or out of good standing. It's one thing for an expression to be used in the making of a certain distinctive kind of normative claim; quite another matter for there to be such a thing as a bearer's *really qualifying for* a judgement of that kind. An error theorist about morals, for example, like John Mackie, would presumably readily grant that moral language is *used* normatively—is used to applaud, or censure, particular actions, for instance.[17] What he will deny, nevertheless, is that there are any real characteristics which respond to this use—any real characteristics by possessing which an action may qualify for a deserved such appraisal.

It is easily seen that deflationism cannot avail itself of any counterpart of this first line of defence. For the deflationist must surely be quite content to allow that all manner of statements *really are true*— when the right circumstances obtain: that grass is green, for instance,

17. Mackie (1977).

really is true just when grass is green; that snow is white really is true just when snow is white; that the earth's orbit is an ellipse is true just in case the earth's orbit really is an ellipse; and so on. For deflationism, there has to be, for each proposition—or at least for those of an objective subject matter—*an objective condition,* namely, the very one specified by the appropriate instance of the Equivalence Schema, under which it qualifies as true. So there is no possibility of refuge in error theory in this context. The Equivalence Schema itself determines what the conditions of rightful application of 'true' to a particular proposition, p, are; if as a matter of fact they obtain, then this, coupled with the distinctive normativity of the predicate, enforces the recognition that there really is such a thing as p's complying, or failing to comply with the distinctive norm of truth. It is not merely that our concept of truth calls for such a norm; the call is answered.[18]

We should conclude that two characteristic claims of deflationism are lost. It is not true, first, that 'true' *only* functions as a device of (indirect, or compendious) endorsement; it also functions, for each proposition, to advert to the satisfaction of a distinctive norm, whose satisfaction is—at least for a proposition with an objective subject matter—a real matter of fact. Second, it is hard to hear a distinction between that last point and the admission that truth, for each such proposition, is a real property. But there is still a final line of defence—one last characteristic deflationary claim which a proponent might try to salvage. The question remains so far open whether the property in question should be regarded as *the same* in all cases. Perhaps the deflationist can dig a last ditch here. For if the property were not the same, we might yet have the resources to undercut the classical debates about the *general* constitution of truth; and that those debates were bad was one major point that deflationism wanted to make.

18. This simple observation is a partial response to a recent tendency of Richard Rorty's, namely, to dismiss those features of our practice with 'true' which are recalcitrant to 'pragmatist' interpretation as mere reflections of the concept's absorption of a misguided representationalist metaphysic. See, for instance, Rorty (1995). But it is to be expected, of course, that he would refuse to hear any but a metaphysically inflated reading of 'an objective subject matter'.

A line of thought with that tendency is nicely expressed by Simon Blackburn:

[C]ompare 'is true', . . . with a genuine target of philosophical analysis: 'is conscious', or 'has rights', for example. We investigate these by looking for the principles which determine whether something is conscious, or has rights. These principles are intended to govern any such judgement, so that we get a unified class: the class of conscious things, or things that have rights. Each item in such a class is there because it satisfies the same condition, which the analysis has uncovered. Or, if this is slightly idealised, we find only a 'family' of related conditions or 'criteria' for the application of the term. Still, there is then a family relationship between the members of the class. But now contrast 'is true'. We know *individually* what makes this predicate applicable to the judgements or sentences of an understood language. 'Penguins waddle' is a sentence true, in English, if and only if penguins waddle. It is true that snow is white if and only if snow is white. The reason the first sentence deserves the predicate is that penguins waddle, and the reason why the judgement that snow is white deserves the predicate is that snow *is* white. But these reasons are entirely different. There is no single account, or even little family of accounts, in virtue of which each deserves the predicate, for deciding whether penguins waddle has nothing much in common with deciding whether snow is white. There are *as* many different things to do, to decide whether the predicate applies, as there are judgements to make. So how *can* there be a unified, common account of the 'property' which these quite different decision procedures supposedly determine? We might say: give us any sentence about whose truth you are interested, and simply by 'disquoting' and removing the reference to truth, we can tell you what you have to judge in order to determine its truth. Since we can do this without any analysis or understanding of a common property of truth, the idea that there is such a thing is an illusion.[19]

Blackburn here captures with characteristic felicity a thought which has unquestionably influenced many deflationists—though he does

19. Blackburn (1984), pp. 230–1.

not himself explicitly endorse it. However, it surely provides no very good reason for the intended conclusion—that truth is no single property. For the pattern it calls attention to is a commonplace, exemplified by a host of properties which we should not scruple to regard as unitary or as potentially open to philosophical account. *Many* properties, that is, are such that their satisfaction conditions vary as a function of the character of a potential bearer. Consider the property of having fulfilled one's educational potential. What it takes to instantiate this will depend naturally on other characteristics of the individual concerned; but that ought to be quite consistent with the substantiality and commonality of the property in question since there is a clear sense in which anyone who has fulfilled his educational potential has done the same thing as anyone else who has done so, and what they have both done may be expected straightforwardly to allow of a uniform account. In general, how x has to be in order to be F can depend in part on how things stand in other respects with x, and vary accordingly, without any motive thereby being provided for regarding it as an error to suppose, or to try to characterise, a general condition which being F involves satisfying. Otherwise you might just as well say that there is no single thing in which being twice as old as one's oldest child consists (being a *doubletenarian*), since for me it would involve being twice as old as Geoffrey, for Prince Charles being twice as old as William and for Blackburn being twice as old as Gwen.

The general pattern, it should be evident, is that of properties whose satisfaction consists in an individual's meeting a condition implicitly involving existential quantification over the right field of a relation. To fulfil one's educational potential is for there to be certain levels of academic attainment such that under certain normal educational conditions it is possible for one to meet them, and such that one has met them. To be twice as old as one's oldest child is for there to be some individual of whom one is a father or mother and whose actual age is half one's own. In general, to be the bearer of such a property will be to stand in a relation of a certain kind to an appropriate instance or instances of this implicit quantifier, and the identity of that instance or instances may vary depending on the identity and character in other respects of the bearer in question. It is in the *nature* of properties of this general character to admit such variation, and it compromises their unity not at all.

There is accordingly no comfort for a deflationist in the platitude that how things have to be in order for particular propositions to be true varies. Propositions vary in *how they claim matters to stand*—as parents vary in how old their children are, or people vary in what their educational potential is—and propositions' truth values will naturally be a function of the specific such claims they make. To impose the rubric explicitly: for any proposition p, it is true that p just in case *there is a way things could be* such that anyone who believed, doubted, and so on that p would believe, doubt, and so on that things were that way, and things are that way.[20] This paraphrase is doubtless wholly unilluminating—it offers little more than a longhand version of the Correspondence Platitude. Its merit is merely to serve as a reminder how truth is naturally conceived to share a conceptual shape with, for example, doubletenarianship or fulfilment of educational potential, and thus to bring out why no conclusions follow about its integrity from the line of thought outlined in Blackburn's remarks.

A sympathiser with deflationism may essay a final throw. It may be contended that the position at which we have arrived, although inconsistent with the traditional formulations of deflationism, is still nothing terribly at odds with its spirit. Maybe it has to be recognised that truth is a property after all, contrasting with justification, and normative over assertion and belief. But the conviction of the traditional debate is that it is a *metaphysically deep* property, whose essence is unobvious and controversial. By contrast, the characterisation of it now offered by way of rebuttal of the tendency of Blackburn's remarks is nothing if not obvious and *trivial;* and this triviality surely just as effectively cuts the ground from under the traditional debate as would the findings that truth is no unified property, or no

---

20. For truth as a property of sentences, the rubric might naturally be applied to issue in something along the lines: for any sentence, s, an utterance of s in a particular context is true just in case there is a proposition, that p, which such an utterance would express, and which is true.

property at all. The victory over deflationism is therefore pyrrhic: the skirmishing has led us to say what truth in general is in such a way as to drain all metaphysical interest from the question in the process.[21]

Someone inclined to resist this would not be prudent to stake all on the possibility of a less trivial account of truth. Where the rejoinder goes astray is in its oversight, rather, of the contrast, drawn at the start, between the project of analysis of the concept of truth and the debate about the structure and objectivity of the property of truth. One meritorious claim in the deflationist portfolio—though not its exclusive possession—may well be that the success of any purported analysis of the concept must pay a price in terms of triviality. But the above account of truth for propositions, trivial as it may be, simply does not engage the structural alternatives charted earlier nor the debate they delimit. Anyone who has mastered the concept of truth and does not scruple to quantify over 'ways things could be' can accept it as necessary and sufficient for the truth of a proposition that there be a way things could be which anyone who believes that proposition will suppose realised, and which is indeed realised. To accept that much enjoins so far no commitment on the matter of what kind of characteristic—intrinsic, relational (if so, what are the terms of the relation?) and so on—the truth of a proposition is, nor on whether or to what extent its possession may be viewed as objective. Exactly those are the metaphysically substantial matters.

V

The third and last alternative to a correspondence account of the structure of truth is coherentism. Here is an expression of an old and sometimes very influential objection to the coherence theory:

> [T]he objection to the coherence theory lies in this, that it presupposes a more usual meaning of truth and falsehood in constructing its coherent whole, and that this more usual meaning, though indispensable to

21. Compare the remarks of Horwich quoted in note 9 above.

the theory, cannot be explained by means of the theory. The proposition 'Bishop Stubbs was hanged for murder' is, we are told, not coherent with the whole of truth or with experience. But that means, when we examine it, that something is *known* which is inconsistent with this proposition. Thus what is inconsistent with the proposition must be something *true:* it may be perfectly possible to construct a coherent whole of *false* propositions in which 'Bishop Stubbs was hanged for murder' would find a place. In a word, the partial truths of which the whole of truth is composed must be such propositions as would commonly be called true, not such as would commonly be called false; there is no explanation, on the coherence theory, of the distinction commonly expressed by the words *true* and *false,* and no evidence that a system of false propositions might not, as in a good novel, be just as coherent as the system which is the whole of truth.[22]

The Right Reverend W. Stubbs died of natural causes. Russell's point is that we may nevertheless envisage a comprehensive *fiction* part of which is that he was hanged for murder, and that in point of coherence such a fiction may very well stand comparison with what we take to be the truth. In order, then, to recover the idea that such a fiction *is* fiction, we need recourse to a notion of truth which the coherence account is powerless to explicate. Whatever 'coherence' is taken to involve in detail, it seems likely that mutually incompatible, equally comprehensive, internally coherent systems of beliefs will be possible; more, *any* self-consistent proposition is likely to participate in *some* coherent system of belief with whatever degree of comprehensiveness you want. So the coherence theory cannot discriminate truth from falsehood—and it cannot justify principles like non-contradiction:

If p is true, not p is not true.

Yet surely any correct account of truth has to sustain such principles. Notice that this objection in no way depends upon the detail of any

22. Russell (1906–7), pp. 33–4.

particular proposed conception of coherence, and thus does not presuppose that the coherence account is being offered as an *analysis* of truth. The objection is purely structural. The driving thought is that whatever coherence is taken to consist in, the suggestion that the truth of a proposition consists in its participation in a coherent system in effect falls foul of a dilemma: if *fiction* can constitute such a system, then participation in such a system is clearly insufficient for truth. If it cannot, then it appears that truth is not constituted purely in inter-propositional relations—the propositions in question have to meet some other condition, so far unexplicated, and Russell's hostile suggestion is that the only available such condition is: truth as ordinarily understood.

There are two possible lines of response. First, the coherentist may go relativist, conceding that there is indeed no *absolute* truth and embracing the contention that, to the contrary, truth is relative to a system. Thus the proposition that Bishop Stubbs was hanged for murder can indeed be true, relevant to a sufficiently coherent and comprehensive body of propositions which includes it. What we are pleased to regard as *the* truth merely reflects the actually entrenched such system. Principles, like non-contradiction, which seem to require that the truth cannot extend to every conceivable coherent system of propositions, are misconstrued when taken to have that implication. Sure, they are valid *within* systems: no proposition can participate in a coherent system for which its negation is already a member. But they have no valid application *across* systems.

Alternatively, a coherentist might try to avoid this extreme and rather unappealing form of relativism by earmarking certain propositions as in some way *privileged,* and construing truth not as participation in any old sufficiently comprehensive, coherent system of propositions, but as participation in such a system which is required in addition to include the privileged propositions. To be sure, thinking of truth as having such a structure does not by itself guarantee its uniqueness. But the resources may be available to do so if the theorist chooses the privileged base class cannily and interprets the relation of coherence in some suitable way. For instance, the base class might consist of a large sample of our most basic beliefs. Then what might ultimately defeat the truth, conceived as by coherence, of the proposition that Bishop Stubbs was hanged for murder would be its inability to participate in a maximally coherent and comprehensive system of belief incorporating that particular membership.

This manoeuvre, however, appears open to an extremely powerful objection. The objection does, admittedly, make an assumption about the general character of the inter-propositional relationships which coherence, conceived as a structural proposal, might regard as important—albeit an assumption suggested by the very term, 'coherence', and validated by all the actual proposals which have been made under its head. That assumption is that the relations in question are *internal* relations: that the coherence, or otherwise, of a system of propositions is grounded *purely in their content*. The salient question is then: How can any proposal of this kind handle *contingency?* The general form of account proposed is that p's truth consists in its participation in a coherent system based on a specified base class, that is, its coherence with the other propositions in that system. But that situation, when it obtains, should be a matter of relations of a purely internal character holding between p and the other propositions in the system. If p coheres with those propositions, it will therefore do so in *all possible worlds*. So how could the truth of p, when it is true, ever be a contingent matter?

There is only one possible line of response. If p, although true, could be false, and if its truth consists in its sustaining internal—necessary—relations to a system of propositions, then what contingency needs is the possibility of a switch in the system—a change in which are the propositions coherence with which determines truth—and the possibility that p may fail to cohere with the new system. If we say that a system is *dominant* if it is coherence with *it* that constitutes truth, then what contingency demands is flexibility in the matter of dominance. (Dominance might be interpreted just as a matter of incorporating lots of what we actually believe, and its flexibility would then be secured by the flexibility in the identity of our beliefs.)

Now, though, interestingly, we find we have come full circle with the reemergence of a version of the Bishop Stubbs objection. All contingency is now being construed as turning on contingencies of dominance. So the obvious next question is what properly coherentist account is to be given of the truth of a proposition of the form

(K) S is dominant.

Naturally, the coherentist has to view the truth of an instance of K, like that of any true proposition, as a matter of its coherence with a system. But which system? Presumably any coherent system S will be such that it will cohere with S to suppose it is dominant even if it is not in fact so—if, for example, dominance is construed as a matter of what is actually believed, it ought in general to cohere perfectly with a system of beliefs that we do not in fact hold to suppose that we do hold them. So in general, for each comprehensive, coherent system S, whether dominant or not, the relevant instance of K will cohere with S with the consequence, first, that the fact of dominance—the actual truth value of that instance—goes unrecovered; and second, that we remain powerless to explicate the contingency of a system's dominance, since the coherence of the relevant instance of K with the system in question will be a matter of necessity.

There is thus no prospect of explicating what it is for a proposition of the form, S is dominant, to be true in terms purely of relations of coherence if the truth in question is conceived as contingent—as it has to be, if contingency in general is to be recovered in terms of a coherentist account. What has to be said, it seems, is that for that proposition, like any other, truth is a matter of relations with *what is in fact* the dominant system. But then exactly the move has been made that Russell triumphantly anticipated: for this appeal to the notion of *what is in fact so* has not been, and apparently cannot be, explicated in terms of coherence.

The upshot is that coherentism, taken as a proposal about the general nature of truth-constituting relations, has no means—provided the relations in question are all internal—to recover the notion of contingent truth except that the cost of, one way or another, an appeal to an unreconstructed notion of *what is in fact true* of particular belief systems (that they are based on what we mostly believe, or otherwise dominant in some sense to be supplied) whose contingency is taken for granted and whose obtaining cannot be construed in terms of coherence. In brief, coherentism demands exceptions to its own account.[23] It thus has nothing to offer as a general account of the structure of truth.[24]

23. This moral is repeatedly emphasised in Ralph Walker's excellent study (Walker (1989)). See note 1 above.

24. The explicit argument has been against a response to the original Bishop Stubbs objection—the privileging manoeuvre—which was canvassed as an alternative to relativism about truth. Briskly, then, to review how a similar difficulty afflicts the relativistic move. The relativist proposal has it that truth is always coherence with a system, but that there are thus as many versions of the truth as there are coherent comprehensive systems. Thus the proposition that Bishop Stubbs was hanged for murder, while unfit to participate in any comprehensive coherent system which is controlled by what we actually believe, may—presumably will—participate in other comprehensive and coherent systems. Well, we should now immediately press the question: what account has this relativism to offer of the truth of contingencies about belief—of propositions of the form, S is believed? Again, it should cohere with any particular coherent comprehensive system to suppose that it is in fact believed—so such a proposition should be true relative to each particular system. So now the fact of actual belief seems fugitive. Suppose there is a single comprehensive and coherent system, S, incorporating (most of) what we actually believe, and that the proposition that Bishop Stubbs was hanged for murder is not a participant. Consider by contrast such a system, S', in which that proposition is a participant. Add to each the proposition that it is believed by most human beings. Clearly a Martian, presented only with axiomatisations of each system, would have no way of telling, just on the basis of facts about coherence, which, if either, we *did* believe. So the truth of the proposition, that it is S we believe, if constituted just in facts about coherence, must reside in other such facts. The relativist-coherentist will offer, presumably, that it will be a matter of coherence with the Martian's own beliefs. But that is to appeal to an unreconstructed notion of *what is in fact believed* by the Martian—and it was exactly the counterpart fact about us that the proposal seems to have no means to construe. So there is no progress.

VI

I have reviewed each of the three possible structural alternatives to a correspondence conception of truth, and found that each is subject to seemingly decisive difficulties. It may seem to have been established, accordingly, that among the four paths on the original tree, only the feathered path to the correspondence conception is viable—that, contra deflationism, our ordinary concept of truth requires us to think of a proposition's being true as, so to speak, a distinctive accomplishment, and that, contra intrinsicism and coherentism, we may not satisfactorily conceive of this accomplishment as an intrinsic property of a proposition or a characteristic conferred upon it by dint of its relation to other propositions. It would follow that even if no satisfactory *analysis* of truth in terms of correspondence can be given, we are nevertheless squarely committed to a correspondence *conception* of truth—that there is no alternative but to think of the truth of a proposition as conferred upon it, in the general case, by its relations to non-propositional reality.

That is, in effect, the second main contention of this essay earlier advertised. But two very important qualifications are needed here. First, in the traditional debate, as we remarked, the correspondence theory was conceived as expressing a form of metaphysical *realism,* standing opposed to the idealism which kept company with the coherence theory. It merits emphasis that even if the effect of the foregoing arguments is indeed to impose a conception of truth as conferred on a proposition by aspects of non-propositional reality,[25] that conclusion certainly carries no direct implications for the realism debate in its modern conception. For example, nothing is yet implied about the *nature* of the relations in question, so there is consequently no immediate implication of the idea that the truth of a proposition consists in its successfully *representing* an aspect of reality, in any distinctively

25. Except in cases, naturally, where the proposition is actually about other propositions.

realist sense of 'represent'. There may in general be no alternative to thinking of propositions as made true when they are true, by, inter alia, non-propositional matters. But there is so far no commitment to any specific general conception of the kind of relations that may be involved in truth, or of the nature of the non-propositional items in their fields. Any broad view which assigns a role in the constitution of truth to a domain outside the bearers of truth would be consistent with our findings; and that much most modern anti-realisms, for example those canvassed by Dummett and Putnam, certainly do. In particular, nothing is implied about *cognitivism*—about whether the factors involved in appraising truth are invariably wholly cognitive; nor about *evidential constraint*—about whether it is possible for truth to outrun all evidence available in principle. Someone who thought, for example, of moral truth as broadly a matter of what *we* find acceptable in the light of a full appreciation of the non-moral facts and certain non-cognitive dispositions to moral sentiment would be making no demands on the notion to take him off the feathered path; on such a view, moral truth would be a complex matter, but one essentially implicating certain relations to aspects of the non-propositional world. Likewise, a proponent of a broadly Peircian conception of truth, that truth is what would be agreed upon by thinkers operating under epistemically ideal conditions, would be quite at liberty to think of the status of such propositions as owing in part to the impingements of a non-propositional world which such thinkers would feel. In sum: our findings at this point have almost no impact on the second of the great issues associated with the classical debate about truth, namely, the issues of realism and objectivity.

However—this is the second necessary qualification—there ought in any case, I believe, to be no presumption in favour of a *monistic* view of truth.[26] If the difficulties which we have been exploring are to

26. That is, in favour of the view that truth everywhere consists in the same thing. (This kind of 'monism' about truth contrasts, of course, with that of Bradley and Joachim, for whom the thesis of monism is rather that reality is an intrinsically unified whole which is distorted when conceived as a totality of individual states of affairs, each apt to confer truth on a single proposition considered in isolation.)

dispose of all the alternatives to correspondence once and for all, then it needs to be assumed that truth everywhere must possess a *uniform constitution:* that the truth of any true proposition always consists in the same sort of thing. Yet why should that be so? For instance, both intrinsicist and coherentist conceptions of truth fell into difficulty over the construal of contingent truth, but a proponent of either view could conceivably retrench if it could be argued that truth is only *sometimes* to be conceived as an intrinsic property of a proposition, or a property bestowed upon it by its relations of coherence with certain other propositions, while in other cases the structure of truth is best conceived as by correspondence. The upshot of the argument is that if truth has a single uniform constitution, then that constitution must be conceived along broadly correspondence lines. But what enforces the assumption of uniformity?

I think the answer is: nothing. In fact, an opposed pluralistic outlook is intuitively quite attractive. It is quite appealing, for instance, to think of the true propositions of number theory as those which sustain certain internal relations—an appropriate kind of semantic consequence—to a certain base class of propositions, for instance, the Dedekind-Peano axioms. Such an account, it should be noted, would extend to the axioms themselves (assuming the reflexivity of the relevant internal relation). What it would not comfortably extend to would be truths of the form: p is a Dedekind-Peano axiom (more generally, p is a member of the relevant base class). But once coherentism forswears the ambition to a *comprehensive* account of the structure of truth, that limitation need not be a difficulty. An account along broadly similar lines might also be attractive for truth as it applies to general moral principles (as opposed to their applications).

A pluralistic conception of truth is also philosophically attractive insofar as an account which allows us to think of truth as constituted differently in different areas of thought might contribute to a sharp explanation of the differential appeal of realist and anti-realist intuitions about them. But I acknowledge, of course, that more detail and a sharper theoretical setting is required for the proposal before it can really be clear that it makes genuine sense, let alone possesses merit.

In particular, an account is owing of what would make it *truth* that allowed of variable forms of instantiation in different areas—what would make for the relevant *unity*. (This is not work that one might excuse oneself by pleading that truth is a 'family resemblance' concept, or whatever. Even that suggestion would at least require that there be a network of marks of truth, any true proposition qualifying as such by its exemplification of some sufficiently substantial set of them; and the task of characterising these marks would remain.)

In order to clarify the cast which a defensible alethic pluralism might assume, it will help to revisit the conception, dominating the traditional debate, that the winning position would be the provision of a satisfactory necessary-and-sufficient-conditions analysis of the concept. Earlier, I was concerned to point out that scepticism about that project remained consistent with the interest of many of the questions, about structure and objectivity in particular, which provided the driving force of the traditional debate, and that these questions could survive in a setting in which the idea of analysis of the notion of truth had been abandoned altogether. Now, though, it is time to reconsider and qualify that scepticism. For misgivings about the project are driven by the particular conception we had in play of what a successful analysis—of truth, or anything—would have to accomplish. And on that score there is clearly some scope for relaxation. Such a necessary-and-sufficient-conditions analysis, after all, even if it could be provided, would only culminate in one particular a priori—presumably, conceptually necessary—claim. Why should not other such claims—even if not biconditional or identity claims—not provide illumination of essentially the same kind? To be sure, if one wants conceptual clarity about what truth—or beauty, or goodness, and so on—is, then the natural target is an identity (or a biconditional). But perhaps the point of the enquiry can be equally if less directly served by the assembly of a body of conceptual truths which, without providing any reductive account, nevertheless collectively constrain and locate the target concept and sufficiently characterise some of its relations with other concepts and its role and purposes to provide the sought-for reflective illumination.

Faced, then, with the manifest improbability of an illuminating necessary-and-sufficient-conditions analysis of truth, there is still a different, more relaxed programme of analysis which we might undertake before despairing of the whole business and falling back on the issues to do with structure. This more relaxed project will see us trying to build an overall picture of the concept of truth—of its contents and purposes—by the assembly and integration of as wide a variety as possible of basic a priori principles about it—'platitudes', as I've elsewhere termed them.[27] What would such principles be for the case of truth?

The method here should be initially to compile a list, including anything that chimes with ordinary thinking about truth, and later to scrutinise more rigorously for deductive articulation and for whether candidates do indeed have the right kind of conceptual plausibility. So we might begin by including, for instance,

> the transparency of truth—that to assert is to present as true and, more generally, that any attitude to a proposition is an attitude to its truth—that to believe, doubt or fear, for example, that p is to believe, doubt or fear that p is true *(Transparency)*
>
> the opacity of truth—incorporating a variety of weaker and stronger principles: that a thinker may be so situated that a particular truth is beyond her ken, that some truths may never be known, that some truths may be unknowable in principle, and so on *(Opacity)*
>
> the conservation of truth-aptitude under embedding: aptitude for truth is preserved under a variety of operations—in particular, truth-apt propositions have negations, conjunctions, disjunctions and so on which are likewise truth-apt *(Embedding)*
>
> the Correspondence Platitude—for a proposition to be true is for it to correspond to reality, accurately reflect how matters stand, 'tell it like it is' and so on *(Correspondence)*

27. The limitation to a priori cases effects, of course, a restriction on the standard lay use of 'platitude', which applies to anything which no one would dispute (and also carries an unwanted connotation of tedium).

the contrast of truth with justification—a proposition may be true
without being justified, and vice-versa *(Contrast)*

the timelessness of truth—if a proposition is ever true, then it
always is, so that whatever may, at any particular time, be truly
asserted may—perhaps by appropriate transformations of
mood, or tense—be truly asserted at any time *(Timelessness)*

that truth is absolute—there is, strictly, no such thing as a proposition's being more or less true; propositions are completely true if
true at all *(Absoluteness)*

The list might be enlarged,[28] and some of these principles may anyway
seem controversial. Moreover it can be argued that the Equivalence
Schema underlies not merely the first of the platitudes listed—Transparency—but the Correspondence Platitude[29] and, as we have seen in
discussion of deflationism, the Contrast Platitude as well.

There's much to be said about this general approach, and many
hard and interesting questions arise, not least, of course, about the
epistemological provenance of the platitudes. But such questions arise
on *any* conception of philosophical analysis, which must always take
for granted our ability to recognise truths holding a priori of concepts
in which we are interested.

Let us call an analysis based on the accumulation and theoretical
organisation of a set of platitudes concerning a particular concept an
analytical theory of the concept in question.[30] Then the provision of

28. One possible addition is reviewed in section VII below.

29. For elaboration of this claim, see *Truth and Objectivity,* pp. 24–7.

30. Readers familiar with Michael Smith's work will note a point of contact here
with the conception of a *network analysis* which he derives from Ramsey and Lewis;
see esp. Smith (1994), chap. 2, section 10. The principal contrast with the approach to
truth here canvassed is that a network analysis has to be based on a comprehensive set
of platitudes whose conjunction so constrains the target concept that the replacement
within them of all expressions for that concept by a variable and its binding by the
description operator results in a definite description which is at the service of an analytically true identity,

Φ–ness is the property, F, such that $\{\ldots\ldots F\ldots.\&\ldots\ldots F\ldots\ldots\&\ldots.\}$

an analytical theory of truth in particular opens up possibilities for a principled pluralism in the following specific way: that in different regions of thought and discourse *the theory may hold good, a priori, of—may be satisfied by—different properties*. If this is so, then always provided the network of platitudes integrated into the theory were sufficiently comprehensive, we should not scruple to say that truth may consist in different things in different such areas: in the instantiation of one property in one area, and in that of a different property in another. For there will be nothing in the idea of truth that is not accommodated by the analytical theory, and thus no more to a property's being a truth property than its furnishing a model of the ingredient platitudes. In brief: the *unity* in the concept of truth will be supplied by the analytical theory; and the *pluralism* will be underwritten by the fact that the principles composing that theory admit of collective variable realisation.

One important question is whether any unmistakably coherentist conception of truth is indeed such a truth-realiser for a particular region of thought.[31] Another candidate I have explored elsewhere is the notion of *superassertibility*.[32] A proposition is superassertible just in case someone investigating it could, in the world as it actually is, arrive at a state of information in which its acceptance was justified, which justification would then persist no matter how much more relevant information was acquired. Clearly a notion of this kind must make sense wherever the corresponding notion of justification makes sense—wherever we have a concept of what it would be to justify a particular proposition, it will be intelligible to hypothesise the attainment of such a justification and its stability through arbitrarily extensive further investigation. It turns out that in any region of discourse meeting certain constraints, superassertibility will satisfy each of the

---

which thus effectively supplies a reductive analysis of the concept Φ. An analytical theory, by contrast, need not—though it may—subserve the construction of such an analytically true identity.

31. For exploration of one local case—arithmetic—see the appendix to this essay.

32. See *Truth and Objectivity*, chap. 2; an earlier discussion is reprinted in Wright (1993a), chap. 14.

platitudes listed above, so a prima facie case can be made that, with respect to those regions, the concept of superassertibility is a truth concept.[33] In these areas, it is consequently open to us to regard truth as consisting in superassertibility. In other areas, by contrast, where the relevant background conditions arguably fail—in particular, if we can see that there is no essential connection between truth and the availability of evidence—then the concept of truth will not allow of interpretation in terms of superassertibility, and the constitution of truth must accordingly be viewed differently. It is perhaps superfluous to remark that a superassertibilist conception of truth chimes very nicely with the semantic anti-realism which Michael Dummett has presented as a generalisation of mathematical intuitionism, whose cardinal thesis may indeed be taken to be that truth is *everywhere* best construed in terms of superassertibility.

To be sure, the method of analysis incorporated in the analytic-theoretical approach is, as far as it goes, consistent with a monistic view of the target concept—but the approach cautions against prejudice in that respect since such an account, may, in any particular case, prove to allow of multiple realisation. That is a matter which will depend on the detail of the account, on whether it includes all relevant platitudes, and on whether the concept in question may justifiably be taken to have further components which are necessarily omitted by such an account (for instance, a component fixed by ostensive definition). Here, I have meant only to sketch how a principled pluralism about truth might conceivably emerge.

VII

I conclude by noting a different potential corollary of the analytic-theoretical approach to truth. If its satisfaction of the platitudes suffices for a concept to be a concept of truth, then wherever we can introduce a concept which is such a satisfier with respect to a particular

33. For relevant details, see the appendix to this essay.

class of contents, that fact on its own will justify us in regarding the contents in question as *apt for truth*. Or put another way: wherever the word 'true' operates in a fashion agreeable to each of the theorems of a satisfactory analytical theory of truth, then we should think of it as expressing a genuine concept of truth, and of the contents being expressed as genuinely truth-apt accordingly. And this will always be so just when we are dealing with contents which meet certain constraints of syntax and discipline. Roughly: the contents in question must allow for combination and recombination under the connectives—negation, the conditional, conjunction, disjunction—of ordinary sentential inference; they must allow of embedding within expressions of ordinary propositional attitudes; and their affirmation must be subject to recognised standards of warrant.[34] If that is right, then it falls out of the very analysis of the notion of truth that the aptitude for truth is a comparatively promiscuous property. Comic, moral, aesthetic and legal discourses, for instance, all exhibit the requisite syntax and discipline and so presumably pass the test. The upshot is thus a tension with one traditional form of anti-realism

34. How does it follow that a satisfier of the platitudes will be definable on such contents? Very straightforwardly. First, if we are dealing with a range of genuine contents—to the extent ensured by the hypothesis of discipline—for which we have the conditional construction, then nothing can stand in the way of the definitional introduction of a predicate, or operator which is subject to the Equivalence Schema:

That p is Φ if and only if p.

As noted, that will then suffice for versions of Transparency, Contrast, the minimal degree of Opacity that attends Contrast and a Correspondence platitude for Φ. It will further be open to us to insist that Φ be defined for all combinations of specified kinds of the contents in question and thereby secure Embedding. Assuming that the contents in question allow of tensed expression, Timelessness—effectively the principle that whatever may truly be thought or expressed at any particular time may, by appropriate variations of tense, be truly thought or expressed at every time—may be secured by stipulating that Φ is to be governed by analogues of the usual truth-value links between differently tensed counterparts. (If the contents in question are tenseless, then Timelessness will hold by default.) Absoluteness, for its part, will hold by default in any case unless we explicitly fix the use of a comparative.

about such discourses: the idea, typified by 'expressivism' in ethics, that a target discourse whose surface exhibition of these features is not questioned may nevertheless not really be dealing in truth-apt contents—in 'genuine' propositions—at all.

Some recent critics, however, have objected that this upshot depends on focusing only on a selection of the platitudes which constrain the notions of truth and assertion, and ignoring in particular equally platitudinous connections of those notions with *belief*.[35] Their thought is that one may be forced to look below the propositional surface of, for example, ethical discourse if one takes it as a platitude that an assertion is a profession of belief[36] but also accepts, with Hume, that no belief can be, in and of itself, a *motivational* state and regards it as clear that whatever is professed by an ethical 'assertion', it *is* such a motivational state.

One who advances this line of thought need not, it merits emphasis, be offering any criticism of the analytic-theoretical approach to truth as such. Moreover the general point being made is obviously perfectly fair: conclusions drawn from a proposed analytic theory of a concept are, of course, liable to be vitiated if that theory omits to recognise what are in fact valid conceptual ties between the target concept and others. But what of the specific objection?

It might seem that the only clean way to dispose of it would be to controvert one of its two auxiliary premises; that is, to argue directly that certain kinds of belief *are* intrinsically motivational after all,[37] or to make a case that the attitudes expressed by sincere ethical claims are, appearances notwithstanding, not *intrinsically* motivational.[38] On reflection, however, it is not evident that it is necessary to take on

35. See, for instance, Jackson, Oppy and Smith (1994).

36. Of course, an assertion may be insincere. For an utterance to be a *profession* of a certain state means that one who accepts its sincerity must be prepared to ascribe that state to the utterer.

37. This is a view often taken to be defended by John McDowell; see McDowell (1978).

38. Michael Smith himself eventually takes such a view in Smith (1994).

either of those projects (even if either might very well succeed). Rather, the anti-expressivist may respond that insofar as the questions—whether a belief can be, in and of itself, a motivational state, and whether the states professed by ethical utterances are indeed intrinsically motivational—are taken to be open, philosophically substantial questions, to that extent it is simply *not* a platitude that the assertion of any truth-apt content is a profession of belief. Or better: for one who accepts that those issues are open, *belief* is not the notion in terms of which to articulate the platitude which lurks in the vicinity. Instead, an alternative expression can be found by taking over for the purpose a term which Simon Blackburn conveniently introduces in his writings on these issues: *commitment*.[39] Blackburn's 'commitments' are typically expressed by indicative sentences; they may be argued for and against, reasoned to and from, accepted, doubted and entertained. So the notion ought to provide everything here required: the relevant platitude is, in effect, that the assertion of any truth-apt content is the profession of a commitment. Since the two auxiliary premises are not simultaneously good for commitments, the objection accordingly lapses.

Someone who sympathises with the view that only some commitments are pukka *beliefs* owes an account of what is distinctive of the narrower class. I know of no reason to reject out of hand the suggestion that a worthwhile such distinction may exist; and if it exists, the annexure of the term 'belief' to the narrower class might conceivably be a well-motivated linguistic *reform*. Until then, the fact remains that our ordinary practice does not scruple to use 'belief' across the range of cases where the expressivist would have us worry about it; and the anti-expressivist is free to respond to the objection by charging that it is only with this more generous notion that there is a platitudinous connection with assertion, and that the two auxiliary premises which the objection exploits cannot both be acceptable if it is the more generous notion of belief that is in play.

39. See Blackburn (1984), passim but especially chaps. 5 and 6.

APPENDIX: TWO ILLUSTRATIVE SATISFIERS
OF THE PLATITUDES FOR TRUTH

We shall reckon with just the seven platitudes proposed above: Transparency, Opacity, Embedding, Correspondence, Contrast, Timelessness, and Absoluteness. First, we note the following dependencies:

(i) *Transparency* is tantamount to the validity of the Equivalence Schema,

> It is true that p if and only if p

for all propositional contents, p, which in turn ensures that of the Disquotational Scheme,

> 'p' is true if and only if p,

assuming only the validity of the corresponding instance of

> 'p' says that p

and the stipulation that the truth of a sentence is to enjoin and be enjoined by that of the proposition it expresses.

(ii) *Correspondence* is a platitude, whether for propositions or for sentences, only if suitably neutrally interpreted—that is, interpreted so as to be neutral on the status of the correspondence *theory*. As a platitude it thus carries no commitment to a real ontology of facts—'sentence-shaped' worldly truth-conferrers—nor to any seriously representational construal of 'correspondence', but merely claims that talk of truth may be paraphrased by any of a variety of kinds of correspondence idiom. We may thus take the Correspondence Platitude for propositions to be, for example:

> (CPP) It is true that p if and only if matters stand in
> conformity with the proposition that p.

CPP is an immediate consequence of the Equivalence Schema, together with the analogous equivalence controlling correspondence idiom itself:

> Matters stand in conformity with the proposition that p if and only if p.

Likewise the Correspondence Platitude for sentences may suitably neutrally be taken to be:

> (CPS) 'p' is true if and only if matters stand as 'p' says they do.

Now wherever we have that

> 'p' says that p

it follows that

> Matters stand as 'p' says they do if and only if p.

CPS is immediate from the last together with the Disquotational Scheme.[40]

(iii) *Contrast*—the contrast between truth and justification—is straightforwardly derived from the Equivalence Schema (or Disquotational Scheme) together with Embedding (specifically, its instance that every truth-apt content has a negation which is likewise truth-apt) and a very basic proof theory for negation. For propositions, the derivation runs as follows. Negation of both halves of the Equivalence Schema provides that

> It is not true that p if and only if not p,

40. For parallel discussion, see *Truth and Objectivity*, pp. 25–7.

while substitution of 'not p' for 'p' at each of its occurrences in the Equivalence Schema provides that

It is true that not p if and only if not p.

Transitivity of the biconditional then yields what I termed the 'negation equivalence':

It is not true that p if and only if it is true that not p

—the commutativity of truth and negation. It then suffices for Contrast to reflect that, for any range of propositions for which neutral states of information are a possibility, negation does *not* commute with justification. For in such a neutral state, a lack of justification for p precisely does not convert into justification for its negation.

The upshot, then, is that our illustrations need address only the following: the Equivalence Schema, Opacity, Embedding, Timelessness and Absoluteness.

Illustration I: Pure Arithmetical Truth Conceived as Coherence

Assume a language, L, containing just the usual resources of first-order logic with identity plus the non-logical constants: Nx ('x is a natural number'), Sx ('the immediate successor of x') and the decimal numerals, '0', '1', '2', '3'. . . . and so on. Take as the coherence base, **B**, the Peano axioms suitably formulated in this language as:

(i) $N(0)$
: Zero is a number

(ii) $(\forall x)(Nx \rightarrow NSx)$
: Every number is immediately succeeded by a number

(iii) $(\forall x)(\forall y)(\forall z)(\forall w)(Nx \ \& \ Ny \rightarrow (Sx = Sy \rightarrow x = y))$

: Numbers are the same if their successors are the
same

(iv) $(\forall x)(Nx \rightarrow \neg 0 = Sx)$
: Zero is not a successor

(v) $(F0 \,\&\, (\forall x)((Nx \,\&\, Fx) \rightarrow FSx))) \rightarrow (\forall x)(Nx \rightarrow Fx)$
: Any characteristic possessed by zero and by the
successor of any number which possesses it is
possessed by all numbers

plus the standard recursive clauses for '+' and '±':

(vi) $(\forall x)x + 0 = x$
(vii) $(\forall x)(\forall y)\ x + Sy = S(x + y)$
(viii) $(\forall x)\ x \pm 0 = 0$
(ix) $(\forall x)(\forall y)\ x \pm Sy = (x \pm y) + x$

and axioms to govern the definition of the regular decimal numerals
from '1' onwards in terms of iterations of 'S' on '0'. The proposal,
then, is that a statement's being a *pure arithmetical truth of first-order*
may be identified with its *cohering with* **B**. How is coherence here to
be understood? Intuitively all the significant statements of first-order
number theory fall into one of two classes: a *simple-arithmetical*
base class whose members draw on no expressive resources save the
numerals, the expressions for addition, multiplication and identity,
and expressions for other operations which may be (recursively)
defined in terms of those notions; and a remainder, each of which can
be formed by (iterated) introductions of the logical constants into sentences of the base class in accordance with the standard first-order
formation rules. From a classical point of view, it is quite intuitive
that the truth value of every first-order pure arithmetical sentence
supervenes upon the truth values of sentences in the base class: specifically, determine the truth value of each of the latter and you have
implicitly settled the truth value of every pure arithmetical thought
which may be expressed at first-order. (The crucial point, of course, is

that simple arithmetic has the resources to name every element in the domain of quantification of full first-order arithmetic.) A natural version of truth as coherence, which should be attractive to those of broadly formalist disposition, simply follows through on this intuition, characterising the coherence of simple-arithmetical sentences in terms of their syntactic derivability from ingredients in **B**, and that of the remainder in accordance with the sort of recursive clauses familiar from standard truth theories. It could run as follows:

(i) If A is a simple-arithmetical sentence of L, then A coheres with **B** just if A may be derived from elements of **B** in standard (classical) first-order logic with identity.

(ii) If Ax is any open sentence of L in one free variable, x, and A is $(\forall x)Ax$, then A coheres with **B** just if each of $A0, A1, A2,$ ..., coheres with **B**.

(iii) If Ax is any open sentence of L in one free variable, x, and A is $(\exists y)(Ay)$, then A coheres with B just if at least one of $A0,$ $A1, A2, \ldots,$ coheres with **B**.

(iv) If A is B & C, then A coheres with **B** just if both B and C cohere with **B**.

(v) If A is B ∨ C, then A coheres with **B** just if either B coheres with **B** or C coheres with **B**.

(vi) If A is B → C, then A coheres with **B** just if it is not the case that B coheres with **B** and C does not.

(vii) If A is ¬B, then A coheres with B just if B does not.

To the platitudes, then.

(i) First, does this proposal validate the Equivalence Schema? Can it be affirmed, for all first-order expressible pure arithmetical statements, p, that

(E^C) p coheres with **B** if and only if p?

Dialectically, the status of a positive answer is somewhat akin to that of Church's thesis, that all effectively calculable arithmetical functions are general recursive. A formal proof of Church's thesis would demand some independent formal characterisation of the effectively calculable functions—the very thing that Church's thesis purports to provide. Likewise a proof of (E^C) would demand some independent characterisation of the first-order arithmetical truths. So, as with Church's thesis, it seems it cannot be definitely excluded that *intuitive* counter-examples to (E^C) might be forthcoming: sentences of the relevant kind which intuitively ought to rank as true yet which there is no reason to regard as cohering with **B** in the light of the stated clauses; or conversely, sentences which intuitively ought *not* to count as true, yet which do apparently so cohere. What can be said to make it plausible that there are no such cases?

Well, if (E^C) did have counter-examples, then—assuming the consistency of **B**—they could not come from within simple arithmetic, which comprises a complete and consistent system which is axiomatised within **B**. So their provenance would have to be of one of two kinds. *Either* truth in first-order arithmetic does not supervene upon simple-arithmetical truth, so that some arithmetical truths are determined by factors beyond the truth-value assignments in simple arithmetic and the semantics of the constants (that is surely excluded by the fact that '0', '1' and their suite collectively name everything in the domain); *or*, conversely, coherence as characterised outruns arithmetical truth (as it would if **B** were inconsistent or if, say, some quite different—perhaps intuitionistic—account of the truth conditions of universally quantified arithmetical sentences was thought appropriate than that which informs clause (ii)). Prescinding from the scenario of inconsistency, then, it does seem reasonable to doubt—or at least that one of realist inclination should doubt—that intuitive counter-examples of either kind will be forthcoming.

Of course, some kinds of arithmetical realist will doubtless regard truth, so characterised, as at best merely *extensionally equivalent* with the real thing. But even for such a realist, the coincidence in extension would be necessary. What, if anything, is wrong with the coherentist account would not be its extensional inaccuracy.

(ii) How much Opacity should be required of a truth predicate is controversial but the arithmetical coherentist proposal is generous on this score. Matters of syntactic derivability, even though effectively decidable, can be mistaken or unknown by any single competent judge, or group of judges, in practice. And the presence of clause (ii) ensures that coherence in effect follows the Omega Rule, so that the proposal is hospitable to the idea that some arithmetical truths may be unknowable in principle.

(iii) Embedding: any statement couched purely in first-order arithmetical vocabulary can be regarded as in the relevant sense apt to cohere with the Peano axioms. Since the logical constants are part of that vocabulary, aptitude for coherence with the Peano axioms is thus conserved under the usual logical operations.

(iv) Timelessness: relations of coherence as defined are eternal.

(v) Absoluteness: relations of coherence as defined do not admit of degree.

Illustration II: Truth Conceived as Superassertibility

Recall that a statement is superassertible just in case it is justified by some accessible state of information and will continue to be so justified no matter how that state of information is improved. (When *I* is such a state of information with respect to a statement, S, I say that *I* is S-stable.) Superassertibility models the truth platitudes under three assumptions concerning the region of discourse, D, with which we are concerned:

(I)   that it is a priori that all truths of D are *knowable;*
(II) that the states of information which specifically bear on the characteristic claims of D are of a timelessly accessible kind;
(III) that it is a necessary condition of knowledge (at least of the subject matter of D, if not in general) that it exists only where a claimant is not thereby laid open to a charge of irrationality.

(I) is a repudiation of evidence-transcendent truth for D. (II) has the effect that the opportunity for justification of a particular claim within

D is never ephemeral but remains eternally open in principle for any suitable enquirer, no matter what her circumstances. (Note, however, the qualification: *suitable* enquirer. Suitability may demand, in particular, a certain innocence. It may be impossible for one who *knows too much* to justify a certain statement, even though evidence speaking defeasibly on its behalf is timelessly available.) (II) also implies that states of information may be conceived as *additive*—accessing one such state never costs you in principle the opportunity to access another (though again, since warrant is a function of one's *total* state of information, the import of a body of information under addition may naturally be different from what it would have been in isolation). (III) imposes a boundary on externalist conceptions of knowledge: let it be that, at least with respect to certain subject matters, knowledge should be viewed as grounded purely in the exercise of what are in fact reliable cognitive powers and stands in no need of further internal qualification—still, it should not be open to internal *disqualification*. There is no knowledge, even of such subject matters, in any case where persistence in a knowledge claim would commit a subject to disregarding the balance of the available evidence and so convict her of irrationality.

Pure mathematics and issues of moral and aesthetic principle may arguably be thought to supply examples of discourses meeting these conditions under only relatively modest idealisations of the powers of their practitioners. Discourse concerning the spatially and/or temporally remote would do so, if at all, only under more elaborate idealisations—maybe of dubious coherence, like the possibility of time travel.

The platitudes of Opacity, Embedding, Timelessness and Absoluteness are all straightforward under these assumptions. To take them in that order:

First, it is clear that the superassertibility of a statement can *in practice* elude any single competent judge, or group of judges. On the other hand it cannot be undetectable *in principle*: if a statement is superassertible, then that fact will show in the S-stability of the relevant—superassertibility-conferring—state of information and hence will be detectable, albeit inconclusively, in just the same way that such S-stability is detectable. But that is no objection under the assumption

(I) that we are operating in a region where it is a priori that all truths are knowable. For that is to suppose that the truths are detectable in any case.

Second, any statement is apt to be superassertible which is apt to be warranted in the first place, since its superassertibility is merely a matter of the S-stability of some warrant-conferring state of information. But aptitude for warrant itself is, of course, inherited under embedding within the standard logical operators. So such embeddings conserve aptitude for superassertibility.

Next, since one of our assumptions is exactly that states of information are accessible timelessly, it follows that superassertibility is, likewise, an eternal characteristic of any statement that has it.

Last, the definition of superassertibility—though the notion must inherit any vagueness in the notion of (all things considered) warrant—manifestly makes no provision for degrees: one statement may be more warranted than another, but if both are nevertheless all-things-considered warranted, and if their warrants are respectively stable, then they are equally and absolutely superassertible.

The key issue is accordingly the status of the Equivalence Schema with 'true' interpreted as superassertible:

(E^S) It is superassertible that p if and only if p.

There are some subtleties here[41] but our discussion is simplified by the announced assumption (I), that we are working in a region where the schema

p → It is knowable that p

holds good a priori.

We consider each direction of (E^S) in turn. First, suppose that it is superassertible that p but that it is not the case that p. Then, by (I), it can be known that it is not the case that p. But that is absurd. For

41. See *ibid.*, chap. 2, section V.

whatever state of information was possessed by one who had that knowledge, it would have—by the implication of additivity in (II)—to be able to co-exist with the enduring all-things-considered warrant for p ensured by its superassertibility. And no one could be said to know that not p whose total state of information warranted, to the contrary, a belief in p unless—contrary to (III)—the belief that not p can be an example of knowledge even when irrationally held.

Now suppose that p but that it is not superassertible that p. Since p is not superassertible, we have it that there is no p-stable state of information—that any warrant for p can be defeated. So any subject who claims to know that p is nevertheless destined to lose a debate with a sufficiently resourceful agnostic; for—by additivity—the agnostic will always be able to come up with some consideration which will spoil whatever case the believer advances for p. It follows that it will not be possible rationally to sustain a belief in p. So, by (III), p cannot be known; whence by (I) it cannot be that p, contrary to hypothesis.

*

A version of this essay was originally written for delivery as a lecture in the series, "Unsere Welt—gegeben oder gemacht? Wissensproduktion zwischen sozialer Konstruktion und Entdeckung" held at the Johann Wolfgang Goethe-Universität in Frankfurt in the spring of 1996. It is published in German in Matthias Vogel and Lutz Wingert, eds., *Unsere Welt gegeben oder gemacht? Menschliches Erkennen zwischen Entdeckung und Konstruktion* (Frankfurt am Main: Suhrkamp, 1999). Thanks to the discussants on that occasion and also to participants at colloquia at University College, Dublin, the University of Kent at Canterbury, Columbia University and the 1998 Austin J. Fagothey S.J. Philosophy Conference on Truth at Santa Clara University; and to Bob Hale, Fraser MacBride, Stewart Shapiro and Charles Travis.

11   Truth as Sort of Epistemic:
Putnam's Peregrinations

Two major changes of mind have characterised Hilary Putnam's philosophy: from the early realism to the 'internalism' of the late 1970s and 1980s, and then in the last decade back to a qualified—'commonsense' or 'natural'—realism supposedly innocent of the objectionable features against which internalism had justly reacted. Someone who wants to understand what is essential to the ingredient positions in this progression, and the motives for the moves from one position to the next, will need to shoulder a broad philosophical agenda. But some of the key issues concern, of course, the concept of truth. The 'metaphysical realism' which Putnam attacked in his middle period was associated with a concept of truth which is evidentially utterly unconstrained—a concept which would permit an empirical theory which was ideal by all internal and operational criteria to be false—whereas internalism proposed a notion whereby truth would coincide with some kind of idealisation of rational acceptability. So much is well known. What may seem less clear is in what respects, if at all, purely as far as the concept of truth is concerned, metaphysical realism and Putnam's most recent 'common-sense' or 'natural' realism should differ.

In this essay I offer a possible answer to that question by showing how one influential line of criticism, canvassed by Alvin Plantinga,[1] of what many commentators (mistakenly) took to be the Peircean conception of truth defended in *Reason, Truth and History*[2] leads naturally to a modified, though still evidentially constrained conception of truth: a conception which not merely has resources to handle Plantinga's and other recent lines of objection to broadly Peircean accounts, but also permits the type of 'recognition-transcendence' of truth to which common sense is attracted and to which Putnam gave his recent blessing in the Dewey Lectures.[3] I shall suggest that this concept of truth, though utterly foreign to metaphysical realism, does properly belong with 'the natural realism of the common man' that Putnam now defends.[4]

I

The mistake of the commentators I just referred to may well have been compound. For it is unclear whether even C. S. Peirce himself ever actually endorsed exactly that conception of truth which modern commentary thinks of as 'Peircean'. The passage usually cited runs:

> Different minds may set out with the most antagonistic views, but the progress of investigations carries them by a force outside themselves to one and the same conclusion. This activity of thought by which we are carried, not where we wish but to a fore-ordained goal, is like the operation of destiny. No modification of the point of view taken, no selection of other facts to study, no natural bent of mind even, can enable a man to escape the predestinate opinion. This great law is embodied in the conception of truth and reality. *The opinion which is fated to be*

1. Plantinga (1982).
2. Putnam (1981).
3. Putnam (1994a).
4. *Ibid.*, p. 483.

ultimately agreed by all who investigate is what we mean by the truth, and the object represented in this opinion is the real.[5]

This statement by Peirce incorporates a number of elements associated with the pragmatist tradition by contemporary commentators— in particular, the repudiation of evidence-transcendent truth, and the implicit inbuilding into the very notion of truth of the cognitive values of human investigators. However the *alethic fatalism* of the passage is no part of the 'Peircean' conception of truth as nowadays most often understood. Peirce seemingly believed in a predestined march towards a stable scientific consensus among 'all who investigate'; but the received understanding of the 'Peircean' view has come to be, rather, that the true propositions are those on which investigators *would* agree if—which may well not be so—it were possible to pursue enquiry to some kind of ideal limit. I do not know whether an unmistakable advocacy of this type of conception of truth—whereby a biconditional like

P is true if and only if, were epistemically ideal conditions to obtain, P would be believed by anyone who investigated it,

is supposed good a priori for all truth-apt claims—is anywhere to be found in the actual writings of Peirce.[6] But the terminology is entrenched, and in this essay I abide by the prevailing understanding of what it is for a view of truth to be 'Peircean'.

II

Whatever the truth about Peirce, Putnam should never confidently have been read as a 'Peircean'. Recall the famous passage in *Reason,*

5. Peirce (1935), vol. 8, p. 139 (emphasis added).

6. He may have moved to something closer to such a view of truth later in his life. See Peirce (1935), vol. 5, p. 495, where he writes 'Truth's independence of individual opinions is due (so far as there is any "truth") to its being the predestined result to which sufficient enquiry *would* ultimately lead'. (Emphasis added.)

Truth and History which has regularly been so interpreted. Having rejected the identification of truth with what he calls rational acceptability,[7] Putnam there suggested that

> truth is an *idealization* of rational acceptability. We speak as if there were such things as epistemically ideal conditions, and we call a statement 'true' if it would be justified under such conditions.

He explains that, as he intends the notion, 'epistemically ideal conditions' are an idealisation in the same way that frictionlessness is: they are conditions that we cannot actually attain, nor—he adds interestingly—can we 'even be absolutely certain that we have come sufficiently close to them'. Putnam is explicit that he is not 'trying to give a formal *definition* of truth, but an informal elucidation of the notion'. And he goes on to say that

> the two key ideas of the idealization theory of truth are (i) that truth is independent of justification here and now, but not independent of *all* justification. To claim a statement is true is to claim it could be justified. (ii) Truth is expected to be stable or 'convergent'.[8]

So far as I am aware, this is the nearest that Putnam ever came to explicitly endorsing the Peircean conception, and it is clear that his words leave considerable latitude for interpretation. In particular, there was no clear suggestion of some *single* set of 'epistemically ideal conditions', apt for the appraisal of any statement whatever.

Putnam himself subsequently returned to clarify that point. In the preface to *Realism with a Human Face*[9] he again endorsed the idea that to claim of any statement that it is true—'that is, that it is true in its place, in its context, in its conceptual scheme'—is, roughly, to claim that it could be justified were epistemic conditions good enough. And he goes on to allow that 'one can express this by saying

---

7. We may take it that this is the notion which is now standardly called 'assertibility'.
8. Putnam (1981), p. 56.
9. Putnam (1990).

that a true statement is one that could be justified were epistemic conditions ideal'. But he proceeds immediately to repudiate the idea

> that we can sensibly imagine conditions which are *simultaneously ideal* for the ascertainment of any truth whatsoever, or simultaneously ideal for answering any question whatsoever. I have never thought such a thing, and I was, indeed, so far from ever thinking such a thing that it never occurred to me even to warn against this misunderstanding . . .[10]

Putnam continues:

> There are some statements which we can only verify by failing to verify other statements. This is so as a matter of logic (for example, if we verify 'in the limit of enquiry' that *no one ever will verify or falsify P,* where P is any statement which has a truth value, then we cannot decide the truth of P itself, even in 'the limit of enquiry' . . . I do not by any means *ever* mean to use the notion of an 'ideal epistemic situation' in this fantastic (or utopian) Peircean sense.

Rather, the notion of ideal epistemic circumstances stands in need of specialisation to the subject matter under consideration:

> If I say 'there is a chair in my study', an ideal epistemic situation would be to be in my study, with the lights on or with daylight streaming through the window, with nothing wrong with my eyesight, with an unconfused mind, without having taken drugs or being subjected to hypnosis, and so forth, and to look and see if there is a chair there.

Indeed, Putnam now suggests, we might as well drop the metaphor of idealisation altogether. Rather

> there are *better and worse* epistemic situations *with respect to particular statements.* What I just described is a very good epistemic situation with respect to the statement 'there is a chair in my study'.[11]

10. *Ibid.,* p. viii.
11. *Ibid.*

These remarks might encourage the following regimentation. Let us, for any proposition P, call the following the *Peircean biconditional* for P:

> P is true if and only if were P appraised under conditions
> U, P would be believed,

where U are conditions under which thinkers have achieved some informationally comprehensive ideal limit of rational-empirical enquiry. And let us call the following the corresponding *Putnamian biconditional* for P:

> P is true if and only if were P appraised under topic-specifically sufficiently good conditions, P would be believed.

Then—the suggestion would be—the view endorsed in the preface to *Realism with a Human Face,* and thereby offered as a gloss on the *Reason, Truth and History* account, was indeed a biconditional elucidation of 'true'. But rather than endorsing the Peircean elucidation, Putnam was suggesting that Peircean biconditionals should be dropped in favour of Putnamian ones: we should dispense with the fiction of a single, comprehensive, utopian limit of enquiry and localise the idealisation to the particular proposition, P, concerned; or better, we should drop the idea of ideal epistemic conditions in any case, supplanting it with that of 'very good' conditions for the appraisal of P—to be detailed by a constructive account, along the lines illustrated for 'There is a chair in my study', of a topic-specific such set of conditions.

III

Whether or not this is the right account of what was happening in the preface to *Realism with a Human Face,* it merits remark that the reason Putnam there gave for discarding the Peircean biconditionals is not a convincing one. Let it be true that there are consistent pairs of propositions, P, Q, such that—whether for broadly logical, or quantum mechanical, or other reasons—the achievement of knowledge whether or not P precludes the achievement of knowledge whether or not Q. That, so far as I can see, presents a problem for the idea that the truths and falsehoods are just the propositions which we would know to be true or false under conditions U only if we assume that each member of such a pair is *determinate in truth value* in any case— that is, if we assume that the principle of bivalence holds without restriction.[12] But why should any Peircean hold that? Michael Dummett, whose thought about these issues ran parallel in many (not all) ways to Putnam's erstwhile 'internalism', has always rightly emphasised that one casualty of the adoption of an epistemically constrained conception of truth is the classical principle of bivalence. Very simply: if truth requires knowability (in principle, at the ideal limit of enquiry, or whatever), then we possess no guarantee that either P or its negation is true if we possess no guarantee that either P or its negation is so knowable. All statements, then, about which there is no guarantee of any verdict under conditions U are statements for which we have no justification for assuming bivalence. And in that case the fact that we know now that there are pairs of mutually consistent statements not both of which can be known under conditions U should provide no motive for thinking that there are (or may be) *truths* which would not be known under conditions U.

IV

Myself, I think it doubtful in any case whether Putnam's view of the late 1980s (the view of the author of the preface to *Realism with a Human Face*) could be neatly captured merely by emphasising that it was Putnamian rather than Peircean biconditionals that were to

---

12. Putnam realised this, of course: note the occurrence of the words 'where P is any statement which has a truth value' in the passage quoted above.

feature in the internalist 'elucidation' of truth. If that is what he had meant, he would presumably simply have said so. What we get instead are seemingly deliberately indefinite remarks like: 'I am simply denying that we have in any of these areas [quantum mechanics, moral discourse, common-sense material object discourse] a notion of truth that totally *outruns* the possibility of justification'.[13] Later, he offers merely that 'the truth and justification of ideas are closely connected'.[14] I think the fact is that Putnam at this time was not satisfied with *any* particular formulation of the evidential constraint on truth which he wanted his internalism to require. The imprecise formulations to which he resorted in this period reflect that dissatisfaction.

The matter may seem academic since, by the early 1990s, Putnam had, by his own admission, ceased to defend any conception of truth in the broadly Peircean tradition.[15] In the Dewey Lectures, indeed, a 'recognition-transcendent' conception of truth is repossessed on behalf of the 'common-sense' realism which Putnam now defends.[16] Here is an illustrative passage:

> How, then, do we understand 'recognition transcendent' uses of the word 'true', as, for example, when we say that the sentence 'Lizzie Borden killed her parents with an axe' may well be true even though we may never be able to establish for certain that it is? . . . If we accept it that understanding the sentence 'Lizzie Borden killed her parents with an axe' is not simply a matter of being able to recognise a verification in our own experience—accept it, that is, that we are able to conceive of how things that we cannot verify *were*—then it should not appear as 'magical' or mysterious that we can understand the claim that that sentence is *true*. What makes it true, if it is, is simply that Lizzie Borden killed her parents with an axe. The recognition transcendence of truth comes, in this case, to no more than the 'recognition transcendence' of some killings. And did we ever think that all killers can be recognised

13. Putnam (1990), p. ix.
14. *Ibid.*, p. xi.
15. See the preface to Putnam (1994b).
16. See esp. Putnam (1994a), pp. 488–517.

as such? Or that the belief that there are certain determinate individuals who are or were killers and who cannot be detected as such by us is
a belief in magical powers of the mind?[17]

These rhetorical questions do indeed evoke a plausibly commonsensical conception of the world and our cognitive situation within it: one
according to which our epistemic opportunities and powers are essentially limited in space and time, so that it can be a matter of *sheer
good luck* whether evidence is available to us here and now of what
took or will take place there and then. But must a conception of truth
which is tolerant of this commonsensical conception be one about
which Putnam's middle-period denial 'that we have . . . a notion of
truth that totally *outruns* the possibility of justification' is simply mistaken? I shall argue not: that the spirit of the view about truth which
is expressed in the internalist statements Putnam now disowns can
accommodate his recent reversion to 'common sense'. This is where
it will help to work through the objection to Peircean accounts advanced by Alvin Plantinga in "How to be an Anti-Realist".

V

Here is a generalisation (and, in one respect, simplification—see note
19 below) of Plantinga's objection. Assume any purported analysis—
or 'informal elucidation'—of truth of the form

> (o)   P is true $\leftrightarrow Q \to Z(P)$,

where Q expresses a general epistemic idealisation, $Z(\ldots)$ is any
condition on propositions—for instance, being judged to be true by
the ideally rational and informed thinkers whose existence is hypothesised by Q, or cohering with the maximally coherent set of beliefs
whose existence is hypothesised by Q, and so on—and ' $\to$ ' expresses
the subjunctive conditional. Since this is purportedly a correct analy-

17. *Ibid.*, p. 511.

sis—or at least a correct elucidation—of a concept, it presumably holds as a matter of conceptual necessity; thus

> (i)   Necessarily: (P is true $\leftrightarrow$ (Q $\rightarrow$ Z(P)))

Now suppose

> (ii)   Possibly (Q & Not Z(Q)).

Then, by logic and the Equivalence Schema, P is true $\leftrightarrow$ P, we have that

> (iii)   Possibly (Q is true & (Q & Not Z(Q)))

But (iii) contradicts (i),[18] with 'Q' taken for 'P', which therefore entails

> (iv)   Not possibly (Q & Not Z(Q)).

So

> (v)   Necessarily (Q $\supset$ Z(Q)).

A necessarily true conditional ought to be sufficient for the corresponding subjunctive, so

> (vi)   Q $\rightarrow$ Z(Q).

So, from (i),

> (vii)   Q is true.

So, by the Equivalence Schema again,

> (viii)   Q.

18. Assuming—surely correctly—that a subjunctive conditional, no less than an indicative, is controverted by the actual truth of its antecedent and falsity of its consequent.

The upshot is, it seems, that anyone proposing an account of truth of the shape typified by (o) must accept that the idealisation, Q, *already obtains:* thus the Peircean must accept that conditions are already 'epistemically ideal'; and a coherence theorist must accept that there already is a maximally comprehensive and coherent set of beliefs.[19] Obviously that is unacceptable.

VI

How might a Peircean—or a defender of some other 'conditionalised' account of truth—respond? One germane reflection is that the reasoning after line (vi) depends on a movement from right to left across (o) and thus would not engage an anti-realist who proposed merely a one-way evidential constraint on truth, rather than an analysis or some other allegedly a priori biconditional. But the obvious question is how abstention from the right-to-left direction of (o) might be motivated: Is it after all to be allowed that propositions believed in epistemically ideal circumstances might yet be *false?* In that case, it would seem, an ideal theory could be false—and how could that admission possibly be reconciled with anything in keeping with the spirit of pragmatism?

A prima facie more promising thought is that the problem should not afflict a proponent of Putnamian rather than Peircean biconditionals. For the key to the proof is the licence, implicit in the Peircean conception of truth, to assume that the conditions which are ideal for the appraisal of the proposition Q are the very conditions depicted

---

19. Plantinga's version of this argument exploits the S4 principle—that what is necessary is necessarily necessary—to drive the conclusion that the idealisation Q holds of necessity. But the derivability of Q, unnecessitated, is quite bad enough. A proponent of the Peircean conception, or a coherence account of truth, certainly would not intend that the obtaining of epistemically ideal conditions, or the actual existence of a maximally coherent belief set, should be consequences of the account; indeed these conditions are precisely thought *not* to obtain—hence the counterfactual analysis.

by that proposition—it is that assumption that sanctions the substitution of 'Q' for 'P' in (o). Suppose instead that, with Putnam, the anti-realist drops the idea of such a comprehensive set of epistemically ideal conditions and that (o) gives way to a range of Putnamian biconditionals:

$$(o)' \quad P \text{ is true} \leftrightarrow Q_P \rightarrow Z(P)$$

where Q_P is the hypothesis that conditions are epistemically ideal—or sufficiently good—for the appraisal of P. We can advance as before to

$$(iii)' \quad \text{Possibly } (Q_P \text{ is true } \& \ (Q_P \ \& \ \text{Not } Z(Q_P))).$$

But nothing harmful need follow unless one of our Putnamian biconditionals is

$$Q_P \text{ is true} \leftrightarrow Q_P \rightarrow Z(Q_P)$$

which will be available only if conditions Q_P are ideal (or sufficiently good) not merely for the appraisal of P but also for the appraisal of the proposition Q_P itself—that is, if $Q_P = Q_{QP}$. And why should that be so?

Fine. But the question should be: is it certain such an identity is never realised? Consider Putnam's own example: an ideal—or sufficiently good—epistemic situation for appraisal of 'There is a chair in my study'. That would be, he said, to be in my study, with the lights on or with daylight streaming through the window, with nothing wrong with my eyesight, with an unconfused mind, without having taken drugs or being subjected to hypnosis, and so forth. But wouldn't those conditions likewise be ideal conditions in which to appraise the claim that I was indeed in my study, with the lights on or with daylight streaming through the window, with nothing wrong with my eyesight, with an unconfused mind, without having taken drugs or being subjected to hypnosis, and so forth? Maybe not— maybe there is some condition whose addition would not improve my epistemic situation with respect to 'There is a chair in my study' but would significantly improve it with respect to the complex proposition just stated. Let the reader try to think of one. But even if there is such a condition in the particular example, must that *always* be so? Unless we can see our way to justifying an affirmative answer, there can be no assurance that Plantinga's problem can be resolved by a fall-back to Putnamian biconditionals.

And in fact it is clear that the most basic problem with the Peircean biconditional cannot be resolved by that fall-back. Plantinga made a difficulty by taking Q for P in (o). But suppose instead we take 'Q will never obtain', thus obtaining

$$Q \text{ will never obtain} \leftrightarrow Q \rightarrow Z(Q \text{ will never obtain}).$$

Then if the right-hand side is interpreted as in the Peircean biconditional, we have a claim to the effect that conditions will always be less than epistemically ideal just in case thinkers who considered the matter under epistemically ideal conditions would suppose so. That is obviously unacceptable. And it is an illustration of a very general point: that no categorical claim, P, can be a priori (or necessarily) equivalent to a subjunctive conditional of a certain type—roughly, one whose antecedent hypotheses conditions under which a manifestation, depicted by the consequent, of the status of P takes place— unless it is likewise a priori (or necessary) that realisation of the antecedent of the latter would not impinge on the actual truth value of the categorical claim. More specifically , it cannot be a priori—or necessary—that

> P is true $\leftrightarrow$ were conditions C to obtain, such-and-such an indicator, M, of P's status would also obtain

unless it is a priori (or necessary) that the obtaining of C would not bring about any change in the actual truth value of P. For suppose that P is true, but that were conditions C to obtain, it would cease to be so: would M then obtain? Yes. For by hypothesis, P is actually true. So the biconditional demands that M would obtain if C did. So not P would hold alongside conditions C and M. But in that case M would not be an indicator of P's status in those circumstances. In particular, if M consists in the believing that P by suitably placed thinkers, then the effect will be that their beliefs will be *in error* under conditions C—exactly what the internalist proposal was meant to exclude.

This point—or anyway the general thought, epitomised in the phrase 'the Conditional Fallacy', that subjunctive conditional analyses are almost always unstable—is nowadays very familiar from the literature on dispositions and response-dependence.[20] What is clear for our present purpose is that it is no less a problem for Putnamian biconditionals than for Peircean ones. Unless, that is, it is given a priori that the implementation of conditions QP would not impinge on the circumstances actually conferring its truth value on P, it cannot be supposed to hold purely in virtue of the concepts involved that

$$P \text{ is true} \leftrightarrow QP \rightarrow P \text{ would be believed}$$

except at the cost of allowing that even under QP circumstances P might be believed when false. And, again, that is just to surrender the idea that belief under (topic-specifically) ideal—or sufficiently good—circumstances is guaranteed to track the truth: the cardinal tenet of Putnam's internalism.

VII

However, to be persuaded by this style of point that *any* broadly internalist conception of truth is unsustainable is, I believe, to overreact. Reflect that Plantinga's original *reductio* does not need a proposed analysis or 'informal elucidation' of truth to get its teeth into but will engage any putatively necessary equivalent of 'P is true' of the appropriate subjunctive form. Even a realist might accept, albeit not

20. A useful early discussion is Shope (1978).

in the spirit of any kind of analysis or elucidation of 'true', that there can be a necessary biconditional link between 'P is true' and a counterfactual about the beliefs of a *sufficiently* idealised subject—if, say, to go to extremes, the idealisation would ensure that the thinker in question would track *all* truth. But such a realist is, on the face of it, put in difficulties too. Is not such a biconditional, indeed, characteristic of the ordinary conception of an omniscient God? The intent of the Peircean conception is, after all, precisely that (a dispositional form of) omniscience would be the reward for reaching the limit of rational-empirical enquiry. Even if we doubt that we have any clear conception of what such a limit might consist in, it may nevertheless seem quite clear that a (dispositionally) omniscient being would stand to the truths as occupants of that putative limit would stand if the Peircean conception were intelligible and correct. So Plantinga's argument, if good, lends itself to a proof of the existence of the Christian God, or at least of a being possessing something like His traditional epistemic powers! Clearly there is something the matter with such an argument.

Let's go carefully. The suggestion is to take as an instance of (o) the result of letting Q be: 'There is a Unique Omniscient Being'—one who believes all truths and no falsehoods—and letting Z(. . .) be: '. . . would be believed by the Unique Omniscient Being':

> (Omn.1) P is true ↔ were there to be a Unique Omniscient Being, P would be believed by the Unique Omniscient Being.

The reasoning sketched then takes us to a proof of the existence of such a being. Plantinga himself might welcome that finding; but not, surely, by this route. So where is the mistake? Are not the true propositions, after all, exactly those which would be believed by such a being?

Well, obviously enough, this argument too is running foul of a version of the Conditional Fallacy. Again, no subjunctive conditional with an 'indicator' consequent can be strictly equivalent to a categorical proposition if the realisation of its antecedent cannot be guaranteed not to impinge on the truth value of that proposition. So an instance of (Omn.1) has a chance of being a priori correct only if P and 'there is a Unique Omniscient Being' are independent. If there were an omniscient being, He would indeed believe exactly the truths. But it cannot be correct to represent the purport of that by something of the form of (o) if we want both 'there is a Unique Omniscient Being' and its negation to be admissible substituends for P. If the range of P is to be unrestricted, then the claim must be, rather, that a Unique Omniscient Being would believe all and only the truths *that would obtain if such a being existed:* that is the conceptual truth about omniscience which (Omn.1) is trying—ineffectively—to express. Not (Omn.1) but

> (Omn.2) Necessarily: were there to be a Unique Omniscient Being, then (P would be true ↔ P would be believed by the Unique Omniscient Being)

is what is wanted.[21]

The obvious next thought is: Should not a supporter of the Peircean conception have made the *same adjustment from the start?* The 'informal elucidation'—of course, it *cannot* now be an analysis, since no straightforward equivalence is being proposed—should have taken the form not of

> (o)   P is true ↔ Q → Z(P)

21. This type of adjustment will be very familiar to a reader who is au courant with the move from 'Basic Equations' to 'Provisional Biconditionals' in the setting of recent discussions of the 'Euthyphro Contrast'; see, e.g., *Truth and Objectivity,* pp. 117–20. The structural prototype of the move is made, of course, by Carnap when he contrasts the definition of a term like 'soluble' with its *reduction sentence;* see Carnap (1936a); see also Carnap (1936b), pp. 440–4. However, I ask the reader to keep it in mind that a theorist who proposes this adjusted form of evidential constraint *need have no pretensions to be giving an elucidation of the concept of truth*—in contrast to the intent betrayed by Carnap's terminology of 'reduction'. Some of the comments in Putnam (2001) depend on his missing this.

but of

$$(o^*) \quad Q \to (P \text{ is true} \leftrightarrow Z(P)).$$

Of course we may still want to allow that there are good reasons for localising Q to topic-specific conditions—for replacing it by QP, as it were. But that is fine-tuning: the crucial point is that, if the analogy with omniscience—the idea that we would stand to the (topic-specific) truths under (topic-specific) epistemically ideal conditions as an Omniscient Being would stand to the truths *tout court*—is apt, then the Peircean conception, as usually formulated, involves a simple structural *faux pas*, whose correction should be entirely consonant with its spirit; and those criticisms of it which cluster around the Conditional Fallacy, rather than being fundamental, do no more than highlight that avoidable mistake.

VIII

The suggestion, then, is that an internalist conception of truth as evidentially constrained might find its best—most resilient—expression not in the endorsement of Peircean or Putnamian biconditionals, nor in the vague idea that truth is somehow intimately connected with justification—that it cannot 'totally outrun' it—but in the specific proposal that *provisional biconditionals* of the form of (o*) hold for all statements—or at least, for all statements for which internal realism is proposed.[22] The proposal of the *moderate internalist* about a given discourse, that is, is that for each statement P of that discourse, the concept of truth is constrained by a principle of the form

> Were P to be appraised under (topic-specific) sufficiently good epistemic conditions, P would be true if and only if P would be believed.

22. Putnam himself never wrote as though internalism would be anything other than a global position. But that's a matter of the detail of its best motivation—and it is not to be ruled out in advance that the best motives might be selective as between one region of discourse and another.

And the *global* moderate internalist will hold that *all* truth-apt claims P are subject to an instance of that schema which holds good.

Obviously more will need to be said. Such a principle is no real constraint on the notion of truth unless certain controls are imposed on the way in which its antecedent is to be understood. If 'sufficiently good' epistemic conditions are understood simply as conditions which incorporate whatever features it might take to enable a thinker to track the relevant facts—if there were no obligation for a constructive specification of what conditions those might actually be—then no realism, however extreme, need hesitate to accept provisional biconditionals everywhere. However, such a caveat already applied, of course, to the Peircean and Putnamian biconditionals: there too, there could be no cause to object—other than on grounds of Conditional Fallacy—to the formulations that result if 'ideal' or 'sufficiently good' are interpreted in non-constructive, 'whatever it takes' terms. Of course, it is another question exactly what it is, for any particular proposition P, to specify *constructively* what it is for conditions to be epistemically ideal, or sufficiently good, for P's appraisal. But the central contention of the moderate internalism that we are now considering must be that it holds a priori of each truth-apt proposition—or at least each such proposition of a targeted discourse—that a constructive specification is possible of what sufficiently good epistemic conditions for its appraisal would consist in of such a kind that a suitable provisional biconditional will hold when so understood; that such a specification will proceed by elaboration of *our ordinary practical understanding* of what would constitute best or good enough conditions for the appraisal of such a proposition; and that the availability of such a provisional biconditional belongs to the very concept of truth.[23]

---

23. To avoid misunderstanding, I am not claiming that the moderate internalist should insist that it has to be possible for each truth-apt claim P to provide a detailed and constructive specification CP such that a provisional equation,

> Were P to be appraised under conditions CP, P would be true if and only if P would be believed

IX

So far, we have merely seen that the moderate internalist conception of truth is not vulnerable to one very basic type of difficulty in Peircean proposals. The next question is whether the Putnam of *Reason, Truth and History* might as well have proposed this view: Is moderate internalism in any way inferior to Putnam's internalism, in its actual historical form, as a reaction against metaphysical realism?—does it contain the resources to provide a stable and adequate vehicle for Putnam's original critique?

Indeed it does. Metaphysical realism, as the view emerges from Putnam's various characterisations of it during his internalist period, is a complex doctrine, involving a number of separable strands: for instance, that 'the world consists of a fixed totality of mind-independent objects', that 'there is exactly one true description of the way the

---

will hold a priori. What, for the internalist, is a priori is rather that there *are* constructively specifiable conditions in terms of which such a provisional equation will hold; that is, it is to be a priori that

> There are conditions which allow of fully constructive specification such that were P to be appraised under such conditions, P would be true if and only if P would be believed,

where a specification counts as relevantly constructive only if it avoids explicit (or implicit) appeal to 'whatever it takes' to be right about P, restricting itself to detailing and building on our ordinary conception of what it does take, but allowing for empirical additions to that conception. (For it should not be inconsistent with internalism to allow that empirical science may teach us of new sources of potential unreliability of observations, for example.)

All this is vague, to be sure. A fully satisfying account would take steps to remedy that. But the vagueness does not matter for our present purposes; first, because the issues here already arose for Putnam's middle-period position—they are not distinctive problems for *moderate* internalism; and second, because—and this will be the crucial point for the connection I want to urge later with Putnam's most recent views—the vagueness involved is perfectly matched by—indeed, just is—that of the *direct realist* conception of what it is for something to be visible, tangible, or audible: in short, of what it is for a state of affairs to be directly available to our awareness.

world is' and that 'truth involves some sort of correspondence between words or thought signs and external things and sets of things'.[24] Putnam regarded (and still regards) these ideas as unintelligible. But one awkwardness with the stated characterisations is, to the contrary, that they tend to allow of more or less deflationary or commonsensical readings, by the light of which any reaction against them carries an implausible air of paradox—the last thing that the sensible, less extravagant form of realism for which Putnam was seeking ought to do. However, Putnam was always clear that, on the intended non-deflationary understanding, such ideas had one quite concrete and discussible consequence: that even an ideal theory (a theory that is 'epistemically ideal for humans'—ideal by the lights of the operational and internal criteria by which we assess the merit of theories) may nevertheless be, in reality, false.[25] According to metaphysical realism, the success of our cognitive endeavours is a matter of *sheer contingency* in the sense that a proposition's compliance with our very best standards of acceptability stands in no necessary—and, in particular, in no rationally scrutable—relation to its being true. An ideal empirical theory—one unimprovable by reference to any standard on whose basis a change in a theory might ordinarily be supported—may, on such a conception, just be a tissue of falsehoods.

That—the sheer contingency of cognitive success—is the notion which is the target, for instance, of Putnam's model-theoretic argument and is implicitly at stake in his famous discussion of the spectre of brains-in-a-vat. The conception of truth enshrined in both the Peircean and Putnamian biconditionals is a direct repudiation of it. Whatever 'epistemically ideal' or 'sufficiently good' conditions for the appraisal of an entire theory would be, they would have to be conditions under which the merits of the theory would be rationally evident, so that a theory which met *all* operational and internal criteria for excellence would be bound to be endorsed under such conditions.

24. See Putnam (1981), p. 49, where the metaphysical realist stance is characterised as *externalism*. Cf. "A Defense of Internal Realism" in Putnam (1990), p. 30.
25. See Putnam (1980), pp. 12–13.

So for each ingredient statement, P, in the theory, the right-hand side of either the Peircean or the Putnamian biconditional would be met, and the biconditional would then preclude the possibility that P be false. But now it's notable, if that is right, that the same would be true if the a priori epistemic constraint on truth proposed was given not by Peircean or Putnamian biconditionals but instead by provisional biconditionals:

> Were P to be appraised under (constructively specified) sufficiently good epistemic conditions, P would be true if and only if P would be believed.

For such formulations still entail, of each ingredient P in an ideal empirical theory, that the opinion about it by one who considers it under the appropriate conditions—conditions under which its merits are rationally evident—cannot be other than correct. So, again, there is no possibility that such a theory could be false if provisional biconditionals are generally in force. Moderate internalism thus clashes with metaphysical realism over exactly the clearest, single most important issue in Putnam's original internalist crusade: the possibility of a false but empirically ideal theory. More generally, it takes issue with metaphysical realism concerning the latter's entire background conception of the place of human cognitive subjects in the world and the conditions on the success of our cognitive endeavours. For metaphysical realism, it is, to stress, always a sheerly contingent question whether our best cognitive efforts—best by our standards, that is— put us broadly in touch with the world or leave us potentially victim to massive error. For moderate internalism, by contrast, it belongs to the concept of truth that each truth-evaluable statement P is associated with conditions of assessment which (a) allow of a constructive specification involving at most empirically acceptable additions to our ordinary idea of what reliable assessment of P would demand; and (b) are such that opinions formed under them are *eo ipso* truthful. The position thus squarely confronts what I take to be the core metaphysical realist thought: a conception of the objectivity and independence of the world so fashioned as to leave the connection between the prosecution of (by our standards) the very best cognitive procedures and the attainment of the truth an ultimately inscrutable matter.

X

So far, so good. It is therefore striking that truth as conceived by moderate internalism—in contrast with the standard understanding of the internalism of *Reason, Truth and History*—can 'outrun' the evidence in what may seem a perfectly intelligible and domesticated fashion. Provisional biconditionals ensure that for each statement, P, within their range, the obtaining or lack of obtaining of a state of affairs depicted by P is humanly accessible under the relevant epistemically ideal conditions. But there is no reason to suppose that the implementation of such conditions has to be feasible in any arbitrary situation. The best—or a 'sufficiently good'—situation for the appraisal of what is stated by 'Lizzie Borden killed her parents with an axe' might be that of a contemporary witness of her action, or of Lizzie herself. There is nothing in the moderate internalist thesis—that each truth-evaluable claim admits of some constructively specifiable set of conditions under which its truth value could be recognised—that entails that such conditions are accessible by an arbitrary subject from an arbitrary starting point in space and time.

There is a basic point that needs emphasis here. Any proposed form of constraint on the truth of a statement in terms of what would be recognisable by thinkers operating under hypothetical idealised circumstances has to allow that the occupation of such circumstances might necessitate a change in the spatio-temporal circumstances of a thinker—or in other aspects of her 'point of view'—of such a kind as to call for some measure of reexpression of the target statement. Consider, to take a trivial instance, 'Somebody is standing behind you', said by you of me. That is surely a statement whose truth ought to be recognisable by me under 'sufficiently good' epistemic circumstances—

and such circumstances will no doubt involve my turning round and looking! But once I've turned, the form of words appropriate to the expression of the statement can no longer be what it was, if only because the preposition 'behind' must disappear. Still, it would seem absurd to deny that I can ever verify your claim 'Someone is standing behind you' simply on the grounds that putting myself in position to do so would necessitate its reexpression. And if that is agreed to be absurd, then it would follow that in all the biconditional forms of constraint which we have so far considered, 'P' needs to be taken as ranging over claims—*propositions*—rather than entities identified by indexical sentence-type. If this were not so, what was just proposed about the Lizzie Borden example would indeed be quite beside the point: so long as the range of 'P' was understood to be over entities specified as essentially involving particular forms of indexical vocabulary—tenses, adverbs of place, and so on—it would remain questionable whether we have any clear, constructive conception of 'sufficiently good' conditions to ensure that an opinion about the example would be true just in case it was arrived at under those conditions. But against that, I am setting the thought that it should no more seem to be a cheat to invoke conditions whose obtaining would require a thinker to use the present tense in order to engage the claim about Lizzie than it should seem a cheat, in trying to show that I know how to appraise the claim, made of me, that 'There is someone standing behind you', to about-face and look and see.[26]

---

26. These remarks may seem to undercut the entire thrust of the sort of anti-realist concern about past-tense discourse that Michael Dummett, in particular, has drawn to our attention. Whether they really do is a large issue which I will not try to engage here. But I think it fair to say that it has to be an assumption of Dummett's concern that our abilities, here and now, to recognise the truth value of present-tensed claims *have no role to play* in an appropriately practical—manifestable—account of our understanding of past-tense discourse. Against that, one might naturally feel that the theory of understanding should treat grasp of the tenses as a holism: that there can be no accounting for our grasp of the present tense in isolation, just as there is no properly understanding the numerals for even numbers without grasping the numeral system in general. That is not to reject Dummett's *ur*-thought that grasp of the past tense must somehow be exhausted in certain manifestable abilities; but it is to suggest that

It may be rejoined that Putnam's position on evidence-transcendent truth in the Dewey Lectures is more generous than can be accommodated by this moderate internalist treatment of examples which essentially turn on distance in space and time. Speaking of the extension of our conceptual abilities brought about by a vocabulary which includes not just tenses but the quantifiers, he adverts to

> the possibility of formulating conjectures that transcend even 'ideal verifiability,' such as 'there are no intelligent extra-terrestrials.' The fact that this conjecture may not be verifiable even 'in principle' does not mean that it does not correspond to a reality . . . [I]dentifying understanding with possession of verification abilities . . . makes it mysterious that we should find these words intelligible.[27]

Here, it may seem clear, knowledge of a truth value may be beyond not merely those who, for reasons of spatio-temporal distance, or other accidents of circumstance, are not in sufficiently good position to appraise the statement in question. Rather, it may be supposed,

---

the abilities in question may be no more localisable, so to speak, than those concerned with tensed discourse as a whole.

For all the attention expended on this issue over the last thirty years, it remains obdurately difficult to be sure what to think. But even when Putnam, in his internalist period, came closest to Dummett's views, I don't think his motivation ever required him to regard the kind of manoeuvre proposed on behalf of the moderate internalist with respect to the Lizzie Borden example as an evasion. The bottom line, so to speak, is that the emphasis on understanding as a complex of practical abilities had better go along with the recognition that abilities can be possessed in circumstances where their exercise is preempted or frustrated for incidental reasons. Of course, one who would ascribe such an ability nonetheless then owes an account—a testable account—of what kind of change in the circumstances would enable the subject once again to manifest her ability. But if the ability in question is one to do with an indexical sentence, the possibility is thereby opened up that such a change in the circumstances might render some of the indexical components in that sentence inappropriate. So the only candidate for a *practical* ability associated with the original will have to be something which associates that sentence with an appropriate reformulation together with a practical manifestation of an understanding of the result.

27. Putnam (1994a), pp. 503–4.

that type of statement might be essentially beyond *all* evidence, no matter what the cognitive starting point from which a thinker went at it. If 'common-sense' realism is tolerant of allowing that it might nevertheless record the fact of the matter, then it surely leaves even moderate internalism behind with that concession.

I think more care is needed with such examples. We may take it that Putnam's remarks about the particular case do not involve reposing any particular weight on the fact that it is a negative existential quantification over an unsurveyable domain. That point entails merely that it cannot be known on the basis of a search, not that it cannot be known at all. It might yet be known—or anyway perfectly justifiably regarded as true—under circumstances of sufficiently good theoretical information. If there is to be any chance of constructing a true provisional biconditional for such a case, we have to expect that the relevant 'sufficiently good' epistemic circumstances should involve a thorough understanding of the physical conditions for the emergence of intelligent life (of whatever form) and enough understanding of the distribution and diversity of matter in the cosmos to allow the assignment of a well-grounded probability to the supposition that such conditions are replicated elsewhere besides on this earth. If moderate internalism can accommodate the example as a truth-apt claim, then the view has to be that under such informationally fortunate circumstances, thinkers would take the correct view of the question. The move that *would* necessitate parting company with moderate internalism is accordingly of one of two kinds: *either* it is denied that there is any such thing as the appropriate kind of understanding of the conditions for the emergence of intelligent life and of the likelihood of a happy intersection of the relevant parameters elsewhere in the universe *or* it is granted that one could have all that information and yet the fact of the matter could just be brutely different from what one then fully justifiably took it to be. The first is tantamount to thinking that there is no ideal—or sufficiently good— theory of this particular subject matter; the second to the view that here even an ideal theory could be false. Either possibility would be inconsistent with the existence of an appropriate true provisional biconditional.

Putnam's text does not make it completely clear whether he would want to advance either claim. Certainly, moderate internalism can allow that the truth value of 'There are no intelligent extra-terrestrials' may transcend our knowledge if the explanation of its doing so is our inability (even in principle) to *access* the needed, sufficiently good informational state—which is not implausible, since accumulation of the data on which to construct the best theory of such matters would presumably call for observation of spatio-temporal regions which are too far away. But suppose Putnam had something stronger in mind: that it is a brute possibility that there simply not be enough information out there, even 'in principle', that would enable us to advance to the 'sufficiently good' understanding called for—or alternatively that even the achievement of that informational state and the construction of a theoretical understanding that would ground a high degree of rational certainty on the issue might still, through sheer bad luck as it were, point us in the wrong direction. If he intended to endorse either of those possibilities, then the question is simply: What did metaphysical realism hold about the nature of our cognitive relations to the world that common-sense realism can consistently discard while endorsing such possibilities? I shall return to this.

XI

It would be disingenuous not to correct any impression that a tolerance of knowledge-transcendent truth is something which comes only with the shift to *moderate* internalism. The insufficiently recognised fact is that an internalism which favoured Peircean or Putnamian biconditionals had the same resources all along! True, Peirce's own explicit view entailed that all truths will eventually be known, and hence that all are knowable. But that is not an implication carried simply by the unrestricted endorsement, for all truth-apt claims, of either Peircean or Putnamian biconditionals. Those formulations do no more than ensure that opinions formed under 'epistemically ideal' or (topic-specific) 'sufficiently good' circumstances will track the facts. To derive from them that any truth is *knowable,* two lemmas would need to be established: first, that opinions formed under such circumstances would thereby amount to knowledge; and second, that an opinion formed under such circumstances is always a *possibility* (where the modality involved is the same as that involved in the relevant concept of knowability). If one is externalist enough to allow that any true opinion formed under what are in fact appropriately fortunate circumstances counts as knowledge, then the first consideration need be no obstacle—though the issues concerning such epistemological externalism are controversial and substantial.[28] We can set them aside, however, since the second lemma is the crux. Let it be that a proposition is true just in case I would know it if I could appraise it under the right circumstances: it remains that it may be impossible to know it precisely because I *cannot* achieve those circumstances. Thus an internalism based on Putnamian or Peircean biconditionals can and should take just the same view of Evidence Transcendence as moderate internalism. Whether or not Putnam himself was sufficiently clear about the point, it is evident that his middle-period internalism need never have been antithetical to the idea of recognition-transcendent truth as such. What it was essentially antithetical to is the notion that recognition-transcendent truth can arise for some reason other than the unavailability of sufficiently good epistemic conditions (or—if it matters on one's preferred account of knowledge—the unrecognisability of such conditions when they arise). But in this respect, that form of internalism and moderate internalism are exactly on a par.

28. Ought knowledge not to demand, in addition, an assurance that the circumstances in question *are* so fortunate and, as Putnam himself earlier emphasised, is there any guarantee that such an assurance would have to be available, that occupants of 'sufficiently good' epistemic circumstances would have to be in position to know that they were? (Of course, there would be potential difficulty with that question if 'sufficiently good' epistemic circumstances are Peircean, that is if one such set of circumstances is supposed to suffice for all cases. For then the idea that we might occupy such circumstances yet not be able to realise it is the idea of a truth that would not be believed under sufficiently good epistemic circumstances. For related discussion, see *Truth and Objectivity*, p. 46.)

XII

Nevertheless there is a more specific—and much-discussed—problem to do with recognition transcendence on which an internal realism based on Putnamian biconditionals arguably founders, but with which moderate internalism is perfectly comfortable. I am referring to the so-called Paradox of Knowability, due to Fitch, concerning claims which are very plausibly taken as truth-apt yet entail limitations on their own knowability.[29] Take F as some proposition of the form: Q and no thinker will ever rationally believe that Q.[30] We would ordinarily suppose that there must be *countless* truths of this kind—for there are countless propositions, including ones we could if we chose quite straightforwardly decide, which are true but will never actually be (rationally) believed by anybody, because nobody will ever actually take the trouble to check. For a Putnamian internal realist a proposition like F can, in the nature of the case, never be believed under the relevant 'sufficiently good' epistemic circumstances.[31] For such circumstances must include the rationality of the thinker. But rational acceptance of F would require rational acceptance of both its conjuncts, and rational acceptance of either conjunct under 'sufficiently good' epistemic circumstances precludes rational acceptance of the

---

29. Fitch (1963).

30. Fitch actually took: Q and no one will ever know that Q. But it is more convenient in the present context to work with rational belief. (Doing so necessitates some departure from Fitch's own reasoning, however, which exploited the factivity of knowledge.)

31. Do there even have to be such circumstances in this case? As noted, Putnam observed that 'sufficiently good' epistemic circumstances for the appraisal of one proposition may exclude 'sufficiently good' epistemic circumstances for the appraisal of another. But I see no reason to suppose that the conjuncts of a Fitch example provide such a case. And—the important point—if they did, then there necessarily would be no 'sufficiently good' circumstances for the appraisal of the Fitch conjunction, and the relevant Putnamian biconditional would consequently get F's truth conditions wrong. (For whatever one's preferred verdict about counterfactual conditionals with necessarily false antecedents, it will presumably be uniform; but F is a contingency.)

other.[32] So whatever specific 'sufficiently good' conditions are germane to the right-hand side of a Putnamian biconditional for a particular such F, it would appear that the resulting subjunctive conditional will never hold good. Someone who operated under sufficiently good circumstances never would (rationally) accept F. Putnamian internalism would seem, accordingly, to have no resources to explain the possibility that such an F could be true in the first place.

For moderate internalism, by contrast, Fitch-type examples bring out no more than that there are some propositions whose very appraisal under 'sufficiently good' circumstances would be sufficient to bring about their untruth. For instance, 'sufficiently good' circumstances for the appraisal of F as above would have to be circumstances in which one was in position to appraise each conjunct of it. So on the one hand one would be in position to carry out the procedure appropriate to determining whether or not Q is true, and on the other hand one would be in a state of ongoing reflective lucidity concerning what one was/was not in position rationally to believe. Maintaining the latter through implementation of the former procedure would thus have one of two effects: either one would consciously verify Q and, coming thereby rationally and self-consciously to believe it, consciously falsify 'No thinker will ever rationally believe that Q' and thereby F; or one would consciously falsify Q and thereby consciously falsify F directly. Either way: if F were to be appraised under suffi-

---

32. To spell that out: suppose C constitute sufficiently good epistemic circumstances for the appraisal of 'Q and no thinker will ever rationally believe that Q', and hence for both its conjuncts. If Q—the first conjunct—is rationally believed under C, then it is not true that no thinker will ever rationally believe that Q, so not rationally believed either—since, remember, the internalist position requires that if either conjunct is rationally believed under C, then it is true. On the other hand, if under C the second conjunct is rationally believed—namely, that no thinker will ever rationally believe that Q—then indeed no thinker ever will; so in particular there will be no rational belief that Q under conditions C.

ciently good circumstances, it wouldn't be true. But that result is perfectly consistent with

> If **F** was to be appraised under sufficiently good
> circumstances, **F** would be true just in case it was believed
> to be true

precisely because under those circumstances, as noted a moment ago, **F** wouldn't be believed either. Thus, in contrast with the situation with Putnamian biconditionals, the provisional biconditional for **F** is indeed an a priori truth. Provisional biconditionals accordingly involve no misrepresentation of the intuitive truth conditions of such examples, which are perfectly compliant with the constraint on truth which moderate internalism involves precisely because both their being true, and their being believed, are inconsistent with their appraisal under optimal conditions.

Under this perspective, the Fitch Paradox emerges as, in effect, a special type of Conditional Fallacy difficulty for the Peircean and Putnamian biconditionals: just one more example of the kinds of awkwardness that can be generated for them by non-independence between the target proposition and the antecedent of the relevant subjunctive conditional—and, like such problems in general, it is finessed by the shift to provisional biconditionals. It remains, to be sure, that such a proposition can be true only if an appraisal of it under sufficiently good circumstances never takes place, so that its truth is, in that sense, essentially recognition-transcendent. But that there are such recognition-transcendent truths—like the case of Lizzie Borden and in contrast with the situation of 'There are no intelligent extra-terrestrials' when pushed beyond the reach of even the very best theory—is indeed merely common sense and nothing which a recoil from metaphysical realism should provide any motive to deny.

XIII

Let's take stock. So far I have offered considerations in support of a number of claims:

that a moderate internalist conception of truth would have served as well as any conditionalised, 'Peircean' proposal as a vehicle for Putnam's middle-period opposition to metaphysical realism;

that a moderate internalist conception of truth can handle certain well-known structural difficulties for Peircean (and other essentially evidentially constrained) conceptions of truth, including Plantinga's problem and Fitch's paradox;

that a moderate internalist conception of truth is friendly to at least two important classes of potentially recognition-transcendent truths, typified by the Lizzie Borden and Fitch examples.

All of that is to suggest that Putnam's middle position allowed of stronger play than perhaps it historically received; and that it need not have been inhospitable to certain ideas which it has later seemed important to him to accommodate and emphasise. What is still to be clarified is how far, if at all, Putnam's recent views genuinely demand a departure from this refashioned version of those of *Reason, Truth and History* and *Realism with a Human Face*. If moderate internalism had been the view which Putnam had adopted at the time of *Reason, Truth and History*, would there have been any need for the *further* recantation of the early to mid 1990s? Or does moderate internalism have a case to be regarded as faithful to 'the natural realism of the common man'?

What precisely are the key differences between the philosophical syndrome which for Putnam constitutes 'metaphysical realism' and 'the natural realism of the common man'? Earlier we noted some aspects of Putnam's own conception of the contrast: the idea of the world as consisting in some fixed totality of objects (and hence of some fixed totality of things falling under some uniform conception of 'object'); the conception of the variety exhibited in the world as determined by some fixed totality of properties (and hence of any interest-relativity in our classifications as a matter simply of *which* such properties we have chosen to take an interest in); the conception of truth as consisting in some fixed relation of correspondence between our sentences, or thoughts, and the world (and hence of ascriptions of truth as making, more than a claim about the world, claims about the obtaining of such a relation of correspondence); the conception of a sharp and meaningful contrast—dictated of course by the metaphysical-realist ontology of genuine properties—between the areas of discourse where we *describe* how matters objectively stand and areas of discourse where we rather 'project' aspects of our own reactions onto the world—all these notions Putnam continues, with his common-sense realist hat on, to reject as unintelligible.[33] However, these aspects of Putnam's continuing 'recoil' do not seem directly to help with the specific question: How, if at all, do the conceptions of truth respectively involved in metaphysical realism and common-sense realism differ? Certainly, common-sense realism will not accept the particular version of the correspondence theory of truth held by metaphysical realism, since it will not accept the associated 'metaphysical' ontology of objects and properties. But the key question specifically concerns the evidence-transcendence of truth: Does a return to 'the natural realism of the common man' involve any kind of disagreement with metaphysical realism about that?

I believe that it does. The issue of evidential constraint—of whether truth requires the possibility of verification and, if so, what notion of possibility of verification is germane—has loomed so large in the secondary literature that almost no thought has been given to what range or gradation of views may open up if a negative answer is returned. However, admissions that truth may be evidence-transcendent may be driven by two quite different kinds of motive. One such motive is benign. It is indeed part of common sense to view ourselves as finite creatures, whose knowledge-gathering powers are

33. See especially the first of the Dewey Lectures, *passim*, and in particular note 41 at p. 463.

limited. We are limited by our range of sensory susceptibilities—our vision and hearing, for instance, are restricted to quite small bands of frequencies of light and sound. We are limited by our intellects: there are surely many problems which we are too slow or unimaginative to solve. We live short lives, and the spatial distances within which we can investigate are further restricted by the slowness of our means of travel. We cannot travel in time at all (other than forwards at the usual rate). All these ideas go to the core of our common-sense self-conception: it thus goes with that conception that there can be no end of possible ways things might be which we can fully understand—since they allow of characterisation within our conceptual reper-toire—but which we cannot know to obtain or not because we are grounded in the wrong place, or the wrong time, or because the issues raised are too difficult for us. A conception of truth which denies this, like the kind of anti-realism about the past canvassed in Dummett's famous papers,[34] will indeed seem paradoxical and revisionary; for instance, the idea that there are no truths about the past save those for which confirming evidence is available in the present just flies in the face of the intuitive conception of the past as a *removed present*, a realm of states of affairs no less determinate than the present but no longer directly accessible to us and whose surviving traces are partial and contingent.

This benign form of Evidence Transcendence is conceived as going with—in the broadest sense—*contingencies of epistemic opportunity*: in all cases where we have a conception of this kind of how the truth value of a particular statement could be unverifiable, a developed spe-cific account of that conception will consist in detailing limitations of opportunity, or spatio-temporal situation, or perceptual or intellec-tual capacity, which stop us getting at the relevant facts but to which we, or others, might easily not have been subject—or at least, to which we can readily conceive that an intelligible form of investigat-ing intelligence need not be subject. The hallmark of this general range of cases is thus that in providing an account of how and why it

34. The *locus classicus* for Dummett's treatment of the issues is Dummett (1969).

is that they may transcend our epistemic powers, we will simultaneously begin to provide an account of a suitable set of conditions to figure as the antecedent of an appropriate provisional biconditional: a set of conditions which creatures very much like us, but situated elsewhere in space and time, or finitely idealised in certain respects, could occupy and, by doing so, ensure that a judiciously formed opinion about the relevant matter would be correct.

The opposed, malignantly motivated cases arise quite differently. Here we are concerned not with contingencies of opportunity but with putative *necessities of limitation*. And it is here that we find a connection with perhaps the single most emphatic theme in the Dewey Lectures: the repudiation of any form of 'interface' between the knowing, perceiving, or thinking subject and the worldly subject matter of his thought. Putnam writes:

> Winning through to natural realism is seeing the *needlessness* and the *unintelligibility* of a picture that imposes an interface between ourselves and the world.[35]

The 'interface' conception is, of course, very old. It is just a generalisation and intensification of the predicament of the thinkers in Plato's Cave. On the interface conception, large sweeps of fact are essentially inaccessible not just to us (cave dwellers) but to *any* sentient, intelligent creature, no matter where and when situated. The classic way for this to happen, of course, is by restriction of all sense experience in its very nature to a domain—of sense data, or mere seemings otherwise construed than as sense data—which are then conceived as standing in merely causal, potentially inscrutable relations to an ulterior material reality. Knowledge of the external world is thus made to rest upon a chancy, backwards inferential leap across those causal relations. An exactly analogous predicament arises, of course, on a dualist conception of the mental with respect to knowledge of other minds; and also with respect to knowledge of the past, when memory is conceived

35. Putnam (1994a), p. 487. See also *ibid.*, p. 505.

merely as the tokening of memory images, conceived as phenomenal proxies, in consciousness. In all these cases, Evidence Transcendence is not down to contingencies of opportunity. Rather, it is held, we have no coherent conception of the workings of perception, or memory, or of the recognition of others' mental states, save in terms which see the proper operation of the faculties in question precisely as stopping short at an *interface:* that is, at a domain of facts which are *categorically distinct* from those in which we are really interested, and which stand to the latter merely as effects to strictly inscrutable causes. On this type of view, Evidence Transcendence is a product not of contingencies of opportunity, or of contingent limitations of our powers, but of *metaphysical* shortcomings and divides: consciousness—unless it is the consciousness of God, of which we have no satisfactory conception—is necessarily and essentially insular.

The essence of metaphysical realism, we might say, is thus *interface-realism.* And the evidence-transcendent conception of truth which metaphysical realism brings in train is of a malignant kind, the kind that goes with an interface-conception of mind's interaction with the world. About these ideas, there is nothing 'natural' or 'commonsensical'. Rather, it is supposed to take philosophical sophistication to appreciate their point. (They are naturally viewed as Cartesian. But for Putnam, the structural mistake which they embody is a cardinal feature of much modern philosophy of mind—what he therefore calls 'Cartesian materialism'—which thinks of 'representations' as brain states whose connections with what they represent are essentially merely causal.)

If it is no part of common-sense realism to accept this picture of cognitive alienation, to tolerate interfaces, then the Evidence Transcendence that needs to be provided for should be solely of the benign sort. But the benign conception has it that no genre of states of affairs is essentially beyond our powers of knowledge: under the right—in principle constructively specifiable 'sufficiently good'—circumstances, our powers will 'reach out' to the very facts in question, and opinions formed will be correct. So the holding of an appropriate range of provisional biconditionals should belong with our very conception of the states of affairs in question, and will thus be a priori. Conversely, if interfaces are allowed, then whatever states of affairs are open to our perceptual, or other faculties will constitute *distinct existences* from those behind the interface, and even if any provisional biconditionals do hold good for the latter, they will do so only courtesy of a harmony with the former for which there will be no a priori ground. In brief, the epistemology of direct realism, surely part and parcel of 'the natural realism of the common man', goes with the provisional biconditional as an a priori constraint upon truth. If we want no truck with interfaces, then every kind of state of affairs of which we are capable of conceiving must be one of which we can attain a concrete conception of what kind of powers and situation would place us, or relevantly similar beings, into a position from which it would be assured that our, or their, opinion that it did, or did not obtain, would be correct. That is exactly what the possibility of *direct* cognition demands.[36]

36. One line of resistance to the foregoing, put to me by Timothy Williamson, is worth mention. Direct realists take the view that perception is a certain kind of *tracking ability:* we have the ability to be immediately receptive to aspects of our local environment. They also hold, presumably, that the successful exercise of this ability is the norm. Since their thesis is an article of philosophy, it is presumably considered to hold good a priori (even if the materials to counter various forms of sceptical attack are not immediately to hand). But is saying that our senses normally put us in direct touch with our local environment a commitment to holding that, under in principle constructively specifiable circumstances, they *always* do, as would be demanded by the holding of the appropriate kind of provisional biconditional? Might not episodes of cognitive dissonance beset even the best perceivers among us, so that occasional misfires occur even under the most favourable conditions, perceivers forming false beliefs, or failing to form appropriate true ones, for no reason anyone can produce? Surely it is no part of the concept of possessing an ability to provide a *guarantee* that, under some specifiable set of suitable circumstances (including dominant motivation of the subject) successful performance is entrained: perhaps even the most adept cyclist would sometimes fall off her bicycle under perfectly unremarkable conditions.

It may be tempting to reply that if that were so, it would merely be because of our imperfect understanding of the conditions sufficient for success: that it should always in principle be possible to isolate some further specification of the conditions under which such an aberration would occur and thereby, correlatively, of conditions under which a given ability will invariably show in performance. But how could it be *a priori*

It follows that it must still be part of the stock-in-trade of common-sense realism, if it is to be a *thoroughgoing* direct realism, to hold that an empirically ideal theory could not be false. For to suppose other-

---

that this is so? (What if the most basic laws governing certain relevant brain events are merely statistical?)

The question is pertinent. I think, however, that we are entitled to proceed, as I have, without engaging this complication. For the wider question is not whether direct realism must involve a commitment to there being true, in principle constructively specifiable suitable provisional biconditionals, but whether its commitments concerning truth and knowability coincide with those of moderate internalism. And it should be clear that the objection poses no obstacle, actually, to the coincidence. Let it be that for indeterministic reasons—if I may so put it—any human ability fails to guarantee successful performance even under the most favourable conditions. Then this is a complication which the entire internalist tradition should have reckoned with from the start, and none of the biconditionals—Peircean, Putnamian, or provisional—which we have canvassed ever had any chance of holding a priori and absolutely. Rather each could only hold in some appropriately *statistical* form. A Peircean should have proposed, for instance, that the true is what thinkers judging under epistemically ideal conditions would *mostly* take to be true. Putnam's internalist should have proposed that the proposition that there is a chair in my study is true if and only if were it appraised under topic-specifically sufficiently good conditions, it would be believed in the (overwhelming) majority of cases. And a moderate internalist about some region of thought should hold, for instance, not that under certain constructively specifiable circumstances, thinkers' judgements whether P and the fact of the matter would be covariant, but that they would *usually* be covariant—that a series of trials would converge on one verdict and that cases of conflict would be isolated and unlikely. But just that, presumably, is what a direct realist who takes seriously the mooted complication will hold about our perceptual thought.

I leave it to an enthusiastic reader to consider in detail whether the dialectic of this essay would have differed in any significant respect had it been organised in terms of these various statistical conceptions of evidential constraint. But notice at least that the Conditional Fallacy difficulties besetting the Peircean and Putnamian proposals still apply; for instance,

Epistemically ideal conditions will never obtain ↔ were epistemically ideal conditions to obtain, thinkers would mostly judge that epistemically ideal conditions will never obtain

is still a singularity for a would-be Peircean. Thus the passage to the (correspondingly statistical) provisional biconditionals proposed by the moderate internalist will still be well motivated.

wise, to suppose that a theory which was operationally and internally ideal—which saved all empirical phenomena and was best by all criteria by which we might assess the competing claims of pairs of empirically adequate theories—might nevertheless be false would be exactly to conceive of its proper subject matter as standing behind an interface: it would be to conceive of the states of affairs in virtue of which its distinctive theoretical claims were true or false as items for our knowledge at best only via proxies.

In sum: the crucial difference between the philosophy of truth of common-sense realism and that of metaphysical realism concerns the proper way of conceiving of the *possible sources* of evidence-transcendent truths. For common-sense realism, they arise because of contingencies of epistemic opportunity. For metaphysical realism, they arise because—according to that view—it is in the nature of most types of states of affairs to influence consciousness, if at all, only via proxies. It goes with the latter conception, just as Putnam always said, that a theory of such states of affairs which is ideal by our standards can be false. It goes with the direct realism of the former conception that appropriate provisional biconditionals should hold and hence that an ideal theory cannot be false. Thus the latter contention should still be part of the common-sense realism which Putnam now advocates, if that position is to incorporate a thoroughgoing direct realism. And a moderate internalist conception of truth should be recognised as part of 'the natural realism of the common man'. That is my principal conclusion.

If these ideas go in the right direction, then it would be unhappy to see the thrust of Putnam's most recent views as a partial rapprochement with metaphysical realism after a period of (over)reaction against it. Rather, they are best seen as a continuing working out of that reaction in a consistent direction. And an epistemic conception of truth, of the moderate internalist sort, should be a continuing part of the picture. But what remains to be settled, of course, is *how big* a part: whether a direct realist epistemology, and consequent endorsement of a moderate internalist conception of truth, should indeed be generalised across the whole gamut of possible states of affairs of which we can claim any clear conception. Putnam spoke of the needlessness and unintelligibility of the interface picture. Did he mean 'everywhere'? It is essentially the interface picture that we will need to make sense of the idea that 'There are no intelligent extra-terrestrials' might be true beyond all evidence available in principle, beyond the verdict of even the very best possible empirical theory. Can one have a stable and coherent *mixed* view—one with merely local interfaces, so to speak, restricted to areas of discourse where knowledge, if attainable at all, essentially depends, even in the very best conceivable case, upon defeasible inference? Those like Putnam (and of course John McDowell, by whose John Locke Lectures[37] Putnam's recent work is influenced) who have wanted to press the claim of a sophisticated direct realism (the 'second *naïveté*' Putnam approvingly finds in Austin) still owe a statement, it seems to me, of the point, if any, beyond which they do *not* want to press the direct realist claim—and indeed an account of how permitting *any* boundary could spare our conception of what lies beyond it the range of problems—to do, for example, with content and reference—which they urge against those philosophies that would confine our *direct* knowings within more traditionally conceived (interior) boundaries.[38]

Postscript

Hilary Putnam has recently responded to a number of aspects of the preceding essay.[39] I hope to react to his responses in more detail in another place. Here I shall be concerned with just two—albeit the principal—claims that he makes.

The first claim is that the differential treatment meted out in the later sections of 'Putnam's peregrinations' to the Fitch sentence, F,

37. Published as McDowell (1994).
38. Thanks to Alvin Plantinga, Sven Rosenkranz and Tim Williamson for comments.
39. Putnam (2001).

and to the example, 'There are no intelligent extra-terrestrials'—which he calls Π—is based on confusion. On my account of the matter, it is open to a moderate internalist to regard the possibly evidence-transcendent truth value of instances of F as benign: as attributable to what I termed contingencies of epistemic opportunity, broadly understood. By contrast, to suppose that Π might be true, although even the very best possible empirical theory, making best sense of all data available in principle, would assign it a very low probability, would be a commitment to the 'malignant' type of evidence transcendence, characteristic of 'interface realism'. Putnam cannot see a relevant difference: 'that proposition [i.e. Π]'—he writes—

> is falsifiable-though-not-verifiable just as F is. Its truth value, like F's, can be 'appraised under sufficiently good circumstances'—circumstances in which it is false! For if Π is false, then there are intelligent extra-terrestrials, and we may easily imagine there being observers who know this. We can even formulate a 'provisional biconditional' for N. . . .[40]

That is a superficial analogy, however. It fudges the difference which it was the whole point of moderate internalism's notion of evidential constraint, formulated in terms of provisional biconditionals, to bring out. A statement offends against that notion of evidential constraint if it is a possibility that the antecedent of the relevant provisional biconditional can be true—conditions are optimal, or good enough, for the appraisal of the statement—while the consequent is not, the statement in question failing to be adjudged true under the relevant conditions although it is, or being adjudged true although it is not. As enlarged on in the essay, this is not a possibility for instances of F: when appraised under sufficiently good circumstances, instances of F will be adjudged to have the truth value they then actually have. It is different with Π: if the very best theory we can in principle construct

40. *Ibid.*, p. 597.

misrepresents its truth value—specifically, takes it to be very probably false when it is true—then ideal epistemic circumstances for its appraisal (namely, circumstances in which a thinker is fully informed of this theory and of its virtues) may obtain even though it is then adjudged to have a truth value other than the one it actually has. So Π, so conceived, is a potential counter-example to moderate internalism's version of evidential constraint. And to suppose that it may, in this kind of way, be true beyond the ken of even an in principle unsurpassably well-situated judge is to attempt to conceive of a species of fact which essentially outreaches us and of which we can apprehend only local and finite manifestations ('There are no extra-terrestrials here').

That, indeed, does not introduce *exactly* the idea of an interface—not if that is to be the kind of notion that goes with a Lockean 'veil of perception': the situation Putnam thinks it is natural common sense to allow is more like having one's vision restricted to modest parts of an immense object, some of which is too remote ever to be perceived, than being confined to watching shadows (proxies) reflected on the wall of a cave. But it is for Putnam to tell us why that is a relevant difference—why the one image betrays a pernicious metaphysical realism when applied to ordinary perception while the other is something which common sense can take in stride as epitomising the situation of the empirical scientist. I'll return to that in a moment. The distinction remains: the truth value of a suitable instance of F will not elude a judgement made under sufficiently good circumstances—sufficiently good, that is, for the appraisal of each of its conjuncts; whereas the truth value of Π, according to what Putnam wants to regard as mere common sense, may.

As is apparent from the quotation above, Putnam encourages an oversight of this distinction by helping himself to the idea that 'sufficiently good circumstances' for the appraisal of Π may be stipulated to be circumstances in which it is false! This is of course illicit. We cannot, it is true, assume that a constructive specification of optimal or sufficiently good circumstances for the appraisal of a particular proposition will always be neutral on the truth value of the proposition in question—that is, after all, exactly what Fitch-type examples show is not the case. Nevertheless, optimal or sufficiently good conditions for the appraisal of a Fitch conjunction may be specified, just as they should be, as a combination of conditions which are sufficiently good for the appraisal of, but neutral on, the truth value of the conjunct they respectively concern. Sure, an investigation under the joint obtaining of these conditions then proves to be incompatible with the Fitch conjunction itself. But that's a far cry from the idea that Putnam apparently has, that we may simply pick on one or other truth value for a targeted proposition and deem that its possession of that truth value should be accounted as part of the obtaining of optimal or sufficiently good circumstances for its appraisal.

Actually, Putnam could concede this. What is more important to him (for he does after all still wish to renounce metaphysical realism) is not the—alleged—similarity between F and Π under the aegis of moderate internalism, but his second claim: that there is a relevant distinction between the potential Evidence Transcendence that he wants to accord to Π and the malignant form that goes with metaphysical realism, and that my 'analogising' the two is a further confusion.

So what exactly is the distinction? We may envisage that the 'very best possible empirical theory' assigns a high probability to the replication elsewhere in the cosmos of the physical conditions which, according to that same theory, fostered the emergence of life on Earth, so assigns quite a high probability, *albeit one falling short of certainty*, to the denial of Π.[41] But in that case, Putnam reasons,

> it is a conceptual truth . . . that what is [merely] highly probable does not always happen. Thus it is internal to physical theory itself . . . —and not the product of some metaphysical conception of 'the kind that goes with an interface conception of mind interaction with the world'—that Π may be true.[42]

So he is claiming a distinction between metaphysical realist forms of Evidence Transcendence and a third kind of case, contrasting alike

41. *Ibid.*
42. *Ibid.*, pp. 597–8.

both with the former and with the cases (generated by limitations of epistemic opportunity) with which moderate internalism is perfectly comfortable. The third kind covers cases where, while there is no epistemic vantage point which could in principle allow anyone to ascertain the truth value of the proposition in question, the conception of its Evidence Transcendence flows not from the malign workings of some dubious metaphysics but from the very content of respectable empirical theory.

I do not think this passes muster, for three reasons. It is, to begin with, tendentious to regard it as 'internal to'—part of the content of—a theory which assigns a less-than-maximum probability to a hypothesis that the hypothesis in question may be false. The most that follows is that the falsity of the hypothesis—*if* allowed as a possibility—would be consistent with the theory, not that the possibility of its being false is part of the theory's content. More generally, and that point apart, Putnam's reasoning here seems to confuse metaphysical with epistemic possibility—for that my evidence for a certain proposition entitles me to assign to it no more than a less-than-maximum probability has no implication whatever for its metaphysical modal status. But finally, it is in any case wholly unclear why a *scientific* provenance for the conception of statements like Π as evidence-transcendent—if indeed there were one—would, just by itself, tend to establish its innocence of the failings which Putnam continues to find in similar conceptions generated by metaphysics. What if the one conception arises in the course of (hypothetical) scientific theorising while the others arise in the course of philosophising? What was objectionable about metaphysical realism was surely the *content* of the outlook; how should it become less objectionable if endorsed by science?

I continue to think, then, that moderate internalism, while it can accommodate interestingly many, cannot accommodate *all* aspects of Putnam's position in the Dewey Lectures—and in saying that, I intend to acknowledge that what he now wants to say about examples like Π would indeed probably pass for 'common sense' in many contemporary circles. The question is whether the concessions to common sense that moderate internalism *cannot* accommodate and that Putnam wants to make do indeed belong to a principled position, properly contrasted with and importantly more moderate than metaphysical realism. We have still to see a clean distinction of principle that makes the contrast out.

12

Minimalism and Deflationism

I

Deflationists have offered views about truth differing significantly in detail. But they characteristically maintain that, as far as philosophy is concerned, there is nothing to say about truth that is not captured by a suitably generalised form of one (or both) of the following two schemata:

(ES) It is true that P iff P
(DS) 'P' is true iff P,

and that this point in turn entails deflation—that the traditional metaphysical debates about truth, as well as more recent ones, are about nothing substantial.

It is worth noting that these are separable claims. Someone could allow that the two schemata—the Equivalence Schema for propositions and the Disquotational Scheme for sentences—are each a priori correct[1] and (together) somehow fully encapsulate all proper uses of the truth predicate without conceding that (it follows therefrom that) truth is somehow not a proper object of further philosophical enquiry, that no further metaphysical or semantic issues arise. Conversely someone broadly in agreement with the anti-metaphysical spirit of deflationism might hold that a correct characterisation of the use of the truth predicate demands something more complicated than the two schemata.

The minimalist[2] view about truth I have defended rejects each of these deflationist claims, contending both that the two schemata are insufficient to capture all that should properly be reckoned as belonging to the concept of truth and that the anti-metaphysical message of deflationism, globally applied, represents a philosophical mistake. Still, there are points of affinity between minimalism and deflationism. Minimalism agrees that, as far as the *conceptual* analysis of truth is concerned, matters should proceed by reference to a set of basic a priori principles in which (ES) and (DS) are preeminent candidates for

---

1. That is, yield instances whose truth is knowable a priori by anyone who is in a position to understand them. As is familiar, the right-to-left directions of these equivalences become contestable if truth-value gaps or many truth values are admitted. This complication is pursued in the first discussion note of chapter 2 of *Truth and Objectivity*. But I do not think that any deflationist should go out of her way to accommodate it since rejection of the right-to-left direction of the Equivalence Schema flies in the face of what seems to be an absolutely basic and constitutive characteristic of the notion of truth, that P and 'It is true that P' are, as it were, attitudinally equivalent: that any attitude to the proposition that P—belief, hope, doubt, desire, fear and so on—is tantamount to the same attitude to its truth. For if that's accepted, and if it is granted that any reservation about a conditional has to involve the taking of *differential* attitudes to its antecedent and consequent, then there simply can be no coherent reservation about: P → it is true that P.

2. It is an unhappy situation that the leading contemporary theorist of deflationism, Paul Horwich, uses both 'minimalism' and 'deflationism' to characterise his view. However, both his use of 'minimalism' and my contrasting one are now entrenched. Probably nobody is confused.

membership; and agrees too that aptitude for truth and falsity goes with surface assertoric content and is not the kind of deep property which, for instance, expressivist views about moral judgement standardly take it to be. However, minimalism rejects the idea that the analysis of the concept of truth exhausts the philosophy of truth: rather, even if the *concept* may be fully characterised by reference to certain basic a priori principles concerning it, the question of which *property* or *properties* of propositions, or sentences, realise the concept can still sensibly be raised for every discourse in which truth has application. Not that an answer to this question has necessarily to provide an identification of truth in the form 'x is true iff x is F'. Minimalism only requires that each discourse that deals in truth-apt claims is associated with such a property, whose character need not be fully determinable just from the list of basic principles serving to characterise the concept but which, relative to the discourse in question, serves as truth by dint of satisfying those principles. The fuller characterisation of this property will depend on specific features of the particular discourse; and it will ultimately depend on these features whether or not the relevant truth property can be explicitly identified by, for instance, a biconditional of the above type.[3]

Minimalism thus incorporates a potential *pluralism* about truth, in the specific sense that what property serves as truth may vary from discourse to discourse. And it is this point that allows it to provide hospitality for the discussion of metaphysical—realist or anti-realist—ideas which have fuelled those other traditional conceptions of truth that deflationists sought to undermine from the start. This potential pluralism is itself in opposition to the more traditional posi-

3. Contrary to what is suggested by Horwich (1998a), pp. 143–4. Horwich there seems to conflate the substantiality of a property with the feasibility of what he calls a 'theory of constitution' for this property, that is, a theory that identifies this property by means of a non-circular equation of the form 'x is true iff x is F', where 'F' is replaced by a predicate that does not contain any semantic terms, a fortiori no cognates of 'is true'. But that seems to be a mere prejudice. It is evident from the example of scientific-theoretical predicates, for instance, that there can be no compelling reason to tie expression of a substantial property to explicit definability.

tions, insofar as they claim to uncover *the* universal nature of truth, something common to all truth-apt discourse. But it can still allow that some regions of discourse may be subject to a truth property congenial to broadly realist thinking about them, while in other regions the character of the truth property may be more congenial to anti-realism.

All this may seem to suggest that the key difference between minimalism and deflationism resides in the fact that while the latter concedes the significance of the predicate 'true' and hence grants that there is a discussible *concept* of truth,[4] it holds—in contrast to minimalism—that there is no *property* of truth: no property that all truths in a given area have in common. This view of the matter would be encouraged by some of the literature in the field, but it is not the happiest way of putting the differences. For once the currency of a concept of truth is granted, it ought to be allowed that all truths have at least the following property in common: the property of falling under this concept.[5] No doubt this move may not illustrate the most natural or fruitful way of conceiving the relationship between concepts and their associated properties in general. But, for all that, it would be misleading to suggest that (most) deflationists would embrace the view that 'Coal is black' and 'Snow is white' have no more in common than do coal and snow.

The real distinction between minimalism and deflationism in respect of the issue whether truth is a property is not that deflationism cannot consistently allow that it is, but rather that minimalism allows more: precisely, that the character of the property (in a particular region of discourse) may not be transparent from the analysis of the

4. There are deflationists that go so far as to deny that 'is true' is a genuine predicate at all, but most deflationists are ready to concede that there is such a thing as the *concept* of truth. A deflationist proposal of the first kind can be found in Grover et al. (1975).

5. That is: of having 'true' correctly predicable of them. This is presumably what Horwich has in mind when he says that truth denotes a property in the sense in which 'every term that functions logically as a predicate stands for a property' (Horwich (1998a), pp. 141–2).

concept. So in that respect there is a rough analogy with the relation-ship—to have recourse to a tired but still useful example—between the concept of water and the property (that of being composed of H_2O molecules, I suppose) which it denotes. Not that minimalism suggests that it should comparably be an a posteriori matter what property truth (locally) is. It will be a matter for further *conceptual* reflection what (kind of) property best fulfils (locally) the role circum-scribed by the concept. (That is why the water analogy is imperfect.)

This kind of substantial distinction between a concept—F—and the property it denotes—being F—is called for whenever we stand in need of some sort of general explanation of a characteristic of items which are F that cannot be elicited solely from materials directly implicated in those items' falling under the concept in question.[6] To take a simple instance: suppose, to pursue the tired example, that the concept of water is a natural kind concept after the fashion of Put-nam's well-known paradigm: that it is, for example, given as the con-cept of that colourless, odourless, tasteless liquid that is typically found in lakes and rivers, assuages thirst, and so on. If we allow that it makes good sense to ask *why* water typically presents with the sur-face features mentioned in its concept, we accept that there is a good explanatory question which cannot—obviously—be answered by appeal to water's falling under its concept, since it is of the very fea-tures involved in its so doing that an explanation is asked. To allow the legitimacy of the question thus involves conceiving of whatever makes water what it is as distanced from the characteristics presented in its concept—as something which can potentially be invoked in explaining their habit of co-occurrence. But what makes water what it is is just its having the property of being water.

Now, it is plausible enough that there are no such explanations that might be given by appeal to the 'thin' truth property which we envis-aged the deflationist as admitting—the property of *falling under the concept of truth*—that we could not equally well give by appeal to the concept of truth itself. What the minimalist should claim, accordingly,

6. Cf. Hilary Putnam's "On Properties" in Putnam (1975a), pp. 305–22.

in contradistinction to the deflationist, is that there *are* certain legitimate explanatory burdens which can be discharged only if we appeal to a property (or properties) of truth conceived in a more substantial sense of 'property'.[7] And note that this claim can be true—in contrast with the situation of the kinds of explanation that might be given by appeal to the property of being water—even if truth, locally or globally, admits of no naturalistic (physicalistic) reduction. (It all depends on whether the things that need explaining are themselves so reducible.) As we shall see in due course, however, the minimalist's argument has no connection with the question of the feasibility of any such reduction.[8]

II

The inflationary argument of *Truth and Objectivity* is to the effect that the legitimacy of thinking of truth, in any particular discourse, as substantial in a fashion deflationism cannot accept, is already guaranteed by the very principles characterising the concept of truth to which deflationism gives centre stage—at least when they are taken in conjunction with certain further uncontroversial principles. Thus minimalism does not just go beyond what deflationism allows but contends in addition that deflationism is incoherent: that, in coupling the thesis that (ES) and/or (DS) yield(s) a complete account of truth with the contention that truth is a property only in the aetiolated sense we have just reviewed, its proponents withdraw with one hand what they just tabled with the other.

---

7. Thus, the minimalist opposes Horwich's suggestion that truth presents a special case in that an account of the property (or properties) denoted just coincides with an account of the concept that does the denoting. See Horwich (1998a), p. 136.

8. On Horwich's interpretation of 'substantive property', such a reducibility is precisely a necessary condition for a property to be substantive. His suggestion that minimalism (in my sense) is based on the idea that truth is substantive on this understanding thus misconceives the position. See *ibid.*, pp. 142–3.

We begin with the observation that truth-apt contents, or sentences expressing such contents, demand a distinction between circumstances under which asserting them is warranted and those under which it is not. And competent thought and talk requires an ability to tell the difference: I need to be able to tell which assertions I am warranted in making in a given state of information and which I am not. So if I am warranted in asserting P, that fact will be recognisable to me and I will thereby be warranted in claiming that I am so warranted. Conversely, if I am warranted in thinking that the assertion of P is warranted, I will be beyond relevant—that is, epistemic—reproach if I go on to assert it. But that is to say that I will be warranted in doing so. We accordingly obtain

> There is warrant for thinking that [it is warrantedly assertible that P] iff there is warrant for thinking that [P].

Given the Equivalence Schema, this in turn will yield

> There is warrant for thinking that [it is warrantedly assertible that P] iff there is warrant for thinking that [it is true that P].

And now, since warranted assertibility is, in a perfectly trivial sense, a normative property—a property possession or lack of which determines which assertions are acceptable and which are not—it follows that truth is too; for by the above equivalence, to be warranted in thinking that P is true has exactly the same normative payload as being warranted in thinking that it is warrantedly assertible. More, our finding is that truth, as characterised by the schemata, and warranted assertibility *coincide in positive normative force*.

That is hardly a startling finding. But the relevant point is not the result itself but its provenance: that truth's being normative in the fashion noted is not merely plausible anyway but is a consequence of what ought to be uncontroversial considerations about the concept of assertibility and a central tenet of deflationism: the conceptual necessity of the Equivalence Schema. So now observe that the Equivalence Schema will also entail any instance of the following *Negation Equivalence:*

(NE) It is true that [Not P] iff it is not true that [P],

given only the further assumption that any P apt for truth has a significant negation that is likewise apt for truth.[9] And this shows that, coincident in positive normative force though they may be, we cannot in general *identify* truth and warrant. For most propositions about most subject matters allow of neutral states of information: states of information in which there are neither warrants for asserting P nor for asserting its negation. In any such case, an invalid schema results if we substitute 'is warrantedly assertible' for 'is true' in (NE). More specifically, if the propositions which make up the substitution class for P allow in principle of neutral states of information, the following conditional is *not* valid:

It is warrantedly assertible that [Not P] if it is not warrantedly assertible that [P].

Thus, we can already conclude from (NE), and hence from (ES), that truth and warranted assertibility, even if coinciding in positive normative force, are *potentially divergent in extension.*[10]

9. Proof: derive the two biconditionals one gets from (ES) by respectively negating both its halves and taking 'Not P' for 'P'. Transitivity of the biconditional then yields (NE).

10. If they were necessarily co-extensive, the Negation Equivalence would have to hold for both if for either.

To offset misunderstanding, two points may merit emphasis. First, warranted assertibility is here understood to be a notion that is always relativised to a particular state of information. If no such state of information is explicitly mentioned, claims involving this notion will always be understood to relate to the present state of information. Second, the modality involved in 'warranted assert*ibility*' does not signify the potential possession of warrants for an assertion, but the actual possession of

It is an immediate consequence of this observation that for any assertoric practice which allows the definition, on the contents of the moves it permits, of a truth property satisfying (ES)—that is, for any assertoric practice whatever—there must be a further kind of distinction between circumstances in which making these moves is in good standing and circumstances in which it is not—a distinction that need not coincide with the distinction between circumstances in which such a move can warrantedly be made and those in which it cannot. The concept of truth as characterised by (ES) precisely calls for a norm—a way an assertion may be in good standing—which warrant is essentially warrant to suppose satisfied but which, because of the point about potential extensional divergence, may nevertheless not be satisfied when an assertion is warranted (or may be satisfied when it is not). And a fully intelligent participation in such practices will involve grasp that they essentially involve submission to a standard the meeting of which need not just be a matter of possessing warrants for the claim that it is met.

Minimalism now claims that these facts about assertoric (and doxastic) practices stand in need of explanation. In particular, it maintains that it needs to be explained what this further norm of correctness amounts to in such a way that it becomes clear how it and warranted assertibility, although potentially divergent in extension, coincide in normative force: how it can be that warrant is essentially warrant to think that this other norm is satisfied when there is no guarantee that they are always *co*-satisfied. And such an explanation, it is contended, while it will have to do much more than this, must at least begin by finding something for the truth of a proposition to consist in, a property which it can intelligibly have although there may currently be no reason to suppose that it has it, or may intelligibly lack even though there is reason to think that it has it. Warrant can then be required to be whatever gives a (defeasible) reason to think that a proposition has that property.

---

warrants for a potential assertion. So in particular merely provable mathematical statements—for which we so far have no proof—do not qualify as warrantedly assertible. I believe a confusion of this distinction drives the criticisms in Tennant (1995).

The deflationist account of truth would appear, however, to have no resources to give such an explanation. For all we can elicit from the Equivalence Schema is the *problem*. The point of the inflationary argument is precisely that the basic principles on which deflationism builds its account spawn the concept of a norm—a way a proposition can be in good or bad standing, as I put it a moment ago—which contrasts with its current evidential status. But they keep silence when the question is raised, what the satisfaction or nonsatisfaction of this new norm consists in and how it can fail to be a substantial property.

So at any rate the inflationary argument contends. But the deflationist is likely to believe that she has a good rejoinder. 'There is no silence on the point', she will reply. 'On the contrary, my theory is very explicit about what the satisfaction of your "norm" consists in. The proposition that snow is white satisfies it just if snow is white; the proposition that grass is green satisfies it just if grass is green; the proposition that there is no life on Mars satisfies it just if there is no life on Mars'. However, this response is of course to no avail unless we *already* understand the difference between the proposition, for example, that there is no life on Mars and the proposition that that proposition is warranted. And clearly that distinction cannot be recovered from any contrast between the circumstances under which the two propositions are *respectively* warranted, since—as in effect noted right at the start of the argument—there is none. The difference between them resides, rather, precisely in a difference in correctness conditions of another sort (sotto voce: *truth* conditions). In order to understand the contrast between the two propositions, I precisely have to understand that the former is in principle hostage to a kind of failure which can occur even when it is warranted, and which will not then affect the latter. So the debate is rapidly brought back to the point before the deflationist made her putative 'good response', with the minimalist charging her to explain (i) how the relevant contrast can so much as exist unless there is something substantial in which such failure—or more happily, success—consists; and (ii) how a *grasp* of the contrast can anywhere be possible unless we are familiar with a (perhaps local) property which behaves as the concept characterised by the basic principles demands.

The kind of rejoinder I just envisaged a deflationist making is of course pure deflationist stock-in-trade. Supporters of deflationism characteristically view the whole debate as turning on whether it can be shown that all legitimate uses of the word 'true' can be somehow explained on the basis of the Equivalence Schema (and/or the Disquotational Scheme) together with a repertoire of contexts free of 'true' and its cognates, and put all their effort and (often considerable) ingenuity into the attempt to show that they can.[11] It therefore merits emphasis that success in that project is entirely beside the point if the contents of the relevant 'true'-free contexts, to which deflationists simply help themselves, cannot be explicated by construing them merely as subject to norms of assertibility but demand an additional truth-like constraint. To show that we can deduce some aspect of our use of the predicate 'true' by appeal just to the Equivalence Schema and certain 'true'-free contexts cannot just be assumed to have reductive significance, without further ado. The initial position in the debate is one in which nothing yet stands against the opposed thought that, instead of reading the Equivalence Schema from left to right, as if to eliminate the truth property, we should read it from right to left, as highlighting the fact that, implicit in any content in the range of 'P', there is already a tacit invocation of the norm of truth. Deflationism needs to get to grips with that reading: to make a case that no implicit prior grasp of the concept of truth, nor implicit reference to a property that concept denotes, lurks buried in the materials to which its 'explanations' appeal. The thrust of the inflationary argument is that no convincing such case can be made—that whether or not we can somehow eliminate or otherwise 'deflate' the *word*, a corresponding property, and its contrast with assertibility, is part and parcel of assertoric content itself.[12]

11. Thus for instance Horwich (1998a), at pp. 20–3, 139–40.

12. In *Meaning* (Horwich (1998b)), Horwich himself tries—as he must—to develop a general account of meaning in which truth plays no explanatory part. I shall, however, not discuss his proposals here, except to record the belief that they do not succeed in addressing the needed distinction.

III

The last claim requires that there is no explicating the contrast in content between the proposition that P and the proposition that P is assertible without recourse to the notion of truth in the *explanans*. Robert Brandom, for one, would disagree. His recent ambitious pragmatist project holds out the prospect of an account of that contrast constructed out of truth-free materials.[13] Brandom himself is no deflationist, of course. But the question is whether his arguments might nevertheless serve to deflect the thrust of the inflationary argument.[14]

Brandom's project is assertibilist: the sought-after contrast is to be explicated in terms of contrasts in the assertibility conditions, normatively understood,[15] of the two types of proposition in question. More generally, Brandom sets himself to explain how, in a practice initially disciplined merely by norms of assertibility, contents can emerge which are *objective* in the specific sense that they do not concern the situation of the assertor—do not concern what is or is not permitted, or prohibited, for her in that particular context, or other features of her attitudes. That P is assertible is relative to an assertor, to her context and state of information in relevant respects. But the content of what is asserted—that P—is, typically, not so relative.

Say that two claims are co-assertible just in case any body of information warranting the one warrants the other and conversely. Then any claim which is objective in Brandom's sense—that is, is not about the attitudes or informational situation of any particular subject or group of subjects—will be co-assertible with certain non-objective claims. Such are the respective pairs,

'The swatch is red'   'That the swatch is red is properly assertible by me now'

13. See Brandom (1994), chap. 5, and (2000), chap. 6. I focus on the latter in what follows.

14. Brandom himself is confident: 'The fact is that the distinction between sentences sharing assertibility conditions and sharing truth-conditions . . . can be made out in terms of commitments and entitlements, without the need to invoke the notion of truth' (Brandom (2000), pp. 201–2).

15. That is, understood as conditions of *proper* assertion.

'I will write a book on Hegel'	'I foresee that I will write a book on Hegel'
'All ravens are black'	'We have a body of evidence corroborating the claim that all ravens are black and no significant counter-evidence'

How can the assertibilist properly differentiate these contents? The immediate difficulty is that, on a natural understanding of 'assertibility conditions', the paired propositions *share* their assertibility conditions. No doubt their differences are indeed manifest in differences in the assertibility conditions of more complex claims in which they are respectively embedded: for instance the *negations* of each of the contrasted pairs will have different assertibility conditions, as will *conditionals* in which they are the respective antecedents. But these differences are apt to seem unintelligible so long as the assertibilist allows, what may seem undeniable, that the content of a negated or conditional claim must be construed as a function of the content of the claim negated or of the antecedent and consequent. The problem posed for the assertibilist by these pairs is not to find differences in conditions of warranted assertion to reflect what are the intuitive differences in their contents, but to do so in a way which respects semantic compositionality.

Brandom's interesting response is that assertibilism needs to operate with a more finely discriminated notion of assertibility. Specifically, we are to distinguish between what a speaker ought to assert, or be prepared to assert, *qua entitled* to it (justified in accepting it) and what a speaker ought to assert, or be prepared to assert, *qua committed* to it (by other things she accepts).[16] How is this to help the distinction of the co-assertible pairs? The notions of entitlement and commitment are open to interpretation in detail, of course, but one would expect—in effect, the consideration already emphasised, that sets the problem—that the members of such pairs would have the same *entitlement*

16. For elaboration, see Brandom (2000), pp. 190 ff.

conditions. The expectable proposal is therefore that they can, in effect, be distinguished as commitments. But what Brandom suggests, while in keeping with that, is actually more subtle. Reflect that the intuitive differences in content between members of the pairs issue in differences in their *compatibility relations*—in which claims they are respectively compatible or incompatible with. For instance, the non-objective members of the pairs will in general be compatible with the falsity of the objective members; and the objective members will in general be compatible with the non-satisfaction of certain necessary conditions for particular subjects' being in the informational states described in the corresponding non-objective claims. Brandom's idea is to construct a notion of incompatibility to reflect these intuitive differences out of materials provided by his finer-grained conception of assertibility. Specifically, what he proposes is this:

> We can say that two assertible contents are incompatible in case commitment to one precludes entitlement to the other. Thus commitment to the content expressed by the sentence 'The swatch is red' rules out entitlement to the commitment that would be undertaken by asserting the sentence 'The swatch is green'.[17]

Given this notion of incompatibility, we can then define a corresponding notion of entailment: one content entails another just if everything incompatible with the latter is incompatible with the former. And then we may hope to distinguish objective from non-objective contents in terms of systematic differences in what they entail and are entailed by.

IV

It seems to me very unclear whether this project can succeed. I'll canvass three specific doubts—though in fact they are all aspects of the same problem: that there seems to be no understanding of 'preclusion' that delivers the result Brandom wants.

17. *Ibid.*, p. 194.

(i) First, it is hard to see how there can *ever actually be* a 'preclusion' in the relevant kind of case. For presumably there is to be no requirement of ancestral entitlement in one's commitments—consequences of beliefs which I hold prejudicially, or dogmatically, or otherwise without entitlement, are no less *commitments* on that account than those which flow from beliefs to which I am entitled. Indeed, this is no mere presumption but a presupposition of Brandom's whole approach. If he were to restrict the idea of commitment in such a way as to require, to the contrary, that commitments must be based on anterior entitlements, then—assuming the transmissibility of entitlement across entailment and other relations of commitment—his account of incompatibility would collapse into one of preclusion between entitlements and the entire point of the bipartite refinement of the notion of assertibility would be undermined. Commitments, then, may have no ultimate ground in entitlement. But now: How can there ever be a conflict between a groundless commitment and an entitlement? The facts may simply be that I am committed to a certain claim, p, because it follows from things I accept; and simultaneously that I'm entitled to not p, because my epistemic situation fully warrants it. Commitment—so long as it does not have to be entitlement-based—and entitlement simply pass each other by. What I ought to accept because I am committed to it is one thing; what I ought to accept because my informational input warrants it is quite another. There are, intuitively, no collisions or 'preclusions' between these domains.

(ii) It is clear that *merely* (somehow) distinguishing objective contents from (putatively) co-assertible non-objective ones is not enough. In addition, they have to be distinguished *fully and correctly:* the assertibilist has to show specifically how he can make a contrast between the members of such pairs which is a correct reflection of the *semantic* compatibility and incompatibility relations which the contents in question actually respectively bear to contents at large. The challenge is not merely to get *some* kind of distinction going between objective/non-objective pairs but to track the detail of the semantic compatibility/incompatibility relations which they respectively actually sustain across contents in general.

Now reflect that the relevant kind of incompatibility—the semantic incompatibility which obtains between 'That the swatch is red is properly assertible by me now' and, say, 'No one knows anything about the colour of the swatch', but does not obtain between the latter and 'The swatch is red'—is of course symmetric. So any successful assertibilist surrogate for it had better be symmetric too. We may take it therefore that Brandom's surrogate—that a commitment to one content precludes entitlement to the other—is a symmetric relation. (If it isn't, that is an independent objection.) Hence if we are trying to determine whether the pragmatic surrogate correctly reflects the different semantic compatibility relations which a pair of contents, p and p^*, bear to a particular content, p^+—let it be, for instance, that intuitively p^* is incompatible with p^+ but p is not—it won't matter whether we put the question as

> Is an entitlement to p^+ precluded by a commitment to p^*,
> but not by a commitment to p?

or as

> Does a commitment to p^+ preclude an entitlement to p^*,
> but not an entitlement to p?

Focus, therefore, on the latter form of the question, and suppose that p and p^* are *co-entitlements* (that is, that any situation in which one is entitled to one is a situation in which one is entitled to the other). Let it be that a commitment to p^+ does indeed preclude entitlement to p^*. And—notwithstanding the first worry above—let preclusion just be this: that the norms governing the relevant assertoric practice be such as to require that any situation in which one is committed to p^+ is a situation in which one is not entitled to p^*. Well, since p and p^* are co-entitlements, it follows that the situations in which one is not entitled to p* are all and only situations in which one is also not entitled to p. So commitment to p⁺ must preclude entitlement to p as well.

In other words, provided the listed type of pairings of objective and non-objective contents are all cases of co-entitlement, Brandom's proposal has to be impotent to reflect the intended semantic distinctions in full and correct detail. The contents of 'That the swatch is red is properly assertible by me now' and 'The swatch is red' are indeed distinguished by their differing incompatibility relationships to 'No one knows anything about the colour of the swatch'. But if this distinction has to be recovered in terms of the norms of the practice proscribing simultaneous commitment to 'No one knows anything about the colour of the swatch' and entitlement to 'That the swatch is red is properly assertible by me now', but allowing simultaneous commitment to 'No one knows anything about the colour of the swatch' and entitlement to 'The swatch is red'—it goes fugitive. For the norms require—indeed, this might just seem like a restatement of the datum for the problem—that any situation in which I am not entitled to the second is one in which I am not entitled to the third either, and conversely.

To be sure, this assumes that the relevant kind of objective/non-objective pairs are co-entitlements. But if that is wrong, then there already is the solution to the assertibilist's initial problem! Brandom's proposal, and the attendant break-up of assertibility into commitment versus entitlement, will not be needed. In short: if Brandom allows that the objective/non-objective pairs are co-entitlements, it seems his proffered apparatus cannot get their semantic compatibility/incompatibility relationships right; and if he doesn't so allow, he doesn't need that apparatus to distinguish them.

(iii) It is very telling, I think, that Brandom's proposal fails to deliver what is wanted even when the preclusion of entitlements by commitments is understood in a way that presupposes an *independently achieved* conception of assertoric content and the rationality of the agent: specifically, that commitment to p precludes an entitlement to q just when, because of their respective contents, one cannot *rationally and clear-headedly* endorse both contents simultaneously—

cannot rationally and clear-headedly recognise the entitlement along-side retention of one's antecedent commitments. Even *this* notion—whose unreconstructed appeal to rationality surely must anyway put it outside the legitimate base materials of Brandom's own project—won't deliver just the intended contrasts.

To see why, consider how the proposal might work in response to a particular example—say, the third pair above:

(i)   All ravens are black, and
(ii) We have a body of evidence corroborating the claim that all ravens are black and no significant counter-evidence.

Now, (i) is, whereas (ii) is not, semantically incompatible with

(iii) A grey raven is nesting in the Cairngorm Mountains.

Hence a commitment to (i), but not a commitment to (ii), should preclude entitlement to (iii). But while it's true that one could not rationally and clear-headedly welcome an entitlement to the belief that a grey raven is nesting in the Cairngorms alongside a commitment set that included the belief that all ravens are black, the same would also be true if one's commitment set included the belief (ii), whereby there is a body of evidence corroborating the claim that all ravens are black and no significant extant counter-evidence. For while (iii) is not inconsistent with (ii), *an entitlement to it is.*

The pair, (i) and (ii), are a prototype of the kind of difference—between an objective content and a corresponding non-objective content—which Brandom has set himself to differentiate. Yet it seems that even when we understand a commitment's precluding an entitlement—surely illicitly, in the present context—in terms of the rational impossibility of accepting the entitlement alongside continuation of the commitment, we fail to recover an appropriate contrast between (i) and (ii) in relation to (iii). Recognition of an entitlement to (iii) is *rationally incompatible* with a continuing commitment to (ii), no less than to (i). True, it is the *fact* of an entitlement to (iii) which is inconsistent with (ii), and the *content* of an entitlement to (iii) which is inconsistent with (i). But that's just the crucial distinction which Brandom's proposal, however interpreted in detail, seems to have no prospect of recovering. To recover the difference, we have to appeal not merely to rational incompatibilities between acceptances of entitlements and commitments in general but to the narrower subclass of such in which the rational incompatibilities are sustained *purely by the contents*—I want to say: *truth conditions*—of the commitments and entitlements in question. In brief: even when the preclusion by commitments of entitlements is understood as a rational relation, sustained by the contents in question, it is a broader relation than the semantic incompatibility which Brandom seeks to reconstruct, and is therefore bound to lead to misrepresentation of the contents in question when they are identified by the corresponding 'entailment' relations.

PART FIVE

RESPONSE-DEPENDENCE

AND COGNITIVE COMMAND

The three essays in this final part are the most recent in the collection, all having been completed since the turn of the millennium. They are variously concerned with issues arising in connection with the crux of Cognitive Command, or response-dependence and the Euthyphro Contrast. Essay 13 is the culmination of a line of research which was stimulated by conversations with my Ph.D. student, the late Mark Powell, tragically killed in a fire in 1994.[1] It is concerned with the famous argument of Saul Kripke, outlined in the third lecture of *Naming and Necessity* (Kripke 1980) that pain—and sensations generally—cannot be anything physical. The driving ideas of the essay are two: first, that Kripke's argument has the resources to withstand the most commonly received objections against it; and second, that if good at all, it will generalise both to subject matters which qualify as Euthyphronic by the specific conditions imposed on that notion in *Truth and Objectivity*, and to subject matters meeting more

---

1. Mark's ideas on some of the relevant issues were published posthumously in the *European Review of Philosophy* (Powell 1998). This essay is a sequel to my published response to him in the same volume (Wright 1998a).

relaxed conditions of response-dependence—sufficiently relaxed conditions, indeed, to qualify the semantic, the moral and the intentional-psychological in general. The upshot is an outstanding challenge to the prospects of any form of reductive naturalism about these and other controversial areas: unless fault can be found with the Kripkean style of argument, the conclusion looms that naturalism is unsustainable, that there can be no solution to (what has recently come to be termed) the 'placement problem' not merely for sensations and colours but for meanings, values and mental states in general. However, the chapter concludes by suggesting that there is indeed a cogent but (so far as I am aware) unremarked form of objection to the Kripkean strategy of argument, one which teaches us something important about the epistemology of the metaphysical modalities.

If the generalised Kripkean argument should not be sustained, that merely removes a barrier to the solution to the 'placement problem'. It still remains to solve it. Essay 14 is directed against those philosophers who, holding that—for their own various reasons—there is no solution to the problem for ordinary intentional ('folk') psychology in particular, have been drawn to some form of anti-realist response. The central question of the essay is: What specific form should an anti-realism about ordinary psychology best assume? It is suggested that, in the light of the foreseeable motivation for anti-realism in this area, there are just four relevant possibilities. The anti-realist may embrace eliminativism, contending that ordinary psychology is at best false, at worst incoherent empirical theory, and should be abandoned in favour of the development of a more satisfactory explanatory theory of human behaviour. Or she may go instrumentalist, arguing that ordinary psychology does not need to be regarded as credible in order for it to serve as a useful heuristic tool. There is, third, the option of contending, in the tradition of expressivism in ethics, that the 'statements' of ordinary psychology do not purvey genuinely truth-apt contents, but are the products of a type of illocutionary act distinct from assertion. And there is, finally, what seems to me by far the most attractive option: an application of the minimalism of *Truth and Objectivity*, according to which ordinary psychological statements, while indeed truth-apt and very often justifiably regarded as true, are merely *minimally* truth-apt, and thus are not even in potential competition with empirical science, realistically conceived. On this view, no problem of placement—of locating the states and entities of ordinary psychology under fundamental ontological categories—arises.[2] The argument of the essay, however, is that none of these four positions is dialectically stable: each of the four distinguished kinds of anti-realist view—error-theoretic, fictionalist, expressivist and minimalist—turns out to have, one way or another, an implicit investment in ordinary psychology of such a kind that to attempt to apply it to psychological discourse is to attempt a position that, in one way or another, bites its own tail. The result, it appears, is not merely that there is no tenable positive thesis available to the would-be anti-realist about psychological discourse, but that there is not even any self-coherent one. This is not a finding that imposes realism—that would still have to be supported independently, in a fashion which addressed the various specific anti-realist arguments in the field. The immediate moral is rather a kind of local *quietism:* failing considerations sufficient to enforce realism about it, ordinary psychology must be granted a kind of 'diplomatic immunity', as it is expressed in the essay, in realist versus anti-realist debate.

The final essay in the collection returns to an outstanding item of unfinished business. Central to the project of *Truth and Objectivity* is the distinction between merely minimally truth-apt discourses and those exerting cognitive command. Cognitive Command is characterised as involving that all disputes formulable in the discourse in question and meeting certain collateral conditions should involve something worth regarding as a cognitive shortcoming. So it is natural to suppose—and in places encouraged by my wording in *Truth and Objectivity*—that merely minimally truth-apt discourses allow the opposite: disagreements which can be expressed within the discourses in question and meet the various collateral conditions yet

---

2. More needs to be said, of course, about how minimalism enables placement issues to be finessed.

where nothing worth regarding as cognitive shortcoming is involved. This is not only natural, but rather chimes with an intuitive conception of what it is for a region of thought to be most apt for the traditional kind of *relativism*. As various critics of *Truth and Objectivity* rapidly pointed out, however, the conception of the possibility of cognitively blameless disagreements is unstable under normally uncontroversial reasoning. Whether it is held to suffice for cognitive shortcoming that there merely be a mismatch between a thinker's belief and the truth value of what he believes, or whether it is held to be necessary in addition that there be some defect in the process whereby a belief is formed, it is straightforward to show that, at least under the supposition that truth in the discourse obeys a form of evidential constraint, the supposition of cognitively blameless disagreement—one involving no cognitive shortcoming on either side—leads to contradiction.

Essay 15 offers what I believe to be the solution to this problem. The issue, in effect, is not just that of stabilising the distinction between merely minimally truth-apt discourses and those exerting Cognitive Command, but as giving content to a coherent form of relativistic thesis which might be held to apply to, for instance, matters of comedy or, much more controversially, of fundamental moral principle. The central suggestion of the essay is that what merely minimally truth-apt discourses allow, and those exerting Cognitive Command do not, are disagreements which exhibit a certain kind of *indeterminacy*. Specifically, the essay proposes and commends a *broadly epistemic* conception of indeterminacy covering both cases of semantic vagueness as ordinarily understood and also cases—certain kinds of dispute about comedy would again be prime examples— where our inclination is to say that there is no 'fact of the matter' for reasons other than the vagueness of the ingredient comic concepts. It is argued that the logic for discourses exhibiting this kind of indeterminacy should be not classical but intuitionistic, and that in the presence of a certain standard intuitionistic distinctions—for instance, between a negated universal statement and its classically equivalent existential negative—the arguments that threaten to collapse the distinction between mere minimal truth-aptitude and the exertion of Cognitive Command can be neutralised. Two interesting corollaries of this line of response, explored in some detail in the essay, consist in the provision of a basic intuitionistic form of solution to the Sorites paradox and a better understanding of what I believe to be the most powerful kind of case for intuitionistic revisions of classical logic.

13

The Conceivability of Naturalism

A central dilemma in contemporary metaphysics is to find a place for certain anthropocentric subject matters—for instance, the semantic, moral and psychological—in a world as conceived by modern naturalism: a stance which inflates the concepts and categories deployed by (finished) physical science into a metaphysics of the kind of thing the real world essentially and exhaustively is. On one horn, if we embrace this naturalism, it seems we are committed either to reductionism: that is, to a construal of the reference of, for example, semantic, moral and psychological vocabulary as somehow being within the physical domain—or to disputing that the discourses in question involve reference to what is real at all. On the other horn, if we reject the naturalism, then we accept that there is more to the world than can be embraced within a physicalist ontology—and so take on a commitment, it can seem, to a kind of eerie supernaturalism. John McDowell[1] has proposed a distinctive, intendedly 'non-eerie' accommodation, involving our habituation into a more 'relaxed' conception of what should rank as natural, a conception of nature which would

1. McDowell (1994).

357

be hospitable to meanings, to ethical and other norms and to psychological properties. But the position he proposes—I am speaking just of my own reaction—can too easily seem more like a triumphant reaffirmation of the common-sense categories at issue than a real response to the metaphysical dilemma they pose.

This problem provides the background to the present essay, rather than its topic. Its topic is the famous argument, outlined in the third lecture of Saul Kripke's *Naming and Necessity*,[2] that pain—and sensations generally—cannot be anything physical. What gives this argument its interest in the context of the concerns of the present volume is the manner in which it draws on considerations of (apparent) conceivability to substantiate a metaphysical conclusion. In the first part of what follows, I shall outline the background to the argument, develop its detail somewhat, and sustain it against what are, according to my understanding, the two most influential received objections against it. Then I shall make a case that, if good at all, it should generalise to cover not just sensations but all items falling within the extensions of (in a sense to be explained) *transparent* concepts, with colour concepts (an example we shall stalk throughout) and secondary quality concepts generally the obvious next port of call. At that point, the dialectical situation will be that to the extent that the distinctive concepts of semantic, moral and psychological discourse also approximate the relevant model of transparency, the Kripkean argument presents an outstanding challenge to any form of reductionist reaction to the metaphysical dilemma. But I do not think that dialectical situation is stable. My concluding suggestion will be that there is still an outstanding objection to the overall strategy of the argument: the assumption which drives it, that counter-conceivability is a defeater for claims of metaphysical necessity of all kinds, both a priori and a posteriori, stands in need of a (to the best of my knowledge) unremarked form of qualification. If this is right, the argument is balked even for the basic case of sensations, and the fascinating prospect of a wide-reaching exclusion of physicalism on purely conceptual grounds evaporates.

2. Kripke (1980).

I. KRIPKE'S ARGUMENT

Natural Kinds and Natural Kind Concepts

Are colours natural kinds?[3] The philosophical question, of course, is not—in the first instance, anyway—about the actual constitution of coloured things but about the *concept* of colour. According to the usual template, a concept is a natural kind concept if, roughly, its extension is standardly explained by reference to indicators whose status as such is viewed as contingent, and if we conceive of the real determinant of the extension as a natural property, presumed to be explanatorily associated with the indicators, of whose character we may have—and anyway need—no clear idea in ordinary commerce with the concept. The concept of water, for instance, is characteristically explained by reference to the indicator properties: tasteless, colourless liquid, occurring naturally in lakes and rivers, satisfying thirst, essential to life, solvent for many substances and so on. But if, as is usually supposed, **water**[4] is a natural kind concept, then these marks serve not to define it but merely as pointers to an underlying natural essence—to the best of our present knowledge: that of having the chemical constitution, H_2O—whose instantiation is what canonically determines whether or not a sample is water. If **water** is a natural kind concept, the indicators serve merely as *reference fixers:* the concept of water may be glossed as, roughly: that kind of stuff whose being the kind of stuff it is explains its characteristic satisfaction of the indicators in question. A natural kind concept thus incorporates an assumption: that there is an underlying natural essence which discharges—near enough, often enough—that explanatory role. This assumption may be wrong. In that case, the concept will suffer from reference failure.[5]

---

3. One philosopher who has argued so, in a much travelled talk some years ago, is again Kripke. An account of his arguments may be found in Mark Johnston (1992).

4. Except where no ambiguity arises, I shall use boldface type to indicate reference to a concept.

5. I am going past issues to do with whether such a concept could *survive* reference failure.

Colours themselves are natural kinds if colour concepts are natural kind concepts *and* they are not so afflicted.

All this is familiar. The idea that many of our general, prescientific concepts are concepts of this kind came into prominence with Putnam and Kripke[6] and contrasts with an older model, associated (on no clear evidence, actually) with the later Wittgenstein, according to which the indicator properties do not bear a *contingent* relation to an underlying determinant of the extension of the concept but determine that extension intrinsically, after the fashion of a cluster of *criteria*— in the specialised sense of the term that arose in the first generation of commentary on the *Philosophical Investigations*. Clearly there could be concepts—let's call them *criterially governed* concepts—for which this model was correct. Even if our actual concept of water is indeed a natural kind concept, we might have employed instead a concept— **schwater**—for which the water-indicators did play a criterial rather than merely reference-fixing role. To be schwater would just be to satisfy (enough of) the (more important) indicator properties.

How is it manifest which is our actual concept? Well, if 'water' expressed a natural kind concept, then should it turn out that there is no interesting, explanatorily unifying property underlying the presence of the water-indicators in enough cases, we ought to regard the case as one of reference failure: water, like phlogiston, would be a fiction, exploded by science. But if the concept expressed by 'water' were criterially governed—if it were **schwater**—no such conclusion would be warranted; the use of the concept would be indefeasible by any such empirical scientific development. That's only one type of case, though. What about the other—when a criterially governed concept is such that science *does* nevertheless disclose a natural property underlying the characteristic co-manifestations of the relevant criteria, so that a corresponding natural kind concept, had we employed it, would have been successful? That would presumably be the actual situation if the concept expressed by 'water' were **schwater**: schwater

6. The *loci classici* are Putnam (1975b), chaps. 8, 10–12; Kripke (1980) lecture III.

would turn out to be H_2O. What in *that* case would show that the concept was nevertheless criterially governed?

It might be thought that the difference would emerge in our attitude to certain counterfactual conditionals, for instance:

> Had it turned out that there was no underlying explanatorily unifying property, we would have regarded 'water' as failing of reference.

We will affirm that counterfactual, the natural thought would be, if but only if our concept of water is a natural kind concept. But this isn't good enough. For the counterfactual could be wrong even if the concept expressed by 'water' *is* a natural kind concept—provided that, were nature to have let us down in that way, we would then have *changed* the concept expressed by 'water' in the light of that discovery—falling back on the criterially governed analogue, as it were. And of course the question, whether in continuing to regard the term as referential we would have assigned to it a concept of a different status, can be answered only in the light of some *independent* determination of how possession of one or the other status would show. So the counterfactual account is no help—it needs back-up by the very thing it purported to provide.

Kripke's discussion offered a different answer, in terms of modal intuition. If water is a natural kind—say H_2O—then it is *essentially* of that kind: something which manifested all the indicators but was not so constituted would not be water but some other kind of stuff. By contrast, if **water** is actually criterially governed, then such a substance would fall under that concept, so would be water, whatever its constitution, and we ought to allow that while water is normally made up of H_2O, it could be composed of something else. So if **water** is a natural kind concept, and it is true that water is H_2O, it is *necessarily* true that water is H_2O. But if **water** is a criterially governed concept, it is *contingent* what constitution water has—or indeed whether it has any uniform or typical constitution at all. To determine the status of our concept of water, then, we may check our intuitions about claims such as

> Water is H_2O, but it might not have been,

or

> Water might have had no typical physical constitution.

If **water** is indeed a natural kind concept, these should impress as conceptual solecisms. For natural kind concepts distinctively sustain certain forms of necessary (a posteriori) claim of which these are violations.

In what follows, I am going to assume that this proposal is broadly adequate: that the difference between natural kind concepts and others can be found in the kind of modal distinctions Kripke highlighted.

Primary and Derivative Natural Kind Concepts

A further qualification is wanted, however. Intuitions about the necessity of identity statements have to draw on assumptions about the status of *both* the configured terms—for instance, in the particular example, it is taken for granted that 'H_2O' is itself an expression rigidly denoting a natural kind. In general it is obvious that the class of natural kind concepts which fit the Putnam–Kripke template—concepts which purportedly denote an essential underlying property targeted by surface reference-fixers—is a secondary class, adverting by its very characterisation to a contrasting background class of elite concepts—usually assumed, tacitly or otherwise, to be those of developed physical science[7]—by means of which such underlying essences may be canonically identified. For modern naturalists, indeed, the natural coincides with the physical as (best) physics understands it. Call these elite background concepts, whether or not exclusively physical, the *primary* natural kind concepts: concepts of which it is

---

7. Though not, I think, by Kripke.

independently given that they demarcate—if anything—what are properly regarded as natural divisions and substances, properties and stuffs.[8] A *derivative* natural kind concept will then show itself by sustaining[9] an a posteriori but necessarily true identity statement whose other term expresses a primary natural kind concept.

A proponent of the thesis that colour concepts are natural kind concepts thus in principle has the option of maintaining that they are primary natural kind concepts. I take that to be the view of the so-called simple theory of colour.[10] But I shall not return to that idea in the present discussion. The more usual way of taking the thesis is that—like **water**—colour concepts are derivative natural kind concepts: that our understanding of the concept **red,** for instance, tacitly calls for an identification,

Redness is the property thus and such,

whose modal and epistemic status will be exactly comparable to that of:

Water is H_2O.

What Is the Importance of Natural Kind Concepts?

If many of the concepts for which the criterial model might initially seem attractive are in fact natural kind concepts, that is something which it is as well to know. And the adjustment will call in turn for some reconfiguration of our ideas about what is involved in thinking thoughts in which such concepts are constituents—a reconfiguration closely analogous to that involved in dropping the description theory

8. Naturally, the identification of these concepts will be hostage to the fate of contemporary scientific theory. We take it that 'H_2O' expresses a compound such concept; but the notion that hydrogen and oxygen are primary kinds is of course empirically defeasible.

9. Or at least: requiring that there be, if it is instantiated.

10. See Campbell (1993).

of proper names, even in its most sophisticated forms, and accepting that such expressions typically facilitate the thinking of thoughts *de re,* thoughts directly targeted upon specific objects, rather than mediated via complex descriptive conditions. In short, issues are at stake here—as Kripke saw—about the character of the relation between a thought and the objects and properties it concerns.

But those issues are not our present business. Our agenda is set, rather, by a line of thought which begins with a certain simple picture of the nature and limits of natural science. The picture has it that natural science just *is* the empirical theory of natural kinds and their functional relationships: the project of natural science is to taxonomise what kinds of thing naturally occur and to describe how they are causally and explanatorily related, to detail the laws to which they are subject. If this is right, then—here is the line of thought—the spectre is raised that a concept which is not a natural kind concept—but which is nevertheless, intuitively, a concept of a *kind* of thing, state or event—may go on to prove, in a certain sense, *scientifically recalcitrant,* and any truths which it is needed to express may consequently lie outside the domain which natural science can illuminate. In short, at least if the simple picture is accepted, the demarcation of important groups of kind concepts which are demonstrably not natural kind concepts may be just what is needed, for those philosophers inclined to want to do so, to challenge the physical naturalism that for so many has come to seem like common sense.

Any such challenge, however, will need to surmount the simple distinction touched on above. That a criterially governed concept should be intractable for physical science is certainly possible in one kind of case, namely, where it actually has a *physically heterogeneous* extension. In that case, since there will be nothing uniform at the level at which physical science operates in which the instantiation of the concept consists, there may be no physical laws connecting its instantiation with the instantiation of other physical properties.[11] What,

---

11. This is only a possibility, of course. The heterogeneous instances of a concept may still divide up into a manageable variety of physical types, each associated in parallel law-like ways with other kinds of physical states and events.

though, if a criterially governed concept does have a physically unified extension nevertheless—as **schwater** actually has? In that situation we could still affirm the identity, that schwater *is* H_2O, since the
term 'schwater' has a complex descriptive content—to be cashed out
in terms of the indicator properties—of such a kind as to allow the
identity to be true as a matter of *contingency*. The force of the identity
would be that

> the satisfier of [a certain descriptive condition somehow
> factoring in the water-indicators] = H_2O

and this could be a contingent truth because of the non-rigidity of the
term on its left-hand side. So schwater—the actual stuff—would still
be a natural kind—namely, H_2O—even though the *concept* of schwater was not that of a natural kind; and mention of schwater, so use of
the concept, could correspondingly occur in (low-level) scientific generalisations and explanations.

That is a reminder, then, that there is—of course—no *direct* way of
drawing conclusions about the limitations of science from the status of particular concepts. It will be one thing—if indeed it can be
done—to make a case that colour concepts, say, are not natural kind
concepts; but no immediate conclusion is to be expected about the
physical-scientific role of colour. The interesting question this raises
is: what sort of additional philosophical argument could encompass
the stronger conclusion?

The Counter-Conceivability Principle

In *Naming and Necessity,* Kripke deployed his new apparatus of rigid
designation, a posteriori necessities and the rest to outline a new argument—though he did not himself endorse it—against all possibility of
the physical reduction of sensation, focusing on the case of pain.

Recall that any statement identifying the essence of a natural kind
will be, if true at all, necessarily so. If **water** is a natural kind concept,
and it is true that water is H_2O, then it is necessarily true. It follows
that evidence against the necessity of such an identification is evidence

against its truth. But what should count as evidence against its necessity in the first place? Kripke's discussion turns on a major assumption on which we should pause: that *all* purportedly metaphysically necessary statements, even those—of constitution, identity or origin, for instance—whose justification is *a posteriori*, are hostage to what we can, to borrow Descartes' happy phrase, clearly and distinctly conceive, for—short of its actuality—a clear and distinct conception of a situation is the best possible evidence of its possibility. This principle—the *Counter-Conceivability Principle*—invites us, of course, to provide an account of when a conception should rank as relevantly clear and distinct. But without taking that issue on, we can cash the principle's operational content as being that if one has what at least *appears to be* a lucid conception of how it might be that not P, then that should count as a good, albeit defeasible ground for its not being necessary that P.[12] By the Counter-Conceivability Principle, all putative metaphysical necessities, even a posteriori ones, thus have to face the tribunal of what we can, as we think, clearly and distinctly conceive; and their defeat may consequently be a priori even if their sole possible form of justification is not.[13]

12. The Counter-Conceivability Principle is something which might really have *deserved* the title of 'Hume's Principle', now of course purloined by the neo-Fregean programme for the foundations of arithmetic. Recall *Treatise* Bk. I, pt. II, section II: '*whatever the mind clearly conceives, includes the idea of possible existence,* or in other words, *that nothing we imagine is absolutely impossible*'.

13. Kripke does not explicitly articulate the Counter-Conceivability Principle but it is striking how naturally it seems to have come to him implicitly to assume it. It did not occur to him to respond to the hypothetical objector, who thinks she can conceive of Hesperus turning out to be other than Phosphorus, or of heat being something other than molecular motion, by saying: 'So what? What has conceivability to do with it? I didn't claim these things were *conceptually* necessary'. Rather the validity of the objector's prima facie conceptions, and their prima facie relevance, are straightaway conceded. The defence is rather that they are not of what they appear to be—that what is actually conceived in these cases goes no further than *qualitative* similarity to what was intended. But I anticipate.

Is the Counter-Conceivability Principle correct? Naturally, it is uncontroversial for conceptual necessities: any claim that a certain truth is *conceptually* necessary has to be answerable to what we can coherently and lucidly *conceive*. But to suppose that *all* absolute necessities, a posteriori ones included, are subject to constraints of conceivability may seem to be at best a substantial epistemological claim in need of a correspondingly substantial defence. Indeed, at worst it would appear the merest blunder: the retention of an intuitively conceptualist epistemology of modality for a range of cases where modal status originates not in the character of concepts at all but in underlying essences which may go quite unreflected in our concepts of the items whose essences they are.

That is one concern. But in addition, if accepted, the Counter-Conceivability Principle may seem to enforce an objection to the necessity of certain kinds of statement which, if they configured natural kind concepts fitting Kripke's idea of them and were true, would have to be necessary. For instance, it may seem readily conceivable that water might have turned out to have a very different chemical constitution to the one it actually has. So it cannot be necessary that water is H_2O, even if it is true that it is. And indeed, since the point will generalise, it may look as if no such identity statement—no identity statement linking a derivative natural kind concept with a specification of the purported essence of its instances—will pass the test. So the Counter-Conceivability Principle, dubious in any case, might also seem to be inconsistent with Kripke's own view of the modal status of such statements.

Kripke's argument about pain is set up by a lemma constituted by his response to this objection. What is wrong with the objection is its premise. It is no doubt conceivable that scientific investigations with the *same physiognomy* as those which disclosed that water is H_2O might have had a different upshot—that an investigated substance, displaying all the surface indications of water, might have turned out to be XYZ instead. But then, Kripke rejoins, it would not be *water* that would have turned out to be XYZ. The problem for the objector is how to characterise the stuff of the imaginary scientific investigations.

The characterisation can hardly proceed except in terms of satisfaction of the characteristic indicator-properties of water. But how exactly? If as: the *actual* satisfier of those indicator-properties, then that is a rigid designator, which will therefore produce a necessary identity when linked with 'H_2O'. And the suggestion that it is nevertheless prima facie conceivable that the stuff which actually has those properties, namely, H_2O, might not have been H_2O is counter-intuitive indeed. What *is* conceivable is that *something* that satisfies the indicator properties, or the most widespread satisfier of the indicator properties, might have turned out not to be H_2O—but that is perfectly consistent with the necessity of *water's* being H_2O.

Essentially the same point addresses the first, more general concern. Any a posteriori necessity, N, will be associated with a seemingly intelligible imaginative scenario in which the a posteriori investigations which confirm it turn out to disconfirm it instead. So much is a consequence of those investigations' being a posteriori. But it does not follow that N will be prima facie counter-conceivable unless it is granted that the imaginative scenario involves an appropriate play with the very concepts configured in N. And that is not granted. If **water** is a natural kind concept, then which concept it is depends on what is the essence of water. The impression that the Counter-Conceivability Principle is all at sea as soon as necessities originating *in rebus* are countenanced turns on the tacit assumption of a separation between concept and essence: that, as it was expressed above, 'underlying essences . . . may go quite unreflected in our concepts of the items whose essences they are'. That assumption simply misunderstands what is being proposed about the character of the relevant concepts that feature in necessities of identity, origin and constitution.

The Counter-Conceivability Principle is thus under no immediate threat. But the manner of its defence may raise a concern about its utility. Will not the principle be impotent if a presumed necessity which is apparently open to counter-conception can always be excused by charging that an objector's scenario fails genuinely to involve the relevant concepts? Indeed it will, unless such excuses are required to be backed up by a properly principled explanation of what the alleged shortfall consists in. If **water** is the concept of a physical natural kind, such an explanation will be available when the scenario fails to distinguish between instantiation of that kind, whatever it is, and presentation of the indicators. The crux of Kripke's argument about **pain** is that no correspondingly principled excuse is possible: that a counter-conceivability challenge against the necessity of any particular physicalistic identification of pain actually *succeeds*—or at least, stands undefeated.

The Argument about Pain

Suppose C-fibres are a kind of nervous pathway actually occurring in human beings. And let the proposal be that pain is C-fibre stimulation. Still, it seems readily conceivable that physiological investigation might have found no C-fibre activity in subjects suffering pain, or even that, without change in the range of our sensory afflictions, we might have lacked C-fibres altogether. So it cannot be necessary that pain is C-fibre stimulation. Ergo, since it would be necessary if true, it cannot be true. But this would go for any purported physical identification of pain. So **pain** isn't the concept of a physical natural kind.

Why is this argument any better than that about water? Because in this case the premise really does seem to be conceivable. Suppose we try to block the argument as before: so we put the question, how is the putative scenario to justify characterising the imagined scientific experiment as one in which it turns out that no C-fibre stimulation takes place in a *pain-afflicted* subject? Well what are the relevant indicators? Just one, presumably—namely, a distinctive form of discomfort. But then the difference is that to conceive of something that satisfies the indicator is, in contrast with the case of water, already enough to conceive of *pain*. There is a potential difference, provided by the concept, between a substance's giving the indications of water and its being water; but there is no more to a sensation's being pain than its giving the indications of pain—that is, hurting. So while there is an epistemic gap between conceiving of something which satisfies the indicators of water and conceiving of water, there is no such gap in the case of our basic concepts of sensation. The claim to have counter-conceived the identity of pain with C-fibre stimulation thus stands undefeated.

A Naturalist Response

But has a physicalist any cause to object to the argument so far? After all, the conclusion, properly understood, is only that **pain** isn't a physical natural kind *concept*. Even if that is good as far as it goes, isn't the striking conclusion which Kripke himself proposed, that pain is no physical kind of thing, out of reach? As we noted, it is consistent with it's being perfectly proper to conclude that **pain** is not a physical natural kind concept to reserve the thought that pain might yet be a physical natural kind. The position would be exactly analogous to the case for water, the stuff, and **schwater,** the criterially governed concept. The extension of such a concept may always be a natural kind—as indeed it presumably is in that case. So it might be with pain, **pain** and 'pain'. If **pain** were a criterially governed concept, then anything which satisfied the indicators of **pain**—that is, felt uncomfortable in the distinctive way—might indeed count as pain, and 'pain' would be thereby apt to feature in true *contingent* identities in which it was linked with physical terms.

Why do I say that the conclusion of the argument, properly understood, is only that **pain** isn't a physical natural kind *concept*? After all, if the identity statement

Pain is C-fibre stimulation

is, if true, necessarily true, then a standing objection to its necessity has to be reckoned a standing objection to its truth; and since 'C-fibre stimulation' is, in effect, just a place-holder for any physicalist reduction, that is therefore a standing objection to any such reduction. The conclusion of the argument properly concerns pain, and not just **pain**.

But this is to forget that the argument is driven by a more complex conditional than the objector implicitly allows. What we have is not

If pain is C-fibre stimulation, then it is necessary that it is

but

> If **pain** is a natural kind concept, then if pain is C-fibre
> stimulation, then it is necessary that it is.

So if the major antecedent is discharged, pain's actually being C-fibre
stimulation (or whatever else) will be consistent with its being so as a
matter of contingency. Sure, in that case 'pain' would not be a rigid
designator, just as 'water' would not be if it expressed **schwater**. And
Kripke's argument against physicalism assumes that 'pain' *is* a rigid
designator. But where did that premise come from? If it is put up for
reductio that **pain** is a physical natural kind concept, then that, to be
sure, enjoins that its expression, 'pain', is rigid. But once the argument is allowed to proceed to the point where the first assumption is
discharged, then—unless some independent argument on the point is
supplied—it is open to the physicalist to fall back on the view that
pain is, rather, a (very simply) criterially governed concept, that 'pain'
is consequently flexible with respect to its reference among physical
kinds, and that the identity of pain with any particular neural state is
consequently a possibility. And this is just the classical—as we may
call it, 'Australian rules'—physicalism about the mental, originally
proposed by writers such as Jack Smart, which the Kripkean framework has been standardly regarded as squeezing out.

Rebuttal

This line of naturalist resistance arguably fails, however, and the manner of its failure is instructive. Let's for a moment go along with the
idea that 'water' expresses a criterially governed concept—that is,
schwater. 'Water' accordingly has as its sense a complex descriptive
condition, fashioned out of the relevant criteria, its possibly constitutionally variable referents so qualifying by dint of their satisfaction of
that condition. Nevertheless water itself is a *stuff* rather than a state,

so there has to be a contrast between the sense of the term 'water', standing for that stuff, and that of the description 'the state of satisfying the criteria for being water', standing for the state which the stuff distinctively occupies. Is the description rigid or flexible? Presumably, since the criteria for a criterially governed concept are *essential* to it and thus invariant, the state of satisfying them will likewise be invariant. So the latter description—'the state of satisfying the criteria for being water'—should be rigid in any case, that is, should denote the same state in talking of any possible world, even if 'water', whose reference in the present scenario is to whatever is in that state, is not. What follows is that in order for there to be any chance of assimilating the function of 'pain' to that of 'water' as presently conceived, so that it can serve as a correspondingly flexible designator, there has to be a corresponding distinction between the use of 'pain' and that of the description 'the state of satisfying the criteria for being in pain'. For the latter, by an analogue of the argument just given, will be rigid. But here's the point: *there is no such distinction.* 'Pain', unlike 'water', *does* denote a state; moreover, and crucially, if the (single) criterion for being in pain is that mooted above, namely, feeling 'uncomfortable in the relevant distinctive way', then our ordinary concept brooks no distinction between the state of being in pain and the state of satisfying the criteria for being in pain. So if, on the grounds reviewed, the descriptive phrase—'the state of satisfying the criteria for being in pain'—is rigid, then 'pain', too, must be rigid; for only a rigid term can sustain a necessary identity with another rigid term.

So Hey Presto! Kripke's considerations, unless otherwise faulted, can indeed be extended to argue not merely that **pain** is not a physical natural kind concept but to distinguish the reference of 'pain' from any physical kind of state.

Notice that it has not been suggested that no type of physical state is *associated* with pain, and thus to that extent characteristic of it. How could philosophy establish that? The (nonetheless remarkable) conclusion is only that no such type of state *is* pain—that our very concept of pain contains the ingredients to prohibit any such identification.

The Boyd Objection

Let's review the essential moves of the argument. Its essence is that whatever physical identification of the state of pain is proposed, it will be prima facie conceivable that it might be empirically confounded. But the identification must then hold, if at all, of necessity (if only for the rather complex reasons just reviewed). Any claim of necessity may be defeated by conceiving—albeit *genuinely* conceiving—of scenarios in which what it affirms to be necessary does not obtain. So, absent some reason to think that the relevant scenarios about pain somehow fail to portray what they purport to portray, we should (defeasibly) conclude that no identification of pain with a physical state is necessary, nor therefore true. Such a reason is available in the case of the apparently conceivable scenarios in which water turns out not to be H_2O, since it has to be ensured that the stuff of the conceived scenario really is water rather than something that merely possesses water's surface symptoms. But no such difficulty afflicts the case of pain and, say, C-fibre stimulation since any 'surface-symptomatic' counterpart of pain is pain.

The crux, then—the point that is supposed to make all the difference—is that to conceive of a symptomatic counterpart of pain is to conceive of pain, whereas to conceive of a symptomatic counterpart of water is not, *per se*, to conceive of water. But on reflection, how can this be enough to make the difference? In order to conceive of an identity statement's failing to hold, it suffices to conceive of one term in being while the other is not. Kripke thinks we can conceive of a pain's occurring without any C-fibre stimulation taking place, or vice versa. And sure, it seems prima facie completely straightforward. Just imagine a situation in which you suffer pain yet even the most sophisticated apparatus detects no C-fibre stimulation within you; or a situation in which, conversely, the C-fibre activity detectors go off the dial while you lie relaxed in utter comfort. But the fact is that, before we can be entitled to take any prima facie conception of the falsity of an identity statement at face value, it has to be that *both* its terms are resistant to the difficulty Kripke makes for the attempt to conceive of water's turning out not to be H_2O. *Both* the identified items must be such that we are entitled to regard the thought experiment as really engaging *them,* rather than mere symptomatic counterparts. Yet Kripke only considers pain. The other half of the imagined scenario—that there is or is not C-fibre stimulation involved—is not considered at all.

Now, situations in which C-fibres are stimulated would presumably form a natural kind. So as in the case of water, the objection continues, there ought to be a distinction between instantiation of the kind and mere symptomatic imitation. That would be enough to create a problem for the suggestion that the necessity of 'Pain is C-fibre stimulation' might be defeated by conceiving of a situation in which C-fibres were stimulated yet no pain was felt. For while, presumably, the absence of pain, too, is a state which has only to seem to be in order to be, there ought, if there is a gap with water, to be a corresponding gap between conceiving of a genuine case of C-fibre stimulation and conceiving of a symptomatic counterpart. So that form of attempt to rebut the necessity of 'Pain is C-fibre stimulation' would be blocked by Kripke's own move. Conversely, while the concept **situation in which C-fibres are not stimulated** is not a natural kind concept at all—since not a concept of a type of state of affairs with a unified underlying nature—essentially the same point may still seem good against the other relevant kind of counter-scenario: pain without C-fibre stimulation. Maybe I cannot fail to conceive of a pain when there is no C-fibre stimulation by dint of failing to conceive a genuine pain. But surely I may so fail by dint of failing to conceive of a *genuine lack of C-fibre stimulation.* For just as one does not conceive of a lack of water by conceiving of an absence of satisfaction of the indicator properties of water—the concept leaves provision for non-standard instances—so, it may be suggested, one will not have conceived of an absence of C-fibre stimulation merely by conceiving of a lack of satisfaction of the indicators of C-fibre stimulation, whatever they are. It will not be enough merely to conceive of an absence, as assessed by whatever operational tests are appropriate, of the *appearances* of C-fibre stimulation.

The analogy is therefore apparently restored, and now a dilemma arises. If Kripke was successful in defeating the conceivability objection to the necessity of 'Water is H_2O', then his argument against physicalism collapses for want of a relevant disanalogy between 'Pain is C-fibre stimulation' and 'Water is H_2O'. But if he wasn't successful, then the whole apparatus of a posteriori necessities on which the argument against physicalism depends is put in jeopardy in any case.

Call this the *Boyd objection*.[14] It is apt to seem a very damaging objection. But I do not think that it is persuasive at all. Let me try to explain why.

The failure of the attempted thought experiment in which water supposedly turns out not to be H_2O hinges on the claim that—when it seems that conception is possible—what turns out not to be H_2O is not distinguished from a mere water imitator, as it were. It is crucial to understand the source of this claim. In particular, it is *not* an instance of a general thesis about the limits of conceivability—there is no suggestion, for instance, that the conceiving faculty cannot encompass water *per se* at all but only the appearances of it. The challenge to the author of the thought experiment is to specify how its subject is identified. He is not allowed just to reply, 'As water'. Matters cannot be left there or claims of counter-conceivability will become unnegotiable, since a proponent will have no explanatory obligations. An account is owing, accordingly, of what *makes* it water that is the subject of the imagined scenario—of why what is imagined should be regarded as water—and the (plausible) suggestion is that the thinker will prove to be relying on imagined satisfaction of the surface indicators. So it is perfectly fair to reply that, according to the view that is being opposed, that is insufficient to ensure the relevance of the thought experiment. But notice, to stress, that there is no claim here that mere conceiving can make nothing of the difference between genuine water and a symptomatic imitation—that the differences between them are, so to say, opaque to the conceiving faculty—so that *any* attempt to conceive of water would be bound to be no more

14. Boyd (1992).

than a conception of a display of indicators; on the contrary, to conceive of water, as opposed to conceiving of a symptomatic imitation, is to conceive of a purported natural kind—a substance with a certain underlying essence from which those symptoms characteristically flow. And still less is there a general claim to the effect that conceiving can make nothing of the difference between an appearance and reality—that its movement is confined among imagined *appearances*. That would be a hopeless claim, for a reason to be noted in a minute.

Nevertheless the Boyd objection would seem to be feeding on some such idea. To see this, reflect that in order for it to work, there has to be *as* good a reason to suppose that any apparently lucid conception of a situation in which there is, for example, pain but no C-fibre stimulation fails to represent a genuine lack of C-fibre stimulation *as* there is reason to think that the water/H_2O thought experiment succeeds in engaging no more than a symptomatic counterpart of water. Consider, then, what sort of thing might happen when someone—let her be an expert physiologist—who knows about C-fibres and their characteristic forms of activity, tries to conceive a scenario in which they are inactive. Well, she'll no doubt imagine certain tests and microphysiological investigations turning out in a certain kind of way. And one conceptual gap that there will be is that between the appearance—the *seeming* that the tests and investigations turn out that way—and the reality: their actually doing so. So it would certainly serve the purpose of the Boyd objection if it were right that the conceiving faculty cannot cross this gap: that any thought experiment can engage no more than appearances. However, that's a radical error (and no part of Kripke's original point). The price of that contention would be that any apparent contingency whatever could be claimed with impunity to be a posteriori necessary—since any apparently perfectly lucidly conceived scenario in which it failed would be properly describable merely as one in which it *appeared* to fail. The link between conceivability and possibility may be subtle and qualified; but it is genuine—and to confine conceivability to appearances would be to sever it altogether. Thus, failing some independent reason for thinking her conception comes short, it should be granted that the physiologist really can conceive not just of an appearance but of the *reality* of the relevant tests' militating against the hypothesis of C-fibre stimulation.

A proponent of the Boyd objection may try to regroup. Probably there will still be a gap—the tests may not be conclusive or they may be liable to operational error. A situation which, by the most refined and painstaking tests that we have, must be classified as one in which no C-fibres are stimulated may still be *mis*classified as such. Agreed; but *this* gap will not suffice to drive the objection. Someone challenged to explain what makes it *water* that turns out not to be H_2O in his thought experiment does not—from the point of view of one who accepts that water is a natural kind—have a good answer; for the answer involves mere satisfaction of the indicators. But if our physiologist is challenged to explain what makes it a *lack of C-fibre stimulation* that figures in her thought experiment, she has available the best possible answer: namely, its seeming and continuing to seem by the most refined tests that no C-fibre stimulation is taking place. That is to be compared not to mere satisfaction of the indicators of *water* but to the most refined evidence of the presence of H_2O. If someone thinks it is not a good enough answer, then forget about pain for a minute and ask: What could conceiving of a situation in which it turned out merely that *there was no C-fibre stimulation* consist in? But the conceivability of *that*—on its own—wasn't supposed to be in doubt.

To confirm that one who presses this objection is tacitly shifting the goal posts—is making a move quite different to Kripke's—it ought to suffice to reflect that it would presumably be conceded on all sides that, were **water** to be supplanted by **schwater,** there should be no difficulty concerning the conceivability of a variety of substances turning out to be schwater. It is granted on all sides, in particular, that we can conceive of a symptomatic counterpart of water turning out not to be H_2O. But the attempt to disqualify the physiologist's thought experiment along the lines just reviewed demands rules of conceivability which would also disqualify that seemingly straightforward conception. For how is it given that the conceived substance is not H_2O—wouldn't it be merely that it turned out not to be such by the most refined extant chemical tests, and wouldn't they bear a merely defeasible relation to the fact?

In summary: what I have been saying boils down to the point that the Boyd objection misses the distinction between primary and derivative natural kind concepts, and the attendant different constraints involved in conceiving of instances of them. **H_2O** and **C-fibre stimulation,** we may suppose, are primary natural kind concepts. Accordingly, their reference is not fixed by adverting to indicator properties but directly, in the light of the explicit content of those concepts themselves. They are thus associated with no analogues of the distinction between water and symptomatic counterparts of water, and thought experiments in which they feature cannot be faulted for insensitivity to such distinctions.[15] A primary natural kind concept does provide, to be sure, for two other types of distinction: between something's appearing to be P and its genuinely being so; and between something's passing the most refined extant tests for being P and its genuinely being so. But to insist that the Kripkean thought experiments about pain and C-fibre stimulation are flawed by insensitivity to the second of these distinctions is implicitly to disable a whole range of perfectly valid conceivings; while to fault them for insensitivity to the first is implicitly to confine conceiving to the realm of appearances and thereby to forfeit altogether the connection between conceivability and modality.

The McGinn Objection

A second very widely received objection to Kripke's argument was first advanced by Colin McGinn.[16] Actually, McGinn's objection presents itself as more of an accommodation; it does not abrade at all against the argument as I have so far presented it. Distinguish three claims: that **pain** is the concept of a physical natural kind; that pains

---

15. At least as far as relate to those two concepts, though there may of course be such faults in connection with the involvement of other, derivative natural kind concepts.

16. McGinn (1977).

form a physical natural kind; and that *pains are physical.* It is the third that is the essential thesis of physicalism. But it is at most a rejection of the first two that is supported by the considerations which we have reviewed. Even if pains are not a physical kind, each and every individual pain may nevertheless be a physical state. Pains may be *token*-identical with physical states, even if not *type*-identical.

That was McGinn's point. It is an objection to Kripke's argument only when it is interpreted as directed against physicalism *per se* (an interpretation which Kripke's own formulations did not do enough, perhaps, to discourage). Grant that any particular (neuro)physical type of event may coherently be conceived as dissociated from the occurrence of pains, and that this consideration can indeed be worked into a demonstration that pains are not a physical type. Still, the consideration seems powerless to engage the thought that *the particular pain* I am feeling now is token-identical with some aspect of *the particular physical state* I am in. Suppose the aspect in question is actually one of physical type F. So the supposition is that the pain I am now feeling is my being in the particular F-state that I am presently in. Plausibly 'The pain I am now feeling' and 'The F-state which I am currently in' are both rigid designators. So the identity statement linking them, if true, holds of necessity. In the presence of the Counter-Conceivability Principle, it would therefore make trouble for the purported identity if I *could* coherently conceive of that statement's failing to hold. But while I am granted a conception of how it could be that I was in pain without being in an F-state at all, that is not to conceive of my having *this* pain without being in an F-state, a fortiori without being in *this* F-state. For, it is very plausible, nothing in such a thought experiment engages the *numerical* identity of my present pain. No doubt I could conceive of having a *qualitatively indistinguishable* pain, under the very same circumstances, on the very same occasion. But if token–token physicalism is true, such conceiving may be regarded as portraying the pain I actually feel only if it involves nothing inconsistent with the actual physical identity of that pain. This is not to say, note, that conceiving is necessarily insensitive to the distinction between numerical identity and quantitative identity among token pains. It is to say, rather, that the content which may be permissibly assigned to a conceived scenario has to be sensitive to the essential characteristics of the items it involves.

If this is right, then the Kripkean argument may after all be consistent with physicalism. The strongest conclusion that it will be permissible to draw will be, not that mental states—or at least, all mental states which are akin to pain in having a purely phenomenal essence—are not physical in nature, but that their physical identity is not that of a physical type.

The Explanatory Potential of Token-by-Token Physicalism

McGinn's point seemingly provides a way of reconciling Kripke's argument with the ontology of physicalism. But is the resulting form of physicalism worth having? In particular, to what extent can it preserve physicalism's traditional advantages? Paramount among those was the prospect of the complete intelligibility of the world via the categories of physical science. That may now seem to be in jeopardy if the identity of, say, sensations with physical states goes merely token by token.

The line of concern, more fully, is as follows. To make scientific sense of the role of any state, property or event in a world conceived as purely physical, it will be necessary to bring the item under concepts which render physical scientific laws applicable to it. The very generality which is of the essence of physical law, however, ensures that such laws will concern physical *types*. So if—while sensations, say, may all be physical, token by token—there are no physical properties with whose possession being in particular sensational states may generally—type by type—be *identified*, then in order to make sense of the role of such states in the physical world by the application to them of physical laws, it will be necessary to bring them under concepts which are at best, as it were, fortuitously co-extensive with the concepts they fall under *qua* sensations. Suppose, for instance, that—as it happens—everyone in pain *is* in a state of C-fibre stimulation, and vice versa. Still, by the Kripkean argument, the state of being in pain is not the state of C-fibre stimulation. The concepts **pain** and **C-fibre stimulation** must still be reckoned to present different properties. Since the former property is not to be identified with any physical property, it follows that physical science can make no sense of—can give no scientific insight into—the co-extensiveness that happens to obtain. And if it cannot do that, then it can never explain, for example, why aspirin eases a headache, no matter how convincing an account it has to offer of the effects of aspirin on C-fibre stimulation. By contrast, if the identity of pain and C-fibre stimulation goes type-to-type, then the scientific tractability of the latter just is that of the former. If headaches *are* a kind of C-fibre stimulation, then explaining the effects of aspirin on (that kind of) C-fibre stimulation *is* explaining its effects on headache.

In brief: if being in pain is the same thing as being in a state of C-fibre stimulation—if the identity goes type-to-type—then explaining aspirin's effects on C-fibre stimulation is explaining its effects on headache. Headaches become potentially scientifically tractable. But for token-by-token physicalism, it seems that the best that can be said of the types is that they are co-extensive. Since this co-extensiveness is then left explanatorily surd, we do not get explanations of the patterns of instantiation in one of the types merely by explaining the corresponding patterns in the instantiation of the other.

The concern is prima facie compelling. But it makes an unsupported and crucial assumption. It assumes that if we may not identify pain with a physical type, then we are barred from identifying tokens of pain with tokens of a single physical type. That seems unwarranted. Consistently with rejecting the identity of pain, as a type of state, with the state of C-fibre stimulation, we might retain all explanatory advantages of that identification—if the empirical circumstances allow—by identifying each subject's *individual pain* with *a particular episode of C-fibre stimulation*. Then, if best science were to find that, and explain why whenever a subject is in a state of C-fibre stimulation, its mitigation is indeed a normal effect of taking aspirin, the fact that C-fibre stimulation could not legitimately be *identified* with pain *per se* would be no obstacle to adapting this finding to the explanation of aspirin's effect on head*aches*. True, there would now be no way of converting the explanation of why aspirin mitigates C-fibre stimulation into an explanation of why aspirin relieves head*ache*— but if each, or enough, individual headaches are token-identical with individual episodes of C-fibre stimulation, we still get an explanation of why aspirin relieves *them*. And isn't that good enough?

If this is right, it points up something important, namely how merely token-by-token identifications with the physical can always tap into the explanatory advantages that would have been secured by corresponding type–type identifications. Thus token-by-token theories need not, *per se,* involve any consequences about *anomalousness*. Sure, physical laws are essentially general, so naturally formulated in terms of types of property, event and state. Thus in order to harness such laws to the explanation of what we presume to be the causes and effects of sensations, it might seem that we have to find types of physical state for the sensations to be. And then, if such identifications are proscribed, it may seem as though some form of anomalousness, or scientific opacity, of sensation must be the upshot. But not so fast: the simple countervailing thought is that if a law connects one type of state with another, it thereby connects their tokens. So to treat of sensation in a fully intelligible but physical-scientific way, we do not need type–type identifications: it is enough that token sensations be token physical states of (some manageable range of) types that are tractable at the level of physical law.

A Discomfort about Supervenience

Nevertheless I do not think that token-by-token physicalism offers a satisfactory accommodation with the Kripkean argument. One general difficulty with the proposal concerns supervenience. Most of us believe in some form of supervenience of the psychological upon the physical. Of course supervenience relations come in many varieties. But I am referring just to the general idea that psychological differences demand physical ones, that had the psychological history of the world been different in any respect at all, then its physical history would have had to have differed too.[17] Is this a rational belief? It is hard to be certain what exactly is its provenance. It is not empirical. Experience might suggest that many psychological differences tend to go with physical ones. But it could not suggest that they *must* so do. And if we seemed to alight upon psychological changes that went unreflected in any physical differences, we would insist that there must be physical differences all the same, though perhaps of a kind—arcane variations in brain state, maybe—of which we have no present conception.

This supervenience is certainly a rejectable thesis. It would, for instance, be rejected by Cartesian dualism. The supervenience requires that, as a matter of necessity, any change in a subject's psychological condition must be attended by a change in her physical condition. This would be utterly incomprehensible if dualism were true: how could change in one ontological realm necessitate change in another? Dualism has it that the psychological and physical are distinct existences. There is therefore no room for them to be linked as a matter of necessity. To that extent, the entrenchment of psychological-on-physical supervenience in our ordinary beliefs is indicative that our fundamental conception of the psychological is not Cartesian. But Wittgenstein—no Cartesian—also effectively rejects the supervenience (not there so termed, of course) in *Zettel* 608–10. And it is not clear that his stance is anything which we can readily confound by direct argument, either empirical or a priori.

If we have any justification for believing in psychological-on-physical supervenience, it would seem it must have less to do with what we can support by direct argument than with a sense of commitment to it flowing from our basic metaphysics of the psychological. But what metaphysics of the psychological would account for it? How could it be *necessary* that change in one range of states of affairs

---

17. This very general form of supervenience need not involve, of course, that the psychological supervenes upon the *internal* physiological states of the bearers of psychological properties. It is uncompromised by views which see certain psychological and semantic characteristics as *broad*.

might necessitate change in another? The only possible answer, it seems, is if they are not fundamentally of different categories but are at bottom states of one and the same sort, though presented in very different conceptual vocabularies. In short, if we do not believe that psychological states and processes fundamentally *are* physical ones, the claimed supervenience, so far from being basic to our conception of the psychological, would be unintelligible, and the belief in it totally unmotivated.

Only some form of physicalism, it seems, can make sense of the supervenience. Thus it may appear that not only is a token-by-token physicalism *consistent* with the Kripkean argument, but that—if type-to-type physicalism is now ruled out—the supervenience of the psychological upon the physical actually *demands* it. However—and this is the advertised discomfort—it is not clear on reflection how token-by-token physicalism can actually accommodate the supervenience any better than can dualism. To be sure, if my present headache actually *is* some token physical condition of my central nervous system, then had I not had the headache, I would have been in a different physical condition. But psychological-on-physical supervenience, in the form that is usually accepted, requires that a change in which psychological predicates may be truly applied to me requires change in a complete description of my physical state, where the latter description is precisely conceived as a compendium of the *types* of physical state I am in. Token-by-token physicalism simply cannot explain the validity of *that* principle. It requires, to be sure, that if I had not had the headache, I would have been in a different physical state; but it is open on whether that different state could not still have been of a type with that I am actually in. So it allows that my then physical state could have been in every way *type-indistinguishable* from my actual physical state. Psychological-on-physical supervenience, as ordinarily understood, proscribes exactly that.

Note that this is not an objection to token-by-token physicalism's ability to accommodate the Kripkean argument. The point is rather that the accommodation is available only if we either jettison the belief in supervenience altogether or are prepared to retain it in a setting in which we have neither direct argument for it nor any broader metaphysical justification.

Token-by-Token Physicalism and Rigidity

The most fundamental weakness in the token-by-token response to the Kripkean argument, however, is that, so far from providing an accommodation with the conclusion, it proves on reflection to be committed to arguing with the premises. To the extent, then, that someone finds those premises to be well motivated, she is precluded from responding in the way McGinn proposed.

Recall the dialectical situation at the crucial point. We noted earlier that the Kripkean argument was only able to advance beyond the stage of a claim about **pain** (that it is not a physical natural kind concept) to a claim about *pain* (that states of pain are not a physical natural kind) courtesy of the assumption that 'pain' is a *rigid designator*—that 'is in pain' ascribes the same state on all occasions of competent use. We canvassed argument for the assumption, which is indeed independently plausible in any case.[18] But how can it be consistent with mere token-by-token physicalism about pain? For the distinctive thesis of the latter is precisely that while all pains are physical states, no single kind of physical state need be shared by subjects in pain.

More fully: the Kripkean argument appealed to the conceivability of a situation in which no specific type of (presumably) neural state is correlated with the occurrence of, say, migraine. Suppose that situation actually obtains. Still, for token-by-token physicalism, each and every migraine headache is identical to some specific token neural condition. Consider two such token headaches, say of sufferers S_1 and S_2, and the two token neural states, as it happens of utterly different physical types—say F_1 and F_2—with which those headaches are respectively token-identical. What physical states are the respective

---

18. In fact, all the same intuitions kick in as those Kripke appeals to for 'Aristotle': Could pain not have been pain? Could a different state have been the state of being in pain?

referents of the two uses of 'headache' in the two true claims, 'S_1 has a headache' and 'S_2 has a headache'? Since for the physicalist, S_1's headache just consists in her being in state F_1 and S_2's headache consists in her being in state F_2, there seems no option but to allow that the two uses of 'headache' effect reference to these two different physical states. But then for the token-by-token physicalist, 'headache' must be an expression referring *flexibly* among those type physical states whose instantiation, on particular occasions, may constitute a subject's having a headache—it cannot be a rigid designator of any particular such state. So in a physical world—when the only real types of state are physical—it cannot be a rigid designator at all.

Now McGinn's intervention was pointless unless the Kripkean argument succeeds against the identification of pain with a physical type. It so succeeds only if 'pain' is rigid—otherwise the argument can be seen off by 'Australian rules' physicalism. But if 'pain' is rigid, what—physical—state can the token-by-token physicalist regard it as ascribing? The whole essence and being of her view is that no single type of physical state need constitute being in pain, that pains may be constituted by quite different types of physical state. Rather than providing a solution, then, token-by-token physicalism would seem to have no way of construing the data of the problem that McGinn introduced it to address.

The point seems decisive. But a skirmish is possible. The objection could be finessed if we could take it for granted that there are, for instance, *disjunctive* states, or *existentially general* states. Equipped with such a repertoire, the physicalist might straightforwardly allow that the reference of 'headache', on every occasion of use, is indeed rigid—it is always to the disjunctive state of having F_1 *or* F_2 *or* F_3 *or* . . . , where every type of physical state that can constitute a headache features as one disjunct. Or better: let the reference of 'headache' be to the state of being in *some* physical state which . . . and here the theorist plugs in her preferred account of the *functional role* of a headache (or of whatever the unifier is conceived as being). In contrast to type-to-type physicalism, individual pains could then be states of various physical types, united by their featuring in the relevant disjunction, or discharging the relevant functional role. But 'pain' could still be a rigid designator, denoting the same logically compound—disjunctive, or existential—state in every use.

But can physicalism regard such 'logically compound states' as in good standing? To begin with, one might wonder whether there is any satisfactory, principled specification of what might serve to *unify* the disjuncts of the putative disjunctive state, or to complete the specification of the putative existential one. And there is also a serious question whether such construals of the reference of 'pain' can make anything of another datum of the problem: the transparency of pains to their subjects. But, at least in the context of a physicalist ontology, the whole idea seems off-target in a more basic way—specifically, by its illicitly imposing distinctions onto the domain of reference which make genuine sense only at the level of *modes of presentation*: concepts. When we disjoin or existentially generalise on names, the results—for instance, 'Tom or John was to blame', 'Someone was to blame'—had better not be conceived as forms of expression involving reference to disjunctive, or existentially general objects. There are no such objects. Why should it be different with states? Why should 'occupancy of some state with functional role R', be regarded as denoting a state at all? I do not deny the deflated sense of 'state' in which the nominalisation of any significant predicative expression denotes a potential state. But physicalism is a serious ontological thesis, and one of its consequences is that the only genuine states around are physical. Suppose that amongst these are some with functional role R. Clearly 'occupancy of some state with functional role R' denotes none in particular of these, since it suffices to instantiate it that an object be in any of them. Equally, though, since these are the only states that have functional role R, 'occupancy of some state with functional role R' does not denote some state outside that group. It follows that it does not denote a physical state at all, rigidly or otherwise. Since 'is in pain' and 'is in some state with functional role R' would be conceptually equivalent on the present physicalist proposal, it would seem that the latter must repudiate the thesis that 'pain' is a designator at all, let alone a rigid one. But that again is to deny a datum of the problem.

II. GENERALISATIONS

Colour and Euthyphronic Concepts

Now to the case of colour. I choose it because there is a plausible case, so it seems to me, that colour concepts exhibit a germane kind of epistemic transparency. But whatever the facts about colour, it will emerge, if I am right, that any concept which is transparent in this way will lend itself to an argument of the Kripkean kind.

To fix ideas, let me rapidly rehearse the idea of *judgement-dependent* concepts which I have discussed elsewhere.[19] Let a *provisional equation* be an instance of the following schema:

$$C(S, x) \rightarrow (F(x) \leftrightarrow \text{it seems to S that } F(x))$$

—if conditions, C, are met by a subject S and an item x, then x is F if and only if it seems to S that it is. A concept, F, is *Euthyphronic* if such a provisional equation can be written for it meeting each of the following four conditions:

(i)   the provisional equation is true a priori, as a matter of conceptual necessity;

(ii) the conditions, C, are specified in specific, substantial terms;

(iii) the satisfaction of the C-conditions is a matter which is independent of the details of F's actual extension; and

(iv) the provisional equation is *primitively* a priori—it admits of no proof from ulterior principles concerning F of such a kind as to vindicate the idea that the C-conditions merely enable a

19. See the appendix to chapter 3 of *Truth and Objectivity*.

subject to *keep infallible track* of an independently determined extension.

These clauses were proposed as one way of explicating the intuitive idea of a concept whose extension is *constitutively sensitive* to those of our verdicts which are delivered under what we conceive as the very best possible circumstances, rather than merely *reflected* by such verdicts. Whether that idea can indeed be so captured, whether all four conditions are necessary to capture it and how exactly they might need to be modified or elaborated in order to succeed are matters beyond the scope of this essay. However, notice that **pain** plausibly sustains a very simple provisional equation meeting at least three of the specified conditions,[20] namely,

S understands what pain is and is cognitively lucid → (S is in pain ↔ it seems to S that she is in pain).

Moreover—at the price, perhaps, of a surprising degree of complication—a case can be made for thinking that the same is true at least of central colour concepts, like **red.**

The case requires a much more detailed discussion than I can digress to offer here.[21] However, to sample its flavour, consider whether you think you have any clear concept of how the redness of a red surface could escape your judgement, or how its seeming red could be deceptive, if (i) the surface is in full view, and (ii) in normal daylight, (iii) relatively stationary (that is, stationary or slow-moving relative to you, the observer), and (iv) quite close by; and (v) if you know which

---

20. The fourth—anti-tracking—condition is interestingly controversial in this case. John McDowell's view, that sensations are essentially conceptualised modes of experience, is in effect the view that it is satisfied—that there is no brute phenomenal happening, pure pain, whose occurrence is indifferent to the conceptual resources of a sufferer and of which possession of **pain** merely enables him to keep track. But the fourth condition is in any case strictly inessential to the considerations to follow.

21. For further discussion, see Wright (1989).

object is in question, (vi) observe it attentively, (vii) are possessed of actually typical visual equipment and (viii) are free of spots before the eyes, after images, and so on, and (ix) are otherwise cognitively lucid, and (x) are competent with the concept **red.** You can add, if you like, that (xi) the surface be presented against a matt black background,[22] and (xii) that you—the judging subject—be free of doubt about the satisfaction of any of these conditions. Anyway, the thought of one who conjectures that **red** is Euthyphronic is that it is possible in this way to construct a list of substantial conditions whose satisfaction ensures a priori that a presented item is red only if it seems so to an observer, and that the result will be a *primitive* truth about **red:** that the extension of the concept is, in such a fashion, constrained of necessity to be sensitive to our judgements under the elaborated ideal conditions.

Someone might wonder how so relatively complex a claim, which in the nature of the case lies beyond any rigorous proof, can possibly rank as a priori. But that shouldn't be a sticking point. As a rough parallel consider *Church's thesis,* that every effectively calculable function is general recursive, and vice versa. Effective calculability is an intuitive notion; general recursiveness is a mathematically precise one. The thesis is precisely an attempt to give a mathematically exact characterisation of something preformal. In the nature of the case it therefore admits of no conclusive formal proof. Yet if it is true, it is true purely as a reflection of the character of the concepts involved, and to the extent that it can be supported by conceptual reflection— for instance by the striking convergences of other attempted formal characterisations of effective calculability, and a failure to find counter-examples—to that extent, it is supported a priori. It is similar with the provisional equation for **red.** Our concept of the variety of ways in which the redness of an object might in principle be masked by how it seems, or in which how it seems might be deceptive, ought

22. Or maybe viewed through an apparatus—a tube, say—which occludes any background.

to allow of correct circumscription, just as the concept of effective calculability ought. If we alight upon such a circumscription, it will certainly be too complicated to enable its truth to be recognisable immediately, just by the light cast by the analytic understanding, as it were; and there is no basis on which its truth might be recognised inferentially. As with Church's thesis, its a priori correctness, if it is correct, will ultimately be supportable only defeasibly, by the failure of hard reflection to find it wanting.

There is a lot more to say. But our concern here is not with the justification of claims of judgement-dependence, but with the implications if certain concepts are judgement-dependent in accordance with the template described. Now the key point in the Kripkean argument was the claimed counter-conceivability of any physicalistic identification of pain. And the key assumption for that claim was that there is no coherent distinction to be drawn between a state's seeming to its subject, S, to be one of pain and its actually being so. But that equation is not of course unconditional: it is, again, the impressions of a *cognitively lucid* subject, who *fully understands* **pain**, that there is no distinguishing from the fact of pain. And it is the standing prima facie conceivability of a separation between such impressions and any specific type of physical (neural) state that constitutes the crucial point in the argument: what is claimed to be counter-conceivable, in other words, is precisely what results from the provisional equation above when the left-hand side of its biconditional consequent is replaced by a clause ascribing to S any particular physical state taken to be identical with pain:

S understands what pain is and is cognitively lucid → (S is in physical state O ↔ it seems to S that she is in pain).

The crux in the Kripkean argument is thus, in effect, the contention that any provisional equation instantiating that schema on 'O' is counter-conceivable, but that one such would have to hold of necessity if pain was indeed a (type of) physical state.

The possibility of generalisation to **red** is accordingly evident. Assume that we can indeed formulate a (conceptually) necessarily true provisional equation for **red** meeting the outlined conditions:

(1) $C(S,x) \rightarrow (x \text{ is red} \leftrightarrow \text{it seems to } S \text{ that } x \text{ is red})$.

Assume also, for *reductio*, that **red** is a derivative physical natural kind concept. Since there actually are red things, there will therefore be some presumably microphysical property, O, such that

(2) Redness is O

is likewise necessary. We may take it[23] that the necessity issuing a priori from concepts and that issuing a posteriori from essences are the very same, absolute metaphysical necessity, differing in the grounds for ascribing them to particular claims but not in what is ascribed. That being so, since (2) entails that everything red is O and vice versa, we may infer that

(3) $C(S,x) \rightarrow (x \text{ is O} \leftrightarrow \text{it seems to } S \text{ that } x \text{ is red})$

is likewise necessary. But, for reasons exactly analogous to those which applied to **pain**, (3) ought not, it appears, to be regarded as necessary. For no matter what the detail of the physical kind, O, it seems it will be readily conceivable that the C-conditions are met—we are standing out of doors and out of shadow at noon on a typical cloudy summer's day, staring at a stationary object quite close by; we are blessed with statistically normal visual equipment, we are attentive, and so on—and that we judge that the relevant object, which looks manifestly tomato red, is red, and yet microphysical investigation discloses that it is *not* O. (Of course, there is at this point a

---

23. As of course, implicitly, did Kripke. For it is presumably a *conceptual* necessity that there is no distinction between being in pain and being in a state epistemically indistinguishable from pain.

debate to be had about the status of our apparently conceiving that conditions are indeed C and that x is indeed not O; but this will merely recapitulate considerations which we went through in connection with the Boyd objection.) In general, the best case for supposing that, no matter what O might be, (3) is counter-conceivable promises to be exactly parallel to that for the counter-conceivability of 'Pain is C-fibre stimulation'. The only difference is the relative complexity of the C-conditions.

In the first instance, this will be a conclusion not about redness but about the concept **red,** and, as previously, a prima facie accommodation with the argument will be available if the colour-physicalist is willing to maintain that (2), although true, is indeed not necessary, because 'redness' is a flexible designator among physical natural kinds, equivalent in sense, perhaps, to the (unrigidified) description 'the physical state indicated by the property of *looking red under C-conditions*'. Now recall that when we considered the corresponding response in the dialectic concerning pain and 'pain', we confronted the physicalist with the designator 'the state of satisfying the criteria for being in pain', which is plausibly both rigid and necessarily co-referential with 'pain'. Since only a rigid designator can be necessarily co-referential with a rigid designator, it followed that 'pain' is rigid too, and that the physicalist's flexible ersatz is false to the ordinary understanding of the term. Matters can now proceed in an analogous fashion with 'redness'. We form, for instance, the description 'that state which, necessarily, anything is in which looks red under C-conditions' (or—for an arbitrary judgement-dependent concept, F—'that state which, necessarily, anything is in which seems F under C-conditions'). Then, provided the provisional equation is necessary, the intuition is strong that 'redness' and 'that state which, necessarily, anything is in which looks red under C-conditions' are necessarily co-extensive; and the latter must, of course, be rigid if it refers at all, since otherwise there is no state such that *necessarily* anything is in it which looks red under C-conditions. It follows that 'redness' is rigid, that the property it denotes is consequently identical with no physical type—and that all this is called for by our concept of **red:** our concept of the kind of property redness is, if **red** is Euthyphronic. As before, the question may be raised whether some form of token-by-token physicalism can proceed to save the day—and specifically whether it can accommodate the rigidity of the terms in question (for if that rigidity is denied, then the 'Australian rules' version already has all the resources the physicalist needs to see the argument off). And, for reasons analogous to those recently canvassed, we may well feel that it cannot.

Summary of the Recipe

Let us take stock. The suggestion is that Kripke's argument is apt to generalise to any concept, C, of which it holds a priori, as a matter of conceptual necessity, that under certain substantially specifiable, conceivable conditions, it will seem to a thinker that the concept is instantiated just in case it is. For **pain**—as presumably for sensation concepts generally—the conditions in question are very simple: they are merely that the thinker grasps the concept in question and is appropriately cognitively lucid. Other cases will not be so simple: if **red** indeed comes in this category, its C-conditions will be complex. Still, the thesis is a going concern that our concepts of colour, and of Lockean secondary qualities generally, do have the requisite kind of transparency: that even if it is harder than philosophers once supposed[24] to say under what circumstances it is equivalent to an object's being red that it look red, it remains that, with care, one can produce a list of conditions such that nothing counts as an explanation of how, under *those* conditions, an illusion of colour could occur; and that the same holds for sounds, tastes and secondary qualities generally. To have constructed such a list for a given concept F—a list for which no one can produce any prima facie acceptable account of how under the

---

24. Recall Wilfrid Sellars: 'But what, then, are we to make of the necessary truth— and it is, of course, a necessary truth— that x *is* red ≡ x would *look* red to standard observers in standard conditions?' Sellars (1963), p. 142.

Compare Colin McGinn: 'It is a conceptual truth that red things *typically* look red' McGinn (1983), p. 11.

specified conditions it could seem to thinkers that F was instantiated although it was not—will be to have an a priori, albeit defeasible, case for regarding the relevant provisional equation as holding as a matter of conceptual necessity. That, as illustrated, will then suffice to set a form of the Kripkean argument in train.

It will do so by supplying each of two needed premisses. The first premise—the necessitated provisional equation

> Necessarily: for any S and x under C-conditions, x is F iff x seems F to S

—is supplied directly. The second premise—the necessity of any true identity of the form

> F is K,

where 'K' rigidly denotes a physical kind—requires that 'F' too is a rigid designator. But, as we saw, the provisional equation's holding of necessity arguably ensures that as well. It does so provided we may abstract from it to infer that being F is being in that state P such that, necessarily, any object is in P which seems F to a thinker operating under C-conditions. For again, if 'F' were flexible, there would be no single state of which it would be *necessary* that any object—in whatever world—seeming F to a C-conditioned thinker would occupy it; rather being F might be being in P_1 in w_1, and being in P_2 in w_2, and so on, and of no P_k would it be true that in all worlds and for any thinker operating under C-conditions, x's seeming F would be necessary and sufficient for its being in P_k.

The two premisses collectively entail that 'F' may be substituted by 'K' in the first to generate a further necessary truth: that for any S and x in the appropriate C-conditions, x is K iff x seems F to S. But the necessity of this consequence is likely to be in difficulty with the Counter-Conceivability Principle provided conditions C are ones which we can conceive to obtain—which, at least if the kind of list sketched for **red** is any guide, there seems every reason to anticipate.

Moreover, since the list is likely to proceed in quite general terms of idealisation—explaining wherein consist good observation conditions, competent observers and so on—without any reference to how *in particular* things seem to a judging subject or how they actually physically are in other respects, there seems no reason why there should ever be any tension in adjoining to an imaginary scenario in which the C-conditions hold the further detail that the thinkers involved have the impression that x is F; nor to that second scenario in turn the additional detail of x's turning out under examination not to be K.

In general: the Kripkean argument will thus extend to all concepts for which an appropriate conceptually necessary provisional biconditional can be constructed, the obtaining of whose C-conditions is prima facie conceivable and where such a scenario may prima facie coherently be augmented by its seeming to a thinker under the C-conditions in question that a given item instantiates (or fails to instantiate) the concept in question while that item simultaneously lacks (or has) any particular candidate to be the physical property presented by the concept F. To be sure, in view of the prima facie (defeasible) status of the relevant conceivings, the argument is best viewed as a *challenge* to physicalism, rather than a purported refutation. An undefeated impression that one can simultaneously conceive of a thinker's meeting the C-conditions and, say, judging that x is F while x lacks candidate physical property, O, is by the Counter-Conceivability Principle and assuming the rigidity of the relevant terms an undefeated challenge to the physicalist identification. But views which confront undefeated challenges ought not, *ceteris paribus*, to be believed.

Kripke's argument poses such a challenge on behalf of concepts of sensation. The challenge extends, I have suggested, to concepts of colour and, one would expect, to secondary quality concepts generally. However, we should also note that, in moving directly to the case of secondary quality concepts, we have passed over the possibly more straightforward, intermediate case of concepts of *public subjective appearance*—**looks red, feels hot, seems pepperminty**—on which we tend to fall back in cases where there is a potential for a mistake or

illusion about secondary quality for reasons other than the idiosyn-
crasies of individuals, and which one would expect to be associated
with a much simpler set of C-conditions than those for secondary
quality concepts proper. The point is also salient that even if our
actual secondary quality concepts prove recalcitrant, on closer inspection, to the construction of the relevant kind of provisional equations,
that would seem to be the merest *good luck* as far as physicalism is
concerned. For if the primary function of secondary quality concepts
is to provide means whereby we can record aspects of the world of
common subjective appearance, it is not clear that that role would be
compromised in any essential way had they been so fashioned as to
sustain the requirements of the argument after all. Even if **red** is not
transparent in the necessary way, there *could* be a concept, **shred**, of
which it was an a priori essential characteristic that the C-conditions I
listed earlier were exactly right. How would the intelligibility and
utility of ordinary discourse about colours be damaged if **shred** supplanted **red**, and our other colour concepts differed in parallel?

Other Cases

The large metaphysical dilemma with which we started mentioned
semantics, psychology and value. One might now investigate the
prospects for detailed provisional equations for those discourses'
characteristic concepts which satisfy the first three conditions of
Euthyphronism and thereby provide the basics for the Kripkean argument. But a less demanding form of epistemic transparency may
suffice. It is arguably part of our concept of ordinary intentional psychological states that they are standardly manifest to their subjects,
who are in turn standardly authoritative about them. It is no mere
empirical truth, that is to say, that normally a subject will know what
she believes, hopes, wants, intends and so on, and that her opinions
on such matters will be right. At least in cases where one would
expect self-knowledge to be non-inferential (involving no conscious
self-interpretation) it belongs, plausibly, to the very concept of a subject's being an intentional subject at all that her impressions of her

intentional states are generally reliable, and that those states do not generally escape her. We can, to be sure, break the conditional in either direction: sometimes it's fruitful to think as subjects as self-deceived or as self-unaware. But these don't count as good options unless an interpreter is able to back them up with independently attested details about the subject's frame of mind and an explanation of why the circumstances might have been conducive to the mismatch in question. Absent such an account, the rule is that intentional facts should be reckoned to march in step with the subject's impression of them.

This point, if granted, is enough for a variant form of the Kripkean challenge, concentrating on what we might term scenarios of *multiple exception*. Provided it is accepted that expressions denoting types of intentional state do so rigidly, there will be a standing obstacle to any proposed identification of such states with physical types posed by the apparently lucid conceivability of a world in which it is the *normal case* that subjects who have the impression that they are in particular such states fail to instantiate the appropriate physical types, while no considerations are to hand—or indeed emerge—that would allow an interpreter to regard them as self-deceived or self-unaware.

With semantics, the trick is to revert more closely to the Euthy-phronic template but to multiply the judges. It may be arguable whether communally pervasive *ignorance* of meanings is possible: whether our concept of the meaning of an expression allows for the possibility that sentences which are, for instance, too complex or convoluted to be reliably parsed by ordinary speakers might nevertheless have determinate meanings. But it seems we can a priori exclude any possibility of communally pervasive *error*: any possibility that all or a large majority of, by normal criteria, competent speakers should mistake the meaning of an expression—that they should take it, and recognise each other as taking it as meaning one thing when in fact it means another. Rather, if normal speakers are mutually recognised as attaching a particular meaning to an expression, then that is what it means, *punkt*. So again, assuming that expressions of the form 'means that P' are rigid—that they ascribe the same property in speaking of expressions in any world—there will be a standing challenge to the necessity and hence the truth of any proposed identification of such semantic properties with (presumably relational) physical types: the challenge will be posed by the apparently lucid conceivability of a scenario in which the members of a seemingly smooth-running speech community exceptionlessly understand themselves and each other as meaning that P by an expression which lacks whatever natural properties may have been proposed as being those in which meaning that P consists.

The case of moral concepts, finally, is more qualified. There are many, usually theistic, conceptions of morality which view human moral thinking as essentially imperfect; and there are others, for instance some forms of utilitarianism, which view it as almost always limited by ignorance of relevant, non-moral facts. But one would expect a form of the generalised Kripkean challenge to apply on many humanistic or 'ideal-observer' accounts of the moral, according to which there is no gap between moral quality and the assessment of it offered by the most rational, fortunately situated judge. For again, it looks as though there should be no barrier to conceiving of a situation in which, in the context of any particular proposed naturalistic account of some moral quality, M, a thinker rates a situation as, for example, possessing M where the relevant naturalistic features are missing and where there is nothing to impugn the moral credentials of the thinker in question. Assuming the rigidity of moral predicates—that expressions for moral qualities always ascribe the same qualities when used in speaking of hypothetical scenarios—there will then be the same standing difficulty, at least on such transparent conceptions of morality, to the location of moral qualities in the world of modern naturalism.

III. Dénouement

The Counter-Conceivability Principle Again

We have now reviewed a range of variations upon the theme of epistemic transparency, seen why epistemically transparent concepts as a species may offer a Kripkean challenge to naturalist reductions, and noted that the distinctive concepts of many of the subject matters with which modern naturalism abrades seem to be in the frame. Of course, the challenge is potentially reversible. Let it have been shown that naturalism is indeed in difficulties when it tries to accommodate the concepts in question by tending to construe them, after the fashion of **water** outlined at the start, as concepts of underlying physical kinds. That may be taken as bad news for naturalism. But it could be construed instead as bad news for the belief that the concepts in question are of things to be met with in the real—natural—world. Of course, that belief will prove pretty resilient when the concepts in question are concepts of one's own sensations! But the dialectical point remains that there is the option of error theory: it is naturalism as a *descriptive* rather than as a *revisionary* metaphysics which is put under pressure by the Kripkean argument.

But is it really put under pressure at all? An appreciation of the potential generality of the Kripkean argument, so far from deepening one's sense of a crisis for naturalism, is more likely to reinforce the impression that the conclusion is much too easily reached. My final point will be to corroborate that impression.

The Counter-Conceivability Principle says that a posteriori necessities, no less than a priori ones, are defeasible by lucid counter-conception: that if one can construct what appears to be a genuinely coherent scenario in which a putative necessity fails to hold, then unless or until some shortcoming is disclosed in that conception, the claim of necessity should be regarded as defeated. Now, Kripke recognised straight away that with a posteriori necessities in general, a *prima facie* counter-conception will always be available—since one has only, apparently lucidly, to conceive of the relevant kind of a posteriori enquiry as turning out differently. Thus one may apparently lucidly conceive of an investigation into the chemistry of water which finds that it is XYZ; or apparently lucidly conceive of an astronomical investigation which discloses that the Evening Star is actually Jupiter; or apparently lucidly conceive of an investigation into the composition of the Macintosh computer before me whereby it turns out to be made entirely of materials of vegetable origin. It cannot plausibly be denied that some sort of coherent scenario is involved in such cases. But assuming that the examples do involve genuine necessities of constitution and identity, the scenarios in question are not, by one who— like Kripke—accepts the Counter-Conceivability Principle, allowed to count as genuine counter-conceptions. Rather, their claim to concern the items they are supposed to concern is found wanting. It is not water but something which presents itself as water—a mere symptomatic counterpart—that one can lucidly conceive turning out not to be H_2O; it is not the Evening Star but a different though similar-looking body, imagined as occupying the same place in the evening sky, that one can conceive turning out to be Jupiter; it is not this computer but one just like it that one can lucidly conceive as turning out to be of vegetable materials.

What stopped this way of protecting the Counter-Conceivability Principle being totally devoid of interest—what stopped it being simple 'monster-barring'—was that, precisely because the move is unavailable in the case of epistemically transparent concepts, the principle is allowed to retain some teeth. We do not have carte blanche. The claim to have conceived a scenario running counter to a putative necessity involving an epistemically transparent concept cannot be dismissed on the ground that the scenario fails to reflect the difference between a genuine instance of that concept and a mere symptomatic counterpart—for there is no such difference to reflect.

This was the *ur*-thought in the Kripkean argument. But it is sufficient for the purpose only if, where a posteriori necessities are concerned, there is no *other* way in which a lucid putative counter-conception may fall short than by failing to engage the distinction between an item and surface counterparts of it. For suppose there was another way. Then the apparently lucid conception of a scenario in which pain occurred without C-fibre stimulation, while it could not be dismissed as involving nothing distinguished from a mere surface counterpart of pain, might yet come short in this other way. However, it is clear on reflection that we *must* make room for other possible kinds of shortcoming in purported counter-conceptions, however vivid and lucid-seeming they may be.

Here is one example: suppose—Kripke would agree—that I am essentially a human being, and that it is an essential characteristic of human beings to have their actual biological origins. So it is an essential characteristic of mine to be the child of my actual parents. Still I can, it seems, lucidly conceive of my not having had those parents but others, or even—like Superman—of my originating in a different world, of a different race, and having been visited on Earth from afar and brought up as their own by the people whom I take to be my biological father and mother. I can, it seems, lucidly imagine my finding all this out tomorrow. And it is, prima facie, every bit as coherent a scenario as those involved in the water, Evening Star and computer cases. But it cannot be dismissed, in the way that they were, on the ground that it fails to be sensitive to the distinction between myself and a mere epistemic counterpart, a mere 'fool's self', as it were, sharing the surface features by which I identify myself but differing in essence. It cannot be so dismissed because I don't, in the relevant fashion, identify myself by features, surface or otherwise, at all. The point is of a piece with Hume's observation that, in awareness of a psychological state as one's own, one is not presented as an object to oneself. When I conceive some simple counterfactual contingency—say, my being right at this moment in the Grand Canyon—I do not imagine someone's being there who presents themselves, on the surface, as being me. Rather I simply imagine *my* having relevant kinds of experience—imagine, that is to say, the relevant kinds of experience from my first-personal point of view. No mode of presentation of the self need feature in the exercise before it can count as presenting a scenario in which *I* am in the Grand Canyon; a fortiori, no *superficial* mode of presentation, open to instantiation by someone other than myself.

The apparently lucid conceivability of the Superman scenario's turning out to be the truth is in like case. Since it need involve no play with a mode of presentation of the self, it need not be open to any charge of insensitivity to the distinction between the self and a surface counterpart (whatever that would be). And of course it would not help to try applying this complaint to other items in the conceived scenario—for instance, to the people, looking and behaving very much like my actual parents, who are now conceived as having fostered me instead. For even if the scenario is taken to be insensitive to the distinction between those who actually reared me and mere surface counterparts of them, it remains part of it that I was not born to the human race at all. Nevertheless, if I was indeed born to those I take to be my actual parents and the Counter-Conceivability Principle is correct, I cannot genuinely conceive of the Superman scenario. So how am I to describe the content of the scenario which I do seem to be able to entertain, in as great a degree of fanciful detail moreover as may be wished?

Next consider a different kind of example altogether. We can rest assured, I suppose, that Andrew Wiles really has proved Fermat's 'Last Theorem', which therefore holds good as a matter of conceptual necessity. But we can imagine a sceptic about the result who flatters himself that he can still conceive of finding counter-examples to the theorem and of finding mistakes in Wiles' proof. Of course there will be limits on the detail of these 'conceivings', or the sceptic would be thought-experimentally finding *real* counter-examples and mistakes. Still, we should not deny that he could be conceiving *something*, and doing so moreover—subject only to the preceding point—in as vivid and detailed a way as could be wished. The last diagnosis we should propose, however, is that his conceivings are insensitive to the distinction between finding counter-examples to Fermat's theorem and finding counter-examples to an *epistemic counterpart* of it!—or to the distinction between finding a mistake in Wiles' reasoning and finding a mistake in an epistemic counterpart of that. What could that mean? Of course we can imagine someone with only a hazy idea of the theorem or the proof. But our sceptic may be perfectly clear about both—an able (but curmudgeonly) mathematician.

If we are to retain the Counter-Conceivability Principle, then we must provide house room for these cases. There has to be a category of conceivings which fall short of being genuine counter-conceptions to a given proposition, not because their detail fails to be sensitive to the distinction between items that proposition is about and 'fools'-equivalents of them, but because it is insensitive to another distinction: that between genuinely conceiving of a scenario in which P fails to obtain and conceiving, rather, of what it would be like if, *per impossible,* P were (found to be) false. The latter is what the curmudgeonly mathematician does. It is what I do when I conceive, in as much detail as you like, of my originating of a different race, elsewhere in the galaxy (or perhaps, following Descartes, of surviving my bodily death). If time travel is metaphysically impossible, it's what anyone does who imagines himself as a Dr. Who, wandering in time. For a large class of impossibilities, there are still determinate ways things would seem if they obtained.[25] If, *per impossible,* Wiles' proof is flawed and there are counter-examples to Fermat's theorem, we know how things would seem if those circumstances came to light.

The Failure of the Kripkean Argument

To admit such a category of conceivings is not, to stress, to make a concession inconsistent with the Counter-Conceivability Principle. It can remain that a prima facie lucid conception of a scenario in which not P holds is a standing, though defeasible objection to any claim of the necessity of P. But if even a vivid and detailed scenario is to motivate such an objection, then it needs to be able to defend against not one but two charges of potential insufficiency. The first is the original Kripkean charge that nothing in its detail distinguishes its objects from surface counterparts—'fools'-equivalents—of the items that it is supposed to concern; and the second is the charge that it allows of description as a scenario, merely, of how some things would or might be—for instance, what kinds of things would be experienced—if the proposition in question were false. If the scenario can be done full justice by a description of the latter kind, it will not be done less than justice if the description is modified by the insertion of the words, *'per*

25. One reason why semantical treatments of subjunctive conditionals which hold all with impossible antecedents to be true are unfortunate.

impossibile', and in that case it fails to constitute a genuine counter-conception at all.

Both kinds of insufficiency afflict the scenario in which water purportedly turns out to be something other than H_2O. But the price we pay for retaining the Counter-Conceivability Principle is that the second kind of insufficiency—*per impossibile* insufficiency, as it were—must be reckoned to afflict any seemingly lucidly conceived scenario which appears to jar with a necessity, whether a posteriori or not. So if P is a proposition which is known to be necessary if true (and, correspondingly, impossible if false), then in order to determine whether we have constructed a genuine counter-conception to P—as opposed merely to a lucid scenario of how in certain respects things would be if, *per impossibile*, P did not obtain—we need first to know whether P is true. If P is true, then no matter how intricate and coherent, the scenario can embody no more than a *per impossibile* counter-conception; if P is false, then there need be no barrier to its description as a valid counter-conception. But either way, the distinction turns, in the end, on matters beyond the phenomenology of conceiving.

The effect is that, although we save the letter of the Counter-Conceivability Principle, and although—for all I have said—it can continue as a defeasible operational constraint on the ascription of necessity in cases where *contingency is an epistemic possibility*, it is no constraint at all on the ascription of necessity in cases where necessity would follow from truth—as is the situation of all potential necessities a posteriori. The consequence is that the apparent counter-conceivability of physicalistic identifications of the instances of epistemically transparent concepts is of no modal significance whatever. Rather the truth values and hence—on the assumptions of the argument—the modal status of identities of relevant kind must be settled independently, before we can know how properly to describe the scenarios in question.

So, after all, the metaphysical prospects for naturalism cannot be dashed purely by creative exercises of the conceiving faculty, in the extraordinary fashion that the Kripkean argument seemed to promise. But I don't think that we (most of us) ever really believed they could.

✒

Ancestors of this material were presented at colloquia in St. Andrews and Glasgow in 1996, at the Logic and Language conference held at the University of London in April 1998 and at the Language and Mind seminar at New York University in that same month, where Ned Block was commentator. My thanks to the discussants on those occasions for many helpful criticisms and questions, and in particular to Paul Boghossian, Jim Edwards, Bob Hale, Neil Tennant and Ned Block.

14

What Could Anti-Realism about Ordinary Psychology Possibly Be?

✿

I

If you cannot lucidly doubt that you exist as a thinking thing, then nor can there be a lucid doubt about the reality of those psychological states and attributes whose possession is distinctive of thinkers, *par excellence* their being subject to the various kinds of doxastic and conative states involved in goal-directed thought. Thus it seems a short step from the *Cogito* to at least a limited application of the categories of ordinary attitudinal psychology. Yet many leading modern philosophers—for instance, Dennett, Stich, the Churchlands and, above all, Quine—have been united, notwithstanding other differences, in a tendency to scepticism about the reality of (explanation in terms of) attitudinal states.

The connection with the *Cogito* is one reason why such scepticism seems like a denial of the inescapable. More generally, scepticism about the states invoked in ordinary psychology seems to flout their characteristic *self-evidence* to their subjects—the fact that, typically, someone's being in such a state is, as it seems, effortlessly, non-empirically and non-inferentially available to them. Surely each of us does have—really have—beliefs, desires, hopes, intentions, wishes and so on. Can't we each just tell that we do? Don't we do so all the time? Besides, how, save in ways which involve self-ascribing such states, are we to make sense of most of what we do? And how else are we ever to take decisions about what best to do?

These reservations may seem compelling. But they are more protest than argument. For the 'self-evidence' of ordinary psychological states to their subjects really comes to no more than a symptom of the entrenchment of the phenomenon of psychological *avowal*: the fact that people acquire a propensity, on being educated in ordinary psychological talk, spontaneously to affirm claims concerning their own attitudinal states which for the most part, both to themselves and others, seem—by the standards of the practice—to make decent sense of their behaviour and projects. But how we talk, it may be said, is one thing and what the world is really like is another. It is, so it may be contended, quite another matter what metaphysical status should be accorded to our ordinary psychological claims: whether anything real answers to them. And if not, it's a further question again whether the linguistic practices in which they feature are thereby shown to be somehow essentially corrupt or whether, rather, they have a legitimate content and purpose which can be dissociated from a realist view of ordinary psychology.

Confidence in the integrity of ordinary psychology certainly has challenges to answer. My focus in what follows, however, will not be on the pros and cons of the debates those challenges provoke but on the generally unquestioned presupposition that there *is* any such thing in the first place as a coherent anti-realist view of ordinary psychology. In other areas, anti-realism has assumed each of a variety of shapes—error-theoretic, expressivist, instrumentalist, fictionalist and verificationist.[1] I shall review reasons to doubt whether, when it

---

1. The widespread association of 'anti-realism' with verificationist ideas is due, of course, to the work of Dummett. But verificationism is not really to my purpose in the present essay since it would be quite consistent with holding—what is perfectly plausible—that psychological truth cannot outrun verifiability (by all subjects, in prin-

comes to ordinary psychology, there *is* any form of anti-realist thesis which is both internally stable and rationally tenable. Some of the listed types of view about psychology—I am thinking particularly of error theory and instrumentalism—have, of course, already provoked complex and unsettled disputes in a very extensive literature. I make no pretence to settle these disputes here. But I do think the views in question confront much more immediate *structural* difficulties than is often realised and I will outline some of what I take the most serious such difficulties to be. Others of the possible anti-realist positions have received much less attention. The principal contention of the latter half of the essay is that what, as it seems to me, is actually the most attractive anti-realist option in the area faces a potentially lethal problem.

The effect of the discussion as a whole, in my own estimation, will be that we do not, at the present time, have any clear understanding of the shape that a dialectically coherent—let alone cogent—psychological anti-realist position might assume: that the arguments of the sceptics about ordinary psychology, whatever credibility they may or may not seem to possess, have nowhere—or anyway nowhere obvious—to lead.

II

Philosophers understandably worry about the looseness and multiplicity of understandings of the terms 'realism' and 'anti-realism'. Fortunately we do not need to attempt a precise characterisation here. It will suffice to structure the discussion to follow that any realist

---

ciple) to think of the psychological in an intuitively realist way—as an objective domain to which best opinions faithfully correspond. The anti-realist position—*minimalism*, reviewed in the second half of the essay—seems to me to incorporate what is right about the idea that there is a connection between verificationism and anti-realism. But verificationism as such will not feature further in my discussion.

about a given region of discourse is likely to want to maintain versions of two claims:

A semantic claim: something to the effect that statements in the discourse have a content which fits them for representation of aspects of the real world;

A metaphysical claim: something to the effect that the real world comes furnished with states of affairs of the kind which such statements are fitted to represent.

Whatever precise cast particular realists may choose to give to these claims, each will be distinctively denied by some of the well-known anti-realist paradigms listed above, which correspondingly group themselves into metaphysical and semantic forms of anti-realism. Classical ethical expressivism and scientific instrumentalism, for instance, are semantic anti-realisms: they deny that their respectively targeted discourses deal in genuinely representational—truth-apt—contents. Mathematical fictionalism and error-theoretic views of ethics, by contrast, are metaphysical: they allow that their targeted discourses are representational in content but deny that the characteristic objects, states or properties, purportedly denoted or attributed, within the discourse are to be found in the real world.

Modern anti-realists about ordinary psychology have mostly been of the metaphysical stripe, marshalling concerns that call in question whether there are genuinely any such things as the states which ordinary intentional psychology characteristically calls for. But a successful attack on realism's semantic claim—the representationality of psychological discourse—would presumably enjoin rejecting any corresponding category of psychological states in any case. For if there were such states, what could be the barrier to their representation in thought and speech? So it might seem that anti-realists of both kinds must converge on denial of the metaphysical claim. One attractive feature, in my view, of the anti-realist position—minimalism—on which I shall eventually concentrate is that it avoids such a denial.[2] But for the time being we may focus our attention on anti-realist views which, whether for specifically metaphysical or semantic motives, do reject realism's metaphysical claim.

III

The perhaps most influential metaphysical challenges to ordinary psychological realism are posed by metaphysical *naturalism*. One—in the aftermath of the famous sceptical arguments of Kripke, Quine and Putnam[3]—derives from a lingering concern about what content-bearing states might amount to in a world conceived as allowing, ultimately, of complete characterisation in the vocabulary of a fully developed physical science—together with the conviction that such a world is what we actually inhabit. Another closely related challenge worries about the prospects for integrating the—apparently causal—explanations of ordinary psychology within the explanatory framework of a fully developed physical science. We will need to keep the general character of these challenges in mind in what follows but, as I said, I do not propose to add here to the extensive and complex literature that develops and responds to them.

There is, however, a different line of argument towards psychological anti-realism—this time a semantic rather than a directly metaphysical argument—which, because it exploits an idea which will be important to us later and also emphasises a tactical lesson for the discussion to follow, I will briefly review. This argument takes it for granted that psychological interpretation is *indeterminate* in some

2. I must ask the reader's indulgence at this point if it seems puzzling how anything deserving the title 'anti-realism' can avoid such a denial. I return to the matter explicitly in note 20 below.

3. The principal sources are Kripke (1982); Quine (1960), chap. 2; Putnam (1981), chap 3. The last is in many ways a more satisfactory argument than that of Putnam's famous (1980).

important and extensive way—a claim I will not here further consider—and moves from there to an anti-realist conclusion. Some important philosophers—notably Quine and Davidson—have of course
been drawn to this transition. What has not always been clear is how
exactly the passage from indeterminacy to anti-realism is supposed to
be facilitated.

One way of doing it derives from considerations of *Cognitive
Command*.[4] As remarked, realism about a discourse is in part a view
about representation. Unless pessimistic enough to think that its subject matter is altogether beyond our ken, a realist views a discourse as
providing for the proper expression of a representational mode of
cognitive function, rather as a film provides for the expression of the
representational function of a camera. To submit oneself, under conditions of normal cognitive functioning, to the standards of belief
formation and appraisal appropriate to the discourse, is—for the realist—to receive impressions, as it were, of self-standing states of affairs
which are then expressible by the linguistic resources it provides. This
is, no doubt, a vague idea. But even so, it does have certain quite definite obligations. If exposures taken of the *same* scene somehow turn
out to represent it in incompatible ways, there has to have been some
kind of shortcoming in the function of at least one of the cameras, or
in the way it was used. The tariff for taking the idea of representation
in the way the realist wants is that when representations prove to conflict, there has to have been something amiss with the process that
produced them or with their vehicle—with the thinker or with the
way she went about forming her impression.[5] A realist about ordinary
psychology is accordingly obliged to hold that if you and I disagree
about a subject's attitudinal states, then defects of process or thinker
have somehow to be involved in our disagreement.

4. This notion is introduced in *Truth and Objectivity*. See chaps. 3 and 4, for discussion.

5. Qualifications are needed here to accommodate the possibility of vagueness in
the content of conflicting representations. However, it would take us too far afield to
go into the details. For some discussion, see *Truth and Objectivity*, pp. 144–5.

It follows that if there is no assurance to be had that any particular disagreement about a subject's attitudinal states will always involve such a defect, then there is correspondingly no assurance that a realist—seriously representational[6]—view of intentional psychological discourse can be sustained. Just here is the bearing of the thesis of the indeterminacy of radical psychological interpretation. It enjoins exactly that there can be no such assurance.[7] The claim of the indeterminacy thesis will be that, in the nature of the methodology which they follow, interpreters of a given subject's sayings and doings who proceed irreproachably can nonetheless wind up with mutually inconsistent yet respectively unimprovable conceptions of that person's overall psychological set. But if nothing in the methodology of psychological interpretation guarantees convergence among ideal interpreters, then it would appear to follow that forming opinions in a manner constrained by that methodology should not be viewed as, in the sense the realist intends, a representational mode of cognitive function.

To be sure, there was an escape route left open in the possible combination of realism with pessimism. The escape is to allow that the truth values of the conflicting opinions may transcend decision by the methods of radical interpretation. In that case the price of psychological realism becomes what Quine once famously stigmatised as the 'Myth of the Museum'.[8] The basic thought behind the idea of Cognitive Command is that a discourse counts as seriously representational—and the formation of opinions expressible within it counts correspondingly as a representational mode of intellectual function—only if disagreements betoken cognitive shortcoming. But such a shortcoming need not pertain to the way in which opinions are formed

6. 'Seriously' (like 'full-blooded') here marks a contrast whose fuller explanation it will be convenient to reserve until section V below.

7. There are relevant issues here, of course, about the extent of the indeterminacy which the thesis claims. The anti-realist argument under review applies no further than the range of cases about which interpreters may blamelessly disagree. We must finesse this matter here.

8. See Quine (1969), pp. 27–8.

unless the truths in question are ones which best methods, properly pursued, invariably suffice to disclose. The so-styled Myth of the Museum is just the specialisation to psychology of the ordinary realist idea that some domains of fact may strictly transcend the available evidence, which may allow of radically different constructions—theories—of how the facts in question stand. If such were the correct understanding of ordinary psychological claims, then the present semantic anti-realist argument could not get a grip—the indeterminacy of psychological interpretation would just be an instance of the underdetermination of empirical theory by evidence: a consideration which, of itself, has no evident immediate bearing on the viability of a realist view of empirical theory.

To be clear. The indeterminacy thesis says that conflicting views about a subject's attitudinal states may each be impeccably arrived at. But according to the constraint of Cognitive Command, realism about psychology—specifically, the conception of psychological claims as seriously representational in content—requires that conflicting views about a subject's psychological states cannot all be impeccably arrived at—*unless* the relevant subject matter is beyond our ken. The Myth of the Museum allows that it may be. So the semantic argument can only work by jettisoning the Myth of the Museum.

To jettison the Myth is to go for a broadly *interpretationist* view of ordinary psychology. On this view, a *true* account of a subject's motives for an action is just whatever proves to belong with the best (by whatever criteria) overall interpretation of her attitudes and other psychological states—and there is no presumption that will *be* any particular uniquely best overall interpretation, nor that there is any further fact of correctness when there is none. The metaphysical concerns, by contrast, were driven by the belief in an objective, comprehensive, natural causal order and a view of psychological explanation which sees it as, above all else, an attempt to tell truths about aspects of that objective order. They thus presuppose a view of psychology which is actually *in tension* with the implicit interpretationism of the semantic argument.

Indeed, to sustain the semantic anti-realist argument is to cut the ground from under the metaphysical concerns. To sustain the semantic argument is to conclude that ordinary psychology is not really in the business of depiction of the world, that the products of psychological interpretation are not fitted to represent or misrepresent anything real. But the worry of the metaphysical anti-realist was precisely, in effect, one of *mis*representation: it was the misgiving that ordinary psychology calls for states and processes whose nature cannot be reconciled with the (assumed) physicality of the world and the actual natural aetiology of ordinary behaviour. One in the grip of the assumptions which spur these complaints will regard ordinary psychology as *incredible*. But if the semantic anti-realist argument is right, credibility—that is, plausibility as serious representation—is simply not psychology's stock-in-trade in the first place.

Hence the advertised tactical lesson about our leading question: What should a psychological anti-realist best say—positively—about ordinary psychological discourse and the purported explanations it provides for? But now we see that this question needs to be taken with care, for there is reason to expect that the answer may vary, depending on the motivation for the anti-realism: on whether it is metaphysical, driven by the pressure put on the prima facie ontology and explanatory claims of ordinary psychology by a background naturalism; or *non-cognitivist*, driven by consideration of the constraint on representational content involved in the idea of Cognitive Command, an acceptance of the (extensive) indeterminacy of radical interpretation and a repudiation of the Myth of the Museum. The complaints of the metaphysical anti-realist implicitly involve taking a stand on something—the representational ambitions of ordinary psychological discourse—which the non-cognitivist rejects. So we must be wary of assuming that all the options open to them are the same.

IV

With that caveat noted, let's first review the options for metaphysical anti-realism. On this outlook, ordinary psychological ascriptions concern nothing real, and ordinary psychological explanations depict no genuine causes. That would seem to leave a choice between, on the one hand, viewing ordinary psychology as, like phlogiston-theory or any discredited empirical theory, hopelessly compromised—the well-known *eliminativist* response—or, on the other, a *conservative* response, broadly comparable to expressivist construals of the 'statements' of ethics, or fictionalism in the philosophies of science and mathematics, which will try to make a case that ordinary psychological discourse remains acceptable, even while conceding that it serves to represent no real matters of fact, by finding for it some other validly heuristic or instrumentally valuable role.

I do not think that the special obstacles to reconciling any such conservative proposal about ordinary psychology with a metaphysical anti-realist motivation have been sufficiently appreciated. What sort of purpose might intentional psychology, divorced of any claim to represent reality, really serve? One immediately thinks of the kind of instrumentalist or fictionalist 'stance' idea, associated with the writings of Dennett.[9] Dennett's key thought, familiarly, was that the rationalisation of others' behaviour within ordinary intentional psychological categories can prove an economical way of anticipating it—that it is, for instance, much easier to predict the moves of a good chess-playing computer if you just *treat it* as an intentional strategist rather than merely as a physical mechanism, and that the utility of such treatment is quite independent of its fidelity, presumed or otherwise, to anything that is happening with the machine.

The question is whether this idea can offer a fully general account of the role of intentional psychological idiom. One obstacle emerges as soon as one puts aside the other-directed uses of ordinary psychology—by which Dennett himself was preoccupied—and focuses instead on one's own case. To attempt to think of the detail of one's own self-conception as likewise accepted merely as a self-directed 'stance', designed to minimise surprises in one's subsequent behav-

9. See esp. Dennett (1978) and (1987). There is scope for some debate whether Dennett himself really intended his ideas to be taken in an anti-realist sprit. But whatever the view of its author, the idea of 'the intentional stance' has been widely regarded as epitomising a kind of anti-realism about psychology, supposedly apt for a situation in which the *real* explanations of the behaviour of certain 'agents' would be too complex to be useful for practical purposes.

iour, is bizarre and would seem to involve abrogating the intuitive asymmetries between self-knowledge and knowledge of others—asymmetries which are plausibly essential to our ordinary conception of the mental. But there is a more basic structural difficulty. For, even in the other-directed case, is not such a stance itself individuated by its content—by the complex of attitudes one ascribes to the subject? And must the Dennettian theorist not take it as a *matter of fact* that—when one is—one is taking such a stance? According to the proposal, we can somehow deflate the realistic purport of ordinary psychological attributions by viewing them merely as entertained as part of an instrumentally useful stance. But it is thereby presupposed that one does—or can—really take such a stance. So that is then a bit of intentional reality which there is no remaining room to construe as fictional or merely instrumental. To deploy a complex of supposed fictions in the Dennettian manner is already to enter into a complex attitudinal state—in no relevant way distinguishable from regular intentional states like hope, belief and desire. Taking the intentional stance is entering into an intentional state.[10] So the Dennettian anti-realist account winds up with a presupposition at odds with itself.

When it is applied to ordinary psychology under the aegis of metaphysical anti-realism, there is a broadly similar kind of problem with another very familiar anti-realist paradigm—that of the expressivism in ethics classically championed by such writers as A. J. Ayer and R. M. Hare.[11] It might be thought that the expressivist idea is a

10. For related doubts about Dennett's proposal, see Brandom (1994), pp. 58 ff.

11. The *loci classici* are of course the famous "Critique of Ethics and Theology" offered in chapter 6 of Ayer (1936), and Hare (1952). Ayer and Hare proposed the strict expressivist view that moral discourse, properly understood, is only apparently assertoric, and that moral utterances are characteristically governed by a different kind of illocutionary force, serving to fit them for a quite different role than the statement of fact—the expression of attitude, endorsement of norms or whatever. This strict expressivist line is softened in the more recent treatments of Simon Blackburn and Allan Gibbard. Blackburn (1984), chap. 6, remains the best introduction to his view; Alan Gibbard's ideas are developed systematically in Gibbard (1990). It may be wondered, however, whether their proposals would not do better to travel under the banner of 'minimalism' in the sense shortly to follow.

non-starter in this context in any case since, as remarked above, the dominant motivation of the metaphysical anti-realist presupposes a representational interpretation of psychological discourse. But that thought is too quick: it overlooks the possibility that the metaphysical anti-realist's arguments be viewed as a *reductio* of the representational interpretation, with expressivism then proposed as a saving— perhaps revisionary—account. However, the real problem is only a little less immediate. It is, naturally, of the essence of any expressivist view to rely on a distinction between genuine assertions and other forms of speech act which have the surface grammar of assertions but in fact have a different semantic function. But how are such deeper differences in function to be described? The characteristic expressivist answer has standardly been: by reference to the *dominant intentional states* of participants in the discourse in question. Moral expressivists, for instance, have thought they could excuse ethical pronouncements any genuinely assertoric role on the ground that they are—allegedly— characteristically aimed at the expression not of *beliefs,* apt to be true or false, but of certain distinctive *feelings* and at shaping the corresponding feelings of others. However, the details of any particular such proposal do not matter. So long as expressivism accepts that genuinely assertoric discourses are marked off from merely expressive discourses by systematic differences in the psychological attitudes by which competent practice of the discourse is constrained and which it serves to communicate, the very claim that a discourse is expressive will presuppose an underpinning in facts about aspects of the characteristic attitudinal psychology of its participants. But facts of that genre are just what metaphysical anti-realism about psychology is unwilling to countenance. So expressivism can offer it no consistent outlet.

There will be, no doubt, more to say. But the foregoing observations, brisk though they may be, make at least a strong prima facie case: each of the two classic conservative anti-realist options about a discourse—conceding the large-scale literal falsity of its statements but making a case for it as instrumentally useful fiction; and denying that it deals in genuine (truth-apt) assertions at all—would appear to involve presuppositions which are unsustainable within the context of a systematic metaphysical anti-realism about intentional psychology. So neither can present a coherent account of psychology itself from that standpoint.

Such considerations may incline an anti-realist to non-conservatism—to regarding ordinary psychology simply as a primitive and discreditable mode of explanation of human behaviour, which we should aim to supersede. This view—psychological *eliminativism*—has achieved something of a reputation for dialectical resilience. But I think it is moot how deserved this is. Once again, there is a serious question whether the very statement and development of the view can avoid presuppositions which are inconsistent with it. One such presupposition—for a reason I'll give in a minute—would seem to be the existence of *linguistic content*. But how does linguistic content fare on the psychological eliminativist view? Wouldn't one intuitively suspect that the reality of linguistic content must depend on that of intentional states?

Such a dependence would be immediate on a broadly Gricean account of meaning. According to that account, the meaning of any expression is actually constituted in certain characteristic self-reflexive intentions possessed by those who use it. But the intuitive suspicion does not need so much. A sufficient but less committal reflection would be merely that, whatever the correct account in detail, linguistic meanings depend for their existence on *conventions*. For whatever its proper analysis, convention is an intentional notion. Conventions, as opposed to mere regularities, have somehow to be constituted in the beliefs and intentions of those who are party to them. So strip the world of intentional states and properties and you strip it of semantic ones too.

If that is right, then notice that what eliminativism puts in jeopardy is not (merely) the legitimacy of treating meanings as *objects*—the point on which Quine's own early critique of the intensional was largely focused—but the whole idea of expressions' *having meaning at all*; that is, their being semantically differentiated in specific ways. But the eliminativist view is that ordinary psychology is massively false. That fact has to consist in the falsity of the overwhelming majority of its *characteristic type of claims*, and those claims are identified precisely by their *characteristic type of content*. If there is no such thing as linguistic content, how is eliminativism to explain what exactly are the limits of the proposal—which precisely are the kinds of spurious explanatory claim which it is proposed we should try to supersede and which we may retain?

There is a related, more general awkwardness. How, once linguistic meanings are jettisoned along with intentional states, are we to conceive of the determinants of *truth value?* It is—or so one would suppose (with Aristotle)—the merest platitude that the truth of a statement depends on whether what it says is so, is so. So its truth depends on what a statement says. If there is no such thing as what a statement says, how can there be any such thing as its truth or falsity (let alone the massive falsity of an entire discourse)?

Some (Quineans) may have thought they can finesse this point by an emphasis on the Disquotational Scheme:

'P' is true if and only if P

as putatively capturing the determinants of truth independently of any play with meaning or cognate notions. But if so, they are deluded. The Disquotational Scheme is merely another way of articulating the Aristotelian platitude, made possible by the unstated schematic assumption that 'P' says that P.[12]

In sum, the worry is that eliminativism about ordinary psychology requires eliminativism about linguistic content, and that the latter then has two subversive consequences for a proponent of the former: first it throws away the materials for a proper circumscription of the discourse to be supplanted; second it undermines the truth predi-

---

12. There are, no doubt, ways of concealing the semantic character of that necessary assumption—for instance, one may express it as the assumption that 'the metalanguage contains the object language'. But for languages to overlap in the relevant way is just for *lexically* equivalent expressions within them to be *semantically* equivalent.

cate—thus again, in another way, leaving eliminativism without the conceptual resources to identify its own central contention: the massive falsity of ordinary psychology.[13]

An eliminativist might reply that, as far as the first point is concerned, the thrust of the objection is only that our *ordinary notion* of linguistic content has a dependence on convention which in turn, as ordinarily understood, implicates intentionality—and that eliminativism is accordingly in the clear if it can somehow recover a notion of convention, or more generally of linguistic content, which involves no such implication.[14] Moreover, as far as the second point is concerned, the reply may continue, all we really have any right to conclude is that any psychological eliminativist—if indeed committed to dispensing with linguistic content—owes an account of what determines truth value which implicates no parameters of meaning: in effect, that she needs to be able to provide room for *truth values* without appeal to *truth conditions*, semantically conceived. In brief: some kind of intentionality-free ersatz for the notion of linguistic content, and (thereby) some kind of intentionality-free explanation of the determinants of truth value, will indeed need to be supplied if the view is to retain the resources for its own statement. But it has not been shown these needs cannot be filled. Eliminativism is anyway up to its neck in explanatory debts. What are two more? Add them to the slate.

But these are not just any old explanatory debts. The fact is that we have not the slightest inkling of the needed explanations nor any reason whatever to think that they can be given. Accordingly, the idea that there *is* any such identifiable contention as that of the massive falsity of ordinary psychology becomes, for the eliminativist, a mere article of faith. This is not, it is crucial to appreciate, the familiar

13. The contention that error-theoretic views in general are committed to the reality of content—specifically, truth conditions—and that this leads error theory about semantics in particular into aporia is nicely made in Boghossian (1990), pp. 167, 174.

14. Of course, the prospects for a 'naturalised' account of content are more than usually dim in cases where what has to be recovered is a demarcation of the distinctive content of a discourse dealing in *non-existents* (which therefore sustain no causal relations).

grumble that eliminativists are characteristically content to make it a matter of faith that some non-intentional explanatory theory will somehow one day supplant psychology as an account of the sources of human action. The point is that their 'faith' has to extend further: it has to extend to *the very existence of the trademark claim,* namely, that ordinary psychology is massively false. It has to extend to the very existence of the eliminativist position itself. Until at least prima facie viable, intentionality-free reconstructions of linguistic content and the determinants of truth value are available, a systematic doubt about the reality of ordinary psychological states is a commitment to holding that there is no good reason to think that any such thesis as that psychological discourse is massively *false,* and should be abandoned, can be so much as formulated.

To have to take it on faith that empirical science can develop to repair the explanatory gaps left by a philosophical thesis is one thing; but to have to take it on faith that one so much as *has* a thesis in the first place is quite another. As things stand, a metaphysical anti-realist about psychology should regard the very existence of the eliminativist thesis as something there is no reason to accept. So such a theorist cannot—rationally—be tempted by it.

V

If all this is right, then one inclined to sustain any of the metaphysical challenges to realism about ordinary psychology faces a bind. For there appears to be no clearly internally stable position—since if not eliminativism, nor some form of fictionalism, nor some expressivist account, then what?—for a coherent, metaphysically motivated anti-realism about ordinary psychology to assume. But how do matters play if the emphasis is on the other principal anti-realist argument outlined earlier—the alleged failure of ordinary psychological discourse to satisfy the constraint of Cognitive Command, and hence to qualify as seriously representational? We have already observed that a side-effect of this—non-cognitivist—view is to undermine the metaphysical challenges to psychological realism, since the ontology, or explanations, of ordinary psychology can be regarded as incredible—as the metaphysical challenges suggest—only if the discourse is indeed rightly regarded as making a claim to represent what things there really are and what causally explains what. So non-cognitivism does not need to worry about how those challenges might be accommodated if sustained. But what exactly should be its positive view of ordinary psychological discourse? And can it escape binds of its own?

Well, let's take stock. Since non-cognitivism rejects the representationality of psychological discourse, it cannot—for all we have so far said—have any truck with an account which maintains the literal falsity of the massive majority of ordinary psychological statements. So eliminativism, so motivated, and fictionalism are out of bounds. The natural outlet might therefore seem to be some kind of expressivism. But now there will be a close relative of the problem which stood in the way of an expressivist account in a metaphysical realist setting: How could an expressivism about psychology lay claim to the distinction, needed by all kinds of expressivism, between genuinely truth-evaluable and merely expressive utterances without reliance on *statements*—that is, representational, truth-evaluable claims—about the psychological attitudes which constrain and are conveyed by the various illocutionary forces?

Prima facie, then, psychological non-cognitivism seems to be no more comfortably situated than its metaphysical anti-realist cousin. However, that is a premature conclusion. It passes over a radically alternative kind of anti-realist outlet: an anti-realist account of a discourse which disputes neither the *truth-aptitude* of its characteristic claims, nor the *truth* of very many of them. It is this form of proposal, rather than expressivism, which in my view should offer the first port of call for a theorist about ordinary psychology moved by non-cognitivist considerations—a conservative form of proposal differing from fictionalism and expressivism in allowing that we are perfectly entitled to regard those claims which are warranted by the standards of ordinary intentional psychology as both genuine (truth-evaluable) statements and literally true.

Recent work on truth and realism offers the necessary framework for such a proposal. According to the conceptions of truth and truth-aptitude defended by writers such as Paul Horwich and myself,[15] any sentence is a candidate for truth which is possessed of assertoric content, and possession of assertoric content is merely a matter of meeting certain surface syntactic and disciplinary constraints—in essence, assertoric contents are ones which are capable of significant embedding within constructions such as negation, the conditional, and in contexts of propositional attitude, and whose acceptability is subject to acknowledged standards of warrant. When such standards are satisfied, that will then suffice, other things being equal, (defeasibly) to justify the claim that the content in question is true.[16]

If this kind of approach is accepted, almost all the areas which have traditionally provoked realist/anti-realist debate—ethics, aesthetics, intentional psychology, mathematics, theoretical science and so on—will turn out to traffic in truth-evaluable contents, which moreover, when the disciplinary standards proper to the discourse are satisfied, we are going to be entitled to claim to be true.

A reader may be impatient to observe that none of this helps the psychological non-cognitivist unless an acceptance that psychological claims which are warranted by ordinary standards may be regarded as literally true is somehow less than a commitment to psychological *realism*. But what, in that case, *is* realism, if it has not already been conceded with truth-aptitude and truth? According to the type of account I would myself favour,[17] the question most fruitfully taken to be at issue between realist and anti-realist views about a discourse is not whether it deals in truth-apt claims, nor whether those of its

---

15. See Horwich (1998a) and my *Truth and Objectivity*. There are, however, important differences between the views of truth proposed, some of which are outlined in Horwich (1996).

16. These claims would also be accepted by more traditional *deflationary* conceptions of truth, according to which the word 'true' expresses no real attribute of the items in its range of predication. Horwich and I are not deflationists in that sense.

17. And developed in *Truth and Objectivity*.

claims which are justified in the light of its own standards may defensibly be regarded as true, but rather whether their being true involves anything which merits the interpretation which realism places upon it: the interpretation of fit with independent, objective states of affairs. And there are various respects in which what is implicated in the truth of statements of different kinds may so differ as to bear on the propriety of the realist's guiding image of truth as fit—including, for instance, evidence transcendence of truth value, response-dependence of truth value, the extent of the explanatory potential ('cosmological role') of the type of state of affairs concerned, and Cognitive Command. The distinctive claim of the psychological non-cognitivist can thus be that psychology fares relatively badly in relation to these various realism-relevant parameters; that, truth-apt and, in a wide class of cases, true though they may be, the claims of ordinary psychology are *not* apt for the kind of substantial correspondence property aspired to by realism; that when proper controls are placed on such claims, the discourse of intentional psychology proves not to deal in contents which are 'apt for the representation of aspects of objective reality'.

As just indicated, there are a number of plausible candidates for such controls. But the one directly relevant in the present context is, of course, the constraint of Cognitive Command, for it was on this that the semantic anti-realist argument pivoted. Let's look at this idea a little more closely. It is a platitude concerning convergence and representation that

> Representationally functioning systems, targeted on the same subject matter, can produce conflicting output only if working on divergent input or if they function less than perfectly.[18]

Now, in any discourse over which truth operates at all, there can be no good objection to its paraphrase in terms of 'fitting the facts',

18. Cf. *ibid.*, p. 146.

'telling it like it is' and so on—but if the discourse exerts cognitive command, then an important analogy is established between the idea of correspondence between statement and world implicitly featured in such talk and the, as I should like to say, more full-blooded use of the notion of representation as it features in the representation platitude. If a discourse exerts cognitive command, that has the effect of 'beefing up' the idea of truth as correspondence in just the kind of realism-relevant way needed. The idea of correspondence to fact takes on a characteristic which minimal truth-aptitude does not impose, but one it had better have if there is to be real substance in the idea that, in using the discourse in ways which respect the standards of assertoric warrant by which it is informed, we function as representational systems, responsive to objective states of affairs which, when we are successful, our beliefs and statements serve to portray.[19]

There is no doubt much about this specific idea, and the general way of thinking about realism/anti-realism debates which it illustrates, which would stand further discussion. But the relevant point for our immediate purpose is that if the misgivings bruited above about fictionalism, expressivism and eliminativism are well founded, then this kind of truth-tolerant approach would seem to represent the only hope for a coherent psychological anti-realism. So we need to consider how good the prospects really are. Let us appropriate the term *minimalism* about an assertoric discourse for the view that it carries, when correctly conceived, no realist aspiration—that its ingredient claims are merely minimally truth-apt and have no further characteristic which should encourage the idea that they are full-fledged representations, or misrepresentations, of aspects of an objective world.[20] The proposal to be reviewed, then, is that the proper

19. *Ibid.*, p. 147.

20. Recall here the idea mooted in section II above that anything worth regarding as a form of psychological anti-realism will involve denial of the reality of psychological states of affairs. If, as just observed, the identification of truth with 'correspondence to fact' is at one level a platitude, then to grant, in a minimalist spirit, that we are justified in taking certain psychological claims to be true is already a commitment

outlet for the psychological non-cognitivist is minimalism. Such a theorist should allow that psychological discourse is genuinely assertoric, highly disciplined and thereby sustains the introduction over its characteristic claims of a predicate with all the essential features of a truth predicate. But she should insist that nothing is true of psychological discourse which should motivate the interpretation of this predicate in terms of the imagery of correspondence to external, objective matters, in the fashion characteristic of realism.

VI

There is one very immediate challenge to the psychological minimalist proposal. Discourses for which minimalism is the correct view ought peacefully to co-exist alongside others which are more realism-apt. Indeed, that is the whole point: ordinary psychology is supposed to be able, on this proposal, to be credited with *literally true* claims without any risk of competition with the truths of physical science, conceived as by realism. The problem is that it is unclear how competition can be avoided so long as ordinary psychology is viewed as making *causal* claims. For then—so it may seem—it enters the territory occupied by physiology and, ultimately, physics. Just this was one of the principal concerns of the metaphysical anti-realist noted at the start of section III. And it is reinforced by the reflection that the causality of the

---

to recognising the existence, in some sense, of psychological states of affairs. The necessary qualification, then, has to be that it is *only* in a platitudinous, metaphysically non-committal sense that an anti-realist may countenance such states of affairs.

In general, once it is granted that 'true' is open to variously more or less robust—that is, realism-implicating—interpretations, the same will go for its cognates 'fact', 'state of affairs', 'correspondence to fact', 'real' and so on; and it will no longer do to identify anti-realism about a discourse with the range of views converging on the simple denial of the reality of the germane kind of states of affairs. What all such views must deny, rather, is their reality in a sense—(not necessarily the same in every case: realism may admit of kinds and degrees)—cognate to a realist interpretation of 'true'.

explanations offered by ordinary psychology is not just an assumption of its critics but, as Davidson and others have argued, is apparently implicit in the very notion of *acting on* a specific set of motives, which seems to be an essential ingredient in ordinary psychological explanation.

The concern is thus that the causality of ordinary psychological explanations requires their hypotheses to carry a content which *already* puts them out of the running for minimalist construal: that there is an objective and at bottom wholly physical causal order in the world and that once a discourse ventures causal claims, it must be entered into the competition for correct depiction of aspects of this causal order and sink or swim accordingly. If certain of its causal claims do indeed depict such aspects, then it is—at least in that respect—providing for the expression of substantial (not minimal) truths; and if none do, then they are not minimally true but substantially false. Minimalism, the contention is, is not an option for theories of the causes of things. So ordinary psychology, to the extent that causal claims are its stock-in-trade, can no more be excused all substantial representational purport than alchemy—and has to be vulnerable, in principle, to the same fate. Again, this is to presuppose a realist—and a monist—view of the causal order. But psychological minimalism will be the more competitive if it can finesse that presupposition.

I shall not here further consider how this concern might be satisfactorily addressed. Certainly it would be very bad news for minimalism generally if any discourse in which prima facie causal claims are to be found is immediately ruled to be outside its compass. Even so intuitively promising a candidate for minimalism as discourse about comedy has its share of prima facie causal claims. Consider, for instance:

> Lord Hailsham 'hogged' the conversation shamelessly but the other Fellows forgave him because he was such an amusing raconteur,

and

> Always remember: audiences like to laugh. They like that better than they like to hate you, even if sometimes they

kinda like that too. So they're on your side, basically.
They'll more than meet you half-way. And all you gotta do
to make them laugh is: be funny.

Similarly causal-seeming claims are commonplace for the boring, obscene and delightful, and for various kinds of value. If minimalism is
ever to be an interesting option, these kinds of claim have to be shown
to allow of interpretation as non-competitive with those of natural
science—and this for reasons other than the presumed reducibility (by
whatever standards) of the distinctive predicates involved to predicates of (physical) nature.

If this cannot be done, minimalism offers no hope after all for a
coherent outlet for anti-realism about psychology—nor indeed for
anti-realism about very much at all. But I am going to assume, purely
for the purposes of the present discussion, that a careful examination
of the prima facie causal-explanatory claims made in discourses, like
those about the comic, obscene and delightful, where minimalism is at
its most attractive, can disclose considerations and distinctions which
will allow such claims *not* to compete with natural-scientific explanations of the phenomena concerned. And I am going to assume that
ordinary psychological explanations turn out to belong on the right
side of those considerations and distinctions, whatever they are. In
this—perhaps quite fictional—setting, psychological minimalism
would indeed seem to present itself as far and away the most promising vehicle for psychological anti-realism. Or are there other draw-
backs to consider?

VII

When minimalism is accepted as a coherent theoretical alternative, a
realist view of a region of discourse may be characterised as any
which holds that, in addition to the syntactic and disciplinary features acknowledged by minimalism, it is proper to think of truth in
the discourse in question in robustly representational terms. So—
according to the understanding of what that comes to with which we

are presently working—a realist will maintain that Cognitive Command holds for that discourse.[21] The argument to be developed now proceeds through two observations. The first is this:

> Thesis 1:
> It is not possible consistently to be a minimalist about intentional states but realist about *linguistic* content— about semantics.

This parallels our earlier observation that a metaphysical anti-realism about intentional states should enjoin to the same attitude to semantics. Then the thought was that linguistic meanings presuppose conventions, and hence intentions and beliefs. The present point is essentially the same, but needs to draw upon a working formulation of the idea of cognitive command. Here is one.

> A discourse exerts cognitive command if and only if it is a priori that any difference of opinion formulated within the discourse, unless excusable as a result of vagueness in a disputed statement, or in the standards of acceptability, or variation in personal evidence thresholds, so to speak, will involve something which may properly be regarded as a cognitive shortcoming.[22]

Thesis 1 requires that to doubt that discourse about intentional psychology exerts cognitive command commits one to doubt whether discourse about semantics does. To see why this is so, suppose we are concerned with an ascription of content to a sentence, of the form:

> S says that P

---

21. Note that it is not being claimed that its exhibition of cognitive command *suffices* for a discourse to be robustly representational: the claim is that cognitive command is a commitment of realism, not that it is constitutive.

22. *Truth and Objectivity*, p. 144.

and assume that such claims exert cognitive command: that it is a priori that, unless vagueness is implicated in one of the ways allowed for, any disagreement about such a statement will involve some form of cognitive shortcoming—some element of ignorance, error or prejudice. Well, it is obvious enough—again, without presupposing the correctness of any broadly Gricean necessary-and-sufficient conditions *analysis* of what it is for an expression to have any particular specific content—that one way in which such a statement may fall into dispute—between a pair of radical interpreters, for instance—is if the disputants have arrived at quite different views about the attitudinal states that tend to provide the stage-setting for uses of S. If, for example, I believe—perhaps for reasons to do with some knowledge of their ancestry and location—that a certain subject is likely to be taboo to a certain tribe, then I may be forced to find a translation for some of their utterances which in the circumstances would otherwise go over quite nicely into statements about that subject. But it may be that you, for your own theoretical reasons, reject the suggestion that the topic in question is held in taboo and are accordingly free to treat the utterances in question as being about it. In such a case, all hands may be able to agree that we are right to hold our respective conflicting interpretations of a particular utterance in the light of our conflicting views about the tribe members' background attitudinal states. So possession of an a priori guarantee that cognitive shortcoming is involved in the semantic dispute will require a similar guarantee concerning our respective parent views about relevant aspects of the speakers' psychology.[23] On the assumption of minimalism about intentional psychology, however, there is no such a priori guarantee that cognitive shortcoming is involved in the conflicting parent views.

That suffices to validate Thesis 1. Minimalism about intentional

---

23. This claim assumes, of course, that their semantic dispute not merely commits the interpreters to the psychological one but wholly turns on—is fully rationalised by—their conflicting beliefs about speakers' attitudes.

psychology—whatever its motivation[24]—must embrace minimalism about semantics as well.[25]

VIII

One consequence of Thesis 1 is that any demonstration of the *incoherence* of minimalism about linguistic content would convert to a refutation of psychological minimalism. Paul Boghossian has offered precisely such a purported demonstration: specifically, an argument to show that minimalism about linguistic content must wind up committed to incompatible claims about the interpretation of the truth predicate.[26] However, subsequent commentary has suggested that

24. This is important. Lemma 1 might seem unsurprising, even obvious, to someone for whom the only envisaged motivation for psychological minimalism specifically concerned psychological *content,* for it is indeed obscure what sort of argument could select for that while leaving linguistic content alone (cf. note 26 below). However, the considerations just sketched are not so specific but would be good—if good at all—if it were, for example, scepticism about the *attitudes* themselves—hope, belief, desire and their kin—rather than their content that drove a psychological minimalist.

25. For complementary considerations in this direction, see Boghossian (1990), pp. 170–3. Boghossian's observation is, more generally, that the characteristic arguments for anti-realism (of whatever stripe) about psychological content—or at least the best of them—all extend undiminished to linguistic content.

26. *Ibid.,* pp. 175–6. To be specific: the *official* target of Boghossian's argument is what he terms a 'non-factualism' about meaning and content generally. There may be significant philosophical differences between non-factualism as Boghossian conceives it and the kind of position I have introduced as minimalism. However, Boghossian's non-factualist grants both that discourse about linguistic content can quite properly assume an assertoric surface, and that a notion of correct assertibility will operate over it. Such is the detail of his argument, that is enough to ensure there is no difference relevant to our purposes between semantic non-factualism as Boghossian conceives it and semantic minimalism—no difference which might enable his argument to succeed against the former but not the latter.

Boghossian's argument will not perform quite as advertised.[27] I will not recapitulate those discussions now.[28] What is germane is rather a corollary of them, which I here elicit in a more direct manner.

We are currently working with a distinction between truth conceived as serious representation—to which a realist about a given range of statements will have them aspire—and a more minimal conception, apt for the purpose of the anti-realist, which will be some form of (tenseless) projection of the standards of acceptability governing those statements and will not sustain the realist's imagery of correspondence, or representation, except in a thin and merely platitudinous sense. Let's accordingly regiment our terminology, reserving 'true' and its cognates for the substantial, realism-importing notion, and 'correct' for the minimal conception. Minimalism about semantics may therefore now be expressed as the view that statements about linguistic content, and all cognate matters, lack truth conditions. Instances of 'S says that P' and 'S means that P', for example, while governed by conditions of correct and incorrect assertion, will not be apt for truth and falsity. Correlatively, realism about a discourse will be the view that its characteristic statements are apt for truth and falsity; or—as I shall sometimes say—that those statements (or the facts they depict) are *robust*.

Even with 'true' and its kin so regimented, to speak of the truth conditions of a sentence (which has truth conditions) is still, arguably, simply a way of talking about that sentence's content—about the kind of content it has and the specific content of that kind. Statements of the form

S has the truth condition that P

27. See, for instance, Kraut (1993), pp. 247–63; the Appendix to chapter 6 of *Truth and Objectivity;* and Wright (1993d). For further discussion, including formal regimentation of Boghossian's argument, see Tennant (1997), chap. 3.

28. For an indication, see note 29 below.

will thus come within the scope of semantic minimalism, which will accordingly be committed to the following:

For all S and P: 'S has the truth condition that P' is not truth conditional

—ascriptions of realist truth conditions are not apt for realist truth and falsity.

But this has a striking implication: that for the minimalist about semantics, the distinction between truth-apt and merely correctness-apt assertoric discourses emerges as one the details of whose extension are not themselves stateable by *truths,* but only permit of *correct* statement. For reflect that, with 'true' and its cognates now importing realism, a statement of the form, 'S has the truth condition that P', is, as it were, Janus-faced, serving simultaneously both to make a semantic claim about the content of S and to classify its subject—the statement S—as robust. So to attempt to hold simultaneously that ascriptions of robustness are themselves robust while ascriptions of content are not would be—when possession of truth conditions is taken as a hallmark of robustness—a direct commitment to contradictory claims.[29]

---

29. It is this point, in effect, which provides the loophole in Boghossian's argument observed in the discussions referred to in note 27. Boghossian notes that his semantic non-factualist is committed both to the *selectivity* of the truth predicate—since, on his characterisation, all non-factualists hold that some target class of significant declarative sentences do not have truth conditions—and to holding that ascriptions of truth denote no real facts (since ascriptions of truth conditions do not, and how could factual matters functionally depend on non-factual ones?). He takes the first point to imply that truth must be a real property (it cannot allow of deflationary construal since not all indicative discourses are apt for it) and the second to imply that it is not a real property (since ascriptions of it are not factual). But the contradiction is arguably an illusion and disappears under disambiguation of 'real property'. In one—we can call it the *anti-deflationary*—sense, 'true' expresses a real property if it is not promiscuous across indicative discourses. In another—the *non-factualist*—sense 'true' expresses a real property if ascriptions of it generate factual claims. Boghossian shows

Really, this is rather obvious. For however exactly the distinction is drawn, which side of the minimal/robust divide a given discourse falls is going to be, in general terms, a function of the *type of content* which its sentences possess. So the minimality of claims which place a discourse to one side or the other of the minimal/robust divide must follow from a general minimalism about matters to do with content. Imagine that a genie fixes all genuine—robust—facts, as it were, but nothing else. If such a determination would leave content undetermined, then it must likewise fail to determine anything which functionally depends on matters to do with content—including the details of the distinction between minimal and robust discourses. So there could be no *truths* about that distinction.

It may be rejoined that this conclusion follows only so far as the *metalinguistic* classification of discourses is concerned. The observation was that claims about the robustness, or minimality of discourses, construed as ranges of *sentences,* cannot themselves be robust if claims about linguistic content are not. But—the rejoinder runs—nothing directly ensues about the robustness of the distinction between the minimal and the robust when it is drawn at the level of the *contents*—propositions, or Fregean thoughts—themselves. It may be a non-robust question whether S has a robust/non-robust subject matter only and precisely because it is a non-robust question what S means. But there simply is no question, robust or otherwise, about what the proposition that P means: a proposition is an entity *already* individuated as a content, and nothing that has been said bears on the question whether there is not a robust distinction among such entities between those which are apt to represent robust facts and those which are not.

---

that, for the content non-factualist, 'true' expresses a real property in the first sense and it fails to express a real property in the second sense. This is, however—at least prima facie—a perfectly consistent combination. Truth and truth-aptitude can be both selective and non-factual. It is that combination that is shown by the argument in the text to be not just a saving option for content non-factualism (minimalism) but actually integral to the view.

The rejoinder is fair, as far as it goes. But it is very difficult to see how semantic descent could make any important difference in this context. Consider any singular judgement of the form: the F is G. If such a judgement is to exert cognitive command, then so must any particular judgement about which object is the F—for manifestly, it cannot be a priori that disagreements about whether the F is G involve cognitive shortcoming unless the same goes for disagreements—which may be the whole source of the former—about which is the object they concern. Accordingly, if while 'S is truth conditional' is granted to be non-robust for the reason given, we try to conceive of 'The proposition that P is truth conditional' as a robust claim, then which entity *is* the proposition that P had better itself be a robust issue: an issue opinions about which exert cognitive command. But propositions, most philosophers would agree, are not entities which allow of linguistically unmediated acquaintance: an opinion about which proposition is the proposition that P can be nothing other than an opinion about what the particular form of words used to raise the issue—the that-clause, 'that P'—should be taken to mean. And the latter, by Thesis 1, is a non-robust matter.

There is more to say about this.[30] But enough has been done to identify a powerful case for Thesis 2:

> Minimalism about semantics enforces minimalism about
> the minimal/robust distinction itself.

IX

Putting Theses 1 and 2 together, the upshot is that the thesis of psychological minimalism is a commitment to its *own* non-robustness, and that any argument for it is consequently an argument for a non-robust conclusion. The psychological minimalist is making a claim

30. For further discussion, see *Truth and Objectivity,* chap. 6.

which she should regard as no more robust than the claims of psychology itself!

Is that necessarily an uncomfortable dialectical situation? One reason for supposing so is that it seems utterly unclear what possible rationale realist/anti-realist debate can have unless we think of it as answerable to *objective* distinctions. Doesn't one have to be a *meta-realist*—that is, to believe that the protagonists in realist/anti-realist debates are disputing a 'real issue': something where there is a metaphysical 'fact of the matter'—before any interest can attach to the question on which half of the distinction ordinary psychology falls? The brisk reply would be that it need no more be a precondition of the interest of debate about realism that one take a realist view of that very debate than it is a precondition of the interest of ethics, or mathematics, or indeed ordinary psychology that one takes a realist view of them. But that reply seems a little *too* brisk in the present instance: there *is* something disorientating about the thought that while there is an intelligible distinction to be drawn between minimal and robust discourses, there are no robust facts about the proper classification of discourses under that distinction.[31] Why would it not just be a charade to traffic in any kind of distinction between the objective and the non-objective if nothing is *objectively* objective? Besides, a fully satisfying development of the minimalist line about ethics, or mathematics and so on, will involve explaining a legitimate role and purpose for such discourses to have, dissociated from the project of representing the world. But what role and purpose might *metaphysics* have if not the attainment of insight and understanding into how things *really* are?—How could those benefits be the product of an enquiry of which one should take an anti-realist view?

So the psychological minimalist's situation is uncomfortable. But that is hardly a decisive objection. A second, more conclusive line of criticism emerges, however, as soon as we consider the implications of the situation for the tenability of psychological minimalism *as an*

31. For forceful expression of a different view, see Kraut (1993).

opinion. Consider any statement for which one has a cogent a priori case. Presumably it will itself be a fact available to pure reflection that one does so, and hence a priori in turn that anyone who does not accept that statement is guilty of cognitive shortcoming. For there are just two possibilities: if they are unaware of the case in question, that is a material piece of ignorance; and if they are not unaware of it, then they are guilty of failing to appreciate its force. Thus any statement which is cogently grounded a priori will be one which exerts cognitive command. Conversely to regard a statement as failing to exert cognitive command is to be committed to regarding it as one for which one has no cogent a priori grounds. But we have just seen that the thesis that psychology is minimal commits a holder to maintaining that it is itself minimal—does not exert cognitive command. So she must also hold that she has no cogent a priori case for it.

Manifestly, that is not a scenario with which any rational psychological minimalist can rest content, since it is tantamount to something akin to Moore's Paradox. A philosophical claim about the robustness or otherwise of a discourse is, like any philosophical claim, *warranted a priori, by philosophical reflection, or by nothing at all.* So a psychological minimalist would appear constrained to concede both that her position admits of no philosophically sufficient support and that it is a view which, if it deserved to be accepted at all, could be so only by the adduction of philosophically sufficient considerations.

It may be objected that this reasoning depends on a quite mythical view of the kind of persuasiveness exerted by typical philosophical argument. Argument for a philosophical view—for instance, for antirealism about ordinary psychology!—is no doubt a priori in some good sense of that term. But in contrast with a mathematical proof, say, philosophical argument need not be such that, if it can be rationally sufficient for a certain view at all, it must be acknowledged as persuasive by any thinker on pain of cognitive shortcoming. The difference is that, unlike a mathematical proof, a good philosophical argument can be *defeasible*—can be rationally persuasive in one informational setting but cease to be so when further considerations are marshalled. Most philosophical arguments make, implicitly or explicitly, assumptions which, for one reason or another, are found attractive; but their attractiveness may wane when certain of their consequences are elicited. Indeed the dialectic of this essay—if sound—may provide an example: the naturalistic doubts about psychological realism, for instance, might justifiably be found quite forceful just so long as one has not yet bothered to enquire exactly what account of psychological discourse they should motivate.

However, it does no harm to grant this. The argument merely has to cover an additional case. The position becomes that, presented with what are, in my informational context, persuasive a priori grounds for a statement, I have to reckon with *three* possibilities where any dissenter is concerned: that she does not know of these grounds; that she knows of them but underestimates them; or that she rightly discounts them in the light of further considerations. If either of the first two possibilities obtains, she is guilty of cognitive shortcoming; and if the third obtains, I am—*qua* ignorant of the further considerations in question. The characteristic defeasibility of most philosophical argument thus poses no threat to the original conclusion, that to possess a rationally sufficient a priori case for minimalism about psychology is to be entitled to regard that thesis as exerting cognitive command.

Is the upshot we have achieved as strong as the result aimed at by Boghossian's argument in "The Status of Content"? Not quite. The conclusion of Boghossian's argument was to be that semantic minimalism is *contradictory*—that it is committed to incompatible claims about the concept of truth. This would go for psychological minimalism as well if Thesis 1 is correct. The present argument, by contrast, is that the thesis of psychological minimalism is *rationally untenable*— that it is inconsistent with its own philosophical warrantability. For it entails (via Theses 1 and 2) its own non-robustness; whereas the existence of philosophically (hence a priori) sufficient grounds for a thesis entails its exertion of cognitive command. This is a weaker conclusion than Boghossian's; untenability, it hardly needs saying, is consistent with truth. But it is dialectically devastating for psychological mini-malism all the same.

X

Our question has been: What positive account should an anti-realist offer of the status and character of ordinary psychological discourse? Boghossian divided the options into essentially two: error theory and non-factualism. I have suggested we need to distinguish four: ex-pressivism, eliminativism and fictionalism—each of which might belong with a metaphysical anti-realist motivation—and in addition, minimalism, which goes naturally with a non-cognitivist motivation (though that might encourage expressivist proposals as well). Each of the four, however, has given rise to antinomy. Expressivism about any discourse needs illocutionary distinctions whose characterisation, it would seem, must draw on the *statement* of features of speakers' characteristic attitudes (the ones they are characteristically 'express-ing' in that discourse). Fictionalism about any discourse needs the reality of the attitudinal state of working with a (disbelieved) fiction. Eliminativism about psychology is in unresolved difficulty over the circumscription of the discourse to be eliminated and, even more seri-ously, over its right to the notions of truth and falsity—and can accordingly offer at present no reason to believe in its own very for-mulability. And psychological minimalism, finally, relatively attrac-tive as it may be, has emerged as no better than the others; for it follows from its truth that it admits of no cogent philosophical sup-port and hence is strictly rationally untenable.

So—unless some further, quite novel anti-realist paradigm is pro-posed, distinct from these four—we seem to have psychological anti-realism penned within a complete ring-fence of aporia. A resourceful friend of psychological anti-realism will no doubt identify places at which pressure may be put on the fence. But enough has been done to substantiate my original claim: the arguments of the sceptics about ordinary psychology, whatever credibility they may seem to have, have nowhere—or anyway nowhere obvious—to lead.

But I must end on a cautionary note. These considerations, even if they prove to stand the closest scrutiny, are not of the right kind, properly understood, to make a case for realism as the *metaphysical truth* about ordinary psychology. What they collectively tend to show is rather that there can be no rationally compelling argument for psychological anti-realism, in any of its usual guises. That need not be the same thing. For one thing, there may be unforeseen guises. But even if not, the considerations marshalled tend to establish—if correct—not the reality of ordinary psychological categories but that an acquiescence in ordinary psychology is a *commitment* of fictionalist, expressivist and eliminativist positions about *any* region of thought; and that the belief that support for a minimalist position can be rationally cogent anywhere is a *commitment* to regarding psychological discourse as robust. The effect of our arguments is thus that ordinary psychology has a kind of diplomatic immunity in realist versus anti-realist debate, at least as conducted in any familiar form. They drive a conclusion about the *investment* in ordinary psychological discourse to which the various anti-realist paradigms are committed, not one about the soundness of that investment. That, and more generally the significance of the dialectical situation that has emerged, is a further matter, for further consideration.

The foregoing essay pursues a line of enquiry pursuant and complementary to that of Paul Boghossian's "The Status of Content" (Boghossian 1990)—the first sustained discussion known to me of the general issue of the possible varieties, best formulation and dialectical stability of anti-realist views of content. While Boghossian focused on linguistic rather than psychological content, and the overview of the possible positions that his paper utilised is significantly qualified and extended in my discussion, it is appropriate to register a special acknowledgement to it.

The argument of this essay has been leisurely in arriving at its present form. A first version of it was presented at a Birkbeck College reading party held at Cumberland

Response-Dependence and Cognitive Command

Lodge in May 1993. It developed through presentations at the SOFIA conference in Lisbon in 1994, at the Cincinnati conference on Significance in Semantics in the same year, and at subsequent colloquia at Durham, Birmingham, the Irish Philosophical Society, Kings College London, MIT, Ohio State, the conference Being Committed at St. Andrews and a Summer School at Parma in the summer of 2000 and, most recently, at the New York University Mind and Language seminar in spring 2001. My thanks to the discussants on all those occasions and especially to Paul Boghossian, Bob Brandom, John Campbell, Jim Edwards, Bob Hale, Paul Horwich, Christopher Peacocke and Barry C. Smith.

15

On Being in a Quandary: Relativism, Vagueness, Logical Revisionism

In this essay, I shall propose a unified treatment of three prima facie unrelated problems. Two are very well known. One is the challenge of providing an account of vagueness which avoids the Sorites paradox. This has been discussed almost to tedium, but with the achievement, it is fair to say, of increasing variety rather than convergence in the proffered solutions.[1] Another is the problem of formulating a coherent relativism (in the sense germane to matters of taste, value and so on). This is also well known, although it has had rather less intense recent attention; part of my project in what follows (section I) is to recommend a view about what the real difficulty is. But the third problem—an awkward-looking wrinkle in the standard kind of case for revision of classical logic first propounded by the intuitionists and generalised in the work of Michael Dummett—has, I think, not been widely perceived at all, either by revisionists[2] or their conservative opponents.[3]

---

1. I am afraid that the direction of the present treatment will be to add to the variety. My hope is that it will draw additional credibility from its association with resources to treat the other problems.

2. Henceforward, I restrict 'revisionism' and its cognates to the specific form of logical revisionism canvassed by the intuitionists and their 'anti-realist' descendants.

3. An insightful exception to this general myopia is Salerno (2000).

The link connecting the problems, according to the diagnosis here entertained, runs via the notion of *indeterminacy*. Specifically: I propose and commend a—broadly epistemic—conception of what (at least in a very wide class of cases) indeterminacy *is* which not merely explains how vagueness does *not* ground the truth of the major premises in Sorites paradoxes but also assists with the question of what form an interesting relativism (whether global or restricted to a local subject matter) may best assume, and helps to bring out what the basic intuitionistic—'anti-realist'—misgiving about classical logic really is. Though differing in at least one—very significant—respect from the conception of indeterminacy defended in the writings of Timothy Williamson, Roy Sorensen and other supporters of the so-called Epistemic Conception of vagueness,[4] I doubt if it would have occurred to me to explore the ensuing proposal without their precedent. Indeed, a second important subproject of the discussion to follow is indirectly to make a case that the Epistemicists[5] have hold of an insight which may be detached from the extreme and, for many, bizarre-seeming metaphysical realism which—with their own encouragement—is usually regarded as of the essence of their view.

This essay is in eight sections. I–III lay out the problems in the order indicated in the subtitle; IV–VI then take them in the reverse order and develop the advertised uniform treatment. VII comments on the relation of the proposal to the Epistemic Conception of vagueness. VIII is a concluding summary.

---

4. See Sorensen (1998), pp. 199–253; Williamson (1992a) and (1994a). The Epistemic view receives earlier sympathetic treatment in Cargile (1969) and (1979), section 36, and Campbell (1974), and is briefly endorsed in Horwich (1998a), p. 81. For further references, see Williamson (1994a), p. 300, n. 1.

5. I capitalise 'Epistemicist', 'Epistemicism' and so on whenever referring to views which, like those of Sorensen and Williamson, combine a conception of vagueness as, broadly, a matter of ignorance with the retention of classical logic and its associated bivalent metaphysics.

On Being in a Quandary

I. RELATIVISM

§1. Let me begin with a reminder of the crude but intuitive distinction from which the relativistic impulse springs. Any of the following claims would be likely to find both supporters and dissenters:

> That snails are delicious
> That cockroaches are disgusting
> That marital infidelity is alright provided nobody gets hurt
> That a Pacific sunset trumps any Impressionist canvas

and perhaps

> That Philosophy is pointless if it is not widely intelligible
> That the belief that there is life elsewhere in the universe is justified
> That death is nothing to fear

Disputes about such claims may or may not involve quite strongly held convictions and attitudes. Sometimes they may be tractable disputes: there may be some other matter about which one of the disputing parties is mistaken or ignorant, where such a mistake or ignorance can perhaps be easily remedied, with the result of a change of heart about the original claim; or there may be a type of experience of which one of the disputing parties is innocent, and such that the effect of initiation into that experience is, once again, a change of view. But there seems no reason why that should have to be the way of it. Such a dispute might persist even though there seemed to be nothing else relevant to it about which either party was ignorant or mistaken, nor any range of relevant experience which either was missing. The details of how that might happen—how the dispute might be *intransigent*—vary with the examples. But in a wide class of cases, it would likely be a matter of one disputant placing a value on something with which the other could not be brought to sympathise; or with her being prone to an emotional or other affect which the other did not share; or with basic differences of propensity to belief, perhaps associated with the kinds of personal probability thresholds which show up in such phenomena as variations in agents' degrees of risk aversion.

Intuitively, claims of the above kinds—potentially giving rise to what we may call *disputes of inclination*—contrast with claims like these:

That the snails eaten in France are not found in Scotland
That cockroaches feed only on decomposing organic matter
That extramarital affairs sometimes support a marriage
That sunset tonight will be at 7:31 P.M.
That there are fewer professional analytical philosophers than there were
That there are living organisms elsewhere in the solar system
That infant mortality was significantly higher in Victorian times than in Roman.

Any of these might in easily imaginable circumstances come into dispute, and in some cases at least we can imagine such disputes being hard to resolve. Relevant data might be hard to come by in some cases, and there are also material vaguenesses involved in most of the examples, on which a difference of opinion might turn. Then there is the possibility of prejudice, ignorance, mistake, delusion and so on which in certain circumstances—perhaps far-fetched—it might be difficult to correct. However, what does not seem readily foreseeable is that we might reach a point when we would feel the disputants should just 'agree to differ', as it were, without imputation of fault on either side. Opinions about such matters are not to be exculpated, to use a currently modish term, by factors of personal inclination, but have to answer to—it is almost irresistible to say—*the facts*.

This crude but intuitive distinction—disputes of inclination versus disputes of fact—immediately gives rise to a problem. Both types of dispute are focused on straightforward-seeming, indicative contents. But all such contents are naturally treated as truth-evaluable, and truth, one naturally thinks, is a matter of fit with the facts. So the very form of disputes of inclination seems tailor-made to encourage the idea that they are disputes of fact after all: disputes in which, *ceteris paribus,* someone is out of touch with how matters really stand. The problem is therefore: how to characterise disputes of inclination in such a way as to conserve the species, to disclose some point to the lay-philosophical intuition that there are such things at all, genuinely contrasting with—what one's characterisation had better correlatively explain—disputes about the facts.

§2. So far as I can see, there are exactly four broadly distinguishable types of possible response:

(i) *Rampant realism* denies that the illustrated distinction has anything to do with non-factuality. For rampant realism, the surface form of disputes of inclination has precisely the significance just adumbrated: such disputes *do* centre on truth-evaluable contents, and truth *is* indeed a matter of fit with the facts. So, even in a radically intransigent dispute of inclination, there will, *ceteris paribus,* be a fact of the matter which one of the parties will be getting wrong. It may be that we haven't the slightest idea how a particular such dispute might in principle be settled, and that if charged to explain it, we would hesitate to assign any role to ignorance, or prejudice, or mistake, or vagueness. These facts, however, so far from encouraging relativism, are best attributed to the imperfection of our grasp of the type of subject matter which the dispute really concerns.

I mean this option to be parallel in important respects to the Epistemic Conception of vagueness. The Epistemicist holds that vague expressions like 'red', 'bald' and 'thin' actually denote properties of perfectly definite extension. But we do not (or, in some versions, cannot) know which properties these are—our concepts of them, fixed by our manifest understanding of the relevant expressions, fail fully to disclose their nature. There is thus a quite straightforward sense in which when I say that something is, for instance, red, I (necessarily) imperfectly understand what I have said.[6] Clearly there is space for a

---

6. Experience shows that Epistemicists incline to protest at this. Suppose 'tall', say, as a predicate of human beings, applies to an individual just if they are precisely 5'11" tall or more—that *5'11" tall or more* is the property actually denoted by the vague

similar view about the subject matter of a dispute of inclination. It can happen that we express a concept by 'delicious' which presents a property whose nature it fails (fully) to disclose. This property may or may not apply to culinary snails. There is no way of knowing who is right in the dispute, but somebody will be. At any rate, the issue is no less factual than that of whether culinary snails are indigenous to Scotland.

I do not propose to discuss the rampant realist proposal in any detail here. No doubt a fuller discussion of it would recapitulate many of the moves and counter-moves made in the recent debates about the Epistemic Conception of vagueness. Still, there are some interesting, foreseeably additional issues. Here are three:

First, is there any principled ground whereby a theorist might propose an Epistemicist treatment of vagueness but refuse to go rampant realist over what we are loosely characterising as matters of inclination?

Second, can a rampant realist treatment of matters of inclination match the conservatism of the Epistemic Conception of vagueness? The Epistemicist does not, properly understood, *deny* there is any

---

'tall', so used. Then why, in saying that an individual is tall, should I be regarded as understanding what I have said to any lesser an extent than when, in circumstances where I do not know the identity of the culprit, I say that whoever broke the clock had better own up? Why should ignorance of what, in fact, I am talking *about* be described as an imperfection of *understanding*?

Although it is not my purpose here to develop criticisms of the Epistemic Conception, I'll take a moment to try to justify the charge. The foregoing protest assumes that the Epistemicist is entitled to regard us as knowing what *type* of sharply bounded property an understood vague expression denotes, and as ignorant only of *which* property of that type its use ascribes. I know of no justification for that assumption. What type of sharply bounded property does 'red' denote? Something physical? Or a manifest but sharply bounded segment of the 'colour wheel'? Or something else again? On what basis might one decide? And if the understanding of some common-or-garden vague expressions gives rise to no favoured intuitive *type* of candidate for their putative definitely bounded denotations, why should we favour the obvious candidates in cases—like 'tall'—where there are such?

Intuitively, to understand a simple, subject–predicate sentence, say, is to know what object is being talked about and what property is being ascribed to it. To be sure,

such thing as vagueness; rather, she attempts a distinctive account, in epistemic terms, of what vagueness consists in. A similar account would be desirable, if the approach is to be extended to matters of inclination, of what it is that really distinguishes them from those matters which the opposing, mistaken view takes to be the only genuinely factual ones. A satisfying account must somehow *save* the crude and intuitive distinction, rather than merely obliterate it.

Third, the question arises whether rampant realism can be reconciled with the good standing of our ordinary practice of the discourses in question. If irremediable ignorance—for instance, a gulf between our concept of the property denoted by 'delicious' and the nature of that property—is at work in disputes of inclination, one might wonder with what right we take it that there is no serious doubt in cases where there is *consensus* that the property applies. Of course, the same issue arises for Epistemicist treatments of vagueness: if we don't know enough about the sharply bounded property we denote by 'red' to be sure where its boundaries lie, what reason do we have to think we haven't *already* crossed those boundaries in cases where we are

the purport of that slogan should not be taken to require that one invariably has an *identifying* knowledge of the former: I can fully understand an utterance of 'Smith's murderer is insane' without knowing who the murderer is. But it is different with predication. Here what is demanded of one who understands is, at least in the overwhelming majority of cases, that they know—*in a sense parallel to the possession of identifying knowledge of the referent of a singular term*—what property the use of a particular predicate ascribes. Since the overwhelming majority of natural language predicates are vague, that is what the Epistemicist denies us. It would be no good for her to reply: 'But you *do* know what property "red" denotes—it is the property of being red!' On the Epistemic account, I know neither which property that is, nor what type of property it is, nor even—in contrast to, say, my understanding of '. . . has Alex's favourite property' where while ignorant in both those ways, I at least know what a property has to do in order to fit the bill—what would make it true that a particular property was indeed ascribed by the normal predicative use of 'red'. It is the last point that justifies the remark in the text; if you were comparably ignorant in all three respects about the content of a definite description—thus ignorant, in particular, of what condition its bearer, if any, would have to meet—it would be absolutely proper to describe you as failing fully to understand it.

agreed that something is red? However, the problem may be a little more awkward for an epistemic treatment of matters of inclination. For the Epistemicist can presumably rejoin that however the reference of 'red' is fixed, a good account will constrain the word to refer to a property which does at least apply to the paradigms, on which we concur. The possible awkwardness for the extended, rampant realist view is that there are not, in the same way, *paradigms* for many of the examples of matters of inclination. That is: there are shades of colour that must be classified as red on pain of perceptual or conceptual incompetence, but there are no tastes that *must* similarly be classified as delicious. If matters of inclination—for instance, of gastronomic taste—even where not contested in fact, are as a class *essentially contestable,* at least in principle, without incompetence, then in contrast with the situation of 'red' and vague expressions generally, there would seem to be no clear candidates for the *partial* extensions that a competitive account of the reference of the distinctive vocabulary—'delicious', 'oversalted' and so on—might plausibly be required to conserve.

(ii) The second possible response to the problem of characterising disputes of inclination is that of *indexical relativism.* On this view, truth-conditional contents are indeed involved in 'disputes' of inclination, but actually there are no *real disputes* involved. Rather, the seemingly conflicting views involve implicit reference to differing standards of assessment, or other contextual parameters, in a way that allows both disputants to be speaking the literal truth. Snails are delicious *for you*—for someone with your gastronomic susceptibilities and propensities—but they are not delicious *for me*—for one whose culinary taste is as mine is. Hurt-free infidelities can be acceptable to you—perhaps to anyone inclined to judge the moral worth of an action by its pleasurable or painful effects alone—but they are not acceptable to me—to one inclined to value openness and integrity in close personal relationships for its own sake, irrespective of any independently beneficial or harmful consequences.

This, very familiar kind of relativistic move is still supported in recent philosophy—for instance by Gilbert Harman, on morals.[7] Its obvious drawback is that it seems destined to misrepresent the manner in which, at least as ordinarily understood, the contents in question embed under operations like the conditional and negation. If it were right, there would be an analogy between disputes of inclination and the 'dispute' between one who says 'I am tired' and her companion who replies, 'Well, I am not' (when what is at issue is one more museum visit). There are the materials here, perhaps, for a (further) disagreement but no disagreement has yet been expressed. But ordinary understanding already hears a disagreement between one who asserts that hurt-free infidelity is acceptable and one who asserts that it is not. And it finds a distinction between the denial that hurt-free infidelity is acceptable and the denial that it is generally acceptable by the standards employed by someone who has just asserted that it is acceptable. Yet for the indexical relativist, the latter should be the proper form of explicit denial of the former. In the same way, the ordinary understanding finds a distinction between the usual understanding of the conditional, that if hurt-free infidelity is acceptable, so are hurt-free broken promises, and the same sentence taken on the understanding that both antecedent and consequent are to be assessed relative to some one particular framework of standards (that of an actual assertor of the sentence, a framework which might or might not treat infidelity and promise-breaking in different ways).

Of course there is room for skirmishing here, some of it no doubt quite intricate. But it is not clear that we should expect that indexical relativism can save enough of the standard practice of discourses within which disputes of inclination may arise to avoid the charge that it has simply missed their subject matter.

(iii) The third possible response to the problem of characterising disputes of inclination is that of *expressivism*: the denial that the discourses

---

7. Harman has been, of course, a long-standing champion of the idea. The most recent extended defence of his views is in Harman and Thomson (1996), part 1. For many-handed discussion, see Harman, Thomson et al. (1998).

in question genuinely deal in truth-conditional contents at all. Of course, on this view there are, again, no real *disputes* of inclination at all—merely differences of attitude, feeling and reaction. There has been a significant amount of recent discussion of this kind of approach, stimulated by the sophisticated versions of it proposed by writers such as Simon Blackburn and Alan Gibbard.[8] But it confronts a very general dilemma. What is to be the expressivist account of the propositional—seemingly truth-conditional—surface of the relevant discourses? The clean response is to argue that it is misleading—that what is conveyed by discourse about the delicious, the morally acceptable or whatever this kind of view is being proposed about, can and may be better expressed by a regimented discourse in which the impression that truth-conditional contents are being considered, and denied, or hypothesised, or believed, and so on is analysed away. However, it seems fair to say that no one knows how to accomplish this relatively technical project, with grave difficulties in particular attending any attempt to reconstruct the normal apparatus of moral argument in such a way as to dispel all appearance that it moves among truth-evaluable moral contents.[9] The alternative is to allow that the propositional surface of moral discourse, to stay with that case, can actually comfortably consist with there being no genuinely truth-conditional contents at issue, no genuine moral beliefs, no genuine moral arguments construed as movements from possible beliefs to possible beliefs and so on. But now the danger is that the position merely becomes a terminological variant for the fourth response, about to be described, with terms like 'true' and 'belief' subjected to a (pointless) high redefinition by expressivism, but with no substantial difference otherwise.

(iv) Of the options so far reviewed, the first allows that a dispute of

---

8. Blackburn (1984), chap. 6: "Evaluations, Projections and Quasi-realism", still remains the best introduction to his view, but the most recent official incarnation is Blackburn (1998a); Alan Gibbard's ideas are developed systematically in the magisterial Gibbard (1990).

9. For exposition and development of some of the basic difficulties, see Hale (1986), (1992), and (2002).

inclination is a real dispute, but at the cost of conceding that one of the disputants will be undetectably wrong about a subject matter of which both have an essentially imperfect conception, while the other two options deny, in their respective ways, that there is any genuine dispute at all. The remaining option—I'll call it *true relativism*—must, it would seem, be the attempt to maintain that, while such disputes may indeed concern a common truth-evaluable claim, and thus may be genuine—may involve incompatible views about it—there need be nothing about which either disputant is mistaken, nor any imperfection in their grasp of what it is that is in dispute. Opinions held in disputes of inclination may, in particular cases, be flawed in various ways. But in the best case, the true relativist thought will be, such a dispute may oppose two opinions with which there is no fault to be found, even in principle, save by invocation of the idea that there is an ulterior, undecidable fact of the matter about which someone is mistaken. That hypothesis, distinctive of the first option, is exactly what true relativism rejects: for true relativism, genuinely conflicting opinions about a truth-evaluable claim may each be unimprovable and may involve no misrepresentation of any further fact.

§3. In the light of the shortcomings, briefly noted, of the three available alternatives—and because it has, I think, some claim to be closest to the common-sense view of the status of disputes of inclination—it is of central importance to determine whether the materials can be made out for a stable and coherent true relativism. In *Truth and Objectivity*, I proposed—without, I think, ever using the word 'relativism'—a framework one intended effect of which was to be just that. The key was the contrast between areas of discourse which, as it is there expressed, would be merely *minimally truth-apt*, and areas of discourse where, in addition, differences of opinion would be subject to the constraint of *Cognitive Command*.

The idea that there are merely minimally truth-apt discourses comprises two contentions, about truth and aptitude for truth respectively. The relevant—minimalist—view about truth, in briefest summary, is that all it takes in order for a predicate to qualify as a truth predicate is its satisfaction of each of a basic set of platitudes about truth: for instance, that to assert is to present as true, that statements which are apt for truth have negations which are likewise, that truth is one thing, justification another and so on.[10] The view about *truth-aptitude,* likewise in briefest summary, itself comprises two contentions:

> first, that any discourse dealing in assertoric contents will permit the definition upon its sentences of a predicate

10. A fuller list might include:

the transparency of truth—that to assert is to present as true and, more generally, that any attitude to a proposition is an attitude to its truth—that to believe, doubt or fear, for example, that P is to believe, doubt or fear that P is true *(Transparency)*

the opacity of truth—incorporating a variety of weaker and stronger principles: that a thinker may be so situated that a particular truth is beyond her ken, that some truths may never be known, that some truths may be unknowable in principle and so on *(Opacity)*

the conservation of truth-aptitude under embedding: aptitude for truth is preserved under a variety of operations—in particular, truth-apt propositions have negations, conjunctions, disjunctions and so on which are likewise truth-apt *(Embedding)*

the Correspondence Platitude—for a proposition to be true is for it to correspond to reality, accurately reflect how matters stand, 'tell it like it is' and so on *(Correspondence)*

the contrast of truth with justification—a proposition may be true without being justified, and vice versa *(Contrast)*

the timelessness of truth—if a proposition is ever true, then it always is, so that whatever may, at any particular time, be truly asserted may—perhaps by appropriate transformations of mood, or tense—be truly asserted at any time *(Timelessness)*

that truth is absolute—there is, strictly, no such thing as a proposition's being more or less true; propositions are completely true if true at all *(Absoluteness)*

The list might be enlarged, and some of these principles may anyway seem controversial. Moreover it can be argued that the Equivalence Schema underlies not merely the first of the platitudes listed—Transparency—but the Correspondence and Contrast Platitudes as well. For elaboration of this claim, see Truth and Objectivity pp. 24–7. For further discussion of the minimalist conception, and adjacent issues, see Wright (1998a).

which qualifies as a truth predicate in the light of the
minimalist proposal about truth;

and

that a discourse should be reckoned to deal with suitable
such contents just in case its ingredient sentences are
subject to certain minimal constraints of *syntax*—
embeddability within negation, the conditional, contexts
of propositional attitude, and so on—and *discipline:* their
use must be governed by commonly acknowledged
standards of warrant.

A properly detailed working out of these ideas[11] would foreseeably
have the effect that almost all the areas of discourse which someone
intuitively sympathetic to the 'crude but intuitive' distinction might
want to view as hostage to potential disputes of inclination will turn
out to deal in contents which, when the disciplinary standards proper
to the discourse are satisfied, a supporter is going to be entitled to
claim to be true. That, however—the proposal is—ought to be consistent with the discourse in question failing to meet certain further conditions necessary to justify the idea that, in the case of such a dispute,
there will be a further fact in virtue of which one of the disputants is
in error.

What kind of condition? The leading idea of someone—the *factualist*—who believes that a given discourse deals in matters of fact—
unless she thinks that its truths lie beyond our ken—is that soberly
and responsibly to practise that discourse is to enter into a kind of
representational mode of cognitive function, comparable in relevant
respects to taking a photograph or making a wax impression of a key.
The factualist conceives that certain matters stand thus and so independently of us and our practice—matters comparable to the photographed scene and the contours of the key. We then engage in the

11. A partial development of them is offered in *Truth and Objectivity,* chaps. 1–2.

appropriate investigative activity—putting ourselves at the mercy of the standards of belief formation and appraisal appropriate to the discourse in question (compare taking the photograph or impressing the key on the wax)—and the result is to leave an imprint in our minds which, in the best case, appropriately matches the independently standing fact.

This kind of thinking, while doubtless pretty vague and metaphorical, does have certain quite definite obligations. If we take photographs of one and the same scene which somehow turn out to represent it in incompatible ways, there has to have been some kind of shortcoming in the function of one (or both) of the cameras, or in the way it was used. If the wax impressions we take of a single key turn out to be of such a shape that no one key can fit them both, then again there has to have been some fault in the way one of us went about it, or in the materials used. The tariff for taking the idea of representation in the serious way the factualist wants to is that when subjects' 'representations' prove to conflict, then there has to have been something amiss with the way they were arrived at or with their vehicle—the wax, the camera or the thinker.

That's the key thought behind the idea of cognitive command. The final formulation offered in *Truth and Objectivity* was that a discourse exerts cognitive command just in case it meets this condition:

> It is a priori that differences of opinion formulated within [that] discourse, unless excusable as a result of vagueness in a disputed statement, or in the standards of acceptability, or variation in personal evidence thresholds, so to speak, will involve something which may properly be regarded as a cognitive shortcoming.[12]

To stress: the constraint is motivated, in the fashion just sketched, by the thought that it, or something like it, is a commitment of anyone who thinks that the responsible formation of opinions expressible within the discourse is an exercise in the *representation* of self-standing facts.

12. *Truth and Objectivity*, p. 144.

Conversely: any suggestion that conflicts in such opinions can be *cognitively blameless,* yet no vagueness be involved of any of the three kinds provided for in the formulation, is a suggestion that the factualist—seriously representational—view of the discourse in question is in error. Broadly, then, the implicit suggestion of *Truth and Objectivity* was that true relativism about a particular discourse may be formulated as the view that, while qualifying as minimally truth-apt, it fails to exhibit cognitive command.

§4. However there is an awkwardness to be confronted by any proposal of this general kind. The key to true relativism, as we have it so far, is somehow to make out that a discourse deals in contents which are simultaneously truth-apt yet such that, when they fall into dispute, there need in principle be nothing wrong with—nothing to choose between—the disputed opinions. But in granting that the contents in question are minimally truth-apt, the relativist allows, presumably, that they are subject to ordinary propositional-logical reasoning. So, where P is any matter of inclination which comes into dispute between a thinker A, who accepts it, and a thinker B, who does not, what is wrong with the following *Simple Deduction?*

1	(1) A accepts P	Assumption
2	(2) B accepts not P	Assumption
3	(3) A's and B's disagreement involves no cognitive shortcoming	Assumption
4	(4) P	Assumption
2, 4	(5) B is guilty of a mistake, hence of cognitive shortcoming	2, 4
2, 3	(6) Not P	4, 5, 3 RAA
1, 2, 3	(7) A is guilty of a mistake, hence of cognitive shortcoming	4
1,2,	(8) Not (3)	3, 3, 7 RAA

The Simple Deduction seems to show that whenever there is a difference of opinion on *any*—even a merely minimally—truth-apt claim, there *is*—quite trivially—a cognitive shortcoming, something to choose between the views. And since this has been proved a priori, cognitive command holds for all truth-apt discourses. So the alleged gap between minimal truth-aptitude and Cognitive Command, fundamental to the programme of *Truth and Objectivity*, disappears.

Obviously there has to be *something* off-colour about this argument. So much is immediately clear from the reflection that the disagreement it concerns could have been about some borderline case of a *vague* predicate: nothing that happens in the Simple Deduction is sensitive to the attempt made in the formulation of cognitive command to exempt disagreements which are owing to vagueness (one way or another). Yet the Deduction would have it that even these too must involve cognitive shortcoming. And the notion of shortcoming involved is merely that of bare *error*—mismatch between belief and truth value. So if the argument shows anything, it would appear to show a priori that any difference of opinion about a borderline case of a vague predicate will also involve a mismatch between belief (or unbelief) and actual truth value. It would therefore seem that there has to *be* a truth value in all such cases, even if we have not the slightest idea how it might be determined. We appear to have been saddled with the Epistemic Conception! I believe that means, with all due deference to the proponents of that view, that the Simple Deduction proves too much.[13]

13. It may be rejoined (and was, by Mark Sainsbury, in correspondence) that we could accept the Simple Deduction without commitment to the stark bivalence espoused by the Epistemic Conception if we are prepared to allow that A's and B's respective opinions may indeed both reflect cognitive shortcoming where P's truth status is borderline—on the ground that, in such circumstances, both ought to be *agnostic* about P. The point is fair, as far as it goes, against the gist of the preceding paragraph in the text. However, I believe—and this will be a central plank of the discussion to follow—that it is a profound mistake to regard positive or negative verdicts about borderline cases as *eo ipso* defective. If that were right, a borderline case of P should simply rank as a special kind of case in which—because things are *other than P*

So where does it go wrong? It may be felt that the trouble lies with an overly limited conception of 'cognitive shortcoming'. The considerations used to motivate the Cognitive Command constraint—the comparison with the idea of representation at work in the examples of the photograph or the wax impression—license something richer: a notion of cognitive shortcoming that corresponds to failure or limitation of process, mechanism or materials, and not merely a mismatch between the product and its object. Of the two cameras that produce divergent—conflicting—representations of the same scene, one or both must have functioned less than perfectly, not merely in the sense that one (or both) gives out an inaccurate snapshot but in the sense that there must be some independent defect, or limitation, in the process whereby the snapshot was produced. So too, it may be suggested, with cognitive command: the motivated requirement is that differences of opinion in regions of genuinely representational discourse should involve imperfections of *pedigree:* shortcomings in the manner in which one or more of the opinions involved were arrived at, of a kind that might be appreciated as such independently of any imperfection in the result. Once shortcoming in that richer sense is required, it can no longer be sufficient for its occurrence merely that a pair of parties disagree—it needs to be ensured in addition that their disagreement betrays something amiss in the way their respective views were arrived at, some independently appreciable failure in the

---

says—its negation ought to hold. In any case the Simple Deduction will run no less effectively if what B accepts is not 'Not P' when understood narrowly, as holding only in *some* types of case where P fails to hold, but rather as holding in *all* kinds of case where things are not as described by P—*all* kinds of ways in which P can fail of truth, including being borderline (if, *contra* my remark above, that is how being borderline is conceived). So even if bivalence is rejected, the Simple Deduction still seems to commit us to the more general principle Dummett once called *Determinacy:* that P always has a determinate *truth status*—of which Truth and Falsity may be only two among more than two possibilities—and that at least one of any pair of conflicting opinions about P must involve a mistake about this status, whatever it is. That is still absolutely in keeping with the realist spirit of the Epistemic Conception, to which it still appears—at least in spirit—the Simple Deduction commits us if unchallenged.

representational mechanisms. That, it may be felt, is what the cognitive command constraint should be understood as driving at.

Such an emended understanding of cognitive shortcoming is indeed in keeping with the general motivation of the constraint. But it does not get to the root of our present difficulties. For one thing, the Simple Deduction would still run if we dropped all reference to cognitive shortcoming—thereby finessing the issue of how that notion should be understood—and replaced line 3 with

(3*) A's and B's disagreement involves no *mistake*.

The resulting reasoning shows—if anything—that any pair of conflicting claims involves a mistake. If it is sound, there just isn't any fourth, that is, true-relativistic response to the original problem. To suppose that P is merely minimally truth-apt in the sense of allowing of hypothesis, significant negation and embedding within propositional attitudes is already, apparently, a commitment to rampant realism. Surely that cannot be right. But the modified deduction, with (3*) replacing (3), shows that refining the idea of cognitive shortcoming in the manner just indicated has nothing to contribute to the task of explaining why not.

Perhaps more important, however, is the fact that we can run an argument to much the same effect as the (unamended) Simple Deduction even when 'cognitive shortcoming' *is* explicitly understood in the more demanding sense latterly proposed.[14] One reason why rampant realism is unattractive is because by insisting on a fact of the matter to determine the rights and wrongs of any dispute of inclination, no matter how intransigent, it is forced to introduce the idea of a truth-making state of affairs of which we have a necessarily imperfect concept,[15] and whose obtaining, or not, thus necessarily transcends our powers of competent assessment. This is unattractive in direct proportion to the attraction of the idea that, in discourses of the relevant

14. This point was first made in Shapiro and Taschek (1996).
15. See note 6 above.

kind, we are dealing with matters which essentially *cannot* outrun our appreciation: that there is no way in which something can be delicious, or disgusting, or funny, or obscene and so on without being appreciable as such by an appropriately situated human subject because these matters are, in some very general way, constitutively dependent upon *us*. What we—most of us—find it natural to think is that disputes of inclination typically arise in cases where *were* there a 'fact of the matter', it would have to be possible—because of this constitutive dependence—for the protagonists to know of it. Indeed, the ordinary idea that such disputes need concern no fact of the matter is just a modus tollens on that conditional: were there a fact of the matter, the disputants should be able to achieve consensus about it; but it seems manifest in the character of their disagreement that they cannot; so there isn't any fact of the matter. So for all—or at least for a wide class of cases—of claims, P, apt to figure in a dispute of inclination, it will seem acceptable—and the recoil from rampant realism will provide additional pressure—to hold to the following principle of *evidential constraint* (EC):

P → it is feasible to know that P[16]

and to hold that the acceptability of this principle is a priori,[17] dic-

---

16. One substitution instance, of course, is

Not P → it is feasible to know that not P.

17. To forestall confusion, let me quickly address the quite natural thought that, where EC applies, Cognitive Command should be assured—since any difference of opinion will concern a knowable matter—and hence that any reason to doubt cognitive command for a given discourse should raise a doubt about EC too. This, if correct, would certainly augur badly for any attempt to locate disputes of inclination within discourses where Cognitive Command failed but EC held! But it is not correct. What the holding of EC for a discourse ensures is, just as stated, that each of the conditionals

P → it is feasible to know that P
Not P → it is feasible to know that not P

tated by our concept of the subject matter involved.[18]

Consider, then, the following *EC-deduction:*

1	(1)	A believes P, B believes not P, and neither has any cognitive shortcoming	Assumption
2	(2)	P	Assumption
2	(3)	It is feasible to know that P	2, EC
1, 2	(4)	B believes the negation of something feasibly knowable	1, 3
1, 2	(5)	B has a cognitive shortcoming	4
1	(6)	Not P	2, 1, 5 RAA
1	(7)	It is feasible to know that not P	6, EC
1	(8)	A believes the negation of something feasibly knowable	1, 7
1	(9)	A has a cognitive shortcoming	8
	(10)	Not (1)	1, 1, 9 RAA

This time 'cognitive shortcoming', it is perhaps superfluous to remark, must involve less than ideal procedure, and not just error in the end product, since it involves mistakes about feasibly knowable matters.

---

is good for each proposition P expressible in that discourse. That would ensure that any difference of opinion about P would concern a knowable matter, and hence involve cognitive shortcoming, only if in any such dispute it would have to be determinate that one of P or not P would hold. But of course it is of the essence of (true) relativism to reject precisely that—and to do so for reasons unconnected with any vagueness in the proposition that P.

18. The modality involved in *feasible knowledge* is to be understood, of course, as constrained by the distribution of truth values in the actual world. The proposition that, as I write this, I am in Australia is one which it is merely (logically or conceptually) possible to know—the possible world in question is one in which the proposition in question is true, and someone is appropriately placed to recognise its being so. By contrast, the range of what it is feasible for us to know goes no further than what is actually the case: we are talking about those propositions whose actual truth could be recognised by the implementation of some humanly feasible process. (Of course there are further parameters—recognisable when? Where? Under what if any sort of idealisation of our actual powers? and so on.—But these are not relevant to present concerns.)

So: it seems that 1 and EC are inconsistent, that is, evidential constraint is incompatible with the possibility of cognitively blameless disagreement. If the EC-deduction is sound, then it seems that wherever EC is a priori, Cognitive Command is met. And it is plausible that EC *will* be a priori at least for large classes of the types of claim—par excellence simple predications of concepts like *delicious*—where relativism is intuitively at its most attractive, and where a gap between minimal truth-aptitude and cognitive command is accordingly called for if we are to sustain the *Truth and Objectivity* proposal about how relativism should best be understood.[19]

§5. What other objection might be made to either deduction? Notice that there is no assumption of bivalence in either argument; both can be run in an intuitionistic logic. But one might wonder about the role of *reductio* in the two proofs. For instance, at line 6 in the Simple Deduction, the assumption of P having run into trouble, RAA allows us to infer that its negation holds. Yet surely, in any context where we are trying seriously to make sense of the idea that there may be 'no fact of the matter', we must look askance at any rule of inference which lets us advance to the negation of a proposition just on the ground that its assumption has run into trouble. More specifically: in any circumstances where it is a possibility that a proposition's failing to hold may be a reflection merely of there being no 'fact of the matter', its so failing has surely to be distinguished from its negation's holding.

Natural though the thought is, it is not clear that there is much mileage in it. Let's make it a bit more specific.[20] The idea is best treated,

19. To stress: it is not merely *Truth and Objectivity*'s implicit proposal about *relativism* that is put in jeopardy by the EC-deduction. According to the project of that book, Cognitive Command is a significant watershed but is assured for all discourses where epistemic constraint fails and realism, in Dummett's sense, is the appropriate view. Thus if the EC-deduction were to succeed, Cognitive Command would hold universally and thus fail to mark a realism-relevant crux at all.

20. I draw here on a suggestion of Patrick Greenough.

we may take it, as involving restriction of the right-to-left direction of the *Negation Equivalence,*

$$T–P \rightarrow –TP,$$

expressing the commutativity of the operators 'it is true that' and 'it is not the case that'. In circumstances where there is no fact of the matter whether or not P, it will be the case both that –TP and –T–P. The proper conclusion, on the assumptions in question, of the *reductio* at line 6 of the Simple Deduction is thus not that the negation of P holds, but merely that it is not the case that P is true. And from this, since it is consistent with there being 'no fact of the matter' whether or not P, we may not infer (at line 7) that A is guilty of any mistake in accepting P. Or so, anyway, the idea has to be.

Rejecting the Negation Equivalence has repercussions, of course, for the Equivalence Schema itself:

$$TP \leftrightarrow P$$

since one would have to reject the ingredient conditional

$$P \rightarrow TP.^{21}$$

That flies in the face of what would seem to be an absolutely basic and constitutive property of the notion of truth, that P and TP are, as it were, *attitudinally equivalent*: that any attitude to the proposition that P—belief, hope, doubt, desire, fear and so on—is equivalent to the same attitude to its truth. For if that's accepted, and if it is granted that any reservation about a conditional has to involve the taking of some kind of differential attitudes to its antecedent and consequent, then there simply can be no coherent reservation about P → TP.

A more direct way of making essentially the same point is this. At line 6 of each deduction, even with RAA modified as proposed, we

---

21. There will be no cause to question the converse conditional, which is needed for the derivation of the uncontroversial T–P → –TP.

are entitled to infer that it is not the case that P is true. By hypothesis, however, A accepts P. Therefore unless that somehow does fall short of an acceptance that P is true, A is guilty of a mistake in any case. But how could someone accept P without commitment to its truth?

Indeed, there is a residual difficulty with this whole tendency, independent of issues to do with the attitudinal transparency of truth. Simply conceived, the mooted response to the two deductions is trying to make out/exploit the idea that A and B may each be neither right nor wrong because there is 'no fact of the matter', where this is conceived as a *third possibility*, contrasting with either A's or B's being right. That idea may well demand some restriction on the form of *reductio* utilised in the two deductions. But the problem they are bringing to light will persist even after the restriction. For the simple fact now seems to be that A is taking matters to be one way, and B is taking them to be another, when in truth they are *neither*—when, precisely, a third possibility obtains. In that case there is indeed nothing to choose between A's and B's respective views, but only because they are both equally *off-beam*. We achieve the parity between their views essential to any satisfactory working out of a true relativism only by placing them in *parity of disesteem*. This general point—broadly, the intuitive inadequacy of 'third possibility' approaches to the construal of indeterminacy—will recur in the sequel.

So, that's the first of the three problems which I want to work towards a unified approach to: it is the problem of stabilising the contrast between minimal truth-aptitude and cognitive command or, more generally, the problem of showing how there can indeed be a coherent true relativism—a coherent response of the fourth kind to the challenge of providing a proper account of the character of disputes of inclination.

II. THE SORITES

§6. Even after all the attention meted out to it, the simplicity of the Sorites paradox can still seem quite breathtaking. Take any example of the standard sort of series. Let F be the predicate in question. Let x′

be the immediate successor in the series of any of its elements, x. The first element in the series—call it '0'—will be F and the last— 'k'—will be non-F. And of course F will be vague. If it were precise, there would be a determinate cut-off point—a last F-element in the series, immediately succeeded by a first non-F one. It would be true that $(\exists x)(Fx \ \& \ -Fx')$. So since F is vague, that claim is false. And its being false would seem to entail that every F-element is succeeded by *another* F-element: that

$$(\forall x)(Fx \rightarrow Fx').$$

But that is trivially inconsistent with the data that F0 and that not-Fk.

What is startling is that it is, seemingly, child's play to replicate this structure with respect to almost every predicate that we understand; and that the motivation for the troublesome major premise—

$$(\forall x)(Fx \rightarrow Fx')$$

—seems to flow directly just from the very datum that F is vague, that is, from the denial that it is precise. Again: if $(\exists x)(Fx \ \& \ -Fx')$ just *says*—falsely—that F is precise in the relevant series, then surely its (classical) contradictory, $(\forall x)(Fx \rightarrow Fx')$, just says—*truly*—that F is vague. But it was given that F0 and that not-Fk. Seemingly incontrovertible premises emerge—extremely simply, if a little long-windedly— as incompatible. Vague predicates, in their very nature, seemingly have all-inclusive extensions.

§7. Hilary Putnam once suggested that an intuitionistic approach might assist.[22] How exactly? Not, anyway, by so restricting the underlying logic that the paradox cannot be derived.[23] It is true that it takes classical logic to motivate the major premise, $(\forall x)(Fx \rightarrow Fx')$, on the

22. See Putnam (1983b), pp. 271–86.
23. I do not suggest that Putnam was under any illusion about this.

basis of denial of the *unpalatable existential,* $(\exists x)(Fx \ \& \ -Fx')$. But the paradox could as well proceed directly from that denial:

$$-(\exists x)(Fx \ \& \ -Fx')$$

in intuitionistic logic. To be sure, we cannot then reason intuitionistically from F0 to Fk. (To do so would require double-negation elimination steps.) But we can still run the Sorites reasoning *backwards,* from not-Fk to not-F(0), using just n applications of an appropriate subroutine of conjunction and existential introduction and RAA. So what profit in intuitionism here?

Putnam's thought is best taken to have been that there is no option but to regard the major premises,

$$-(\exists x)(Fx \ \& \ -Fx')$$

or

$$(\forall x)(Fx \rightarrow Fx'),$$

as reduced to absurdity by the paradox, and that we are therefore constrained to accept their respective negations,

$$- -(\exists x)(Fx \ \& \ -Fx')$$

and

$$-(\forall x)(Fx \rightarrow Fx')$$

as demonstrated. The advantage secured by an intuitionistic framework is then that, lacking double-negation elimination,[24] we are not thereby constrained to accept the *unpalatable existential:*

$$(\exists x)(Fx \ \& \ -Fx').$$

24. And also the classical rule, $- (\forall x)(\ldots x \ldots) \Rightarrow (\exists x) - (\ldots x \ldots)$, in consequence.

So we can treat the Sorites reasoning as a straightforward *reductio* of its major premise without thereby seemingly being forced into denying the very datum of the problem, namely, that F is vague.

The trouble is that this suggestion, so far, deals with only half the problem. Avoiding the unpalatable existential is a good thing, no doubt. Yet equally we have to explain what is wrong with its denial. And does not recognition of the vagueness of F in the relevant series precisely *enforce* that denial? Does not the vagueness of F just *consist in* the fact that no particular claim of the form Fa & –Fa′ is true? And is not the problem compounded by the fact that the usual style of anti-realist/intuitionist semantics will require us to regard recognition that nothing could justify such a claim as itself a conclusive reason for denying each particular instance of it for the series in question? It is true that intuitionistic resources would avoid the need to treat the Sorites reasoning as a proof of the unpalatable existential claim. But that thought goes no way to explaining how to resist its *negation,* which seems to be both an apt characteristic expression of F's vagueness and mandated by intuitionist style-semantics in any case. And to stress: the negation leads straight to the paradox, whether our logic is classical or intuitionist.[25]

This brings out sharply what I regard as the most natural perspective on what a solution to the Sorites has to accomplish. Since the reasoning *is* a *reductio* of the major premise, we have to recognise that

$$- -(\exists x)(Fx \ \& \ -Fx')$$

is true. So we need to understand

(i)   how the falsity of $-(\exists x)(Fx \ \& \ -Fx')$ can be consistent with the vagueness of F; and

(ii) how and why it can be a principled response to refuse to let

$$- -(\exists x)(Fx \ \& \ -Fx')$$

25. Cf. Read and Wright (1985).

constitute a commitment to the unpalatable existential, and hence—apparently—to the precision of F.[26]

III. REVISIONISM

§8. It is generally though not universally assumed among interested philosophers that anti-realism in something close to Dummett's sense—the adoption of an evidentially constrained notion of truth as central in the theory of meaning—should lead to revisions in classical logic. But why? Truth plays a role in the standard semantical justification for classical logic. Persuasion that truth is essentially—or locally—evidentially constrained might thus lead to (local) dissatisfaction with classical *semantics*—and hence with the standard justification for classical logic. But why should that enjoin dissatisfaction with the logic itself? There would seem to be an assumption at work that classical logic needs its classical justification. But maybe it might be justified in some other way. Or maybe it needs no semantical justification at all.[27] Is there a revisionary argument that finesses this apparent lacuna?

Here is one such proposal—I'll call it the *Basic Revisionary Argument*—advanced by myself.[28] Assume the discourse in question is one for which we have no guarantee of decidability: we do not know that it is feasible, for each of its statements P, to come to know P or to come to know not P. Thus this principle holds

$$(\text{NKD}) \ -K \ [(\forall P)(FeasK[P] \lor FeasK[-P])].$$

---

26. This perspective is not mandatory, of course. In particular, it will not appeal to any dyed-in-the-wool classicists. Supervaluationist and Epistemicist approaches try, in their different ways, to allow us the unpalatable existential while mitigating its unpalatability. But those are not the approaches followed here.

27. I pursued these doubts about Dummett's revisionary line of thought in Wright (1993b), pp. 433–57.

28. Cf. *Truth and Objectivity*, pp. 37–44.

Then given that we also accept

(EC) P → *Feas*K[P]

—any truth of the discourse in question may feasibly be known—
we get into difficulty if we also allow as valid

(LEM) P ∨ –P.

For LEM and EC sustain simple reasoning to the conclusion that any
P is such that either it or its negation may feasibly be known.[29] If we
know that both LEM and EC are good, this reasoning presumably
allows us to know that, for each P, *Feas*K[P] ∨ *Feas*K[–P]. But that
knowledge is inconsistent with NKD. Thus it cannot stably be supposed that each of EC, LEM and NKD is known. Anti-realism supposes that EC is known a priori, and NKD seems incontrovertible (for
doesn't it merely acknowledge that, relative to extant means of decision, not all statements are decidable?). So the anti-realist must suppose that LEM is not known—agnosticism about it is mandated so
long as we know that we don't know that it is feasible to decide any
significant statement. Since logic has no business containing first principles that are uncertain, classical logic is unacceptable in our present
state of information.

---

29. For a reason to emerge in note 30 below, we should formulate the reasoning as
follows:

LEM	(i)	P ∨ –P	
EC	(ii)	P → *Feas*K[P]	
	(iii)	*Feas*K[P] → (*Feas*K[P] ∨ *Feas*K[–P])	
EC	(iv)	P → (*Feas*K[P] ∨ *Feas*K[–P])	(ii), (iii)
EC	(v)	–P → *Feas*K[–P]	
	(vi)	*Feas*K[–P] → (*Feas*K[P] ∨ *Feas*K[–P])	
EC	(vii)	–P → (*Feas*K[P] ∨ *Feas*K[–P])	(vi), (vii)
LEM, EC	(viii)	*Feas*K[P] ∨ *Feas*K[–P]	(i), (iv), (vii) disjunction elimination

Of course, there are *three* possible responses to the situation: to deny, with the anti-realist, that LEM is known; to deny, with the realist, that EC is known; or to accept the reasoning as a proof that NKD is after all wrong. The last might be reasonable if one had provided consistent and simultaneous motivation for LEM and EC. But it is not a reasonable reaction when the grounds—if any—offered for LEM presuppose an evidentially unconstrained notion of truth (or at least have not been seen to be compatible with evidential constraint).

Note that provided disjunction sustains reasoning by cases, it is LEM—the *logical law*—that is the proper target of the argument, not just the semantic principle of bivalence. (And reasoning by cases would be sustained in the relevant case if, for example, the semantics was standard-supervaluational, rather than bivalence-based.)[30] So this really is an argument for suspension of classical *logic,* not just classical semantics.

---

30. Actually, as Tim Williamson has reminded me, this point depends on how reasoning by cases (disjunction elimination) is formulated. If 'P∨Q' is supertrue and so is each of the conditionals, 'P → R' and 'Q → R', then so is R. That is ungainsayable, and enough to sustain the proof in note 29 above and the letter of the argument of the text, that one who believes that EC and NKD are each known should be agnostic about LEM. However, reasoning by cases fails from the supervaluational perspective if the required auxiliary lemmas take the form

$P \vdash R, Q \vdash R,$

rather than the form

$\vdash P \to R, \vdash Q \to R.$

A counter-example would be the invalidity of the inference from 'P ∨ –P' to 'Definitely P ∨ Definitely –P', notwithstanding the validity of each of

$P \vdash$ Definitely P,

and

$–P \vdash$ Definitely –P.

From the supervaluational perspective, we lose the inference from

$P \vdash$ Definitely P

Note too that the argument is for *not endorsing* LEM in our present state of information. It is not an argument that the law allows counter-examples—that it is *false*. That view is indeed inconsistent with the most elementary properties of negation and disjunction, which entail the *double negation* of any instance of LEM.[31]

§9. But there is a problem—the advertised 'awkward wrinkle'—with the Basic Revisionary Argument: what justifies NKD? It may seem just obvious that we do not know that it is feasible to decide any significant question. (What about vagueness, backwards light cones, quantum mechanics, Goldbach, the Continuum Hypothesis and so on?) But for the anti-realist, though not for the realist, this modesty needs to be able to stand alongside our putative knowledge of EC. And there is a doubt about the stability of that combination.

To see the worry, ask: What does it take *in general* to justify the claim that a certain statement is not known? The following seems a natural *principle of agnosticism*:

(AG) P should be regarded as unknown just in case there is some possibility Q such that if it obtained, it would ensure not P, and such that we are (warranted in thinking that we are) in no position to exclude Q.[32]

---

to

$\vdash P \rightarrow$ Definitely P,

so that the premises for the form of disjunction elimination that is supervaluationally sound are unavailable in the particular instance. Cf. Williamson (1994a), p. 152; Fine (1975), p. 290.

31. Here is the simplest proof. Suppose $-(P \vee -P)$. And now additionally suppose P. Then $P \vee -P$ by disjunction introduction—contradiction. So $-P$, by *reductio*. But then $P \vee -P$ again by disjunction introduction. So $--(P \vee -P)$. This proof is, of course, intuitionistically valid.

32. If 'are in no position to exclude' means 'do not know that not', then of course this principle uses the notion it constrains—but that is not to say that it is not a correct constraint.

Admirers of 'relevant alternatives' approaches to knowledge may demur at the

If AG is good, then justification of NKD will call for a Q such that, were Q to obtain, it would ensure that

$$-(\forall P)(FeasK[P] \lor FeasK[-P]).$$

And now the problem is simply that it would then follow that there is some statement such that neither it nor its negation is feasibly knowable—which in turn, in the presence of EC, entails a contradiction. So given EC, there can be no such appropriate Q.[33] So given EC and AG, there can be no justifying NKD. Thus the intuitive justification for NKD is, seemingly, not available to the anti-realist.

§10. There is a response to the problem which I believe we should reject. What NKD says is that it is not known that *all* statements are such that either they or their negations may feasibly be known. So an AG-informed justification of NKD will indeed call for a Q such that, if Q holds, *not all* statements, P, are such that $(FeasK[P] \lor FeasK[-P])$. But the advertised contradiction is in effect derived from the supposition that *some particular* P is such that $-(FeasK[P] \lor FeasK[-P])$. So to refer that contradiction back to the above, we need the step from $-(\forall P)(\,.\,.\,P\,.\,.\,)$ to $(\exists P)-(\,.\,.\,P\,.\,.\,)$—a step which is, of course, not generally intuitionistically valid. In other words: provided the background logic is intuitionistic, no difficulty has yet been disclosed for the idea that there are grounds for NKD which are consistent with AG.

The trouble with this, of course, is that we precisely may not take it that the background logic *is* (already) intuitionistic; rather the context is one in which we are seeking to capture an argument to the effect that it *ought* to be (at least to the extent that LEM is not unrestrictedly acceptable). Obviously we cannot just help ourselves to distinctively intuitionistic restrictions in the attempt to stabilise the argument if the argument is exactly intended to motivate such restrictions.

---

generality of AG as formulated; but it will make no difference to the point to follow if 'there is some possibility Q' is replaced by 'there is some *epistemically relevant* possibility Q', or indeed any other restriction.

33. Epistemically relevant or otherwise.

A better response will have to improve on the principle AG. Specifically it will need to argue that it is not in general necessary, in order for a claim of ignorance whether P to be justified, that we (recognise that we) are in no position to exclude circumstances Q under which not P would be true—that, at least in certain cases, it is possible to be in position to exclude any such Q while *still* not knowing or being warranted in accepting P.

And of course it is actually obvious that the intuitionist/anti-realist needs such an improved account in any case. For while the right-hand side of AG is presumably uncontentious as a *sufficient* condition for ignorance, it cannot possibly give an acceptable *necessary* condition in any context in which it is contemplated that the *double negation of P may not suffice for P.* In any such case, we may indeed be in a position to rule out any Q sufficing for not P, yet still not in a position to affirm P. What the anti-realist needs, then, is a conception of *another* sufficient condition for ignorance which a thinker can meet even when in position to exclude the negation of a target proposition. And that there is this type of sufficient condition needs to be appreciable independently and—since we are seeking this in order to refurbish an argument for revising classical logic—in advance of an endorsement of any broadly intuitionistic understanding of the logical constants.

Is there any such alternative principle of ignorance? Our third problem[34] is the challenge to make out that there is and thereby to stabilise the Basic Revisionary Argument.

IV. REVISIONISM SAVED

§11. I shall work on the problems in reverse order. To begin with, then, how might AG fail—how might someone reasonably be regarded as ignorant of the truth of a proposition who rightly considered that they were in a position to exclude (any proposition entailing) its negation?

---

34. Of course, friends of classical logic are not likely to perceive this as a *problem.*

A suggestive thought is that a relevant shortcoming of AG is immediate if we reflect upon examples of indeterminacy.[35] Suppose we take the simplest possible view of indeterminacy—what I will call the *third possibility view*: that indeterminacy consists/results in some kind of status other than truth and falsity—a *lack* of truth value, perhaps, or the possession of some other truth value. Then it is obvious—at least on one construal of negation, when not P is true just when P is false—how being in position to exclude the negation of a statement need not suffice for knowledge of that statement. For excluding the negation would leave open *two* possibilities: that P is true and that it is indeterminate—that it lacks, or has a third, truth value. Hence if that were the way to conceive of indeterminacy, we should want to replace AG with, as a first stab, something like:

(AG*) P should be regarded as unknown just in case *either* there is some possibility Q such that if it obtained, it would ensure not P, and such that we are (warranted in thinking that we are) in no position to exclude Q *or* P is recognised, in context, to be indeterminate.

This (in one form or another very widespread)[36] conception of indeterminacy is, however, in my view *un premier pas fatal*. It is quite unsatisfactory in general to represent *in*determinacy as any kind of

35. Under this heading I mean at this point to include both linguistic vagueness—the phenomenon, whether semantic, or epistemic or however it should be understood, which is associated with the Sorites paradox—and also indeterminacy *in re*, as might be exhibited by quantum phenomena, for instance, or the future behaviour of any genuinely indeterministic physical system.

36. It is a common assumption, for instance, both of any supervaluational theorist of vagueness who accepts it as part of the necessary background for a supervaluational treatment that vague statements give rise to a class of cases in which we may stipulate that they are true, or that they are false, without (implicit) reclassification of any case in which they would actually be true, or false; and of defenders of degree-theoretic approaches (in accepting that there are statements which are neither wholly true nor wholly false).

determinate truth status—any kind of middle situation, contrasting with both the poles (truth and falsity)—since one cannot thereby do justice to the absolutely basic datum that in general borderline cases come across as *hard cases:* as cases where we are baffled to choose between conflicting verdicts about *which polar verdict applies,* rather than as cases which we recognise as enjoying a status inconsistent with both. Sure, sometimes people may non-interactively agree—that is, agree without any sociological evidence about other verdicts—that a shade of colour, say, is indeterminate;[37] but more often—and more basically—the indeterminacy will be initially manifest not in (relatively confident) verdicts of indeterminacy but in (hesitant) differences of opinion (either between subjects at a given time or within a single subject's opinions at different times) about a polar verdict, which we have no idea how to settle—and which, therefore, we do not recognise as wrong.

In any case, even if indeterminacy is taken to be third-possibility indeterminacy, AG* is indistinguishable from AG in the present dialectical setting. The standard anti-realist/intuitionist semantics for negation will have it that P's negation is warranted/known just when the claim is warranted/known that no warrant for/knowledge of P can be achieved.[38] It follows that for the intuitionist/anti-realist, *recognisable* third-possibility indeterminacy would be a situation where the negation of the relevant statement should be regarded as holding and is hence no ground for agnosticism about anything. (*Unrecognisable* third-possibility indeterminacy, for its part, would be a solecism in any case, in the presence of EC for the discourse in question.)

§12. A better conception of indeterminacy will allow that it is not in general a determinate situation and that indeterminacy about which statement, P or its negation, is true, is not to be conceived as a situation in which neither is. The latter consideration actually enjoins the former.

---

37. Though I do not think it is clear what is the *content* of such an agreement.

38. This account of negation is actually enforced by EC and the Disquotational Scheme—see *Truth and Objectivity,* chap. 2.

For to comply with the latter, indeterminacy has to be compatible both with P and with its negation being true and clearly no determinate truth status can be so compatible: if it is a truth-conferrer for either, it is inconsistent with the other; if it is a truth-conferrer for neither, then neither is true and contradictions result (at least in the presence of the Disquotational Scheme). To reject the third-possibility view is thus to reject the idea that in viewing the question, whether P, as indeterminate, one takes a view with any direct bearing on the question of the truth value of P. I know no way of making that idea intelligible except by construing indeterminacy as some kind of *epistemic* status.

To accept this view—I shall call it the *quandary view*—is, emphatically, less than to subscribe to the Epistemic Conception of vagueness, according to which vague expressions do actually possess sharp, albeit unknowable limits of extension. But it is to agree with it this far: that the root characterisation of indeterminacy will be by reference to *ignorance*—to the idea, as a starting characterisation, of cases where we do not know, do not know how we might come to know, and can produce no reason for thinking that there is any way of coming to know what to say or think, or who has the better of a difference of opinion.[39] The crucial question how a quandary view of indeterminacy

---

39. All three clauses are active in the characterisation. If a subject does not know the answer to a question nor have any conception of how it might be decided, she is not thereby automatically bereft of any ground for thinking it decidable. One such ground might be to advert to experts presumed to be in position to resolve such a question. Another might be some general reason to think that such questions were decidable, even while lacking any specific idea of how. Neither will be available in the range of cases on which we shall shortly focus—simple predications of colour of surfaces open to view in good conditions. A difference of descriptive inclination in such a case among otherwise competent and properly functioning subjects is not open to adjudication by experts, nor do we have any general reason to think that the issue must be adjudicable in principle, in a way beyond our present ken. To be sure, we are forced to say so if we cling to the law of excluded middle while retaining the belief that these predications are subject to EC. But then—again—we owe a ground for LEM consistent with that belief.

I shall add a fourth clause in due course.

---

can avoid becoming a version of the Epistemic Conception will exercise us in due course.

How does AG look in the context of the quandary view? Consider for P a borderline-case predication of 'red'. The materials about it which the quandary view, as so far characterised, gives us are that we do not know, do not know how we might come to know, and can produce no reason for thinking that there is any way of coming to know whether the item in question is correctly described as 'red'. Now if what we are seeking to understand—in our attempt to improve on AG—is how someone could remain ignorant of the correctness of this predication who already knew that no Q inconsistent with it was true, then clearly the quandary view helps not at all. For if I knew that no Q entailing not P was true, that would surely be to *resolve* the indeterminacy, since it would rule out the case of not P and—on the quandary view, though not the third-possibility view—no other case than P is then provided for. If all I am given is, not some additional possibility *besides* P and not P, but merely that I do not know, and do not know how to know, and can produce no reason for thinking that there is any way of coming to know which of them obtains, then there seems to be no obstacle to the thought that to learn that one does *not* obtain would be to learn that the other does.

§13. The situation interestingly changes, however, when we consider not simple indeterminate predications like 'x is red' but *compounds* of such indeterminate components, as conceived under the quandary view. In particular the Basic Revisionary Argument, that LEM is not known to hold in general, arguably becomes quite compelling when applied to instances of that principle whose disjuncts are simple ascriptions of colour to surfaces in plain view. It is a feature of the ordinary concept of colour that colours are *transparent* under suitable conditions of observation: that if a surface is red, it—or a physical duplicate[40]—will appear

---

40. The complication is to accommodate 'altering'—the phenomenon whereby implementing the very conditions which would normally best serve the observation of something's colour might, in special cases, actually change it. Rapid-action chameleons would be an example.

as such when observed under suitable conditions; *mutatis mutandis* if it is not red. Colour properties have essentially to do with how things visually appear and their instantiations, when they are instantiated, may always in principle be detected by our finding that they do indeed present appropriate visual appearances. So, according to our ordinary thinking about colour—though not of course that of defenders of the Epistemic Conception—EC is inescapable in this setting: when x is any coloured surface in plain view under what are known to be good conditions, each of the conditionals

If x is red, that may be known

and

If it is not the case that x is red, that may be known

is known.

Now EC for redness, so formulated, would of course be inconsistent with recognisable *third-possibility* indeterminacy: with our recognition, of a particular such x, that it could not be known to be red and could not be known not to be red. But it is perfectly consistent with our recognition merely that among some such possible predications, there will be a range where we do not know, and do not know how we might come to know, and can produce no reason for thinking that there is any way of coming to know whether the objects in question are red or not—it is only knowledge that we *cannot* know that is foreclosed. (If we could know that we couldn't know, then we would know that someone who took a view, however tentative—say that x was red—was wrong to do so. But we do *not* know that they are wrong—the indeterminacy precisely leaves it open.) The key question is therefore the status of NKD as applied to these predications: the thesis that the disjunction, that it is feasible to know P or feasible to know not P, is not known to hold for all P in the range in question. Sure, in the presence of EC, it cannot be that—so we cannot know that—*neither* disjunct is good in a particular case; that's the point just reemphasised. But we surely do know of suitable particular instances—particular sample surfaces, in good view—that we do not know, and do not know how we might know, and can produce no reason for thinking that there is any way of coming to know what it is correct to say of their colour or who has the better of a dispute. And it may therefore seem plain that, the contradictoriness of its negation notwithstanding, we are thus in no position to affirm of such an instance, x, that the disjunction, that either it is feasible to know that x is red or it is feasible to know that it is not the case that x is red, may be known. Since LEM, in the presence of EC, entails that disjunction, it follows—granted that there is a compelling case for EC over the relevant subject matter—that we should not regard LEM as known.

§14. But there is a lacuna in this reasoning. An awkward customer may choose to query the passage from the compound ignorance described by the three conditions on quandary to the conclusion that we do not know the target disjunction, that either it is feasible to know that x is red or it is feasible to know that it is not the case that x is red. Suppose I do not know, and do not know how I might know, and can produce no reason for thinking that there is any way of coming to know that P; likewise for not P. Then I might—loosely—describe myself as not knowing, and not knowing how I might know, and able to produce no reason for thinking that there is any way of coming to know what it is correct to think about P or who has the better of a dispute about it. Still, might I not have all those three levels of ignorance and still know that it is the case *either that P is knowable or that its negation is?* For not knowing what it is correct to think about P might naturally be taken as consisting in the conjunction: not knowing that it is correct to think P *and* not knowing that it is correct to think not P; likewise not knowing who has the better of a difference of opinion about P might be taken as the conjunction: not knowing that the proponent of P has the better of it *and* not knowing that the proponent of not P has the better of it. And all that, of course, would still be consistent with knowing that there *is* a correct verdict—that *someone* has the better of the dispute.

The objection, then, is that it does not strictly follow from the too-informal characterisation offered of quandary that if 'x is red' presents a quandary, then we have no warrant for the disjunction

*Feas*K[x is red] ∨ *Feas*K[it is not the case that x is red].

All that follows, the awkward customer is pointing out, is that we are, as it were, thrice unwarranted in holding either disjunct. To say that someone does not know whether A or B is ambiguous. Weakly interpreted, it implies, in a context in which it is assumed that A or B is true, that the subject does not know which. Strongly interpreted, it implies that the subject does not know that the disjunction holds. The objection is that we have illicitly mixed this distinction: that to suggest that to treat borderline cases of colour predicates as quandaries enjoins a reservation about the displayed disjunction is to confuse it. It is uncontentious that such examples may be quandaries if that is taken merely to involve ignorance construed as an analogue of the weak interpretation of ignorance whether A or B. But to run the Basic Revisionary Argument, a case needs to be made that borderline cases of colour predicates present quandaries in a sense involving ignorance under the strong interpretation. What is that case?

A first rejoinder would be to challenge the objector to say, in the examples that concern us, what if any ground we possess for the claim that our ignorance *goes no further* than the weak interpretation—what residual ground, that is, when x is a borderline case of 'red', do we have for thinking that the disjunction

*Feas*K[x is red] ∨ *Feas*K[it is not the case that x is red]

is warranted? It will not do, to stress, to cite its derivation from EC and classical logic—not before a motivation for classical logic is disclosed consistent with EC. Yet no other answer comes to mind.

However a second, decisive consideration is to hand if I am right in thinking that the kind of quandary presented in borderline cases has so far been underdescribed. As stressed, it is crucial to the conception of indeterminacy being proposed that someone who takes a (presumably tentative) view for or against the characterisability of such a case as 'red' is *not known to be wrong*. But that is consistent with allowing that it is also not known whether knowledge, one way or the other, about the redness of the particular case is even *metaphysically possible*—whether there is metaphysical space, so to speak, for such an opinion to constitute knowledge. I suggest that we should acknowledge that borderline cases do present such a fourth level of ignorance: that, when a difference of opinion about a borderline case occurs, one who feels that she has no basis to take sides should not stop short of acknowledging that she has no basis to think that anything amounting to knowledge about the case is metaphysically provided for. And if that is right, then there cannot be any residual ground for regarding the above disjunction as warranted. The strong interpretation of our ignorance whether it is feasible to know that x is red or feasible to know that it is not the case that x is red, is enforced.

§15. Let's take stock. Our project was to try to understand how it might be justifiable to refuse to endorse a claim in a context in which we could nevertheless exclude the truth of its negation. For the case of simple predications of colour on surfaces open to view in good conditions, the situation is seemingly this:

(i) that what I termed the transparency of colour enjoins acceptance of EC, in the form of the two ingredient conditionals given above;

(ii) that we know that there is a range of such predications where we do not know nor have any idea how we might come to know whether or not they are correct, and moreover where we can produce no independent reason for thinking that there must be a way of knowing, or even reason to think that knowledge is metaphysically possible.

Nevertheless,

> (iii) we have a perfectly general disproof of the negation of LEM. (See note 31 above.)

If we now essay to view the latter as a proof of LEM, something will have to give: either we must reject the idea that even simple colour predications obey EC—specifically its two ingredient conditionals—and so reject the transparency of colour, or we must repudiate (ii), treating the putative proof of LEM precisely as a ground for the claim that there must be a way of adjudicating all borderline colour predications. But, again, it just seems plain that the proof does not show *that;* what it shows is merely that denial of the law cannot consistently be accommodated alongside the ordinary rules for disjunction and *reductio ad absurdum.* The move to 'So one of the disjuncts must be knowably true' should seem like a complete *non sequitur.*

If that is right, then one who accepts both the transparency of colour and that borderline cases present quandaries as most recently characterised must consider that there is no warrant for LEM as applied to colour predications generally—even though the negation of any instance of it may be disproved—and hence that double-negation elimination is likewise without warrant. Thus there *has* to be a solution to the problem the intuitionist has with the Basic Revisionary Argument if it is ever right to accept EC for a given class of vague judgements and simultaneously allow that some of them present quandaries. And the solution must consist in the disclosure of a better principle of ignorance than AG.

§16. Does the example of colour guide us towards a formulation of such a principle? According to AG it is necessary and sufficient for a thinker's ignorance of P that there be some circumstances Q such that if Q obtained, not P would be true and such that the thinker has no warrant to exclude Q. The improved principle the anti-realist needs will allow this to be a sufficient condition, but will disallow it as

necessary. Here is a first approximation. Consider any compound statement, A, whose truth requires that (some of) its constituents have a specific distribution of truth values or one of a range of such specific distributions. And let the constituents in question be subject to EC. Then[41]

(AG⁺) A is known only if there is an assurance that a suitably matching distribution of evidence for (or against) its (relevant) constituents may feasibly be acquired.[42]

A purported warrant for a compound statement meeting the two stated conditions thus has to ground the belief that some appropriate pattern of evidence may be disclosed for its constituents. In particular, nothing is a basis for knowledge of a disjunction which does not ensure that at least one of the disjuncts passes the evidential constraint in its own right. More generally, when the truth of any class of statements is evidentially constrained, knowledge of statements compounded out of them has to be conservative with respect to the feasibility of appropriate patterns of knowledge of their constituents. One may thus quite properly profess ignorance of such a compound statement in any case where one has no reason to offer why an appropriate pattern of knowledge for its constituents should be thought achievable.

The great insight of the mathematical intuitionists—and the core of their revisionism—was that a thinker may simultaneously both lack

41. As it stands this—more specifically, its contrapositive—provides a second sufficient condition for ignorance, restricted to the kind of compound statement it mentions. That is all that is necessary to explain how someone can be properly regarded as ignorant of a statement who, by being in position to discount any Q inconsistent with that statement, fails to meet the other sufficient condition of ignorance offered by AG.

42. This is, to stress, only a first approximation to a full account of the principle required. Quantified statements, for instance, do not literally have constituents in the sense appealed to by the formulation—though it should be straightforward enough to extend the formulation to cover them. More needs to be said, too, about how the principle should apply to compounds in which negation is the principal operator. But the provisional formulation will serve the immediate purpose.

any such reason and yet be in a position to refute the *negation* of such a compound using only the most minimal and uncontroversial principles governing truth and validity. The proof of the double negation of LEM sketched above in note 31, for instance, turns only on the standard rules for disjunction, *reductio ad absurdum* in the form that no statements collectively entailing contradictory statements can all be true, and the principle (enjoined, remember, by the Equivalence Schema) that the negation of a statement is true just in case that statement is not. These principles are themselves quite neutral on the question of evidential constraint but are arguably constitutive of the content of the connectives—disjunction and negation—featuring in LEM. The assurance they provide of the validity of its double negation is thus ungainsayable. But when the truth of the ingredient statements is taken to involve evidential constraint, then that assurance does not in general amount to a reason to think that the appropriate kind of evidence for one disjunct or the other must in principle be available in any particular case. The assurance falls short in quandary cases—like borderline cases of simple colour predications—where we do not know what to say, do not know how we might find out, and can produce no reason for thinking that there is a way of finding out or even that finding out is metaphysically possible.

Quandaries are not, of course, restricted to cases of vagueness as usually understood. They are also presented, for instance, by certain unresolved but—so one would think—perfectly precise mathematical statements for which we possess no effective means of decision. So add the thought—whatever its motivation—that mathematical truth demands proof and there is then exactly the same kind of case for the suspension of classical logic in such areas of mathematics.[43] That

43. Note that this way of making a case for basic intuitionistic revisions needs neither any suspect reliance on AG nor appeal to specific non-truth-based proposals—in terms of assertibility conditions, or conditions of proof—about the semantics of the logical constants. The key is the combination of epistemic constraint and the occurrence of quandary cases. Any *semantical* proposals offered can sound exactly the same as those of the classicist.

is what the intuitionists are famous for. But if the account I have outlined is sound, then—whether or not there are compelling reasons derived within the philosophy of meaning for regarding EC as globally true—there will always be a case for suspension of classical logic wherever locally forceful grounds for EC combine with the possibility of quandary.[44]

44. An interesting supplementary question is now whether a revisionary argument might go through without actual *endorsement* of EC, just on the basis of agnosticism about it in the sense of reserving the possibility that it might be right. The line of thought would be this. Suppose we are satisfied that the outlined revisionary argument would work if we knew EC, but are so far open-minded—unpersuaded, for instance, that the usual anti-realist arguments for EC are compelling, but sufficiently moved to doubt that we know that truth is in general subject to *no* epistemic constraint. Suppose we are also satisfied that NKD, as a purely general thesis, is true: we have at present no grounds for thinking that we can in principle decide any issue. The key question is then this: Can we envisage—is it rational to leave epistemic space for—a type of argument (which a global proponent of the revisionary argument thinks we already have) for EC which would ground its acceptance but would not improve matters as far as NKD is concerned? If the possibility of such an argument is open, then it must be that our (presumably a priori) grounds for LEM are *already* inconclusive—for what is open is precisely that we advance to a state of information in which EC is justified and yet in which NKD remains true. But in that case we should recognise that LEM already lacks the kind of support that a fundamental logical principle should have—for that should be support which would be robust in any envisageable future state of information.

That seems intriguing. It would mean that revisionary anti-realism might be based not on a positive endorsement of EC but merely on suspicion of the realist's non-epistemic conception of truth.

Would this provide a way of finessing Fitch's paradox—the well-known argument (Fitch (1963)) that, in the presence of EC, it is contradictory to suppose that some truths are never known? No: if nothing else was said, the paradox would stand as a reason for doubting that it *is* rational to reserve epistemic space for a convincing global argument for EC.

V. An Intuitionistic Solution to the Sorites

§17. Our problem was to make out how the Sorites reasoning could justly be treated as a *reductio* of its major premise without our incurring an obligation to accept the unpalatable existential, and further—when the existential is unpalatable precisely because it seems to express the *precision* of the relevant predicate in the Sorites series—to explain how the major premise might properly be viewed as a misdescription of what it is for that predicate to be vague. The essence of the solution that now suggests itself is that the vagueness of F should be held to consist not in the *falsity* of the unpalatable existential claim, but precisely in its association with quandary in the sense latterly introduced.

To expand. Assume that F is like 'red' in that, though vague, predications of it are subject to EC. Then any truth of the form, Fa & –Fa′, would have, presumably, to be recognisably true. The unpalatable existential, (∃x)(Fx & –Fx′), has only finitely many instances in the relevant type of (Sorites) context. So its truth too would have to be recognisable. And to recognise its truth would be to find an appropriate Fa and –Fa′ each of which was recognisably true. We know that there is no coherently *denying* that there is any such instance, since that denial is inconsistent, by elementary reasoning, with the data, F(0) and –F(n). But we also know that we cannot find a confirming instance so long as we just consider cases where we are confident respectively that Fa, or that –Fa′. Thus, if there is a confirming pair, Fa and –Fa′, it must accordingly be found among the borderline cases. If these are rightly characterised as presenting quandary—that is, if we do not know whether to endorse them, do not know how we might find out, and can produce no reason for thinking that there is or even could be a way of finding out—then the status of (∃x)(Fx & –Fx′) is *likewise* a quandary, notwithstanding the proof of its double negation. And the plausibility of its (single) negation, notwithstanding the paradox it generates, is owing to our misrepresentation of this quandary: we are prone to deny the *truth* of the unpalatable existential when we should content ourselves with the observation that all its instances in the series in question are either false or quandary-presenting—an observation that merits denial of no more than its (current or foreseeable) assertibility.

§18. Again, it is crucial to this way with the problem that the quandary posed by borderline cases be exactly as characterised and in particular that it falls short of the certitude that there can be no deciding them. There can be no intuitionistic treatment of the Sorites unless we hold back from that concession. The indeterminacy associated with vague predicates has to fall short of anything that fits us with knowledge that one who takes a determinate—positive or negative—view of such an example, however tentative, makes a mistake. For once we allow ourselves to cross that boundary—to rule out all possibility of finding a confirming instance of the unpalatable existential—EC, where we have it,[45] will enforce its denial and the paradox will ensue.

This limitation—that we lack the certitude that there can be no finding a validating instance of the unpalatable existential—may seem very difficult to swallow. Let it be that atomic predications of vague expressions present quandaries in just the sense characterised; in particular, that we do not know that there is no knowing that such a predication is true, or that it is false. Still, that both P and Q present quandaries is not in general a reason for regarding their conjunction as beyond all knowledge: if Q is not P, for instance, we can know—one would think—that the conjunction is false even though each conjunct is a quandary. It may seem evident that instances of the unpalatable existential are in like case: that even if Fx and −Fx′ are quandaries, we *do* still know that there is no knowing that both are true. In general, quandary components are sure to generate quandary compounds only if verdicts on those components are mutually unconstrained; but the whole point about Sorites series is that adjacent

45. Is EC always plausible for basic Sorites-prone predicates? It does seem to be a feature of all the usual examples. See concluding remarks below.

terms lie close enough together to ensure that differential verdicts cannot be justified—ergo cannot be known.

Plausible as this train of thought may seem, it must be resisted—at least by a defender of EC for the range of predications in question. For suppose we knew that any adjacent terms in a Sorites series lie close enough together to ensure that differential verdicts about them cannot both be known. Then we would know that

$$FeasK[Fx] \rightarrow -FeasK[-Fx'].$$

By EC, we have both

$$Fx \rightarrow FeasK[Fx]$$

and

$$-Fx' \rightarrow FeasK[-Fx'].$$

So, putting the three conditionals together,

$$Fx \rightarrow --Fx'.$$

Hence, contraposing and collapsing the triple negation,[46]

$$-Fx' \rightarrow -Fx.$$

So if we think we know that any adjacent terms in a Sorites series lie close enough together to ensure that differential verdicts about them cannot both be known, we have to acknowledge that each non-F item in the series is preceded by another. Thus we saddle ourselves with a Sorites paradox again.[47]

46. The equivalence of triple to single negation is of course uncontroversial.
47. The general thrust of our discussion involves—as one would naturally expect of an advertised intuitionistic treatment—a heavy investment in EC. As I have said, I

Let me again stress the two morals:

(i) EC plus knowledge of the *irresolubility* of borderline cases is a cocktail for disaster. Any compelling local motivation for EC with respect to a vague discourse enforces an acknowledgement that our ignorance with respect to the proper classification of borderline cases can extend no further than quandary, as characterised, allows. We—innocent witnesses, as it were, to a difference of opinion—don't know what to say about such a case, don't know how to know, cannot pro-

---

believe the principle is plausible for the kinds of statement that feature in the classic examples of the Sorites paradox—though the relationship between vagueness and evidential constraint is a crucial and relatively unexplored issue (see remarks at the end of the essay). But I should stress that I regard the conception of borderline cases which I am proposing, of which it is an essential feature that we do not know that there is no knowledgeable verdict to be returned about a borderline case, as plausible independently of the incoherence of its denial when EC is accepted. Let me quickly rehearse a further corroborative consideration.

According to the opposing view—the *verdict-exclusion view*—a borderline case is something about which we know that a knowledgeable positive or negative verdict is ruled out. The verdict-exclusion view would be imposed by the third-possibility view, but whatever its provenance, it faces great difficulty in accommodating the intuitions that ground the idea of higher-order vagueness. For consider: if a (first-order) borderline case of P is something about which one can know that one ought to take an agnostic stance—a situation where one ought not to believe P and ought not to believe not P—then (one kind of) a higher-order borderline case is presumably a situation where one can know that one ought not to believe P and ought not to believe that P is (first-order) borderline. Since on the view proposed P's being first-order borderline is a situation where one ought not to believe P and ought not to believe not P, it follows that, confronted with a higher-order borderline case, one can know that

(i)   One ought not to believe P;

and

(ii)   One ought not to believe that one ought not to believe P and ought not to believe not P.

However, in moving in the direction of (putative) borderline cases of P and the first-order P/not P borderline, we have moved *towards* P, as it were, and away from not P.

duce any reason for thinking that there is any way of knowing nor even that there could be. But we do *not* know that there is none.

(ii) EC plus knowledge of the *undifferentiability* of adjacents in a Sorites series—the unknowability of the truth of contrasting verdicts about them—is similarly explosive. So we must take it that, where the statements in question are quandaries, we do not know that verdicts of the respective forms, Fa and not-Fa′, can never knowingly be returned. That allows each conjunction of such quandaries, Fa &

Since—according to the verdict-exclusion view—the first-order borderline cases were already cases where it could be known that

(iii)   One ought not to believe not P,

it should follow that the relevant kind of higher-order borderline cases are likewise cases where (iii) may be known. So one gets into a position where one may knowledgeably endorse both (i) and (iii) yet simultaneously know—by dint of knowing (ii)—that one ought not to endorse their conjunction—a Moorean paradox (at best).

In sum: the idea that agnosticism is always mandated in borderline cases cannot make coherent sense of higher-order vagueness. The distinction between cases where a positive or negative view is mandated and cases where agnosticism is mandated cannot itself allow of borderline cases, on the verdict-exclusion view. That is very implausible, and provides a powerful reason to be suspicious of the verdict-exclusion view.

This conclusion would be blocked, of course, if the verdict-exclusion view were qualified: if it were conceded that agnosticism is only mandated for *some* borderline cases and that for others, perhaps less 'centrally' borderline, something like the permissibility conception which I have been recommending—that in such cases those who incline to return positive or negative verdicts are not known to be incorrect but are, as it were, 'entitled to their view'—is the stronger account. Arguably, though, such a compromise would give the game away. For if the permissibility conception is correct at least for cases towards the borderline between definite cases of P and—the alleged—definite cases on the borderline between P and its negation, the question must immediately arise what good objection there could be to allowing the negation of P to cover the latter, agnosticism-mandating cases. None, if they are conceived as by the third-possibility view—for then they are exactly cases where P is other than—so not—true. But after that adjustment, the only remaining borderline cases would be just those where conflicting opinions were permissible, and the permissibility conception would therefore seem to have the better case to capture the basic phenomenon.

–Fa', to be itself a quandary; whence we may infer that the unpalatable existential is also a quandary, by the reasoning outlined in §17.[48]

§19. What are we now in position to say about the following conditional:

$(\exists x)(Fx \ \& \ -Fx') \rightarrow$ 'F' is not vague,

rightly focused on by Timothy Chambers in recent criticism of Putnam?[49] If it is allowed to stand as correct, then—contraposing—any vague expression will be characterised by the negation of the antecedent and the all too familiar aporia will ensue. What fault does the broadly intuitionistic approach I have been canvassing have to find with it?

Well, there *is* no fault to be found with it as a *conditional of assertibility*: to be in position to assert the antecedent with respect to the elements of a Sorites series must be to be in position to regard 'F' as sharply defined over the series. So an intuitionist who insists on the familiar kind of assertibility-conditional semantics for the conditional, whereby 'P → Q' is assertible just if it is assertible that any warrant for asserting P would be (effectively transformable into) a warrant for asserting Q, will be put in difficulty by Chambers' simple point. However, that style of semantics is arguably objectionable in any case, obliterating as it does the distinction in content between the conditionals

  If P, then Q

---

48. Timothy Williamson's otherwise cogent criticisms of Putnam (see Williamson (1996a)—specifically, his *reductio* of the combination of Putnam's proposal about vagueness and the ideal-justification conception of truth which Putnam favoured at the time—precisely assume that our knowledge of the status of borderline cases extends far enough to let us know that there can be no justified differentiation of adjacents, even under epistemically ideal circumstances. But we have seen, in effect, that Putnam should refuse to grant that assumption. A would-be intuitionistic treatment of vagueness must respect the two morals just summarised.

49. Chambers (1998).

and

> If P is assertible, then Q.[50]

What is wrong with the Chambers conditional from our present perspective is rather that, if its antecedent—the unpalatable existential—is rightly regarded as presenting a quandary in cases where F is vague in the series in question, then it is not something whose truth we are in a position to exclude. So for all we know, the antecedent of the Chambers conditional may be true while its consequent is false; for F is vague by hypothesis. So there is—as there needs to be—principled cause to regard the conditional as unacceptable.[51]

---

50. This assumes that 'P' and 'P is assertible' are always co-warranted.

51. A skirmish about this is possible. If the unpalatable existential is justly regarded as presenting a quandary, then we shouldn't rule out the possibility of coming to know that $(\exists x)(Fx \ \& \ -Fx')$ is true. But if we did know it, we should presumably not then know that the relevant predicate, F, is vague—for we would know that it was sharply bounded in the series in question. So it seems we can rule out

> (*) $(\exists x)(Fx \ \& \ -Fx') \ \& $ 'F' is vague

as a feasible item of knowledge. And now, if (*) is subject to EC, it follows that it is false and hence—again, an intuitionistically valid step—that the Chambers conditional holds after all. (I am grateful to Timothy Williamson for this observation.)

On the other hand, if (*) is *not* subject to EC, then the question is why not—what principled reason can be given for the exception when so much of our discussion has moved under the assumption that many contexts involving vague expressions are so?

The answer is that (*) cannot be subject to EC—at least in the simple conditional form in which we have been considering that principle—for just the reason that Fitch's well-known counter-examples cannot be. These counter-examples are all contingent conjunctions where knowledge of one conjunct is inconsistent with knowledge of the other. The simplest case is: P and it is not known that P. Knowledge of the second conjunct would require—by the factivity of knowledge—that the first conjunct was not known; but if the conjunction could be known, so could each conjunct simultaneously. Hence EC must fail if the Fitch schema has true instances. It now suffices to reflect that, on the conception of vague expressions as giving rise to quandary, (*) is merely a more complex Fitch case. For to know that 'F' is vague is to know that predications of it give rise to quandaries in a series of the appropriate kind and hence—by

This is not inconsistent with allowing that the unpalatable existential does indeed characterise what it is for F to be *precise* relative to the series of objects in question. But if that is insisted upon, then we learn that it was a mistake to view vagueness as entailing a *lack of precision*. Rather, the vagueness of a predicate involves the combined circumstances that atomic predications of it are prone to present quandary and that we are unwarranted in regarding bivalence/excluded middle as valid for such predications. Vagueness so conceived is an epistemic notion; precision, if enjoined by the truth of the unpalatable existential, is a matter of ontology—of actual sharpness of extension. I'll return to the issue of the characterisation of vagueness below.

§20. Earlier we set two constraints on a treatment of the Sorites: it was to be explained

(i)   how the falsity of $-(\exists x)(Fx \ \& \ -Fx')$ can be consistent with the vagueness of F; and

(ii) how and why it can be a principled response to refuse to let
$$--(\exists x)(Fx \ \& \ -Fx')$$

constitute a commitment to the unpalatable existential, and hence—apparently—to the precision of F.

The answers of the present approach, in summary, are these. The major premise for the Sorites may unproblematically be denied, without betrayal of the vagueness of F, if F's vagueness is, in the way

---

the reasoning sketched in the second paragraph of §17—that the unpalatable existential is itself a quandary and hence is not known.

Of course this comparison would not be soothing for someone sympathetic to the sketched intuitionistic response to the Sorites who was also a proponent of EC *globally*. But there is no evident reason why the viability of the intuitionistic response to the Sorites should depend upon the global proposition. For one for whom the case for EC always depends on the nature of the local subject matter, there should be no discomfort in recognising that 'blind-spot' truths—truths about truths of which we are, de facto or essentially, ignorant—will provide a region of counter-examples to EC.

adumbrated, an epistemic property—if it consists in the provision of quandary by some of the atomic predications of F on objects in the series in question. And such a denial need be no commitment to the unpalatable existential—or other classical equivalents of that denial which seem tantamount to the affirmation of precision—if the latter are also quandaries and are thus properly regarded as objects of agnosticism. Rather, the classical-logical moves which would impose such commitments are to be rejected precisely because they allow transitions from known premises to quandary conclusions.[52]

VI.   RELATIVISM STABILISED

§21. Our problem was to block both the apparent lesson of the Simple Deduction, that any dispute about a truth-apt content involves a mistake, and that of the EC Deduction, that any dispute about an evidentially constrained truth-apt content involves a substantive cognitive shortcoming—so that, at least with subject matters constrained by EC, the intended gap between minimal truth-aptitude and Cognitive Command collapses. It should now be foreseeable how a principled response to these awkward arguments may run.

The truth is that each deduction is actually fine, as far as it goes (to the stated line 8 in the case of the Simple Deduction, and line 10 in the case of the EC Deduction). The problem, rather, consists in a *non sequitur* in the way their conclusions were *interpreted*. Take the EC Deduction. (The response to the Simple Deduction is exactly parallel.) What is actually put up for *reductio* is the claim that a certain dispute

---

52. The reader should note that no ground has been given for reservations about double-negation elimination as applied to atomic predications, even in quandary-presenting cases. For—in contrast to the situation of the double negation of the unpalatable existential—no purely logical case will be available to enforce acceptance of $--Fa$ in a case where Fa presents a quandary. However, an acceptance of DNE for vague atomic predications will not, of course, enforce an acceptance of the law of excluded middle for them. (Recall that the proof of the equivalence of DNE and LEM requires that the former hold for *compound* statements, in particular for LEM itself.)

involves no cognitive shortcoming. That is a negative existential claim, so the *reductio* is in the first instance a proof of *its* negation, that is, a doubly negated claim: that it is not true that A's and B's conflicting opinions involve no cognitive shortcoming. This is indeed established a priori (if EC is locally a priori). However, to achieve the alleged demonstration of Cognitive Command—that it is a priori that cognitive shortcoming is involved—we have first to eliminate the double negation. And the needed DNE step, like that involved in the classical 'proof' of LEM and the Sorites-based proof of the unpalatable existential, involves a violation of AG⁺. As the reader may verify, the reasoning deployed in the EC Deduction up to its conclusion at line 10 draws on no resources additional to those involved in the proof of the double negation of LEM save modus ponens and the suggestion that one who holds a mistaken view of a knowable matter is *per se* guilty of cognitive shortcoming. Neither of those additions seems contestable, so the EC Deduction should be acknowledged as absolutely solid. However, the transition from its actually doubly negated conclusion to the advertised, double-negation-eliminated result—that Cognitive Command holds wherever conflict of opinion is possible—demands, in the presence of EC, that there be an *identifiable* shortcoming in A's and B's conflicting opinions—for the shortcoming precisely consists in holding the wrong view about a knowable matter. If the example is one of quandary, the DNE step is thus a commitment to the view that an error may be identified in a case where we do not know the right opinion, do not know how we might know, and have no general reason to suppose that there is or could be a way of knowing nonetheless. Once again, the logical and other resources involved in the simple proof (up to line 10) seem manifestly inadequate to sustain a conclusion with that significance. So although indeed in position to rule out the suggestion that any disagreement is cognitively blameless, just as the two Deductions show, we remain—in the light of the enhanced principle of ignorance AG⁺— unentitled to the claim that there will be cognitive shortcoming in any difference of opinion within a minimally truth-apt discourse. We remain so unentitled precisely because that would be a commitment to a *locatability* claim for which the proof of the double negation provides no sufficient ground and for which we have, indeed, no sufficient ground.

The immediate lesson is that it is an error (albeit a natural one) to characterise failures of Cognitive Command—or indeed what is involved in true relativism generally—in terms of the possibility of blameless differences of opinion.[53] Indeed, it is the same root error as the characterisation of failures of bivalence in terms of third possibilities, truth-value gaps and so on. Failures of Cognitive Command, like failures of bivalence, must be viewed as situations where we *have no warrant for* a certain claim, not ones where—for all we know—its negation may be true. We *do* know—the two Deductions precisely teach—that the negation will not be true. But that's not sufficient for Cognitive Command. The distinction once again turns on the intuitionistic insight that one may, in contexts of evidential constraint and potential quandary, fall short of knowledge of a claim whose negation one is nevertheless in position to exclude.

The point does not depend on the *sources* of any potential quandary. But my implicit proposal in *Truth and Objectivity*—the reason why the Cognitive Command constraint was formulated so as to exempt disagreements owing to vagueness—was that it is a feature of discourse concerning the comic, the attractive and the merely minimally truth-apt generally that differences of opinion in such regions may present quandaries for reasons *other than* vagueness. It is not (just) because 'funny' and 'delicious' are vague in the way 'red' is that the kind of differences of opinion about humour and gastronomy are possible which we do not know how to resolve, do not know how we might get to know, and do not know that there is, or could be, any getting to know. Merely minimally truth-apt discourses, in contrast with discourse exerting cognitive command, provide examples of indeterminacy *in re*. But we need to correct the usual understanding of this, epitomised by the rhetoric of phrases like 'no fact of the matter'.

53. Regrettably, the error is encouraged by the wording of some passages in *Truth and Objectivity*. See pp. 94 and 145, for instance.

That rhetoric, it should now be superfluous to say, is simply inconsistent with the most basic constitutive principles concerning truth and negation. The indeterminacy consists rather in the fact that provision exists for quandaries which, because they arise in contexts governed by evidential constraint, enforce agnosticism about principles—like bivalence—which if they could be assumed to hold, would ensure that there was a 'fact of the matter', about which we would merely be ignorant. It is a matter, if you like, of lack of warrant to believe in a fact of the matter, rather than a reason to deny one—a subtle but crucial distinction whose intelligibility depends on a perception of the inadequacy of AG and the basic intuitionistic insight.

VII.   EPISTEMIC INDETERMINACY

§22. Let me return to the issue of the relation between the epistemic conception of indeterminacy I have been proposing and the rampantly realist Epistemic Conception. Writing in criticism of Williamson's and Sorensen's respective defences of the latter, I once observed that

> Perhaps the most basic problem for the indeterminist [the orthodox opponent of the Epistemic Conception] is to characterise what vagueness consists in—to say what a borderline case is. It is also one of the least investigated. The epistemic conception should not be allowed to draw strength from this neglect. There is no cause to despair that the situation can be remedied.[54]

Well, how close do the foregoing considerations come to remedying the situation? My proposal in that earlier paper was that borderline cases of F should be characterised in the natural way, using an operator of definiteness, as cases which are neither definitely F nor definitely not F but—prefiguring what I have been suggesting here—that the definiteness operator should be construed epistemically, with gen-

---

54. Wright (1995a), p. 146.

uine borderline cases marked off from determinate matters lying beyond our ken—including borderline cases as conceived by the Epistemicist—by examples of the latter sort being characterised by the principle of bivalence, there characterised as the hypothesis of 'universal determinacy in truth-value'.[55]

Williamson later responded:

> So far the parties do not disagree; the epistemicist has merely said more than the indeterminist. But that is not the only difference between them. The indeterminist regards the epistemicist's account of borderline cases as *positively incorrect* [my emphasis]. The epistemicist is supposed to regard borderline claims as determinate in truth-value, while the indeterminist regards them as not determinate in truth-value.[56]

This gloss on the differences between the protagonists enabled Williamson to advance the following line of criticism. Part of the indeterminist characterisation of borderline claims is that they are not determinate in truth value. What does 'determinate' mean? If not being determinate in truth value involves *lacking* a truth value, then we are back with third-possibility indeterminacy. But 'not determinate in truth value' cannot just mean 'not definitely true and not definitely false' since that claim—with 'definitely' understood epistemically, as now by both sides in the dispute—is one the Epistemicist is prepared to make; whereas the denial of determinacy was supposed to crystallise a point of disagreement between the indeterminist and the Epistemicist. So, Williamson concluded, the indeterminist bugbear— of giving some non-epistemic account of borderline cases—recurs.

This was a curious criticism, given that the notion of determinacy in truth value was involved in the first place only as a paraphrase of the principle of bivalence. For in that case, Williamson's supposition that my indeterminist was someone who regarded borderline claims as not determinate in truth value would be equivalent to attributing to her the thesis that bivalence *failed* for such claims. And then, given

55. *Ibid.*, at p. 145.
56. Williamson (1996b), p. 44.

that I explicitly did not want any traffic with third possibilities, Williamson would have had a much more forceful criticism to make than merely that the implicated notion of determinacy had still not been properly explained.

In fact, however—the important point for our present concerns—Williamson mischaracterised the opposition in the first place. It was a misunderstanding to suppose that the 'indeterminist'—my theorist in the earlier paper—regarded borderline claims as 'not determinate in truth value'. Rather, the difference between that theorist and the Epistemicist was precisely that the former draws back from, rather than denies, a view which the Epistemicist takes: the negation belongs with the attitude, not the content. The 'indeterminist' regarded the Epistemicist's bivalent view of borderline cases (the view of them as determinate in truth value) not as positively wrong—where that is taken to mean: something she is prepared to *deny*—but as positively unjustified: something which she knows of no sufficient grounds to accept.

Indeed, the involvement of an (unexplicated) notion of determinacy was inessential to the view that was being proposed. The claim of determinacy in truth value just is the claim that bivalence holds in the cases in question. So the heart of the 'indeterminist' thesis was just that borderline cases are these: cases where—in an appropriate epistemic sense of the definiteness operator—a target predication is not definitely true and not definitely false and where there is no extant warrant for the assertion of bivalence. Williamson's short response contained nothing to threaten the stability of this view.

That said, it merits acknowledgement that 'indeterminist' was not the happiest label for the type of position I was trying to outline, and that it may have misled Williamson. For it is hard to hear it without gathering a suggestion of a *semantic* or an *ontological* thesis: of vagueness conceived as involving matters left unresolved not (merely) in an epistemic sense, but in fact, by the very rules of language, or by the world itself. For someone who wants one of those directions made good—and who read my remark quoted above as calling for just that—the direction taken in my earlier discussion, and in this one, will puzzle and disappoint. In any case—save in one crucial detail—it is still no part of the view I have been developing in *this* essay to regard the Epistemicist's account of borderline cases as 'positively incorrect'. There is agreement that the root manifestations of vagueness are captured by epistemic categories: bafflement, ignorance, difference of opinion and uncertainty; and that to conceive of the phenomenon in semantic or ontological terms is to take a *proto-theoretical* step which, absent any coherent further development, there is cause to suspect may be a mistake. The 'crucial detail' of disagreement—prescinding, of course, from the major conflict over warrant for the principle of bivalence—is merely over the thesis that borderline cases are known to defy all possibility of knowledgeable opinion. While the coherence of the quandary view depends on its rejection, Williamson perceives it as a theoretical obligation of his own view to defend it.[57] But setting that apart, it deserves emphasis that the view of vagueness here defended is consistent with the *correctness* of the Epistemic Conception (and on the other hand, *pari passu*, with agnosticism about whether it even *could be* correct). The quandary view is consistent with the correctness of the Epistemic Conception in just the sense in which the intuitionist philosophy of mathematics is consistent with the actual correctness of the principle of bivalence and classical mathematical practice. The basic complaint is not of *mistake*—though the Epistemic Conception may well prove to be committed to collateral mistakes (for instance about the conditions on possible semantic

---

57. I am not myself certain that the Epistemicist does have any obligation to defend anything so strong. Someone who believes that vague expressions have sharp extensions ought to explain, sure, why we don't actually know what they are nor have any clear conception of how we might find out. But there would seem to be no clear obligation to conceive of them as unknowable (though that might be a consequence of the theorist's best shot at meeting the less extreme explanatory demand). I suspect that matters proceed differently in Williamson's thinking: that he regards the impossibility of knowledgeable (positive or negative) opinion about borderline cases as a datum, which would straightforwardly be explained by semantic and ontological conceptions of indeterminacy (could we but explain *them*) and of which he therefore conceives that his own bivalence-accepting conception must provide an alternative explanation. I do not think it is a datum.

reference: on what it takes for a predicate to stand for a property)—
but of *lack of evidence*.

§23. One—albeit perhaps insufficient—reason to retain the term 'indeterminist' for the conception of vagueness defended in my earlier
paper was the retention of a definiteness operator and the characterisation of borderline cases as 'not definitely . . . and not definitely
not . . .'. But I now think *that* was a mistake, and the operator itself at
best an idle wheel. My earlier proposal was that P is definitely true just
if any (what I called) *primary* opinion—any opinion based neither on
testimony nor inference, nor held groundlessly—that not P would be
'cognitively misbegotten', that is, some factor would contribute to its
formation of a kind which, once known about, would call its reliability into question in any case and could aptly be used to explain the
formation of a mistaken opinion. No doubt this proposal could be pres-
sured in detail, but—with the notion of Cognitive Command recently
before us—the guiding idea is plain: the definite truths were to be those
disagreements about which would have to involve cognitive shortcoming *tout court,* with no provision for excuses to do with vagueness.

So a claim which is not definitely true and not definitely false ought
to be one—I seem to have wanted to suggest—about which 'neither of
a pair of conflicting opinions need be cognitively misbegotten'.[58] This
proposal was intended to capture the idea

> that the phenomenon of permissible disagreement at the margins is of
> the very essence of vagueness. . . . [T]he basic phenomenon of vague-
> ness is one of the possibility of faultlessly generated—cognitively un-
> misbegotten—conflict. [59]

However, we have in effect seen that this will not do. What we
learned from the EC Deduction was that, wherever we have evidential
constraint, hence each of the conditionals

---

58. Wright (1995a), p. 145.
59. *Ibid.*

P → it is feasible to know that P, and
−P → it is feasible to know that −P,

the idea of a 'faultlessly generated' disagreement rapidly destabilises. For if the disagreement were faultless, it could not be that it was feasible to know either of the protagonists' opinions to be correct, or there would have to be fault in the generation of the other. And in that case, contraposing on both conditionals, contradiction ensues.

But we know the remedy now: retreat to the double negation and invoke the enhanced principle of ignorance, AG⁺. My proposal should have been not that faultlessly generated disagreements are possible where vague claims are concerned, but that we are in no position to claim that any disagreement about such a claim involves fault. Thus the root phenomenon of vagueness cannot after all, when cautiously characterised, be that of permissible disagreement at the margins; rather it is the possibility of disagreements of which we are in no position to say that they are *im*permissible, in the sense of involving specific shortcomings of epistemic pedigree. We are in no position to say that because, notwithstanding the incoherence of the idea that such a disagreement is actually fault-free, the claim that there are specific shortcomings involved must, in the presence of EC, involve a commitment to their identifiability, at least to the extent of pointing the finger at one disputant or the other. And that is exactly what we have no reason to think we can generally do.

The upshot is that even when 'definitely' is interpreted along the epistemic lines I proposed, we should not acquiesce in the characterisation of borderline claims as ones which are *neither* definitely true *nor* definitely false.[60] Rather, they will be claims for which *there is no justification for the thesis that they are* definitely true or definitely false—again, with 'definitely' epistemic—nor any justification for the application of bivalence to them. But now the former point is swallowed by the latter. For in the presence of EC, justification for

60. I leave it as an exercise for the reader to adapt the EC Deduction to a proof of this claim.

bivalence just is justification for the thesis that any statement in the relevant range is knowably—so definitely—true or false. So the definiteness operator is (harmless but) *de trop*.

One more very important qualification. None of this is to suggest that we may give a complete characterisation of vagueness along these Spartan lines: that vague statements are just those which give rise to quandary and for which bivalence is unjustified. That's *too* Spartan, of course. The view proposed has indeed, after all, no need for the expressive resource of an operator of indeterminacy. But some quandaries—Goldbach's conjecture, for instance—feature nothing recognisable as vagueness; and others—that infidelity is alright provided nobody gets hurt, perhaps—may present quandaries for reasons other than any ingredient vagueness. So the task of a more refined taxonomy remains—the notion of quandary is just a first step.[61] But if the general tendency of this discussion is right, it is a crucial step.

VIII. SUMMARY REFLECTIONS

§24. To recapitulate the gist of all this: a proposition P presents a quandary for a thinker T just when the following conditions are met:

  (i)   T does not know whether or not P.
  (ii)   T does not know any way of knowing whether or not P.
  (iii) T does not know that there is any way of knowing whether or not P.
  (iv)   T does not know that it is (metaphysically) possible to know whether or not P.

---

61. Relevant initial thoughts, already bruited, are these: it is known—in our present state of information, in the absence of proof—that nobody's opinion about Goldbach is knowledgeable; whereas, on the view proposed, we precisely do not know that a positive or negative verdict about a borderline case of 'x is red' is unknowledgeable. And unlike 'red', predications of 'funny' have no definite cases—they are always contestable.

The satisfaction of each of these conditions would be entailed by

(v)   T knows that it is impossible to know whether or not P,

but that condition is excluded by quandary as we intend it—a quandary is uncertain through and through.

Note that, so characterised, quandaries are relative to thinkers (one person's quandary may be part of another's (presumed) information) and to states of information (a proposition may present a quandary at one time and not at another). There are important classes of example which are acknowledged to present quandaries for all thinkers who take an interest in the matter. Goldbach's conjecture is currently one such case. But for the protagonists in an (intransigent) dispute of inclination, it will naturally not seem that the target claim presents a quandary; likewise when conflicting verdicts are returned about a borderline case of some vague expression. Yet to a third party, the contested claim in such cases—and hence the question who is right about it—may always reasonably be taken to present a quandary nonetheless.

It should seem relatively uncontroversial to propose that unresolved mathematical conjectures, borderline cases of vague expressions and the foci of disputes of inclination meet the four defining conditions of quandary. To say that much is simply to report on our epistemic situation in relation to the claims in question. It is to say nothing about their metaphysical or semantical status. What is not uncontroversial, of course, is the contention that clause (v) fails—that we do not know that there is no knowing the truth of either of two conflicting verdicts about a borderline case, or either of the two conflicting views in a dispute of inclination. As I have acknowledged, this modesty may go against the grain. But it is imposed if we accept that the disputed statement is subject to EC.[62] And it is imposed in any case if we are inclined to think that we should be permissive about such disputes—for otherwise we ought to convict both disputants of

62. See also note 48 above.

overreaching, of unwarranted conviction about an undecidable matter, and they should therefore withdraw. The thought that they are, rather, *entitled* to their respective views has to be the thought that we do not know that they are wrong to take them—do not know that neither of their views is knowledgeable.

I do not expect many immediate converts—at least not from among those who start out convinced that clause (v) should be part of the account of vagueness. But maybe I have done a little to erode that conviction—or at least to bring out other intuitions and theses that it holds hostage. In any case. Epistemicists will abjure the role played by Evidential Constraint in the foregoing discussion. And indeterminists proper will equally abjure the suggestion that the proponents of the Epistemic Conception of vagueness have the matter half right: that indeterminacy *is* an epistemic matter, that borderline cases should be characterised as cases of (a complicated kind of) ignorance. According to the present view, the Epistemic Conception takes us in the right general direction. It goes overboard in its additional (gratuitous and unmotivated) assumption that the principle of bivalence holds for all statements, including quandary-presenting ones, so that we are constrained to think of, for example, predicate expressions which are prone to give rise to such statements as denoting—by mechanisms of which no one has the slightest inkling how to give an account—sharply bounded properties of which we may lack any clear conception.[63] But the general conception of vagueness it involves is otherwise—at least in the round—quite consistent with the present proposal.

I have suggested that the intuitionists' revisionism is best reconstructed as driven by a mixture of quandary and evidential constraint: the belief that truth in mathematics cannot outrun proof, together with a recognition that unresolved mathematical conjectures can present quandaries in the sense characterised. If this is right, then, my point has been, the revisionary argument will generalise, and classical logic—especially the law of excluded middle and, correlatively, the principle of double-negation elimination—should not be accepted

63. See note 6 above.

(since it has not been recognised to be valid) for any area of discourse exhibiting these two features. The result, I have argued, is that we have the resources for a principled, broadly intuitionistic response to the Sorites paradox. And we can stabilise the contrast between minimal truth-aptitude and cognitive command against the Deductions that threatened to subvert it, and which do indeed show that it is unstable in the setting of classical logic. To be sure, we do not thereby quite recover the materials for a coherent *true relativism* as earlier characterised—which involved essential play with the possibility of fault-free disagreement. But an *anti-relativistic* rubric in terms of cognitive command, that it hold a priori of the discourse in question that disagreements within it (save when vagueness is implicated) involve cognitive shortcoming, may once again represent a condition which there is no guarantee that any minimally truth-apt discourse will satisfy. The relativistic thesis, for its part, should accordingly be the denial that there is—for a targeted discourse—any such a priori guarantee (or merely the claim that it is unwarranted to suppose that there is). Thus the ancient doctrine of relativism, too, now goes epistemic. I do not know if Protagoras would have approved.

§25. It merits emphasis, finally, that—for all I have argued here— these proposals can be extended no further than to discourses which exhibit the requisite combination of characteristics: quandary propensity and evidential constraint. Without that combination, no motive has been disclosed for suspension of classical logic[64]—but classical logic would serve to reinstate the intended conclusions of the two Deductions and to obliterate the distinction between the proper conclusion of the Sorites paradox—the denial of its major premise— and the unpalatable existential. One question I defer for further work is whether the two characteristics co-occur sufficiently extensively to allow the mooted solutions to have the requisite generality.

Two initially encouraging thoughts are these. First, as noted earlier, people's ordinary willingness to think in terms of 'no fact of the

---

64. But see, however, note 44 above.

matter' in cases of intransigent disputes of inclination is in effect the manifestation of an acceptance of evidential constraint for the relevant discourse. (For if they were comfortable with the idea that such a dispute could in principle concern an undecidable fact, why would they take its intransigence as an indicator that there wasn't one?) I therefore conjecture that whatever exactly it is that we are responding to when we engage in the kind of taxonomy I illustrated right at the beginning with the two 'crude but intuitive' lists, the contents which we are inclined to put in the first list will indeed be cases where we will not want to claim any conception of how the facts could elude appreciation by the most fortunately generated human assessment.

Second, if classical logic is inappropriate, for broadly intuitionistic reasons, for a range of atomic statements, it could hardly be reliable for compounds of them, even if the operations involved in their compounding—quantifiers, tenses and so on—were such as to enable the construction of statements which are not subject to EC. Thus what the intuitionistic response to the Sorites requires is not that *all* vague sentences be both potentially quandary-presenting and evidentially constrained but only that all *atomic* vague sentences be so. The standard examples of the Sorites in the literature—'red', 'bald', 'heap', 'tall', 'child'—do all work with atomic predicates, and all are, plausibly, evidentially constrained. But that is merely suggestive. If a finally satisfactory intuitionistic philosophy of vagueness is to be possible, we need an insight to connect basic vague expressions and evidential constraint. The notions of observationality and of response-dependence would provide two obvious foci for the search. For now, however—in a contemporary context in which a few theorists of vagueness have argued against its prospects but most have simply paid no serious heed to the idea at all—it will be enough to have conveyed (if I have) something of the general shape which a stable intuitionistic philosophy of vagueness might assume.

*

Versions of the material on revisionism were presented at colloquia at the University of Bologna, the City University of New York Graduate Center, and at Rutgers University in autumn 1998. I was fortunate enough to have the opportunity to present a discussion of all three problems at two seminars at the Ohio State University in December of that year, and to have a precursor of the present draft discussed at the Language and Mind seminar at New York University in April 1999, where Stephen Schiffer's commentary resulted in a number of improvements. The NYU draft also provided the basis for three helpful informal seminars at Glasgow University in May 1999. More recently, I took the opportunity to present the material on the Sorites at an *Arché* Workshop on Vagueness which, with the sponsorship of the British Academy, was held at St. Andrews in June 2000. I am extremely grateful to the discussants on all these occasions, and in addition to John Broome, Patrick Greenough, Richard Heck, Fraser MacBride, Sven Rosenkranz, Mark Sainsbury, Joe Salerno, Tim Williamson and a referee for *Mind* for valuable comments and discussion. Almost all the research for the paper has been conducted during my tenure of a Leverhulme Research Professorship; I gratefully acknowledge the support of the Leverhulme Trust.

REFERENCES

Austin, J. L. 1950. "Truth", *Proceedings of the Aristotelian Society* Suppl. Vol. 24, pp. 111–28, *reprinted in* Austin (1970).

——— 1970. *Philosophical Papers,* 2nd ed., Edited by J. O. Urmson and G. J. Warnock. Oxford: Oxford University Press.

Ayer, A J. 1936. *Language, Truth and Logic.* London: Victor Gollancz.

Bennett, J. 1965. "Substance, Reality and Primary Qualities", *American Philosophical Quarterly* 2.

——— 1971. *Locke, Berkeley, Hume: Central Themes.* Oxford: Clarendon Press.

Blackburn, S. 1971. "Moral Realism", *in* Casey (1971).

——— (ed.). 1975. *Meaning, Reference and Necessity.* Cambridge: Cambridge University Press.

——— 1981. "Rule-following and Moral Realism", *in* Holtzman and Leich (1981), pp. 163–87.

——— 1984. *Spreading the Word.* Oxford: Clarendon Press.

——— 1985a. "Errors and the Phenomenology of Value", *in* Honderich (1985).

——— 1985b. "Supervenience Revisited", *in* Hacking (1985).

——— 1986. "Morals and Modals", *in* MacDonald and Wright (1986).

——— 1988. "Attitudes and Contents", *Ethics* 98, pp. 501–17.

References

——— 1993. *Essays in Quasi-realism*. Oxford: Oxford University Press.

——— 1998a. *Ruling Passions*. Oxford: Clarendon Press.

——— 1998b. "Wittgenstein, Wright, Rorty and Minimalism", *Mind* 107, pp. 157–81.

Blackburn, S., and K. Simmons, eds. 1999. *Truth*. Oxford: Clarendon Press.

Block, N., ed. 1992. *Readings in the Philosophy of Psychology,* vol. 1. Cambridge, Mass.: Harvard University Press.

Boghossian, P. 1989a. "The Rule-Following Considerations", *Mind* 98, pp. 507–49.

——— 1989b. "Content and Self-Knowledge", *Philosophical Topics* 17, pp. 5–26.

——— 1990. "The Status of Content", *Philosophical Review* 109, pp. 157–84.

Boyd, R. 1992. "Materialism without Reductionism: What Physicalism does not entail", *in* Block (1992), pp. 67–106.

Bradley, F. H. 1914. *Essays on Truth and Reality*. Oxford: Oxford University Press.

Brandom, R . 1994. *Making It Explicit*. Cambridge, Mass.: Harvard University Press.

——— 2000. *Articulating Reasons: An Introduction to Inferentialism*. Cambridge, Mass.: Harvard University Press.

Butterfield, J., ed. 1986. *Language, Mind and Logic*. Cambridge: Cambridge University Press.

Campbell, J. 1993. "A Simple View of Colour," *in* Haldane and Wright (1993).

Campbell, R. 1974. "The Sorites Paradox", *Philosophical Studies* 26, pp. 175–91.

Candlish, S. 1990. Critical study of Walker (1989), *Mind* 99, pp. 467–72.

Cargile, J. 1969. "The Sorites Paradox", *British Journal for the Philosophy of Science* 20, pp. 193–202.

——— 1979. *Paradoxes*. Cambridge: Cambridge University Press.

Carnap, R. 1936a. "Über die Einheitssprache der Wissenschaft", *Actes du Congrès International de Philosophie Scientifique,* Fasc II (Paris).

——— 1936b. "Testability and Meaning", *Philosophy of Science* 3, pp. 419–71.

Carruthers, P. 1981. "Frege's Regress", *Proceedings of the Aristotelian Society* 1:32, pp. 17–32.

References

Casey, J., ed. 1971. *Morality and Moral Reasoning*. New York: Methuen.

Chambers, T. 1998. "On Vagueness, Sorites, and Putnam's 'Intuitionistic Strategy'", *Monist* 81, pp. 343-8.

Churchland, P. 1984. *Matter and Consciousness*. Cambridge, Mass.: MIT Press.

Copp, D., and D. Zimmerman, eds. 1985. *Morality, Reason and Truth*. Totowa, N.J.: Rowman and Allen.

Craig, E. 1975. "The Problem of Necessary Truth", *in* Blackburn (1975).

—— 1985. "Arithmetic and Fact", *in* Hacking (1985).

—— 1986. "Privacy and Rule-Following", *in* Butterfield (1986), pp. 169–86.

Dancy, J. 1986. "Two Conceptions of Moral Realism", *Proceedings of the Aristotelian Society* Suppl. vol. 60, pp. 167–87.

Davidson, D. 1978. "What Metaphors Mean", *Critical Inquiry* 5, pp. 31–47.

Davies, M., and L. Humberstone. 1980. "Two Notions of Necessity", *Philosophical Studies* 38, pp. 22–5.

Dennett, D. 1978. "Intentional Systems", *in* D. Dennett, *Brainstorms* (Montgomery, Vt.: Bradford).

—— 1987. *The Intentional Stance*. Cambridge, Mass.: MIT/Bradford.

Divers, J. 1999. "Arithmetical Platonism: Reliability and Judgement-Dependence", *Philosophical Studies* 95, pp. 277–310.

Divers, J., and A. Miller. 1995. "Minimalism and the Unbearable Lightness of Being", *Philosophical Papers* 24, pp. 127–39.

Dummett, M . 1959a. "Truth", *Proceedings of the Aristotelian Society* 59, pp. 141–62.

—— 1959b. "Wittgenstein's Philosophy of Mathematics", *Philosophical Review* 68, pp. 324–48.

—— 1969. "The Reality of the Past", *Proceedings of the Aristotelian Society* 69, pp. 239–58.

—— 1973. *Frege: Philosophy of Language*. London: Duckworth.

—— 1976. "What Is a Theory of Meaning? (II)", *in* Evans and McDowell (1976).

—— 1978. *Truth and Other Enigmas*. London: Duckworth.

—— 1981. *The Interpretation of Frege's Philosophy*. Cambridge, Mass.: Harvard University Press.

Edgington, D. 1985. "The Paradox of Knowability", *Mind* 94, pp. 557–68.

Evans, G. 1980. "Things without the Mind", *in* van Straaten (1980).

References

—— 1982. *The Varieties of Reference*. Oxford: Clarendon Press.

Evans, G., and J. McDowell, eds. 1976. *Truth and Meaning: Essays in Semantics*. Oxford: Oxford University Press.

Field, H. 1980. *Science without Numbers*. Oxford: Basil Blackwell.

—— 1986. "The Deflationary Conception of Truth", *in* MacDonald Wright (1986), pp. 55-117.

—— 1989. *Realism, Mathematics and Modality*. Oxford: Basil Blackwell.

—— 1994. "Deflationist Views of Meaning and Content", *Mind* 103, pp. 249–85.

Fine, K. 1975. "Vagueness, Truth and Logic", *Synthese* 30, pp. 265–300.

Fitch, F. B. 1963. "A Logical Analysis of Some Value Concepts", *Journal of Symbolic Logic* 28, pp. 135–42.

Forbes, G. 1986. "Truth, Correspondence and Redundancy", *in* MacDonald and Wright (1986), pp. 27–54.

Frege, G. 1977. "Thoughts", trans. P. T. Geach, *in* G. Frege, *Logical Investigations* (New Haven: Yale University Press).

Geach, P. T. 1960. "Ascriptivism", *Philosophical Review* 69, pp. 221–5.

—— 1969. "Assertion", *Philosophical Review* 74, pp. 449–65.

George, A, ed. 1989. *Reflections on Chomsky*. Oxford: Basil Blackwell.

Gibbard, A. 1990. *Wise Choices, Apt Feelings*. Cambridge, Mass.: Harvard University Press.

Gillespie, N., ed. 1986. *Moral Realism: Proceedings of the 1985 Spindel Conference, Southern Journal of Philosophy* Suppl. 24.

Grice, H. P. 1989. "Logic and Conversation," *in* H. P. Grice, *Studies in the Way of Words* (Cambridge, Mass.: Harvard University Press).

Grice, H. P., and P. Strawson. 1956. "In Defence of a Dogma", *Philosophical Review* 65, pp. 141–58.

Grover, D., J. Camp and N. Belnap. 1975. "A Prosentential Theory of Truth", *Philosophical Studies* 27, pp. 73–125.

Gunderson, K., ed. 1975. *Language, Mind and Knowledge*. Minneapolis: Minnesota University Press.

Hacking, I., ed. 1985. *Exercises in Analysis*. Cambridge: Cambridge University Press.

Haldane, J., and C. Wright, eds. 1993. *Reality, Representation, and Projection*. New York: Oxford University Press.

Hale, B. 1986. "The Compleat Projectivist", *Philosophical Quarterly* 36, pp. 65–84.

—— 1992. "Can There Be a Logic of Attitudes?" *in* Haldane and Wright (1993).

—— 2002. "Can Arboreal Knotwork Help Blackburn Out of Frege's Abyss?" in *Philosophy and Phenomenological Research* 65, pp. 144–9.

Hale, B., and C. Wright, eds. 1997. *Blackwell Companion to the Philosophy of Language*. Oxford: Blackwell.

Hannan, B. 1993. "Don't Stop Believing: The Case against Eliminative Materialism", *Mind and Language* 8, pp. 165–79.

Hare, R. M. 1952. *The Language of Morals*. Oxford: Oxford University Press.

—— 1991. "Universal Prescriptivism", in Singer (1991).

Harman, G. 1977. *The Nature of Morality*. New York: Oxford University Press.

—— 1988. "Ethics and Observations", in G. Sayre-McCord, ed., *Essays on Moral Realism* (Ithaca, N.Y.: Cornell University Press), pp. 119–24.

Harman, G., and J. J. Thomson. 1996. *Moral Relativism and Moral Objectivity*. Oxford: Basil Blackwell.

Harman, G., J. J. Thomson et al. 1998. Book symposium on Harman and Thomson (1996), in *Philosophy and Phenomenological Research* 58, pp. 161–213.

Holtzman, S. H., and C. M. Leich, eds. 1981. *Wittgenstein: To Follow a Rule*. London: Routledge.

Honderich, T., ed. 1985. *Morality and Objectivity: A Tribute to J. L. Mackie*. London: Routledge.

Hookway, C . 1986. "Two Conceptions of Moral Realism", *Proceedings of the Aristotelian Society* Suppl. vol. 60, pp. 189–205.

Hopkins, J. 1973. "Visual Geometry", *Philosophical Review* 3, pp. 3–34.

Horgan, T. 1996. "The Perils of Epistemic Reductionism", *Philosophy and Phenomenological Research* 56, pp. 891–7.

Horwich, P . 1996. "Realism Minus Truth", *Philosophy and Phenomenological Research* 56, pp. 877–83.

—— 1998a. *Truth,* 2nd ed. Oxford: Clarendon Press.

—— 1998b. *Meaning*. Oxford: Clarendon Press.

Hume, D. 1967. *A Treatise of Human Nature*. Edited by L. A. Selby-Bigge. Oxford: Clarendon Press.

Jackson, F . 1994. "Realism, Truth and Truth-aptness", *Philosophical Books* 35, pp. 162–9.

References

Jackson, F., G. Oppy and M. Smith. 1994. "Minimalism and Truth Aptness", *Mind* 103, pp. 287–302.

Joachim, H. H. 1906. *The Nature of Truth*. Oxford: Oxford University Press.

Johnston, M. 1992. "How to Speak of the Colors", *Philosophical Studies* 68, pp. 221–63.

—— 1993. "Objectivity Refigured: Pragmatism without Verificationism", *in* Haldane and Wright (1993).

Klagge, J. C. 1987. "Supervenience: Perspectives v. Possible Worlds", *Philosophical Quarterly* 37, pp. 312–15.

Kraut, R. 1993. "Robust Deflationism", *Philosophical Review* 102, pp. 247–63.

Kripke, S. 1980. *Naming and Necessity*. Cambridge, Mass.: Harvard University Press.

—— 1982. *Wittgenstein on Rules and Private Language*. Cambridge, Mass.: Harvard University Press.

Locke, J. 1969. *An Essay Concerning Human Understanding*. Edited by Pringle-Pattison. Oxford: Clarendon Press.

Lynch, M. P., ed. 2001. *The Nature of Truth: From the Classic to the Contemporary*. Cambridge, Mass.: MIT Press.

MacDonald, G., and C. Wright, eds. 1986. *Fact, Science and Morality: Essays on A. J. Ayer's Language Truth and Logic*. Oxford: Basil Blackwell.

Mackie, J. 1977. *Ethics: Inventing Right and Wrong*. Harmondsworth: Penguin.

McDowell, J. 1978. "Are Moral Requirements Hypothetical Imperatives", *Proceedings of the Aristotelian Society* Suppl. vol. 52, pp. 13–29.

—— 1981. "Non-Cognitivism and Rule Following", *in* Holtzman and Leich (1981).

—— 1985. "Values and Secondary Qualities", *in* Honderich (1985).

—— 1986. Review of Williams (1985), *Mind* 95, pp. 377–86.

—— 1994. *Mind and World*. Cambridge, Mass.: Harvard University Press.

McDowell, J., and P. Pettit, eds. 1986. *Subject, Thought and Context*. Oxford: Clarendon Press.

McFetridge, I. G. 1985. "Supervenience, Realism, Necessity", *Philosophical Quarterly* 35, pp. 245–58.

McGinn, C. 1977. "Anomalous Monism and Kripke's Cartesian Intuitions", *Analysis* 37, pp. 78–80.

—— 1983. *The Subjective View*. Oxford: Clarendon Press.

References

Noonan, H. W. 1987. "Supervenience", *Philosophical Quarterly* 37, pp. 78–85.

Peacocke, C. 1978. *Holistic Explanation*. Oxford: Clarendon Press.

———— 1983. *Sense and Content*. Oxford: Clarendon Press.

Peirce, C. S. 1935. *Collected Papers*, vols. V and VIII. Edited by C. Hartshorne and P. Weiss. Cambridge, Mass.: Harvard University Press.

———— 1966. *Charles S. Peirce: Selected Writings (Values in a World of Chance)*. Edited by P. P. Wiener. New York: Dover Publications.

Pettit, P. 1991. "Realism and Response Dependence", *Mind* 100, pp. 587–626.

———— 1996. "Realism and Truth: A Comment on Crispin Wright's *Truth and Objectivity*", *Philosophy and Phenomenological Research* 56, pp. 883–90.

Plantinga, A. 1982. "How to be an Anti-Realist", *Proceedings and Addresses of the American Philosophical Association* 56, pp. 47–70.

Plato. 1997. *The Dialogues of Plato*, vol. II. Translated by B. Jowett. Bristol: Thoemmes.

Powell, M. 1998. "Realism or Response-Dependence?" *European Review of Philsophy* 3, pp. 1–13.

Price, H. 1988. *Facts and the Function of Truth*. Oxford: Blackwell.

Putnam, H. 1975a. *Mathematics, Matter and Method*. Cambridge: Cambridge University Press.

———— 1975b. *Mind, Language and Reality*, Philosophical Papers, vol. II. Cambridge: Cambridge University Press.

———— 1975c. "On Properties", *in* Putnam (1975b), pp. 305–22.

———— 1975d. "The Meaning of Meaning", *in* Gunderson (1975).

———— 1980. "Models and Reality", *Journal of Symbolic Logic* 45, pp. 464–82, *reprinted in* Putnam (1983a).

———— 1981. *Reason, Truth and History*. Cambridge: Cambridge University Press.

———— 1983a. *Realism and Reason*, Philosophical Papers, vol. III. Cambridge: Cambridge University Press.

———— 1983b. "Vagueness and Alternative Logic," *in* Putnam (1983a), pp. 271–86.

———— 1990. *Realism with a Human Face*. Edited by J. Conant. Cambridge, Mass.: Harvard University Press.

———— 1994a. "Sense, Nonsense and the Senses: An Enquiry into the Powers of the Human Mind", *Journal of Philosophy* 91, pp. 445–517 (originally given as 1994 Dewey Lectures at Columbia University).

References

———— 1994b. *Words and Life.* Edited by J. Conant. Cambridge, Mass.: Harvard University Press.

———— 2001. "When 'Evidence Transcendence' Is Not Malign: A Reply to Crispin Wright", *Journal of Philosophy* 98, pp. 594–600.

Quine, W. V. O. 1960. *Word and Object.* Cambridge, Mass.: MIT Press.

———— 1961a. *From a Logical Point of View,* 2nd ed. New York: Harper and Row.

———— 1961b. "Two Dogmas of Empiricism", *in* Quine (1961a), pp. 20–46.

———— 1969. *Ontological Relativity and Other Essays.* New York: Columbia University Press.

Rasmussen, S., and J. Ravnkinde. 1982. "Realism and Logic", *Synthese* 52, pp. 379–439.

Read, S., and C. Wright. 1985. "Hairier than Putnam Thought", *Analysis* 45, pp. 56–8.

Rhees, R., ed. 1981. *Ludwig Wittgenstein: Personal Recollections.* Oxford: Basil Blackwell.

Rorty, R. 1995. "Is Truth a Goal of Enquiry? Davidson vs. Wright", *Philosophical Quarterly* 45, pp. 281–300.

Rumfitt, I . 1995. "Truth Wronged", *Ratio* 81 (New Series), pp. 100–7.

Russell, B . 1906–7. "On the Nature of Truth", *Proceedings of the Aristotelian Society* 7, pp. 28–49.

———— 1912. *The Problems of Philosophy.* London: Oxford University Press.

Sainsbury, M. 1996. "Crispin Wright: *Truth and Objectivity*", *Philosophy and Phenomenological Research* 56, pp. 899–904.

Salerno, J. 2000. "Revising the Logic of Logical Revision", *Philosophical Studies* 99, pp. 211–27.

Sellars, W. 1963. "Empiricism and the Philosophy of Mind", *reprinted in* W. Sellars, *Science, Perception and Reality* (New York: Humanities Press).

Shapiro, S., and W. Taschek. 1996. "Intuitionism, Pluralism and Cognitive Command", *Journal of Philosophy* 93, pp. 74–88.

Shiffer, S . 1987. *Remnants of Meaning.* Cambridge, Mass.: MIT Press.

Shope, R. K. 1978. "The Conditional Fallacy in Contemporary Philosophy", *Journal of Philosophy* 75, pp. 397–413.

Singer, P., ed. 1991. *A Companion to Ethics.* Oxford: Basil Blackwell.

Smith, M. 1986. "Should We Believe in Emotivism?", in MacDonald and Wright (1986), pp. 289–310.

———— 1994. *The Moral Problem.* Oxford: Basil Blackwell.

References

Smith, M., J. Divers, A. Miller and P. Horwich. 1994. "Expressivism and Truth", *Analysis* 54:1, pp. 1–26.

Sorensen, R. 1998. *Blindspots*. Oxford: Oxford University Press.

Stich, S. 1983. *From Folk Psychology to Cognitive Science: The Case Against Belief*. Cambridge, Mass.: MIT Press.

Strawson, P. F. 1949. "Truth", *Analysis* 9, pp. 83–97.

Sturgeon, N. 1985. "Moral Explanations", *in* Copp and Zimmerman (1985), pp. 49–78.

—— 1986. "What Difference Does It Make Whether Moral Realism Is True?" *in* Gillespie (1986), pp. 115–42.

Tennant, N. 1995. "On Negation, Truth and Warranted Assertibility", *Analysis* 55, pp. 98–104.

—— 1997. *The Taming of the True*. Oxford: Clarendon Press.

Travis, C., ed. 1986. *Meaning and Interpretation*. Oxford: Blackwell.

van Cleve, J. 1996. "Minimal Truth is Realist Truth", *Philosophy and Phenomenological Research* 56, pp. 869–75.

van Straaten, Z., ed. 1980. *Philosophical Subjects: Essays presented to P. F. Strawson*. Oxford: Clarendon Press.

Walker, R. 1989. *The Coherence Theory of Truth: Realism, Anti-Realism, Idealism*. London: Routledge.

—— 1997. "Theories of Truth", *in* Hale and Wright (1997).

Weingartner, P., and G. Schurz, eds. 1987. *Logic, Philosophy of Science and Epistemology*. Vienna: Holder-Pichler-Tempsky.

Wiggins, D. 1987a. *Needs, Values and Truth*. Oxford: Basil Blackwell.

—— 1987b. "A Sensible Subjectivism?" *in* Wiggins (1987a), pp. 185–214.

—— 1987c. "Truth, Invention and the Meaning of Life", in Wiggins (1987a), pp. 87–138.

—— 1987d. "Truth, and Truth as Predicated of Moral Judgements", *in* Wiggins (1987a), pp. 139–84.

—— 1990–1. "Moral Cognitivism, Moral Relativism and Motivating Moral Beliefs", *Proceedings of the Aristotelian Society* 91, pp. 61–86.

Williams, B. 1985. *Ethics and the Limits of Philosophy*. Cambridge, Mass.: Harvard University Press.

Williamson, T. 1992a. "Vagueness and Ignorance", *Proceedings of the Aristotelian Society* Suppl. vol. 66, pp. 145–62.

—— 1992b. "Inexact Knowledge", *Mind* 101, p. 217–42.

—— 1994a. *Vagueness*. London: Routledge.

References

—— 1994b. "A Critical Study of *Truth and Objectivity*", *International Journal of Philosophical Studies* 30:1, pp. 130–44.

—— 1996a. "Putnam on the Sorites Paradox", *Philosophical Papers* 25, pp. 47–56.

—— 1996b. "Wright on the Epistemic Conception of Vagueness", *Analysis* 56, pp. 39–45.

—— 1996c. "Unreflective Realism", *Philosophy and Phenomenological Research* 56, pp. 905–9.

—— 1996d. "Knowing and Asserting", *Philosophical Review* 105, pp. 489–523.

Wittgenstein, L. 1953. *Philosophical Investigations.* Edited by G. E. M. Anscombe and R. Rhees. Oxford: Blackwell.

—— 1964. *Remarks on the Foundations of Mathematics,* 3rd ed. Edited by G. H. von Wright, R. Rhees and G. E. M. Anscombe. Oxford: Blackwell.

—— 1969. *On Certainty.* Edited by G. E. M. Anscombe and G. H. von Wright. Oxford: Blackwell.

Wright, C. 1980. *Wittgenstein on the Foundations of Mathematics.* Cambridge, Mass.: Harvard University Press.

—— 1983. *Frege's Conception of Numbers as Objects.* Aberdeen: Aberdeen University Press.

—— 1984. "Kripke's Account of the Argument against Private Language", *Journal of Philosophy* 71, pp. 759–78.

—— 1985a. "Facts and Certainty", *Proceedings of the British Academy* 71, pp. 429–72.

—— 1985b. "Review of Blackburn's *Spreading the Word*", *Mind* 94, pp. 310–19.

—— 1986a. "Does Wittgenstein have a Cogent Argument against Private Language? Investigations §§258–61", *in* McDowell and Pettit (1986), pp. 209–66.

—— 1986b. "Inventing Logical Necessity", in Butterfield (1986), pp. 187–209.

—— 1986c. "Rule-Following, Meaning and Constructivism", in Travis (1986), pp. 271–97.

—— 1986d. "Scientific Realism, Observation and the Verification Principle", *in* MacDonald and Wright (1986), pp. 247–74.

—— 1987a. "Further Reflections on the Sorites Paradox", *Philosophical Topics* 15:1, pp. 227–90.

References

————— 1987b. "On Making up One's Mind: Wittgenstein on Intention", *in* Weingartner and Schurz (1987), pp. 391–404.

————— 1988a. "Moral Values, Projection and Secondary Qualities", *Proceedings of the Aristotelian Society* Suppl. vol. 62, pp. 1–26.

————— 1988b. "Realism, Anti-realism, Irrealism, Quasi-realism" (Gareth Evans Memorial Lecture). *In* P. French, T. Uehling and H. Wettstein, eds., *Midwest Studies in Philosophy,* vol. XII, pp. 25–49. St. Paul: University of Minnesota Press.

————— 1989. "Wittgenstein's Rule-Following Considerations and the Central Project of Theoretical Linguistics", *in* George (1989), pp. 233–64.

————— 1992. *Truth and Objectivity.* Cambridge, Mass.: Harvard University Press.

————— 1993a. *Realism, Meaning and Truth,* 2nd ed. Oxford: Blackwell.

————— 1993b. "Anti-Realism and Revisionism", *in* Wright (1993a).

————— 1993c. "Anti-Realism: The Contemporary Debate–Whither Now?" *in* Haldane and Wright (1993).

————— 1993d. "Eliminative Materialism: Going Concern or Passing Fancy?", *Mind and Language* 8, pp. 316–26.

————— 1994a. "Realism, Pure and Simple?" *International Journal of Philosophical Studies* 30:2, pp. 147–61.

————— 1994b. "Response to Jackson", *Philosophical Books* 35, pp. 169–75.

————— 1995a. "The Epistemic Conception of Vagueness", *Southern Journal of Philosophy* 33, pp. 133–59.

————— 1995b. "Truth and Coherence", *Synthèse* 103, pp. 279–302.

————— 1995c. "Truth in Ethics", *Ratio* 8 (New Series), pp. 209–26.

————— 1997. "Self-Knowledge: The Wittgensteinian Legacy", *in* Wright, Smith and Macdonald (1997).

————— 1998a. "Truth: A Traditional Debate Reviewed", *Canadian Journal of Philosophy* 24, pp. 31–74. *Reprinted in* Blackburn and Simmons (1999), pp. 203–38.

————— 1998b. "Euthyphronism and the Physicality of Colour", *European Review of Philosophy* 3, pp. 15–30.

————— 2001a. "Minimalism, Deflationism, Pragmatism, Pluralism", *in* Lynch (2001), pp. 751–87.

————— 2001b. *Rails to Infinity.* Cambridge, Mass.: Harvard University Press.

Wright, C., B. Smith and C. Macdonald, eds. 1997. *Knowing Our Own Minds.* Oxford: Oxford University Press.

ADDITIONAL READINGS

Allen, B. 1994. "Putnam and Rorty on Objectivity and Truth", *Deutsche Zeitschrift für Philosophie* 42, pp. 989–1005.

Alston, W. P. 1995. "Realism and Christian Faith", *International Journal for Philosophy of Religion* 38, pp. 37–60.

Banchetti, M. P. 1992. "My Station and Its Duties", *Idealistic Studies* 22, pp. 11–27.

Battersby, J. L. 1996. "The Inescapability of Humanism", *College English* 58, pp. 555–67.

Beall, J. C. 2000. "On Mixed Inferences and Pluralism about Truth Predicates", *Philosophical Quarterly* 50, pp. 380–2.

Bhushan, N. 1996. "The Possibility of a Radically Different Language", *Philosophical Investigations* 19, pp. 237–63.

Binderup, L. 2001. "Moral Minimalism". Ph.D. diss., University of St. Andrews.

Bloomfield, P. 1997. "Of 'Goodness' and 'Healthiness': A Viable Moral Ontology", *Philosophical Studies* 87, pp. 309–32.

———— 1998. "Prescriptions Are Assertions: An Essay on Moral Syntax", *American Philosophical Quarterly* 35, pp. 1–20.

Brower, B. W. 1993. "Dispositional Ethical Realism", *Ethics* 103, pp. 221–49.

Additional Readings

Brueckner, A. 1998. "Is 'Superassertible' a Truth Predicate?" *Noûs* 32, pp. 76–81.

———— 1998. "Realism, Best Explanation, and Cognitive Command", *Philosophical Papers* 27, pp. 69–78.

Burgess, J. A. 1997. "What is Minimalism about Truth?", *Analysis* 57, pp. 259–67.

———— 1998. "Error Theories and Values", *Australasian Journal of Philosophy* 76, pp. 534–52.

Cohen, J. 1997. "The Arc of the Moral Universe", *Philosophy and Public Affairs* 26, pp. 91–134.

Darwall, S., A. Gibbard and P. Railton. 1992. "Toward *Fin de Siècle* Ethics: Some Trends", *Philosophical Review* 101, pp. 115–89.

Divers, J., and A. Miller. 1994. "Best Opinion, Intention-Detecting and Analytic Functionalism", *Philosophical Quarterly* 44, pp. 239–45.

———— 1994. "Rethinking Realism", *Mind* 103, pp. 519–33.

———— 1994. "Why Expressivists about Value Should Not Love Minimalism about Truth", *Analysis* 54, pp. 12–19.

———— 1995. "Platitudes and Attitudes—A Minimalist Conception of Belief", *Analysis* 55, pp. 37–44.

Dodd, J. 1999. "There Is No Norm of Truth: A Minimalist Reply to Wright", *Analysis* 59, pp. 291–9.

Dodd, J., and S. Sterngillet. 1995. "The Is–Ought Gap, the Fact–Value Distinction and the Naturalistic Fallacy", *Dialogue* 34, pp. 727–45.

Dworkin, R. 1999. "Objectivity and Truth: You'd Better Believe It", *Philosophy and Public Affairs* 28, pp. 87–139.

Edgington, D. 1995. "On Conditionals", *Mind* 104, pp. 235–329.

Edwards, J. 1992. "Best Opinion and Intentional States", *Philosophical Quarterly* 42, pp. 21–33.

———— 1992. "Secondary Qualities and the A Priori", *Mind* 101, pp. 263–72.

———— 1994. "Debates about Realism Transposed to a New Key", *Mind* 103, pp. 59–72.

———— 1996. "Anti-realist Truth and Concepts of Superassertibility", *Synthèse* 109, pp. 103–20.

———— 1997. "Is Tennant Selling Truth Short?" *Analysis* 57, pp. 152–8.

———— 1999. "Prizing Truth from Warranted Assertibility: A Reply to Tennant", *Analysis* 59, pp. 300–8.

Gaukroger, S. 1998. "Justification, Truth and the Development of Science", *Studies in History and Philosophy of Science* 29, pp. 97–112.

Golumbia, D. 1996. "Resisting the World", *Science-Fiction Studies* 23, pp. 83–102.

Greenough, P. 2002. "Knowledge, Lies and Vagueness: A Minimalist Treatment". Ph.D. diss., University of St. Andrews.

Habermas, J. 1996. "Rorty's Pragmatic Turn", *Deutsche Zeitschrift für Philosophie* 44, pp. 715–41.

—— 1998. "Rightness versus Truth—The Meaning of the Validity of Imperative of Moral Judgments and Norms", *Deutsche Zeitschrift für Philosophie* 46, pp. 179–208.

Hale, B. 1994. "Is Platonism Epistemologically Bankrupt?", *Philosophical Review* 103, pp. 299–325.

—— 1999. "Realism and Its Oppositions", *in* B. Hale and C. Wright, eds., *A Companion to the Philosophy of Language* (Oxford: Blackwell), pp. 291–308.

Hand, M. 1996. "Radical Antirealism and Neutral States of Information", *Philosophical Topics* 24, pp. 35–51.

—— 1998. "Radical Antirealism and Wright's Antideflationary Argument", *Noûs* 32, pp. 320–30.

Heath, J. 1997. "Foundationalism and Practical Reason", *Mind* 106, pp. 451–73.

Hohwy, J. 1997. "Quietism and Cognitive Command", *Philosophical Quarterly* 47, pp. 495–500.

Holt, J. 1999. "Superassertibility and Asymptotic Truth", *Dialogue* 38, pp. 109–22.

Holton, R. 1992. "Response-Dependence and Infallibility", *Analysis* 52, pp. 180–4.

Hooker, B., ed. 1996. *Truth in Ethics*. Cambridge: Blackwell.

Horgan, T. 1993. "From Supervenience to Superdupervenience—Meeting the Demands of a Material World", *Mind* 102, pp. 554–86.

—— 1995. "Transvaluationism—A Dionysian Approach to Vagueness", *Southern Journal of Philosophy* 33, pp. 97–126.

—— 1995. "Wright's *Truth and Objectivity*", *Noûs* 29, pp. 127–38.

—— 1996. "The Perils of Epistemic Reductionism", *Philosophy and Phenomenological Research* 56, pp. 891–7.

Horwich, P. 1993. "Wright's *Truth and Objectivity*", *Times Literary Supplement* No. 4711, p. 28.

—— 1996. "Realism and Truth", *Philosophical Perspectives* 10, pp. 187–97.

Additional Readings

Humberstone, I. L. 1997. "Two Types of Circularity", *Philosophy and Phenomenological Research* 57, pp. 249–80.

Jacobsen, R. 1996. "Wittgenstein on Self-Knowledge and Self-Expression", *Philosophical Quarterly* 46, pp. 12–30.

Johnson, R. N. 1998. "Minding One's Manners: Revisiting Moral Explanation", *Philosophical Studies* 90, pp. 181–203.

Johnston, M. 1998. "Are Manifest Qualities Response-Dependent?" *Monist* 81, pp. 3–43.

Kennedy, K. 1996. "Paul Weiss's Method(s) and System(s)", *Review of Metaphysics* 50, pp. 5–33.

Kenyon, T. 1999. "Truth, Knowability and Neutrality", *Noûs* 33, pp. 103–17.

Kölbel, M. 1997. "Expressivism and the Syntactic Uniformity of Declarative Sentences", *Crítica* 29, pp. 3–51.

———— 1997. "Wright's Argument from Neutrality", *Ratio* (New Series) 10, pp. 35–47.

Kvanvig, J. L. 1999. "Truth and Superassertibility", *Philosophical Studies* 93, pp. 1–19.

Lafont, C. 1994. "Philosophical Disputes over the Concept of Truth", *Deutsche Zeitschrift für Philosophie* 42, pp. 1007–23.

Lammenranta, M. 1998. "The Normativity of Naturalistic Epistemology", *Philosophia* 26, pp. 337–58.

Lance, M. 1997. "The Significance of Anaphoric Theories of Truth and Reference", *Philosophical Issues* 8, pp. 181–98.

Lievers, M. 1998. "Two Versions of the Manifestation Argument", *Synthèse* 115, pp. 199–227.

Margolis, J. 1997. "The Growing Philosophical Neglect of History and Culture", *Philosophical Forum* 28, pp. 285–99.

McFarland, D., and A. Miller. 1998. "Response-Dependence without Reduction?" *Australasian Journal of Philosophy* 76, pp. 534–52.

McGrath, M. 1998. "The Concrete Modal Realist Challenge to Platonism", *Australasian Journal of Philosophy* 76, pp. 587–610.

Menzies, P., and P. Pettit. 1993. "Found, the Missing Explanation", *Analysis* 53, pp. 100–9.

Miller, A. 1995. "Objectivity Disfigured—Johnston's Missing Explanation Argument", *Philosophy and Phenomenological Research* 55, pp. 857–68.

———— 1997. "More Responses to the Missing Explanation Argument", *Philosophia* 25, pp. 331–49.

—— 1998. "Objectivity", *in* E. Craig, ed., *Routledge Encyclopaedia of Philosophy*, vol. 7 (London: Routledge), pp. 73–6.

—— 2001. "On Wright's Argument against Deflationism", *Philosophical Quarterly* 51, pp. 527–31.

Milo, R. 1995. "Contractarian Constructivism", *Journal of Philosophy* 92, pp. 181–204.

Mintoff, J. 1998. "Hume and Instrumental Reason", *Journal of Value Inquiry* 32, pp. 519–38.

Misak, C. 1998. "Deflating Truth: Pragmatism vs. Minimalism", *Monist* 81, pp. 407–25.

Miscevic, N. 1998. "The Aposteriority of Response-Dependence", *Monist* 81, pp. 69–84.

Nelson, L. H. 1995. "A Feminist Naturalized Philosophy of Science", *Synthèse* 104, pp. 399–421.

O'Leary-Hawthorne, J. 1996. "The Epistemology of Possible Worlds: A Guided Tour", *Philosophical Studies* 84, pp. 183–202.

O'Leary-Hawthorne, J., and G. Oppy. 1997. "Minimalism and Truth", *Noûs* 31, pp. 170–96.

O'Leary-Hawthorne, J., and H. Price. 1996. "How To Stand Up For Non-Cognitivists", *Australasian Journal of Philosophy* 74, pp. 275–92.

O'Neill, J. 1992. "The Varieties of Intrinsic Value", *Monist* 75, pp. 119–37.

Peonidis, F. 1996. "Secondary Qualities and Moral Values: What do We Really Compare?" *Journal of Value Inquiry* 30, pp. 209–11.

—— 1996. "Realism and Truth: A Comment on Crispin Wright's *Truth and Objectivity*", *Philosophy and Phenomenological Research* 56, pp. 883–90.

—— 1998. "Noumenalism and Response-Dependence", *Monist* 81, pp. 112–32.

Pigden, C. R. 1990. "Geach on Good", *Philosophical Quarterly* 40, pp. 129–54.

Pitson, T. 1997. "The Dispositional Account of Colour", *Philosophia* 25, pp. 247–66.

Price, H. 1992. "Agency and Causal Asymmetry", *Mind* 101, pp. 501–20.

—— 1998. "Three Norms of Assertibility, or How the MOA Became Extinct", *Philosophical Perspectives* 12, pp. 241–54.

Railton, P. 1995. "Subjective and Objective", *Ratio* (New Series) 8, pp. 259–76.

Additional Readings

Rosen, G. 1994. "Objectivity and Modern Idealism: What Is the Question?", in M. Michael and J. O'Leary-Hawthorne, eds., *Philosophy in Mind* (Dordrecht: Kluwer), pp. 277–319.

—— 1997. "Who Makes the Rules Around Here? Robert Brandom's 'Making It Explicit'", *Philosophy and Phenomenological Research* 57, pp. 163–71.

Rosenkranz, S. 1999. "Objectivity and Realism—Meeting the Manifestation Challenge". Ph.D. diss., University of St. Andrews.

—— 2001. "Farewell to Objectivity: A Critique of Brandom", *Philosophical Quarterly* 51, pp. 232–7.

Sainsbury, R. M. 1996. "Crispin Wright: *Truth and Objectivity*", *Philosophy and Phenomenological Research* 56, pp. 899–904.

—— 1998. "Projections and Relations", *Monist* 81, pp. 133–60.

Sandoe, P. 1988. "Secondary Qualities, Subjective and Intrinsic", *Theoria* 54, pp. 200–19.

Seel, M. 1998. "To Determine and Let Determine—The Beginnings of a Medial Theory of Cognition", *Deutsche Zeitschrift für Philosophie* 46, pp. 351–65.

Seymour, M. 1995. "Critical Notice of Crispin Wright's *Truth and Objectivity*", *Canadian Journal of Philosophy* 25, pp. 637–58.

Shalkowski, S. A. 1996. "Conventions, Cognitivism, and Necessity", *American Philosophical Quarterly* 33, pp. 375–92.

—— 1997. "Theoretical Virtues and Theological Construction", *International Journal for the Philosophy of Religion* 41, pp. 71–89.

Sher, G. 1999. "On the Possibility of a Substantive Theory of Truth", *Synthèse* 117, pp. 133–72.

Smith, M. 1994. "Minimalism, Truth-aptitude and Belief", *Analysis* 54, pp. 21–26.

—— 1994. "Why Expressivists about Value Should Love Minimalism about Truth", *Analysis* 54, pp. 1–11.

—— 1995. "Internalism's Wheel", *Ratio* (New Series) 8, pp. 277–302.

Tanney, J. 1996. "A Constructivist Picture of Self-Knowledge", *Philosophy* 71, pp. 405–22.

Tappolet, C. 1997. "Mixed Inferences: A Problem for Pluralism about Truth Predicates", *Analysis* 57, pp. 209–10.

—— 2000. "Truth, Pluralism and Many-Valued Logics", *Philosophical Quarterly* 50, pp. 382–5.

Tasiouslas, J. 1998. "Relativism, Realism and Reflection", *Inquiry* 41, pp. 377–410.

Teichmann, R. 1995. "Truth, Assertion and Warrant", *Philosophical Quarterly* 45, pp. 78–83.

Tenenbaum, S. 1996. "Realists without a Cause: Deflationary Theories of Truth and Ethical Realism", *Canadian Journal of Philosophy* 26, pp. 561–89.

Tennant, N. 1998. "The Full Price of Truth", *Analysis* 58, pp. 221–8.

Tersman, F. 1998. "Crispin Wright on Moral Disagreement", *Philosophical Quarterly* 48, pp. 359–65.

Thomas, A. 1997. "Minimalism versus Quasi-realism: Why the Minimalist has a Dialectical Advantage", *Philosophical Papers* 26, pp. 233–9.

Thornton, T. 1997. "Intention, Rule Following and the Strategic Role of Wright's Order of Determination", *Philosophical Investigations* 20, pp. 136–47.

Tietz, J. 1997. "Truth in Philosophy", *Dialogue* 36, pp. 375–80.

Timmons, M. 1999. *Morality without Foundations.* Oxford: Oxford University Press.

van Cleve, J. 1996. "Minimal Truth Is Realist Truth", *Philosophy and Phenomenological Research* 56, pp. 869–75.

Wedgwood, R. 1997. "Non-Cognitivism, Truth and Logic", *Philosophical Studies* 86, pp. 73–91.

Weir, A. 1996. "Ultramaximalist Minimalism", *Analysis* 56, pp. 10–22.

Weiss, B. 1996. "Anti-realism, Truth-value Links and Tensed Truth Predicates", *Mind* 105, pp. 577–602.

Wiggins, D. 1995. "Objective and Subjective in Ethics", *Ratio* (New Series) 8, pp. 243–58.

Williams, B. 1995. "Truth in Ethics", *Ratio* (New Series) 8, pp. 227–42.

Williams, M. 1995. "*Truth and Objectivity* by Crispin Wright", *Philosophical Review* 104, pp. 145–7.

—— 1995. "Does Assertibility Satisfy The S4-Axiom", *Critica* 27, pp. 3–25.

—— 1996. "Cognitive Homelessness", *Journal of Philosophy* 93, pp. 554–73.

Wright, C. 1993. "Scientific Realism and Observation Statements", *International Journal of Philosophical Studies* 1, pp. 231–54.

—— 2002. "Relativism and Classical Logic" *in* Anthony O'Hear, ed.,

Additional Readings

Logic, Thought and Language (Cambridge: Cambridge University Press), pp. 95–118.

Young, J. O. 1997. "Aesthetic Antirealism", *Southern Journal of Philosophy* 35, pp. 119–34.

CREDITS

Essay 1, "Précis of *Truth and Objectivity*", was first published in the Book Symposium on *Truth and Objectivity* in *Philosophy and Phenomenological Research* 56:4 (1996). It is reprinted by permission of the International Phenomenological Society.

Essay 2, "Realism, Anti-Realism, Irrealism, Quasi-Realism", was given as the 1987 Gareth Evans Memorial Lecture in Oxford, and was first published in *Realism and Anti-Realism, Midwest Studies in Philosophy*, vol. XII, ed. P. French, T. Uehling and H. Wettstein (University of Minnesota Press) 1988. It is reprinted by permission of the journal's Editor.

Essay 3, "Response to Jackson", was first published in *Philosophical Books* 35 (1994). It is reprinted by permission of Basil Blackwell Ltd.

Essay 4, "Realism, Pure and Simple?", was first published in the *International Journal of Philosophical Studies* 2 (1994). It is reprinted by permission of Taylor and Francis Ltd.

Essay 5, "Responses to Commentators", was first published in the Book Symposium on *Truth and Objectivity* in *Philosophy and Phenomenological Research* 56:4 (1996). It is reprinted by permission of the International Phenomenological Society.

Credits

Essay 6, "Comrades against Quietism", was first published in *Mind* 107 (1998). It is reprinted by permission of Oxford University Press.

Essay 7, "Moral Values, Projection and Secondary Qualities", was first published in *Proceedings of the Aristotelian Society*, supplementary volume 62 (1988). It is reprinted by permission of the Aristotelian Society.

Essay 8, "Truth in Ethics", was first published in *Ratio* 8 (New Series) (1995). It is reprinted by permission of Basil Blackwell Ltd.

Essay 9, "Truth as Coherence", is a critical study of Ralph C. S. Walker, *The Coherence Theory of Truth,* and was first published in *Synthèse* 103 (1995). It is reprinted by permission of Kluwer Academic Publishers.

Essay 10, "Truth: A Traditional Debate Reviewed", was first published in German in Matthias Vogel and Lutz Wingert, eds., *Unsere Welt gegeben oder gemacht? Menschliches Erkennen zwischen Entdeckung und Konstruktion* (Suhrkamp) 1999. The English version was first published in *Canadian Journal of Philosophy,* supplementary volume 24 (1999). It is reprinted by permission of the journal's Editors.

Essay 11, "Truth as Sort of Epistemic: Putnam's Peregrinations", was first published in *Journal of Philosophy* 97, pp. 335–64. It is reprinted by permission of the journal's Editors.

The first two sections of Essay 12, "Minimalism and Deflationism", were first published as part of my "Minimalism, Deflationism, Pragmatism, Pluralism" in Michael P. Lynch, ed., *The Nature of Truth: Classic and Contemporary Perspectives* (MIT Press) 2001. They are reprinted by permission of the publishers.

Essay 13, "The Conceivability of Naturalism", was first published in T. Gendler and J. Hawthorne, eds., *Conceivability and Possibility* (Oxford University Press) 2002. It is reprinted by permission of the publishers.

Essay 14, "What Could Anti-Realism about Ordinary Psychology Possibly Be?", was first published in *Philosophical Review* 111 (2002), copyright 2002 Cornell University. It is reprinted by permission of the publishers.

Essay 15, "On Being in a Quandary: Relativism, Vagueness, Logical Revisionism", was first published in *Mind* 110 (2001), pp. 45–98. It is reprinted by permission of Oxford University Press.

INDEX

Index

Index

Index

dentially constrained, 50; on superassertibility, 50, 61, 66–70, 69n12; on Cognitive Command, 50, 61, 70–77, 81, 107n, 110–112; on minimalism about truth-aptitude, 50, 61, 81, 115–119; on pluralism about truth, 61, 62, 77–81; on assertoric content, 61, 62–66; on vagueness, 73n, 492n48; on warranted assertibility, 115–117; on direct realism, 323n; on indeterminacy, 444, 444n5, 498–502, 501n; on supervaluational semantics, 471n; on Putnam, 492n48

Wittgenstein, Ludwig: Kripke on, 2, 19n10; on private language, 2, 195; on rule-following, 4, 9–10, 19n10, 144–145, 148–149, 212, 213, 230–235, 238–240; on character and behavior, 17; on meaning, 17, 19n10; Blackburn on, 127, 141–144; on avowals, 133n, 141; on ethics, 141; on mathematics, 141, 143, 144; *On Certainty,* 141; *Philosophical Investigations,* 141–142, 143, 360; and quasi-realism, 141–144; on games, 142; on truth, 197, 241; Walker on, 205, 212, 213–214, 230–235, 230n, 238–240; on community agreement, 230–235, 238–240; and warranted assertibility, 230–235, 238–240; on supervenience of the psychological on the physical, 383; *Zettel,* 383